DISCARDED
Fordham University Libraries

RELIGION AND HEALING
IN MANDARI

Symbolic colours on domestic animals

RELIGION
AND HEALING IN
MANDARI

JEAN BUXTON

OXFORD
AT THE CLARENDON PRESS
1973

Oxford University Press, Ely House, London W. 1

GLASGOW NEW YORK TORONTO MELBOURNE WELLINGTON
CAPE TOWN IBADAN NAIROBI DAR ES SALAAM LUSAKA ADDIS ABABA
DELHI BOMBAY CALCUTTA MADRAS KARACHI LAHORE DACCA
KUALA LUMPUR SINGAPORE HONG KONG TOKYO

ISBN 0 19 823174 1

© *Oxford University Press 1973*

BL
2480
.M28B8

Fordham University Cop. 2
LIBRARY
AT
LINCOLN CENTER
New York, N. Y.

*Printed in Great Britain
at the University Press, Oxford
by Vivian Ridler
Printer to the University*

IN MEMORY OF
LINNET HOWELL

ACKNOWLEDGEMENTS

I HAVE acknowledged elsewhere my indebtedness to many people, in particular to Professor Evans-Pritchard, to officials of the then Anglo-Egyptian Sudan and to those of the Sudan Republic, and finally to the Mandari themselves.

In connection with the preparation of this book, I would like to record my thanks to Professor Daryll Forde, the then Head of the Department of Anthropology at University College London, who arranged for my attachment to his Department during the 1960s, and to the Institute of Social Anthropology at Oxford where I was invited to act as visiting Lecturer in African Sociology from 1965 to 1967. During this time the material in this book formed the basis of lectures. Part of Chapter 5 was read as a paper at Oxford and at Manchester in 1953, and Chapter 21 at University College in 1965 and 1968. Professor Forde made helpful criticisms of the draft of Chapter 12. Some of the material in Chapter 11 was published as an article in *Man*, and I am grateful for permission to use this again.

Mrs. Dewhurst undertook the task of rearranging and correcting the final draft and I would express my thanks for her many helpful suggestions and her encouragement. Dr. Godfrey Lienhardt later read the draft and made invaluable criticisms and recommendations.

No attempt has been made to take into account works published much after 1968 when the book was completed.

Field-work was carried out between 1950 and 1952 and for a short period in 1958.

LIST OF TABLES

CONTENTS

LIST OF ILLUSTRATIONS

PLATES

FIGURES

LIST OF ILLUSTRATIONS

SKETCH-MAPS

INTRODUCTION

I

IN my first book, I described the Mandari political organization
and traced the origins of the different groups which have come
together to form what Mandari consider to be their unique
people and culture.[1] The mixture of stocks, with the affiliation
of groups of different size and origin around established cores of
indigenes and assimilated immigrants, was shown to be clearly
reflected in political institutions. Mandari society shows a continual capacity for assimilation and for allowing dynamic growth
in assimilated populations, and while I do not deal specifically
with this process of adaption here, it should nevertheless be borne
in mind, since it is clear that it has also allowed and provided the
diversity of religious belief and ritual. I was able during my field-
work to observe the assimilation of further new cultural ideas and
influences taken over from the neighbouring Nilotics with whom
the Mandari have established a network of ties during more recent
decades.

It may be helpful to outline briefly the main features of Mandari
local communities, and to assess the position of Mandari in the
contemporary world. I shall also say something about Mandari
attitudes to cattle and the way animals are selected for ritual purposes.

II

The Mandari number around 15,000, and their position in the
Southern Sudan can be seen on the map at the end of the book.[2]
They regard themselves as pastoralists, but they are also indus-
trious cultivators. The population is scattered and of low density,
but although there is no land shortage, shortage of water and
grazing raise very real problems. Herds are never brought into
villages but kept permanently on the move, while at the same time
permanent village communities are maintained.

[1] *Chiefs and Strangers* (Oxford, 1963).
[2] I do not include here the peoples called Tsera and Köbora, or 'Nile-dwelling
Mandari'. See also *Chiefs and Strangers*, Introduction, pp. 3–11.

The country is divided into small localized chiefdoms (some now in administrative amalgamations). Each is under a chief, a member of the landowning clan which provides the political framework in each territory. Additional populations are affiliated to clan lineages and include client retainers, client lineages which have become semi-autonomous, and, sometimes, more powerful immigrant groups which have acquired permanent land rights; there is also a more temporary population arising from individual connections, for instance from living with the maternal uncle or affines.

A local community, for our purpose, and also as a reality for the Mandari, embodies a number of principles of association. In its widest sense it covers a whole chiefdom, and has a fixed structure through the nuclear clan and the exclusiveness of its territorial boundaries. This is the largest permanent community within which ritual for a common purpose is performed. The smaller units—the lineages of the focal clan and the settler and resident groups—also form communities with a high degree of permanence, although not of so absolute a kind. These small units provide the framework for the greater part of personal and family rituals. There is a further, and very important, kind of community which is based on actual everyday contacts and associations and which also has a degree of permanency. Here I refer to the extension of a community's ties across its own boundaries into the communities of neighbouring chiefdoms because of marriages between families of adjacent chiefdoms; out of these links grow short-term classificatory mother's brother, sister's son, and affinal relationships. Between discrete politico-territorial units, therefore, interstitial neighbourhoods flourish.

Another kind of individual network links persons over a much wider area across Mandari and into neighbouring Nilotic areas. These extended ties also arise through marriages, but they are weaker than those I have mentioned since they only last the three generations recognized for such relationships and are then forgotten because the bond of sharing an interstitial community is lacking, and the ties are too widely spread to be sustained without this. While in operation, and particularly at the first generation level, they may be very intense and provide a channel for frequent ritual.

A village is made up of hamlets, some concentrated in a central area, others scattered around the periphery a few   'red yards to a mile or so apart with bush in between. A village never provides continuous settlement. A hamlet is surrounded by fallow land and a light screen of uncleared scrub, a homestead is completely encircled by its cultivations and shielded from neighbours.

Homesteads and fields are 'for women', essentially for wives. Even in a polygynous family there is no husband's homestead apart from the separate and dispersed homesteads of each wife and her children with its own fields; while this may adjoin that of a co-wife, it equally well may be a mile or so away. A homestead is a man's temporary resting place, a place for ritual and for storing weapons, garden implements, and personal possessions. A man sleeps in each wife's hut in turn; he may also sleep in the village goatkraal or in the cattle-camp where all the herding equipment is kept.

The homestead holds the wife's possessions and those of the unmarried children, cooking utensils, clay pots, and gourds, baskets, sleeping-mats, loin-cloths, and goat-skins. The dwelling-hut is raised above six feet above the ground, and the open area underneath provides the living and cooking space and the centre for family life and entertainment. The grindstone (a valuable possession sometimes sought from other tribal areas where volcanic rock is near the surface) is sited at the side of the central hearth. This hearth, marked by the three round stones used to support cooking-pots, has important ritual associations. A second shady area is provided underneath the raised extension built out in front of the hut doorway on which people sit in the evenings out of reach of wild animals. During the rains the wife and young children sleep in the hut; at other times they sleep on the ground around a fire. At the edge of the packed-mud yard, regularly swept and spotlessly clean, is the grain-store, divided into compartments for the different grains. The homestead boundary may be planted with cassava bushes or clumps of climbing gourds. A good homestead has a small shade-tree.

A hamlet is occupied by a senior married man, his married brothers, and some of his paternal cousins; other small nuclei comprise members of other lineages of the same clan living apart from their immediate kin, and extended families of clients, affines, and maternal kin, some of whom may become the founders of new lineages. Those who affiliate permanently from outside the chiefdom through a female link are not usually, however, persons of landowning status, and the more mobile elements in the population are those who have never had this status or have lost it. A large hamlet may comprise twenty to thirty adult males with their families; a small one, perhaps five to ten families. Hamlet elders of both sexes are responsible for much of the spiritual welfare of their people, but sickness rituals often require the services of persons from further afield. This leads to constant coming and going across hamlet, village, and chiefdom boundaries, a consequence of the numerous marriage links between distant groups. A number of hamlets form a village, associated with a large landowning lineage or small landowning clan. Village elders are the senior hamlet representatives.

In general, those who perform ritual together are kinsfolk of one kind or another. The exception is the attendance at rites for rain or to cleanse the community or the meeting-tree which is its symbol. The exclusion of non-kin from family ritual should not however be taken to mean that close neighbours or non-relatives staying in a homestead cannot be present at a rite, but that those people do not take an active part, simply attending as spectators. Even kin entitled to attend may not do so if they live at a distance, the rite is of minor importance, or if the lineage to which each party belongs has divided. Where major ritual for a senior person is involved, however, lineage elders of a whole clan may attend, but again, wider attendance depends on the size of the clan and the degree of dispersal.

The senior men and women elders who are constantly in demand in connection with the performance of ritual, are never special categories with exclusive ritual authority but ordinary married people. In the absence of elders any adult man can perform a rite; although when senior relatives are available, they must be informed and a rite may have to be postponed if a key man or woman is temporarily absent.

Senior kinswomen are important in ritual in that they must be present and can play an active role, but men in most instances take precedence over them. Women may 'invoke' and lead the sacrificial animal around, but it will always be killed by a male member of the lineage.[1] In minor ritual not involving animal sacrifice

---

[1] Women do not kill stock or other animals; in the first place because they are not trained in killing and do not use spears and clubs, and secondly because, as central creative categories, their role is to give life and not to kill.

women act more independently, particularly in the minor sicknesses of women and children. A wife can act for a sick co-wife, for instance, if no man is available. The grandmother is a prominent figure in rituals for dead kin, particularly those involving dead kinswomen. Young unmarried girls never perform ritual and here there is sexual differentiation since a grown youth can act in a small rite and may even take precedence over his mother. Men play a greater part than women unless the women are trained medico-religious practitioners, partly because a woman is not regarded as fully mature until she has borne children. As a mother a woman in her own right has an important role in ritual, for Mandari do not restrict ritual activities to sterile women or those past the menopause, though after the menopause the range of all women's social activities is extended.

III

Cattle occupy a central position for Mandari as they do for their northern neighbours, the Atwot and Dinka, and for the Nilo-Hamitic Bari-speaking Nyangwara who border the Mandari to the south-east, and the Northern Bari who live beyond the Nyangwara on the banks of the Nile.

Reference to the work of Evans-Pritchard on the Nuer will give the reader information on cattle husbandry generally applicable to the Mandari, although variations on points of detail exist.[1] The Mandari probably face a greater problem in keeping their cattle healthy than either the Nuer or the Dinka because of the different nature of their terrain and the environmental factors which enforce a continual movement of herds. In Mandari the herder's life is experienced at its starkest. Cattle can never be brought into villages or even close to them except at a few favourable locations, and to obtain what the Mandari consider to be a balanced cattle diet, herds must move continuously between camps of greater or less impermanence.[2] Movement means that it is not worth while building and maintaining large permanent cattle-byres, and some camps provide no shelter at all, while others have small, open-sided, grass-roofed structures a few feet high

[1] See particularly E. E. Evans-Pritchard, *The Nuer* (Oxford, 1940), chap. i, for a description of the economic uses of cattle and cattle husbandry.

[2] For accounts of these cattle movements, see *Chiefs and Strangers*, chap. ix, sections ii, iii, and iv.

which protect the newly born stock and the herders from the heavier downpours. Apart from a short period after they are born, Mandari cattle never come under cover, but in spite of this do not seem to be in worse condition than those in Dinka, where byres are provided.

The Mandari select their stud bulls from the progeny of good milch cows. The sturdiness and general good points of the calf and, all other things being equal, its colour, are the criteria guiding selection. Stud animals are not generally selected from the piebald and variegated calves, these being reserved for different purposes, but a plain red or black stud bull has an advantage over a white one because it should produce well-marked offspring.[1] Mandari keep very few breeding animals and while there is nothing to prevent any man from owning one, they often come from the herds of rich and powerful lineages who have a selection of animals and can establish the best strains. One bull can serve the cows of other herders in a camp. Ultimately a breeding bull, although the animal of a particular owner, belongs to the whole herd or herding-unit, and it is the balanced requirements of this unit that are at issue. Stud bulls are herd-leaders, seen by the Mandari to guide the herds and hold them together. Clan histories reflect this feeling for stud animals, as instanced in the myths of herd-leaders in their search for grass and water, guiding the people and cattle to new countries. Bulls are the only animals represented as showing qualities of leadership and endowed with the life-giving associations that go with it.

Apart from stud bulls, all male stock is castrated when a few months old. Certain animals are specially selected for neutering because they are of such high quality that they are suitable as display-oxen (sönö, or duöt-sönö).[2] A sönö is said to be 'made from birth'; Mandari describe the delight of an owner who sees the tiny calf with its perfect markings. Being piebald or variegated is the outstanding criterion; other good points, though important, are secondary. Since, however, every youth wants his display-ox eventually, and as the majority of Mandari cattle are a nondescript white, many, as I observed, tend to be rather poorly marked, but

[1] The stud animal is referred to as mönek, but since this is also the word for the male of small stock, it may be qualified as duöt mönek, 'stud bull'. There is also another word ton, but this is not used in general conversation.

[2] Animals similar to the display-oxen of the Nuer and Dinka and also found among those Bari-speaking tribes who still own cattle.

1. Man with
display-ox

I have never seen an entirely plain one. Marking and patterning are very highly estimated in the Mandari visual aesthetic; and the strong contrast markings of black on white, red on white, or a combination of all three, stand out so strikingly in a landscape devoid of strong colour that the importance given to it can be readily understood.

A youth may acquire his display-ox as a child, from a sister's marriage (when it may be a young steer or already mature), or a display-calf may be born to one of his mother's cows. More usually, a youth receives it from his father or mother's brother at initiation. Initiation is not a traditional Mandari practice but has recently been adopted from Nilotic neighbours; even before this, however, a youth received his display-ox at around fifteen or sixteen when the Mandari consider that physiological adulthood has been reached.

The horns of display-oxen are trained by cutting when the animal is a small calf, and grown into characteristic curved shapes. Cutting thickens the horn and great size and weight of horn is another *sönö* characteristic. The horns of ordinary neuters are not trained.[1] Neutering further encourages large body proportions. Because display-oxen do not fight other cattle they are unblemished; they also do not lose condition through expenditure of sexual energy.

The Mandari lavish great care on display-oxen and when other animals are at their poorest and most emaciated they somehow manage to maintain *sönö* in reasonable condition. These animals are therefore absolutely distinct in appearance from other neuters on account of their size, horn formation, and markings, and the Mandari do not regard the run-of-the-mill oxen as in the same category. Display-oxen resemble ordinary neuters only in being non-productive. I do not consider, however, that the fact that display oxen are neuters means that Mandari see a special significance in neutering. They accept its necessity because without neutering, a display-ox of the desired appearance and temperament could not be produced. The whole male is more aggressive than the neuter, though by our standards Mandari stud bulls are docile; but apart from this the whole male would not be amenable to being led about, groomed, petted, and decorated because he is

---

[1] This appears to be in contrast to Nuer practice; the Nuer may cut the horns of ordinary neuters as well.

cow-orientated. A display-ox must be man-orientated, living much of its life actually at its owner's side. Its artificial docility makes it responsive to man, in a relationship which could not be established between a man and a whole animal running with the cows.

It would not be practicable for every youth to have his own bull since too high a ratio of breeding animals would impair the quality of stock, yet the idea that every male has his *sönö* essentially represents the ideal of equality between age-mates who own the display-oxen. A young man and his display-ox are in their youthful prime together, and the beauty of the one enhances the appeal of the other.[1] The image of the man is magnified in the image of the ox, which has been deliberately taken out of the ordinary animal category and artificially modified to this end. In this sense the ox is identified with the man, and perhaps to some degree the man with the ox. But identification is only present for Mandari with this very special animal; it is definitely not extended to other classes of cattle. This may be one of the reasons why cattle play a role in Mandari sacrifice different from that which they play among the Nuer. The animal killed in a Mandari sacrifice represents an exchange for the life or health of the person who offers it, and not the actual offering, through identification, of the sufferer himself. Moreover, unlike the Nuer, they do not use cattle stereotypes to describe social categories. Important family heads are not known as 'bulls',[2] nor are kinship segments equated with herd segments, nor are women verbally identified with cows. Further, masculine and feminine roles are not absolutely defined by cattle duties. Men are not excluded from milking by status and ritual considerations, and will do it if necessary. The change from boyhood to manhood is not marked by ceasing to milk.

Identification with display-oxen seems to be much stronger among the Nuer and Dinka than among the Mandari. One of the clearest illustrations of this is found among the Nuer, where much weight is given to the analogy between the mutilation of youths at initiation and the mutilation of the ox.[3] This is entirely

[1] As Evans-Pritchard and Lienhardt have stressed. See E. E. Evans-Pritchard, *Nuer Religion* (Oxford, 1956), chap. x, and R. G. Lienhardt, *Divinity and Experience* (Oxford, 1961), Introduction, section ii.

[2] E. E. Evans-Pritchard, *Kinship and Marriage among the Nuer* (Oxford, 1951), pp. 27–8, 37.

[3] E. E. Evans-Pritchard, *Nuer Religion*, pp. 256–7, and T. O. Beidelman, 'The Ox and Nuer Sacrifice: Some Freudian Hypotheses', *Man*, N.S., vol. i

absent in Mandari where head-cutting is practised also by girls at about nine or ten years old according to personal inclination, and is not a part of male initiation. Nor do the Mandari wear the heavy brass and copper wire bracelets, which are used by Nuer youths to 'sympathetically' deform their right arms to parallel the deformation of the ox's right horn.

But personally I feel that some of the apparently exaggerated identification may be explained by the greater poetic richness of Nilotic verbal imagery in general. The richness of Nilotic praise-songs, with their wealth of imagery from the natural and animal world, has long since been recognized by the Mandari, who have now given up using their traditional 'ox-names' and 'praise-songs' (*warju*) in preference for Dinka versions. The borrowing is also partly due to the fact that ox-names are now taken at initiation and initiation is a Dinka custom (or more exactly, in the Mandari case, an Atwot borrowing). Much Mandari cattle-based imagery relates to young peoples' activities and dances and is not indulged in by older persons, and it must be seen as part of a whole range of youthful modes and fashions. The shouting of the ox-name in some contexts, however, as when entering a homestead at a chief's mortuary rite, or when charging during an affray, has a deeper significance, representing a challenge, 'myself and my ox', implying 'myself at a moment of power'. But ox-names are never shouted before an invocation in sacrifice, as they sometimes appear to be among the Nuer.[1] This would be totally out of character. The Mandari officient does not aim to stress at a rite his man–ox identity or even his own identity at all. Another example which shows that man–cattle equivalences are less in Mandari than among the Nuer and Dinka is the fact that cattle are not the traditional compensation for human life; in traditional homicide payments a young girl was placed with the victim's kin. The recent homicide compensation by cattle payment was introduced by the Administration. Cattle were traditionally the compensation only for hurt, adultery, and seduction.

The Mandari categorize their cattle very exactly according to their fitness for different kinds of sacrifice. The whole bull, the exceptional animal giving the herd its identity and the basis of

(1966), no. 4, pp. 461–5, where he develops this point as a central theme in his argument.

[1] Evans-Pritchard, *Nuer Religion*, pp. 253–4.

its increase, is sacrificed only in the rite for male impotence. Then the victim's virility is symbolically essential, for a neuter cannot represent those dynamic, virile, life-giving qualities missing in the impotent. On the other hand that very virility makes the whole bull quite unsuitable for ordinary sickness, burial, or mortuary rites.

Fertile cows are scarcely ever sacrificed.[1] Indeed the killing of any productive animal is confined to special situations. Only in the rare mortuary killing at the grave of a landowning chief who has been greatly loved and whose rain powers have been seen to be outstandingly active, should a cow—sometimes with its calf—be sacrificed. Since chiefs are no longer ritually installed and the killing of the cow in milk at burial specifically links the symbolism of burial with that of installation, such sacrifices must now occur very rarely, if at all.

Display-oxen, the beasts most closely identified with human kind, again are not usually sacrificial victims,[2] although they are sometimes among the cattle killed at the mortuary rites of chiefs. The Mandari say that it is rare for a man to sacrifice a display-ox he himself has raised from a calf, but that he may sometimes kill one acquired in exchange for a cow. If, however, the new owner should sacrifice this ox the original owner ought not to eat or drink in his homestead, lest 'the blood revenge itself'. This compares with homicide prohibitions, for 'sönö is like a person' (sönö se ŋutu). The original owner can only eat and drink safely with the killer by providing a neutered sheep to be killed and eaten together by both.[3]

The neuter (budösho) is the standard offering when cattle are killed in ritual, together with the barren female (teŋ baŋsho), which is treated like a neuter. Neuters are appropriate in most situations because, like barren animals, they lack the special qualities of virility and fertility which respectively make bulls inappropriate for rites for women or children, and cows inappropriate for rites for men. Women and children being specially vulnerable physiologically feature very commonly in ritual.

---

[1] The cow is teŋ or, more precisely, since teŋ is also the generic name for all cattle, teŋ nakwan, 'female cow'.

[2] This does not seem to be so with the Nuer who also sacrifice display-oxen. Evans-Pritchard, *Nuer Religion*, p. 222.

[3] A similar prohibition applies if an owner decides to slaughter an aged display-ox. He 'mourns', and abstains from the meat which is eaten by his age-mates.

Neuters and barren animals are most appropriate for representing either sex and all stages of maturity. Mandari symbolism,
distinguishing two main categories of cattle, the productive (bulls
and cows) and the non-productive (neuters and barren), is consistent with economic principle, for breeding animals, economically
the most valuable, are reserved for the most infrequent rites.
Evans-Pritchard notes that in Nuer sacrifice a male animal must
be neutered should it still be whole.[1] This does not arise among
the Mandari since, apart from stud animals, all stock is neutered
whilst very young.

The Mandari have fewer cattle than the Nuer and the Dinka and
most sacrifices are of sheep or goats for which the same rules as
those for cattle apply. In certain rites a sheep or goat may take
precedence over an ox, and a young ox may then be exchanged
for the required full-grown neutered goat or sheep.

IV

I now indicate briefly the position of Mandari in the contemporary world at the time of my field-work, for the reader should
have some idea of the extent and persistence of foreign influences,
some indication of the degree to which the indigenous beliefs and
related practices have been modified, and roughly the proportion
of the population which has been affected by change.

It would, I think, be no exaggeration to say that around 98 per
cent of the population living in Mandari country continues to
accept the ideological background of traditional belief and to practise the indigenous rituals: and that among the remaining 2 per
cent there is partial acceptance, together with acceptance of new
ideas which may conflict with traditional ones. A few Mandari
only have completely cut themselves off from the traditional way
of life, and these live outside the country. The reasons for the
persistence and resilience of traditional forms in a changing world
can be summed up under a few main headings which I shall deal
with in turn:

[1] This seems quite consistent with the importance the Nuer attach to the
productive animal: there also it is allotted a special sacrificial role and to kill
a whole animal is, as a rule, symbolically incorrect. A further point which may
be relevant is that the Nuer, according to Evans-Pritchard, do not castrate
until the animal is between one and two years old, so most of a man's stock may
be young whole beasts.

1. Poor communications, and the fact that there is no township in Mandari.
2. Lack of trade and facilities for a wage-economy.
3. Lack of educational and medical facilities.
4. Lack of a mission in Mandari.

From the Mandari point of view, the main changes have been those directly introduced by the Sudan Administration in the immediate interests of public security and, as might be expected, these relate to political machinery and the operation of courts. These changes have already been referred to elsewhere.[1] As to the new administrative divisions mentioned there, these have modified indigenous political machinery, but they have little influence on daily social activities and virtually none on ritual which continues to be carried out within the indigenous socio-political divisions based on the landowning clans.

The newly appointed administrative chiefs, sub-chiefs, and headmen, while not always the same as those whom the Mandari themselves might have sponsored (though the majority are local candidates, confirmed by the Administration) are still very far from being bureaucratic officials. A chief is always a member of the group he represents; chiefs are not moved about and, except in one case, are neither literate nor Christian. They remain close to the traditional elder in attitude and function, though new duties and responsibilities have been acquired, such as the collection of hut tax. It is true that administrative chiefs are not necessarily the elders now found performing important rituals, but this is partly because some administrative chiefs, the sons of former office-holders, would not have assumed office in the indigenous system so young, and therefore senior elders automatically take precedence over them in ritual. Older administrative chiefs, especially those of Bora chiefdoms still, in the main, carry out important ritual duties particularly those relating to rain.

The establishment of any administration presupposes a widening of communications and contact with outsiders. Mandari are visited at intervals by the District Commissioner, and by the Veterinary Department for the inoculation of cattle. But the Province Head-quarters from which Mandari are at present administered is in Juba, some 190 miles away, and in 1950, when I began field-work, the earth road was not an all-weather road.

[1] *Chiefs and Strangers*, pp. 34–5, 118–19, 127–31.

The geographical position of Mandari country in relation to established townships (see Map 2 at end of book) has meant that it has been included within the boundaries of one province after another, as a kind of appendage to larger peoples. Province boundaries have been changed during this century. Mandari were originally on the edge of the vast Bahr-el-Ghazal Province with headquarters at Wau; during this period, they were administratively on the periphery of the Dinka tribes and under the Sub-District of Yirol. They were missed out of the Belgian-administered Lado Enclave, which later, in 1910, was reconstituted as a part of the old-established Mongalla Province. They were therefore cut off from the rest of the Bari-speaking peoples. They are now back with the latter, but separated from the Dinka, on the boundary of Equatoria Province, which replaced the old Mongalla Province. Their distance from administrative control, and the splitting at different times between different administrative areas with headquarters hundreds of miles apart, are factors of importance to an understanding of the present Mandari situation, since to be accessible to Administration implies a number of other significant potential contacts, which have bypassed Mandari.

Having no town or urban areas in their country, the centre for the dissemination of new influences has been the small police headquarters known as Tali Post, with its court-house where the sittings of the 'B' courts and the recently constituted combined Aliab–Atwot–Mandari courts take place and with its gaol, under the command of a police sergeant and his staff. Tali, which is not a true Mandari village, but an artificially created unit, has a small non-Mandari population including some of the police, the Medical Assistant and the Dresser, and, during my first visit, an Arab merchant, besides a Bari shopkeeper at an adjacent smaller shop. The two shops sold hoe, axe, and spear-heads, beads and other ornaments, cloth of various kinds and sizes, salt, and local tobacco, mostly Dinka grown. Small essentials for the foreign community such as coarse soap and aspirins were also available. The merchant's lorry which plied back and forth was an important, if unreliable, single link with surrounding townships.

The Mandari in a reasonable year can produce all their daily requirements with the exception of trade articles. In good years the small grain surplus is sold to the merchant who also buys, when available, honey and tobacco, and the occasional ox, sold

by the Mandari to buy set-beads.[1] In return the Mandari receive
the cash necessary to pay the 50 piastres (approximately 50p) per
annum hut tax and to buy trade goods; alternatively, they may
receive goods in kind. Although money is not as yet the over-all
medium for exchange within Mandari, many families have small
amounts of cash.

The Mandari have no markets; the selling of produce is on an
individual basis. No cash crop is grown and there are no development schemes either in or near Mandari. For the few men who
do not choose to follow the traditional life there is no alternative
but to leave. This does not imply the existence of a system of
migratory labour, since there is no demand for mass labour in the
Southern Sudan which cannot be already met in areas where pilot
schemes, such as the Azande scheme, have been located. In any
case the Mandari will not undertake what they consider menial
work. They will, however, join the police and the army; the former,
particularly, in which the Mandari have gained a high reputation,
accounts for most adults working outside the country. These ex-
patriates are literate in varying degrees and combine long periods
of living outside Mandari with periods of leave at home; most will
eventually retire there. By that time they will have acquired cattle
—mainly bought from the Dinka by relatives at home out of pay
sent back—and will have married several wives and founded a
number of families, some located in Mandari others travelling
round with them as they are posted from place to place. Their
sons who attend schools in the towns where they are stationed
form the nucleus of a slowly growing, literate, younger generation.
As Mandari country offers no scope for the ambitions of these
young men they remain in the townships, following the father's
profession, or taking up clerical or technical work. Visits are
occasionally made to relatives back home. Expatriate family heads
may, therefore, have sons living in Mandari in traditional style
and others who are literate and living in the urban environment.

The few older men of retiring age appear to settle back into
Mandari communities without much difficulty, concessions made
to their professional life showing in such modifications as building
a homestead on the ground, wearing clothing, and attending the
Tali Dispensary. When necessary they attend family rituals, but
they are not generally called upon to officiate at rites, since there

---

[1] The beads worn by youths after initiation.

are always other elders who have been acting in this capacity during their absence.

Education within Mandari has been fraught with problems and discouraging failure. At the time of my main field-work the bush schools, which provided the only education available, were mission-sponsored. The establishment of bush schools has been difficult if not impossible outside the immediate area of Tali Post for many reasons. The lack of trained Mandari teachers means that teaching must be done by members of other tribes. Non-Mandari teachers, who have come to expect a relatively comfortable standard of living, find that they cannot adapt to the isolation and the conditions of life in remote villages. There is also a problem of language, in that all teaching is carried out in Bari, the language with which Mandari has its closest affinities but which is not immediately understood. Consistent teaching through the year is impossible in many chiefdoms where cattle requirements, together with lack of water, mean that virtually the entire population moves out to camps of one kind or another for the whole of the dry season.

In the past there has been a lack of enthusiasm for schooling—an attitude now beginning to change—and therefore a shortage of pupils. In the few areas where bush schools have survived for any time, boys from the main local lineages have been selected by village consensus to attend, including at least one of the chief's sons.

Scattered in different parts of Mandari, therefore, are boys and youths who, having for a time attended a bush school and acquired the elements of literacy, have drifted away or been unable to continue because of the closure of the school. As I travelled around, I found evidence of attempts to establish schools; in Dari, only ten miles from Tali, there was a school building but neither teacher nor pupils: six years later there was no trace of the building. Schools in the remoter areas almost inevitably failed. At Tali the position was more favourable. The Catholic-sponsored school at Kiritnumbor, sited near permanent water, had around thirty boys when I visited it in 1951. This and all remaining bush schools were later closed, and a government elementary school opened at Tali, offering boarding facilities. Because of food shortage it was not in operation during my field-work. In 1952 I succeeded, with the help of the then Director of Education for the Southern

Sudan, in obtaining places for twelve Mandari boys at the school at Mundri in Moru District. Attempts have also been made in the past to persuade prominent Mandari to send their sons for education outside the country.

The Catholic Verona Fathers and the C.M.S., have long established missions among the Bari, the Dinka, and the Nuer, but the missions seem to have accepted the difficulties involved and have not aimed at making Mandari converts on any scale; indeed this would hardly have been possible without a mission station in the country. The nearest missions to Mandari and situated among tribes with whom the Mandari from time to time have contact—although over a considerable distance—were the C.M.S. mission at Yirol between the Atwot and the Cic Dinka, and the C.M.S. medical mission at Lui in Moru District. Between 1952 and 1958 (when I was away from Mandari), the Verona Fathers opened a bush station in Mandari near Jabor village, but a few years later all mission activity in the Southern Sudan was brought to an end. All the same it may be presumed that elements of Christian belief have been diffused over time among the pupils at the bush schools, there have been conversions among the Mandari at schools outside their country, and perhaps among the pupils at Kiritnumbor. Being literate, however, does not inevitably imply becoming a Christian.

The Mandari are, of course, aware that education, medical treatment, and other benefits are available elsewhere, and those who have visited Juba or other towns have seen examples of these for themselves, but in their own country they have little chance to participate in them. In view of the shortage of money, technical equipment, and trained personnel, it is not surprising that the Sudan Government should have deployed its scarce resources in areas which seemed to promise the greatest return—that is, within the larger and more dominant tribes and those most accessible to established towns.

I have been referring mainly to the situation as I found it from 1950 to 1952, the time of my main field-work: on my return in 1958, there was evidence that Mandari country was being opened up, most directly through much-improved road communications. I have no reliable news of Mandari from 1958 onwards, a decade of political disturbance and military occupation of the Southern Sudan.

PART I

COSMOLOGY AND CULTS

1

COSMOLOGY

I

I SHALL begin with a brief consideration of certain key assumptions of the Mandari regarding the nature of the universe and the principles governing human existence. Many of the ideas which determine religious action cannot be inferred from the observation of ritual itself (although some can) and the Mandari themselves discuss these ideas in the abstract. They not only act out their religion, they think and reflect about it.

The essence of Mandari cosmology is the concept of Ɖun, a word I translate as Creator. When I refer to Creator as a conscious power, seen to explain the fact of the universe and man, Ɖun will be capitalized. In a derived, or secondary, meaning, and here not capitalized, *ɲun* is a category word used to describe functions or states which have a specific association with Creator or which portray a strong element of creativity.

The Mandari consider that Creator explains the fact of the universe and its continuity, and the existence of the natural world, man, and society. The idea of initial creation and continuing involvement in the world are implicit in their view of Creator, the cosmos and the world being directly represented as Creator's 'work'. The Mandari have no myths to explain how the world itself came into being. For them the visible world about them is sufficient proof of the existence of Creator. Their cosmology deals with the emergence of their own social order and the modification of the natural features of Mandari country when the world was already in being. Assumed to have ordained social life, Creator is seen to be the guardian of custom in its particular Mandari forms and in other forms the Mandari know, or assume to exist, for other peoples. The known diversity of human behaviour is accepted, like the diversity of nature, as right and proper and a part of an initially created order; but custom is also seen to have been evolved by men themselves.

These two complementary ideas explain the tolerance the Mandari display for other people's customs and behaviour-patterns, and the ease with which the Mandari make cross-cultural comparisons between their own religious beliefs and those of neighbours. Although surprise and even disapproval may be the first reaction on hearing of an alien belief, this is inevitably followed by the comment, 'No doubt it is all right for them, since Creator made people differently.'

The Mandari see their own society as a part of a wider social order but they also consider it to have unique rightness and validity for them. Certain principles, very generally stated, are regarded as unchangeable, but recognition is also given to the fact of change. At the time of my field-work, the Mandari were seeking, not without much heart-searching, to accommodate new theoretical ideas and to work out their application in practice. Radical change is generally regarded as dangerous and inadmissible, but the long process of historical assimilation whereby many different groups from outside have been welded into the Mandari people seems to have promoted a flexibility of approach and capacity for compromise. Justification of custom (konesi—'actions') in general is given in terms of Creator, but it is the ancestors who are seen to be the more immediate authority for particular procedures. It is they who embody the human element, through their position as former members of kinship groups, while also providing the spiritual authority through their mergence in Creator.

II

The Mandari do not speculate about Creator's nature, use human models to draw analogies, or reduce Creator to the level of known experiences. They use the word Dun when referring to

Creator, rather than the personal pronoun 'he'.[1] Creator is not described as a father nor human beings as his children.[2] The refusal to concretize seems to be deliberate, and substantiated by the comment, 'Creator has not been known or seen.' To leave ultimates undefined allows adjustment at the lower levels of belief without introducing contradictions at the higher.

Although the Mandari do not portray Creator through a father image they suggest something very similar to the father–son relationship in practice. Thus, affective states such as anger and concern are attributed to Creator, and direct intervention in the form of protection and chastening. Because Creator made the world, Creator is also concerned for it and directly accessible to man: 'a person may call on Creator by mouth [in prayer] in trouble' or 'at any time'. The common Mandari phrase, 'Dun kata', 'Creator is', and the more enigmatic, 'gwa sana', 'the way things are', 'in the nature of things', reflect the acceptance of continuity and rightness which stems from the reality of Creator. The Mandari speak of 'Creator being angered' ('Dun wawaran'), and of practices 'Creator hates' ('Dun maman'); but they refrain from making moral evaluations of Creator—'Creator is neither good nor bad'; as the source, the explanation for all things Creator cannot be judged by human standards. Similarly, Creator is not endowed with the symbolic attributes associated with Creator's lesser spiritual manifestations.

Essential aspects of Creator are present in the two complementary divisions of the Universe which are given great religious significance. Division is drawn where it appears perceptually— between the sky and the earth, between what is above and what is below. Creator may indeed be referred to as Ki, the word for 'cosmic', 'sky', 'above', or 'up', and as Kak, meaning 'earth', 'world', 'below', or 'down'. The earth–sky reference is used as a metaphor for Creator because, according to the Mandari, 'Creator is in all places and everywhere.' If he were described by reference to one part alone, it would limit his universality. It is hardly necessary to stress that the use of metaphor does not imply a failure to distinguish the abstract from the concrete. Mandari

[1] All nouns have gender. Dun is masculine.
[2] This is in contrast to the neighbouring Dinka who use the father model to express their idea of Divinity. Lienhardt, *Divinity and Experience*, part i, chap. i, especially pp. 28–46.

make this quite clear: 'Sky is not Creator, neither are the clouds signs of Creator, but only shadows.' 'The sky is what we see above us, in which are clouds which will later fall as rain, the other Ki is Creator.' Similarly, Creator is not earth: 'There is nothing in the ground, it is only dirt [organic matter].'

In order to preserve the distinction between the conceptual divisions, and earth and sky in nature, I translate 'Ki' when used as a proper name as 'Spirit-of-the-Above', and 'Kak' as 'Spirit-of-the-Below'. I also use the terms 'Celestial Spirit' and 'Terrestrial Spirit' for the more general category divisions.[1] Much more is involved in these notions than simply metaphor; the divisions in themselves are seen to be spiritual realities. The contradictions in their nature and attributes at both the ideal and the natural levels are sharply defined and their mutual opposition is stressed. Each embodies something of the nature of Creator, but both together do not embrace Creator who is ultimately outside both—a point made clear in statements like 'It is His [Creator's] Above.' The divisions are created works, although in them Creator is present in a very special way. In certain respects they may be compared with the 'refractions' of the Nuer universe,[2] in that they are spiritual representations or agents seen to have a direct relationship with humanity and nature, but they are different from the Nuer divisions in other important respects. Thus, while the spiritual agents of division represent channels of communication with Creator, the Mandari give them a formal autonomy. It is the *divisions* which are constantly made manifest in Mandari ritual rather than Creator, the whole.

While for the Mandari, this division suggests equality between the parts, in fact the celestial part is the more actively represented. The reason for this and the perceptions which give the upper its dynamic qualities, will become clear. But I would stress at this point that even the word 'up' has a different kind of value and weight from the word 'down' for the Mandari. It carries the association of the good direction—towards the ideal, the spiritual, the dynamic—when contrasted with the more restricted implications of 'down'. In the same way, Spirit-of-the-Above is an active

---

[1] The addition of the words 'Spirit of' immediately distorts the Mandari concepts, making it both too concrete and too limited. The problem here lies not so much in *translation*—in seeking words to describe comparable concepts—as in the fact that we have no concept resembling the Mandari one.

[2] Evans-Pritchard, *Nuer Religion*, especially chaps. i, ii, and iii.

principle directly experienced, while Spirit-of-the-Below is more
passive, known indirectly through intermediaries like the dead kin.

The sky itself is also seen to have a closer association with
Creator than the earth, and it may be implied that Creator is
located there—'At death, life goes up to Creator.' Even the joking
question put by a Mandari, who asked whether I could see
Creator from my aeroplane when I travelled from Khartoum,
reflects the model of sky as the spiritual location.[1]

None the less Creator, in the final analysis, is not bound by any
spatial categories; indeed the cosmic association implies bound-
lessness, since, for the Mandari at any rate, cosmic space means the
supremely unknown experience, the new, the undiscovered, the
unfettered, the free, whereas earth has the associations of old
experience. and the knowledge of good and evil based on human
observation.

In religious situations where the maximum emphasis is to be
placed on the idea of unity, for instance at a rite of blessing, Spirit-
of-the-Above and Spirit-of-the-Below are invoked simultaneously,
together with Creator. After invoking 'You Creator', the officiant
follows with the words, 'You Above, and You Below'. But in those
rites concerned with specific illness or affliction where an agent
of one division only is seen to be involved, this alone is invoked.
More rarely, when both the divisions are involved, each must be
addressed and approached according to its own rules and receive
its accredited sacrifice. On such occasions the inherent antipathy
between each is clearly portrayed through the symbols used, a
primary concern of Mandari symbolism being to separate and so
define and stress the two conceptual and natural divisions. In one
situation, therefore, earth and sky are harmonious parts of one
universe, but at the same time, in other situations they are the
active counter-principles of each other. The expression of this
antipathy is one of the crucial ways in which Mandari cosmology
contrasts with that of the Nuer and Dinka. The two latter peoples
do not feature a universe divided into equal but distinct parts,
each part having distinguishing attributes and associated with
exclusive phenomena.[2] The idea of equal division is not carried

---

[1] Lienhardt reports a similar comment from a Dinka. *Divinity and Experience*, p. 32.
[2] Evans-Pritchard, *Nuer Religion*, *passim*, and Lienhardt, *Divinity and Experience*, *passim*.

through and emphasized in Dinka or Nuer symbolism as it is through the Mandari symbols of opposition. The Mandari way of looking at things has, perhaps, more in common with the Shilluk representation as described by Lienhardt:

The broadest division of space around them recognized by the Shilluk is between what is above (the sky) and what is below (the earth). There is a Shilluk riddle which runs: 'What are the two half-round things (in Shilluk, *opunne*, literally 'loaves') of God (Juok)?' And the answer is 'heaven and earth'.[1]

This is the kind of statement the Mandari would readily appreciate. The Mandari paradigm also has much in common with the two Bari concepts 'God of the Above' (ɲun lo Ki), and 'God of the Below' (ɲun lo Kak). The Bari terminology has been taken by some writers (mistakenly, I believe) to mean that the Bari God is dual. The following quotation brings out the essential complementary opposition in Bari religious thought, and the kind of interpretation Seligman gives.[2]

Ngun is the name given to a superhuman power, or more accurately powers—for there is no doubt that Ngun is regarded as dual. Ngun lo ki (sometimes Ngun ki), equivalent to 'Ngun-in-the-above', i.e. the sky and Ngun lo kak (Ngun kak), signifying 'Ngun below', appeared sometimes to be synonyms of Ngun in different aspects and at other times they seemed to indicate different personalities. According to Mr. Whitehead, *Ngun lo ki is in opposition to Ngun lo kak. . . .*

It is interesting that the perceptive observer, Whitehead, a C.M.S. missionary, recognized the opposition essential to the differentiation of the parts. In Bari, also, greater emphasis is placed on God as the Upper.[3]

The central Mandari theme of an equally divided universe is confirmed in myths which are also accounts of the creation of Mandari country and society. Mandari mythology represents the earth and sky as originally joined by a perpendicular rope which allowed Creator and men to pass at will from the one to the other. In this primordial universe, the lower part (earth) lacked much of

---

[1] R. G. Lienhardt, 'The Shilluk of the Upper Nile', *African Worlds* (London, 1954), ed. Daryll Forde.
[2] C. G. Seligman, *Pagan Tribes of the Nilotic Sudan* (London, 1932), chap. viii, p. 274 (my italics).
[3] Seligman reports that Driberg understood 'Ngun lo kak to be the younger brother of Ngun lo ki and subordinate to him'. Ibid.

the natural and social diversity of the present time and was regulated by different principles. The rope was eventually severed after the sin of fratricide was committed on earth and the parts separated.[1] The celestial division, now inaccessible, continues to exist in idea as well as in the perceived reality of sky, and a partial communication is seen to remain, with the upper part more actively affecting the lower. When sky and earth were joined there was direct communication—'the ancestors came down the rope'; once it was apart communication ceased although 'kinship' was seen to remain. Separation introduced death and death in turn explains separation: 'At separation, Creator remained above together with a proportion of the people who were caught up there.' Death allows one to be reunited with Creator and separated kin: 'They [human beings] must die, since they cannot go to the heavens as flesh.' This statement recognizes the paradox of man's position, who with his physical nature and his spiritual qualities belongs potentially to both parts.

The theme of the physical and spiritual division in man's nature is reduplicated in the person of Logobong, who is contained within the unity of Creator and combines aspects of both Creator and Created, a combination clearly stated in the Mandari reference to him as 'Creator's Logobong' (Logobong lo Dun), and the 'World's Logobong' (Logobong lo Kak). Logobong is Creator associated with the world and humanity, a further symbol of differentiation in that the world and human society are different from the natural universe and yet a part of it. Logobong may be spoken of as 'Dun'(Creator), without qualification and described as 'in the heavens with Creator'; he may also be represented as archetypal man—in the Mandari phrase, 'the first man, the child of Creator'. In myth Logobong is also intimately associated with the specific races of mankind, the brown, the white, and the black, which he is said to have fathered. This myth describes the origin of the Arabs and other races grouped with them by the Mandari

[1] Variations on the 'rope' theme are found throughout the Southern Sudan, particularly among Nilotics. (Cf. Evans-Pritchard, *Nuer Religion*, p. 10 and Lienhardt, *Divinity and Experience*, pp. 33–4.) The myth is central to the Mandari Bora clan histories and these have additional elements (absent in other Nilotic versions) which have important socio-political implications, since the fratricide between clan brothers is seen to lead to social and territorial separation. In the Mandari case specific clan 'charters' are grafted on to what is elsewhere a general creation myth.

(the Turks and Egyptians), the African peoples including the Mandari, and Europeans, typified by the British and including others like the Belgians.[1] It centres around the choosing of a spear, bow, and gun, by the brown (Arabs), black (Africans), and white (Europeans), respectively.[2] It represents what the Mandari see as the 'evolutionary' pattern, with the Europeans, being descended from the son who stayed with his father and so was favoured by God, arriving later in time, already armed with over-riding material advantages.

Logobong, who fathered the races, symbolizes the spirituality of the procreative act in which he is said to be 'assisted' either by the principle of 'Maleness', Kuluŋ, or the principle of 'Femininity', Agoya: 'when a man goes into his hut with his wife, Logobong is present and Kuluŋ or Agoya.' Only Creator can set in motion the process of initial creation, but Logobong 'who followed after' is said 'to have created [ordered to be born]' the first ancestors; in particular the Bora ancestors who 'fell from the sky and were the first Mandari'.[3]

Logobong also figures as the mediating third, and plays a muted role in keeping with the essential nature of an intermediary which bridges a division in order to unite elements of a different order by combining a part only of each. Participating in the nature of Creator and created, Logobong reunites Creator and man divided by the incompatibility of spirit and matter. Because Logobong stands between Creator and man in the first instance, and represents the principle of mediation as such, he lacks the intimate and intense involvement in human affairs and states which is a feature of Spirit-of-the-Above and Spirit-of-the-Below in their varying forms.

Logobong moreover has an ideal association with each spiritual part of the universe. In his role as a creator he is orientated towards Spirit-of-the-Above, a creative principle of a higher order; in his role as archetypal man and guardian of the world and society he is identified with Spirit-of-the-Below. Association with society is stressed when Mandari refer to Logobong when justifying elements of tradition and custom—such and such a thing is done, 'because

[1] While in general the Mandari refer to Europeans as 'white', they may also, less commonly, refer to them as 'red'.

[2] This myth is also found in Dinka; see Lienhardt, *Divinity and Experience*.

[3] For a description of the Bora rain clans and their myths see *Chiefs and Strangers*, pp. 19–26, 51–9.

of Logobong', a statement particularly common in relation to customary procedures which are automatically accepted and not directly justified.

Through Logobong, Creator and the created order are united and at the same time shown to be distinct. Through him also Mandari are able to express the fact that the created order, and particularly man, face a number of paradoxes which cannot be solved by human reason, although they can be stated in symbolic terms. Logobong, associated also with the east–west dichotomy and therefore identified with the opposed qualities of these spatial categories, stands for the unresolved contradictions of the human condition.

Logobong and the east are closely identified in his legend. He journeys from the east to his destination, the west. The symbolic journey lies at the root of the gestures made at the monthly rite which combines purging and elimination on the one hand, and statements of aspiration and new hope on the other. At the rite, officiating elders assign illness, death, sin, and strife to the west— 'where Logobong's journey ended'; then turn to face the east to call for 'peace, freedom from sin, and health from Logobong's point of departure'. It is said that 'Logobong carries sin with him to the west, because his journey was made in an east–west direction, once and for all time: Logobong did not return back.' Sin once consigned to the west is eliminated. Logobong's journey is also likened to the solar movements: 'As the sun rises and sets, so Logobong came from "sunrise" (*yure*) and travelled to "sunset" (*kotiaŋ*).' East symbolizes the promise of good, the west the accumulation of evil, and on no account must these principles be confused as, for instance, by the consignment of evil to the east. Statements regarding the paradox of good–evil, life–death, beginning–ending, sickness–health, inherent and inevitable in created beings, are made each month in every Mandari homestead. But while east and west are used as symbols of the human condition and have a religious character, they are not developed as active principles of the order of celestial and terrestrial.

Explicit reference is further made to Logobong and his associated east–west symbols in relation to the burial position; Mandari state that the body must be correctly positioned because Logobong 'as man' (*lo ŋutu*) 'is also Creator' (Ɖun *gwi*) and 'brought forth man' (*lo gwiunda ŋutu*). Thus a corpse must be laid in the grave

with the head pointing towards the east—the point of departure
and of man's origin—the feet must point to the west to symbolize
the ending, the completion of life. The head faces the direction of
the good, the feet the place where evil accumulates. Because of
these primary associations, it is also inauspicious if the body of a
chicken, killed by beheading when taking an omen or in a minor
protective ritual, falls facing the west.

The monthly rite offered to Creator who alone gives life is
importantly associated with Logobong who exemplifies certain
fundamental principles of being. Indeed, it is only in connection
with prayers for harmony and peace, and with statements and
actions relating to the elimination of evil and the reinstatement of
good, that Logobong features at all in ritual. The role of Logobong
is to represent timeless truths and to establish them in reality, and
not to enter directly into the specific human situations of sickness
and death. Detachment from human events is clear when the
place of Logobong in ritual is compared with that of the spiritual
agents of division. In ritual for the specific agents, immediate
situations of sickness and death are directly represented and dealt
with.

III

Viewed as a system of ideas the Mandari cosmology can be
seen to be organized according to certain well-defined principles
and can be read as a particular kind of pattern. Such completeness
creates the impression of a received whole, a system of ideas
conceived and worked out as a totality. In fact, there is evidence
for quite the contrary; that the present beliefs have evolved
slowly, and at least in part contain randomly introduced elements.
Inevitably human choice is involved. Ideas offered by the culture
and others introduced through external influences may or may
not be developed, depending on historical events and preferences
of various kinds, including also material considerations arising
from new social contacts or economic pressures, as I shall hope to
show. New elements are, however, always arranged according to
certain underlying principles which provide the unchanging framework into which they are slotted. This framework of ideas and
ritual procedures is accepted by Mandari as correct, and is
supported by symbolic referents which are fundamental to the

oppositional principles seen to underlie the Mandari universe. Ultimately any borrowed element must be appraised and modified. The end result gives the appearance of an explicit explanatory model.

While it may appear likely that a particular element is intrusive, it is not always possible to show this, still less to trace its original source. The new Mandari cult of Powers, however, directly acquired from neighbouring Nilotics in recent decades, is a nice example of the penetration of new ideas and the resultant shifting about of these to fit them into a compatible order. There is also, I believe, some evidence that the seemingly established cult of Spirit-of-the-Above may similarly have spread out over Mandari from the original Bora element in the population. Bora rain rituals retain special features lacking in non-Bora rain rites. It is also perhaps significant that on one occasion Logobong was described to me as the 'true Mandari Creator [ƆUun] of old', implying an absolute and fundamental position in Mandari thought.

IV

Philosophical argument and comment in Mandari usually centres around particular ritual action in a particular situation. However, I found that older men and women, especially trained ritual experts, would discuss theoretical ideas in a more general way often with the help of paradigmatic models which they considered would simplify ideas for a foreign observer. During one particular discussion when I had accused a group of elders of inconsistency, they replied that my difficulty in understanding them arose because of the fact that 'in Mandari there is no single path as there is for people with writing'. They were implying that formal and precise definition without which Europeans appear to be lost is not required by them. This discussion had centred on the over-all relationship envisaged to exist between Creator, Spirit-of-the-Above, and Logobong. The elders, in accordance with the dogma that first principles cannot be defined, suggested to me that I should regard 'Ɔun, Ki, and Logobong as "three mouths" (*kutusen musala*)', as three representations or statements of reality. They also implied that the human element inevitably presupposed a variation in the expression of an idea, that 'the story' will be different with the person telling it. 'If you [Europeans] wish to know something you can look it up in paper' (the Arabic word *warraga* is used for writing and books); 'we have no paper.' While there will be variation in the statement of philosophical ideas, important attributes of Creator and his manifestations are known to all adult Mandari, together with the correct ritual actions and the essential religious symbols of differentiation. If the layman needs special guidance he consults a doctor. As a man becomes a family head he frequently has to act in ritual and becomes more knowledgeable; also, according to his temperament, he may begin to think more deeply about the beliefs on which it is based. The same is the case with the older woman.

It is not uncommon for Mandari to represent the different levels of spiritual order in terms of models taken from kinship categories.[1] For instance, Spirit-of-the-Above was described to me as 'the wife of Creator' and 'the mother of Logobong'; minor Spirits-of-the-Above (*kijin*) as children of Spirit-of-the-Above; Kuluŋ, 'black bird of the sky',[2] as 'the mother's brother' of a Dinka spirit, Löi, and so forth. Such models express elements seen to reside in the character of the spiritual principles: thus Spirit-of-the-Above is female and subsidiary to Creator (husband–wife); Spirit-of-the-Above (female) and Logobong (male) are both creators, but the former is primary (mother–son). Kuluŋ is mother's brother to Löi since they are equals, but the Dinka spirit 'enters' Mandari through the marriage of Mandari women with Dinka men. These models must be accepted as explanatory analogies and in no way understood as implying actual relationship.

V

It soon becomes apparent to the observer, that while Mandari lack an explicit theology, they have a body of ideas about the meaning of human existence. While different individuals express themselves differently on this point, they inevitably come down to a few main themes: the acceptance of a planned and ordered universe, the idea of a balanced relationship between Creator and man (spirit and matter), and the necessity for man's co-operation for the continuity of the world as created and ordained.

[1] The Nuer also use this mode of expression. Evans-Pritchard, *Nuer Religion*, pp. 28–33.
[2] This Kuluŋ is not Kuluŋ the male principle.

These themes often appear in simple similes and parables. For example:

People are like fields; they are the grain of Creator. They are born, grow up, and die. Some die at birth and never reach old age; it is the same with seeds which are planted—young plants die to make room for others. When grain is ripe and ready it is cut by man and finished. The field is left and then re-sown with new seeds. So it is with man.

That space must be left for new generations is frequently stressed, sometimes by analogy with the animal world, pests and predators which prey on other animals being likened to the agents Mandari believe they recognize in their own sickness and death. Agents of Creator—Spirit-of-the-Above, the Ancestors, and paranormal phenomena like witches—are represented as the 'servants of death', used by Creator. 'They are working continuously because if all those who were born were to live, in time there would be no room.' It is also explained that 'there must be something to bring about the death of a man, since a man does not die without a reason'. The positive and necessary role of man in sustaining the created world is represented in such comments as: 'We [humans] are also the servants of Creator. We renew the earth—grow food, tend cattle, burn off old grass, plant, and harvest.' Man is also seen to keep order in society: 'When someone does wrong, there is a case and talk: Creator is satisfied when men work well and displeased when they do wrong.'

Creator is seen as the final arbitrator in man's destiny, and his spiritual manifestations (such as Spirit-of-the-Above) are simply the agents—'tools'—of his will. Everyman has 'his death' (*twan ny'it*), ordained by Creator and brought about by Creator's agents: 'If Creator does not desire the death of a man he will suffer for a time and recover with the help of the doctor, who is also a servant of Creator and protects life.' Creator is never given as the immediate *cause* of an individual sickness or misfortune, or the cause of a death. Not only is this clearly implied in the expressed distinctions drawn by Mandari, it is underlined by the fact that sacrifice is never made to Creator, but only to his agents. As the Mandari express it, 'You do not offer back to Creator what is his already.'

In certain circumstances, however, the Mandari see Creator as directly involved in man's suffering and death. Such responsibility is assumed in major disasters whose widespread nature precludes by Mandari definition the action of a particular agent, as, for example, a serious epidemic which sweeps the country, or rain failure and consequent starvation over a wide area. At such times Mandari consider that 'Creator is angered', or 'Creator has rejected', but it is usual once the all-embracing character of the disaster has been recognized to take no further ritual action.

Creator, boundless and not to be confined within any particular cult or ritual, is open to the direct appeal of any individual. His special concern is clearly expressed in the following comments: 'Anyone may call on Creator at any time. Creator watches everyone. He holds the life of a man in his hands. If He does not desire the death of a man, he will suffer for a while and get well.' And: 'A man walks in the bush, a wild beast watches him from the cover of the long grass. It lashes its tail (in anger), but the man walks safely by: his time is not yet come.' The implication here, is that man is protected since his death is ordained and not arbitrary. The special needs of certain categories are also recognized: 'A woman or child walks in the bush without a spear, they do not need a spear because Creator watches them.'

It is accepted that every man's life is planned: 'The years of a person's life are known beforehand and fulfilled.' A Mandari watching me writing in a note-book pointed out that I sometimes went back and crossed-out. On this analogy he commented that 'It is the same with Creator, He has his "note-book"; He creates man and if He wishes He will strike him out; it is the affair of Creator who gives life and can also kill.' Nevertheless, Mandari say that the death of a man 'causes Creator sorrow'. The commonplace phrase 'Djun *kata*', 'Creator is', expresses what Mandari feel about the immanence of Creator, and his protective concern. On the theme of death itself, Mandari refrain from speculation, but will simply comment that 'a man may wonder, or fear, because it cannot be known whether it is good or bad'.

So because Creator is universal, he represents those broad happenings which cannot be socially circumscribed: because he represents the individual—idiosyncratic and free—and no two persons have the same life-plan, Creator is seen also in terms of what is unique and too varied to be categorized. Logically, for both these reasons Creator does not feature in the various cults which have specific ideological and social definition. Thus, Creator is seldom the centre of communal ritual, the ritual most easily observed, although it is true that prayers may be addressed to Creator, and that after them, his blessing will be asked for the congregation before it disperses. Blessings are perhaps the commonest way of invoking Creator, but these often involve only two people, linked in spontaneous and unplanned situations; the exceptions are the public dedication of the newly born to Creator at the naming ceremony, and the prayers offered at the moment when the dead are laid in the grave.

Religious practice relating to Creator is predominantly personal, and personal religion as exemplified by individual action and spontaneous prayer is not easily open to anthropological observation. It can only be assumed from listening to people's comments and admissions. None the less, it was clear to me that some individuals—older men and women and the ritual experts who are responsible in different ways for guiding the religious life of a community—showed a greater outward piety than others, in that they would refer to Creator in the context of daily life more often. They seemed to have a capacity for viewing events in terms of Creator and his beneficial protective power, rather than stressing the adverse manifestations of lesser agents.[1]

The notion of Creator, then, underlies all other Mandari ideas but little formal ritual centres around Creator understood in this ultimate sense. The following chapters explore the various agents and the explicit ideological themes of actual Mandari ritual.

[1] Stress on the overriding power of Creator was constantly on the lips of one pious older man; on one occasion he admonished me for lack of faith, when, laid up with a stomach disorder, I complained of the attack of 'witches'. 'Don't you know Creator is present [Ɗun kata]? What is all this talk of witches?'

2

SPIRIT-OF-THE-ABOVE
AND THE
PATHOLOGY OF THE UPPER PART
OF THE BODY

I

T HE Mandari draw a clear distinction between the sky on the
one hand and the Celestial Spirit as a manifestation of Creator
on the other. Nevertheless, those things which are evidently
overhead, like stars, the sun and moon (described as 'important
persons of the Above, whose light and warmth makes life possible'),
and, nearer the earth, thunder and lightning, rainbows and rain,
reveal the Celestial Spirit in a particularly appropriate way.

The Mandari also assume the presence of Spirit-of-the-Above
to be revealed in certain ills which affect human beings, and in
this chapter I shall consider classification of diseases connected
with the Spirit, the methods of diagnosis and treatment, and the
growth and spread of the cult of the Spirit round an initial illness
situation. I examine the logic whereby Mandari make a direct
link between celestial agents and particular kinds of human
pathology where symptoms reveal characteristics also said to belong to celestial phenomena.

Before examining such relationships in detail, mention should
be made of the complete dependence of the Mandari on rainfall
and the way in which this determines the Mandari pattern of
living, forcing concentration in large groups of humans and cattle
at one season and dispersal into smaller units at others.[1] The
importance the Mandari attach to regularity and a correct balance
in seasonal change is consistent with environmental factors and
weather conditions. Water shortages are chronic, and even during
the rains few areas flood because of the light porous soils. There
are no large rivers, and small rivers and streams form a very

[1] Details of movements and groupings are given in *Chiefs and Strangers*,
pp. 137–42.

unreliable supply network because many are dry for the greater part of the year. With a few important exceptions pools are rain-derived and seasonal. Mandari consequently have an imperative need for regular rainfall at the expected time, for without it vital water supplies are insufficient for minimal economic planning and survival.

Particularly important is the prompt breaking of the early rains, and then that they should fall in a steady downpour. Before they break the scorching days with their harsh dust-filled winds mark a time of fatigue and shortage. Food is in short supply and women-folk living in villages must fetch water from distant sources. Whole villages may be forced to move to temporary camps near pools. Even water on the main grazing lands runs dangerously low, and since it is shared by men and cattle is inevitably polluted. There is overgrazing and cattle are thin and give a poor milk yield. Herders and villagers alike are hungry.

The scattered, thundery showers which mark the early rains are notoriously unreliable since they tend to be followed by further short but very severe droughts, when the unwary who have sowed and planted prematurely may lose a whole seed crop. The obsession with the sensitivity of rain, apparent in the minutely detailed ritual restrictions placed on the use of rainwater, is ex-plained when it is borne in mind that almost every year rain is literally a matter of life and death. In a very real sense the Celestial Spirit, as manifested in the rain, comes for the Mandari as both deliverer and destroyer.[1]

As a principle immanent in the weather and seasonal rhythms, Spirit-of-the-Above is described as 'coming from Creator', or as being 'His Above' (Ki *ny'it*). The feminine gender is consistent with the capacity to give fertility and abundance through rainfall, but also to destroy by withholding rain. Women also give life, but in certain circumstances are seen to kill. Protectiveness, nur-ture, and solicitude which are regarded as feminine virtues are also attributes of Spirit-of-the-Above—'the Above watches (over) the rain and the year', and 'the Above is the guardian' (Ki *a memetant*).

---

[1] Neither Nuer nor Dinka who share some common herding problems with Mandari show quite the same dependence on rainfall, having different soils, vegetation, and water-distribution, and being less tied for survival to crop yields which are completely dependent on rainfall.

The giving of primal rain to the world is expressed in the statement that 'in the beginning water was brought to the world by the Above as rain, which filled the low places as pools and rivers'. The power to perform the rain rites (described in Part IV below) is based on this 'power-of-Above', said to have been given to early clan founders 'for all time, and once lost never regained'. Thus, the fatal inability of an important ancestral chief to provide abundant water for his people is portrayed in myth as leading to fratricide and eventually to the dividing-up of the Mandari people.[1] Brotherly enmity and rain is a widely occuring historical theme. Continuing access to this stream of cosmic virtue allows a chief to fulfil the expectations of his people regarding fertility in man and nature.

II

Where the Mandari consider Spirit-of-the-Above has invaded the lives of chosen people and established relationships with them, the event, and the sickness symptoms which prove this, may show through natural phenomena belonging to the sky or bear signs of denominators considered to exemplify features of it. The Spirit may be shown to be present in its undivided form, or in one of its particular, individualized forms. These latter, corresponding closely to the spiritual refractions described for the Nuer and the Dinka, compose together the category known as *kijin* (literally translated, 'Aboves'); each in turn is distinguished by a name and special characteristics. I refer to these individualized forms as 'free-Spirits-of-the-Above'.[2] When a Mandari practitioner claims to work curatively through association with the Celestial Spirit, he may be referring to the undifferentiated or the refracted form, depending on factors in his own particular heredity and experiences he has himself undergone. The same is the case with family cults centring around shrines.

Nervous disorders and mental sickness with certain clearly distinguishable characteristics are considered by Mandari to be a sign of Spirit-of-the-Above. The sufferer is described as being 'with Above', or 'having Above', (*gwa ko* Ki), or it may be said

---

[1] See the myths of the Bora clans—*Chiefs and Strangers*, pp. 19–24 and 58–9.
[2] This terminology borrows from Lienhardt's word 'free-divinity'; Lienhardt, *Divinity and Experience*, p. 56. Mandari have in fact acquired a number of these Dinka spirits; see below.

of them 'Above has fallen upon them.' This kind of diagnosis is only made where the symptoms of the mental illness are clearly marked and of sudden onset. A quick return to normal health is another indicator that the illness is from this source, and suddenness in the onset and departure of phases or crises suggests the same origin. The Mandari do not necessarily view every attack of this sort as serious and one form of convulsion which passes rapidly but gives the appearance of a 'taking over' of the personality, although a sign of Spirit-of-the-Above is considered harmless.

The notion of entry from the outside is also present in 'celestial illness'.[1] Spirit-of-the-Above is said 'to come down'—literally 'it falls towards them' (*ŋu'du'an ky'it*). Arbitrary and unsolicited selection is also implied in the statement, 'Above comes to them independently' (*Ki po ky'it kardeleken*). Something which falls from a height comes hard and swiftly and the onset of this class of mental illness is swift, coming, as it were, like a bolt from the blue, and generally producing the kind of symptom manifested in a sudden physical trauma like a blow or a shock, which knocks a person off course or even renders him unconscious. The Mandari believe that to be struck by lightning is a direct punishment from Spirit-of-the-Above, and the archetype of this Spirit's action is a disorientating shock to the person or the personality, similar in effect to a lightning strike.

Since sudden onset is the distinguishing symptom, an illness which might be considered in the context of Western medicine to be a slow-developing personality disorder is not seen to be from Spirit-of-the-Above; it may, in fact, not be viewed as illness at all but merely as the idiosyncrasy of the sufferer, who is regarded as becoming a more extreme version of himself. The Mandari will say of such a person, who for example is becoming more unsociable, that 'he always sits by himself, he is always quarrelling and shouting', or simply, he is odd, 'he talks anyhow' (*kulya ashuŋa*), and so forth. Eccentricities of behaviour, particularly loud and unsuitable talk, in an individual who is of peripheral status, such as a client, may also confirm for others that he has the evil eye or is a night-witch. Such eccentricity may be seen to

[1] When I refer to a specific illness seen to originate from this Spirit or its agents, I shall speak of a 'celestial illness'. This is a convenient term and also follows out the implicit, but important, distinction Mandari make between the causal agent and the sickness itself as a bundle of symptoms. Mandari will, however, *refer* to both the agent and the symptoms by the single word 'Ki'.

denote other abnormality, but it would never be classed as 'with Above', since it lacks the qualifying symptom of sudden onset. Another important form of mental impairment, congenital mental deficiency, is also differently classed. The Mandari recognize this to be an *intrinsic* organic impairment and they attribute the malfunction to an act of 'bad creation' on the part of Creator. They make a similar assessment of physical deformity which becomes apparent at an early age—for instance in the case of a child who never learns to walk upright but crawls or drags a leg, or one who grows up with a withered arm. The Mandari explain that these were 'broken' or 'spoiled' by Creator at birth.[1]

I cannot say to what extent those psychoneurotic disorders— anxiety, depression and so forth—which form such a large part of mental illness in the Western context, are present among Mandari or form any health problem for them. During discussions with Mandari practitioners regarding illness classifications, I found that emotional disorders of these kinds were not isolated as conditions requiring treatment.[2]

Within the Mandari classification of mental illness, there is a wide diversity of symptoms and much variation; attacks may be short- or long-term, severely crippling, or offering no impairment after quickly passing; they may be recurrent or isolated, and a few can be chronic for life. This poses a problem of diagnosis for the Mandari. If illness from Spirit-of-the-Above is sudden in onset and relatively sudden in passing, a contradiction can arise when a condition begins by showing these typical symptoms but then develops a chronic pattern, or leads to complete mental deterioration and impairment to the point where participation in social life becomes impossible. The Mandari consider that a different and distinct condition is then involved: 'It is not Above.' I have never myself seen an advanced case of this type although Mandari say such exist; they are not a simple down-coming of Spirit-of-the-

---

[1] Gross deformity showing in a newborn baby is monstrosity and something different again.

[2] The Leightons in their study among the Yoruba, in very different circumstances from those prevailing in Mandari, found it difficult to obtain such information when they posed questions in the context of sickness, and only received the answers they were seeking by asking a quite different kind of question—for instance, by asking about instances of witchcraft, and then trying to deduce whether anxieties regarding it could be considered 'normal' or 'abnormal'. A. H. Leighton *et al.*, *Psychiatric Disorder among the Yoruba* (New York, 1963).

Above, but result from a form of neutral contact with certain elemental celestial phenomena, in association with witchcraft. The individual's mind is first 'spoilt' by a witch—'his head is scrambled up' (*kwe ny'it dyadyaŋgu*). He becomes confused and disorientated, the witchcraft subsequently sends him out to wander about in the bush, so that 'he catches his foot on the point where the rainbow has touched the earth'. This class of mental illness is called *göri* after its source, the rainbow. It is the witch who establishes the fatal contact with the rainbow by sending the person, who is normally sensible and self-controlled, to wander about 'anyhow' (*ashuŋga*): witchcraft is the positive agent, the rainbow is simply resting on the ground—it is a celestial phenomenon but not an active agent and does not seek out a victim. At the contact point, however, Mandari see a dangerous charge remaining, somewhat as a disused electric wire may be live. While the Mandari do not know the scientific explanation of lethal forked lightning which often kills people and stock, they know this to be associated with rain and storm; the rainbow, with one end of its arc touching the earth, is a part of the total rain complex and is assumed to have dangerous properties similar to those of lightning.

The Mandari are constantly aware of things from 'up' coming down upon them; some, like rain, come beneficially, others come destructively. They regard themselves as exposed and open to the firmament and its phenomena as constantly in contact with them.[1] The notion of mental sickness from this source as swift, destructive, and capricious, accords with the character of natural forces as the Mandari observe them.

A further variation on the Mandari mental illness theme, but one where sorcery alone is involved, is *kapur*, where the patient is chronically confused or demented. The victim typically raves and is violent, shouts, mutters, and talks compulsively and irrationally (*ashuŋga*—'anyhow'). The condition, in Mandari theory, is quite distinct from mental disorder of the Spirit-of-the-Above class, but in practice some of the symptoms of *kapur* may be present in a patient suffering from the former, particularly where a Call syndrome (Chapter 13) is involved. *Kapur* is also the word for 'butterfly', since it is believed that a butterfly, placed in the victim's head

---

[1] A number of clan founders are represented as having 'come' or 'fallen' from the sky: cattle, rain-spears, and other rain implements also 'fell' in much the same way. Even now, 'miraculous falls' are still claimed.

by a night-witch or person with the evil eye, causes the mental
confusion by its fluttering. Thus the insane are described as being
'bewitched with a butterfly' (*kwöniju ko kapur*). It is accepted that
witches have the power to place substances in parts of a victim's
body to cause pain and sickness, the particular thing which is so
placed being analogous in some way to the particular sickness
symptoms. Thus the Mandari compare the vibrating wings and
the hovering and fluttering with the sensation of confusion. It is
a moot point, I think, whether in fact it is a real butterfly (or, in
the case of other forms of witchcraft, snake, etc.) which is assumed
to be present; the Mandari themselves certainly give the impression that they consider this is so, but it is clearly the analogous
qualities of the material thing on the one hand, and the sickness on
the other, which determine the selection of the causal agent.

Madness in this style has given rise to the colloquialism, 'having
a *kapur*' (*gwa ko kapur*), which is equivalent to our phrase 'stark
staring mad'; it can also be used loosely to describe anyone who
behaves in an odd way. To refer to a person as '*kapur*' tends to be
derogatory, because this condition emanates from an evil source
and is always seriously incapacitating. I have heard of individuals
who themselves claimed to be possessed by Spirit-of-the-Above,
dismissed spitefully by others as simply mad *kapur kanay*. There
is some reason for doubting the claim, apart from mere malice,
because initial diagnosis can change, and a condition which was
first considered to be Spirit-of-the-Above may later be seen to be
simply 'madness'. The reverse may also be the case. It must be
remembered that the Mandari have no clinical methods of diagnosis, and can only arrive at a decision about a sickness by comparing the specific state with their traditional symptom scale and
then confirming their finding by divination. For this reason there
may be faulty or indecisive diagnoses, as well as differences of
opinion expressed by those who come into contact with the particular case.

The problem of diagnosis is particularly difficult when a person
suffers *periodic* bouts of mental disturbance. A youth I knew whose
deceased father had served as a policeman suffered recurrent aggressive, potentially homicidal phases during which he became violent.
After stabbing an age-mate he was taken into the care of the Police
Post at Tali. He sometimes came over to talk to me and appeared
normal and intelligent. Shortly afterwards I left Tali, but I heard

later that he had returned home cured to his widowed mother. As he received no treatment, only supervision, at the Post, I assume that this meant he had had no further attacks. His mother had never wavered in her conviction that he suffered from sickness of the celestial class and could be cured, but one of the policemen dismissed this claim and assured me 'he is simply mad' (*kapur*).

The standard treatment for those suffering from mental illness caused by the action of Spirit-of-the-Above is the sacrifice of a sheep. If no improvement follows—and the Mandari admit the difficulty, indeed the impossibility, of curing most of these states—an attempt is made to split off the possessing agent by a form of exorcism. This takes place in the open bush, and must be held by a woodland rain-pool, because the rain-link is important, particularly if 'rainbow' sickness is involved. A permanent pool has lost its pristine rain association and may even be river-fed. The offering must be a sheep, the 'cool' animal, coolness being an attribute of Spirit-of-the-Above. The sheep is held over the patient's head, addressed, and divided longitudinally down the belly in the standard style of symbolic severance. The carcass is abandoned because in exorcism, unlike sacrifice, the object is actual transference of the symptoms from patient to animal. Exorcism never takes place in the homestead and there is no ritual meal, for the dead animal, pervaded by the illness, is left outside to be disposed of by predators.

It may be suggested that I introduce a contradiction when I say that celestial illness is sometimes regarded as incurable, but also that celestial illness is typically swift in passing. Here it must be borne in mind that generalizations of the latter kind relate to over-all classifications, and that in practice variations may appear in specific illness cases. Thus an illness may change its course or develop deviant symptoms which tend to take it out of its recognized class, but the original diagnosis is not inevitably changed, though it may be. The patient said to be 'destroyed by Above', suggests a chronic case, and also that this is occasionally identified in the celestial class.

Mental patients of whatever order are generally well cared for by their families. Mandari make no distinction in terms of social attitude between the mentally and the physically ill. They are solicitous towards *all* patients and expend much time and emotional effort on them. Mental patients who require restraint are

immobilized by locking the ankles with leg bracelets joined together by a middle link.

III

A wide range of motor disturbances, some of which occur together with mental illness, are distinguished and explained as
a 'falling' of Celestial Spirit. The typical symptom is a convulsion
known as *molja*. Convulsions seem to be fairly common and,
medically, are clearly related to different causes. Some may occur
in conjunction with a febrile illness, others may result from advanced guinea-worm (*Filaria medinensis*) infections, where the
worm has reached the cerebrospinal region: some may be organic
or due to epilepsy; others, which I shall be dealing with under the
rubric of 'possession' cannot so easily be fitted into the conventional diagnostic pattern.

The Mandari themselves recognize different categories of convulsions; some, which are harmless and temporary, are not considered illness unless they become very frequent; others, which
are very serious and crippling, requiring constant consultations
and expenditure, often with no result, are recognized as permanently incapacitating and the patient lives as an invalid.

One recurrent form is said to occur at the waxing and waning
of the moon, and may result in a chronic sufferer being advised
to raise a shrine. A serious illness called *moon* features another
chronic, recurrent form of convulsion, the symptoms of which
lead me to suspect epilepsy. This is another sickness which
follows 'contact with the rainbow', but here witchcraft is not involved. The two patients I saw gave the impression of normal
intelligence but were severely handicapped; both were considered
ill by the Mandari—in fact, untreatable. A very dangerous form
of convulsion is involved here, during which the patient may
suffer serious injuries. The fits occur unexpectedly at home, during
the night perhaps, or when the victim is alone, and are not confined
to ceremonial or ritual occasions as in the case of most convulsions
of the *molja* class. While the *moon* condition results from a random
contact with something from the category of things *associated* with
Spirit-of-the-Above, the Mandari stress 'it is not Celestial Spirit'.
A doctor, however, pointed out that the seizures which are a
feature of it may lead the layman to view the attacks initially as

simply the harmless convulsions of an ordinary 'falling of Above'. I encountered two cases of this affliction in a village where I was living. I had been treating one of the youths concerned for a severe leg ulceration without being aware of what was involved. Successful treatment was followed by an outbreak of the same sore a few weeks later. Friends pointed out that I was wasting my time as the sore was caused by *moon*. It appeared that in his convulsions the youth repeatedly fell on to the fire, and the sores were burns. A stereotype of this illness is a compulsion to fall towards fire—thus 'Ki makes them fall on the fire, no sooner are their wounds healed than they are thrown on the fire again.' Neither of these youths wore beads or decorations, a sign of mourning, or serious illness. When I raised the question of marriage, I was told this was out of the question—that girls would be 'afraid'.

Trained experts may attempt an exorcism which is a more radical form of the exorcism for mental illness just described.[1] The patient is laid on a bed of leaves in the wasteland and a neutered ram or barren ewe is stretched over his supine form with its legs firmly held. The specialist works over the animal with his divining rattle, then it is turned round and stretched the other way. Eventually, I understand, it bleats and struggles convulsively and finally spasms occur with such violence that force is needed to hold it down. After a time it dies in a rigor. The convulsive death is said to take place simultaneously with the withdrawal of the patient's convulsions, as these make their lethal entry into the animal. It is perhaps significant for my later discussion of the use of rhythmic rattle-shaking to induce possession, that Mandari describe these sheep as 'taking a long time to die'.

All those states which constitute the phenomena generally described as 'spirit possession' are classified as *molja*. Possession may be mild or violent, its typical signs being twitching and shaking and, in extreme cases, what appear to be states of dissociation. In these conditions a temporary but specific displacement of the individual psyche is seen to take place by the Mandari. The individual concerned is 'taken over', and used by the possessing spirit as an instrument of communication. If any pronouncements are made these are seen to be made by the possessing spirit and

---

[1] The following technique is not widely used in Mandari; it is a specialization of the Nyangwara tribe and of the Nile-dwelling Köbora. A doctor living in Jamiŋa, in Western Mandari, claims to use it.

not by the individual who acts as its agent. Although the same word is used to describe the epileptic seizure and the convulsion attending possession, the two conditions are seen to be quite distinct. The one (*moon*) is a serious and incapacitating illness; the other, possession, is not, in general, so regarded (although possession can *become* pathological), but rather is claimed to be the means by which a source of healing power can flow through the possessed vehicle to members of the community.

That type of possession which definitely channels a healing power is confined entirely to the context of medico-religious practice. I shall refer to those who practise this profession as 'doctors' in the sense of medico-religious healers who diagnose by divination, use herbal medicines, and prescribe sacrifice for reconciling their patients with spiritual or other powers influencing their condition.

The possession said to show the presence of Celestial Spirit and used therapeutically as a diagnostic tool, is mild in form. The doctor shakes and twitches as he stands praying in the middle of the yard or at the shrine raised for the Spirit. The convulsion is spontaneous, which distinguishes it from other forms of diagnostic possession which are induced, and are used by doctors trained under foreign instructors and confined to the situation of working foreign celestial spirits and other phenomena. When the spirit 'gives directions' during possession, it is claimed that 'Above takes over the doctor's body and speaks through his mouth.' The speech is rapid, high-pitched, and punctuated by grunts and hiccoughs. It is by no means essential for a practitioner to use possession in his treatments, and many well-established doctors simply work with the divining rattle and a form of sustained questioning, during which they draw out relevant information. I have never seen a woman doctor possessed and Mandari say that they seldom use this method.

Though an established practitioner may be possessed during divination or when administering a rite, he will not become possessed arbitrarily outside the ritual context. Doctors are controlled personalities, and it is the uncontrolled, the non-professional, the sick, and the immature who suffer inappropriate or adventitious possession. It is, however, recognized that instability may mark the initial entry into practice, and I saw an example of such a possession when a young aspirant to the profession had a minor fit in my homestead while some Mandari were practising dance steps while others clapped and sang. This man, whom I did not know, came by and sat down. After a while I noticed he was beginning to jerk and twitch, then to roll, arching his back, hiccoughing, and speaking in short staccato spurts. The spectators later told me that his 'spirit' had been speaking about the current drought. Spirit-of-the-Above, which had 'spoken', had suggested that Gelaba, the son of the chief, should sacrifice a sheep to it in order to release the rain. The man himself explained that he was beginning to practise through a celestial association and that when the 'spirit' heard the singing and clapping it became active. When I later reported the incident to Gelaba, he was amused, agreed that 'no doubt Above had caused him to *molja*', but suggested this should not be taken too seriously—'Everything necessary for the rain is being done.'

A doctor cannot experience and utilize convulsion for the diagnosis of illness, unless he has himself first suffered a mental or physical illness of the celestial class. The latter is an indispensable sign, and after it has been received, he must 'plant' a homestead pole-shrine to mark the permanent association.

A common form of possession, and one which is viewed as incidental and without great significance, is the violent but quick-passing convulsion which is manifested by some adolescent girls during the ceremonial dancing which follows a mortuary rite. The possession is said to be a sign that Spirit-of-the-Above, which is immanent in the whole scene, has found a particular human vehicle. The girl so chosen is not considered to have special powers, neither is she receiving these. She is simply a sensitive instrument responding to spiritual presence. The head and body of a girl used in this way will begin to twitch and jerk, then she falls down and rolls about, beating her head on the ground, shaking and twitching. People stand round her to prevent her being trampled and rub her head and back. She may be carried to the shade for a few minutes until the fit passes and she can return to the dance ground.

Some girls become known for their special sensitivity. They convulse regularly and easily during mortuary dancing and sometimes on other occasions offering the required stimulus. An important point, however, is that even these convulsions have a controlled nature, in that a girl will never injure herself although she appears to be undergoing a mild form of dissociation, and the fits only take place on ritual occasions where people are present, in marked contrast to the fits of the *moon* sufferer. An attractive and intelligent girl known to have this sort of sensitivity lived near to me, and I saw her in a possessed state at a mortuary rite and then again at a mediumistic seance.

Girlhood convulsions are not considered dangerous to health and are never treated unless they continue beyond adolescence. The Mandari seem to be aware of the mild neurosis or simply the innate susceptibility which can be a symptom of growing up in some girls, and do not take this seriously. But if convulsive fits continue into maturity, they see them as a symptom of harmfully protracted adolescence, and the girl as not adjusting to her physical maturation and changed social status as she should. Efforts are then made to deal with this condition by a severance rite, which aims to cut off the old and harmful personality and to channel the new one into its delayed maturity. When a chronic sufferer marries, a precautionary rite may be performed before she goes to her husband's home—'so that Spirit-of-the-Above will not follow her'. This rite is said often to be unsuccessful, the woman's convulsions persisting after marriage; but I have never heard of a mature woman with children continuing to suffer these attacks. Such a case would be looked on as an illness.

Most Mandari with whom I discussed these states were quite clear that they were glad not to be the chosen vehicles of spiritual power, which seems, inevitably, to involve some degree of personal disorientation. Their attitude appears to be that if spiritual power is to be revealed in an appropriate situation—and a mortuary rite is an appropriate one—someone must be the vehicle. Here, then, possession is 'good' in that it shows 'Spirit-of-the-Above is present'. In a secular situation possession is inappropriate and will be considered aberrant and, perhaps, pathological. Girlhood possession-states are almost invariably confined to the correct ritual situations and are in that sense acceptable, but are not otherwise considered significant; they are neither dangerous nor beneficial to the victim or the community.

IV

One important way in which the Mandari consider Spirit-of-the-Above to link-in with human beings is when it features in the religious Call of an aspirant for the doctor's profession. All Calls do not specifically show the presence of this spirit, but a syndrome with many features of mental sickness of the celestial class appears often to form a part of the pre-training experiences of some practitioners. Whether the patient is eventually regarded as simply ill, or is revealed to be showing religious power, depends on a number of factors which will be amplified when I deal with the vocational Call.

What I have named 'the Call syndrome' is typified by mental crisis involving withdrawal to the bush, wandering there aimlessly, and refusal to eat, speak, or take part in social life. Symptoms may last for a relatively short time or for several months or years. If the condition becomes permanent or is followed by dementia—raving or complete deterioration—the person is considered seriously ill, and this kind of case is likely to be finally diagnosed as *kapur*, unless other evidence is overriding.

The following case showing Call symptoms was being treated as illness at the time I saw the patient, a young girl, and was causing her family great distress. The girl had begun the typical solitary wanderings, and withdrawal from her former activities and friends. I first noticed her standing apart from the crowd of young people who came to flirt, gossip, and buy tobacco at the Tal bush shop. She appeared withdrawn, so I eventually went up and greeted her. She stared at me without replying. To surprise her into some sort of response I asked her for tobacco—an extraordinary request from a European. The normal reaction would have been to laugh, but she silently handed me a piece. Friends later commenting on this unusual behaviour suggested that, 'no doubt her Above recognized your Above and so she made you a gift'—a joking reference to my nickname 'Awuk', the name of a female celestial spirit. I was told that the girl had been gay and popular with eligible suitors until a few months previously. Then 'Above fell upon her', and after this she had begun to wander in a trance-like state, shunning friends and refusing to speak. Attempts to restrain and reason with her had no effect. Diviners were consulted and a sheep sacrificed to Above, but there was as yet no sign of improvement. It was suggested to me that if she recovered she might eventually practise as a doctor, a profession open to both men and women, as her condition showed a typical Call syndrome.

At the onset of symptoms which may later be reassessed and

shown to be Call, a family's first reaction is to fear serious mental illness and to make every effort to effect a cure. Those who go on to recovery and practise will raise a shrine to Spirit-of-the-Above which becomes their spiritual guide.

V

The Mandari also isolate certain physical symptoms and class them as celestial illness. Theoretically, and often in practice, they affect the upper part of the body; one group centres round the head, and includes, for example, all kinds of severe headache, loss of consciousness, and eye infections where the eye is inflamed and watering. Another group affects throat and chest and includes sore throats, colds and coughs, and serious and often fatal chest disorders. These latter, which are probably of the pneumonia-pleurisy type, have a violent onset and are quick-killing, exhibiting that suddenness which suggests Above origin.

The sickness often has a link with 'cold' both as a cause and a symptom of disease. Getting wet and chilled 'when Above is raining', leads to head colds (*jwe*) and coughs (*yoka*), and in the rainy season many people suffer in this way. These minor ailments are not taken seriously, and a doctor will not be called unless grave illness is feared. As coldness can be the cause of illness, so it can be the symptom. The patient may feel cold. A distinction is made between chest complaints where the body is 'hot' (Spirit-of-the-Above is not present) and where it is cold and shivering (Spirit-of-the-Above is present). Here the Mandari may well be making true observations of the stages of physical fever.

Their classification of morbid symptoms is the logical consequence of their observation of the properties of natural phenomena. What is up falls down. Mental illness is a 'falling down' of a celestial agent on to the victim.[1] Where the symptoms are revealed in physical form, it is the head, the upper part pointing to the sky, and the chest, the top of the trunk, that are most typically affected. Cold is represented in the classification by the ideal associations between rain, water, cold, cold illness, and cold

---

[1] To describe this action, an adverbial suffix indicating linear movement out from a point towards the principal person concerned is used: thus, '*du'un*', 'to fall towards', '*ky'it*', 'to themselves'. Such adverbial suffixes are typical of the Bari languages. See Fr. L. M. Spagnolo, *Bari Grammar* (Verona, 1933).

celestial agent, a classification which may be completed by cold in the patient's body.

This theoretical classification often breaks down in practice, however, because, of course, many diseases affect several different parts of the body at once, but also because the evidence the Mandari use in diagnosis includes much material other than the patient's physical symptoms; thus I have seen on several occasions a clear-cut case of dysentery, which obviously affects the lower part of the body, diagnosed as Above, because evidence of the patient's previous history outweighed evidence of the physical symptoms. When all the diagnostic data for a particular case are taken into account several possible causes usually suggest themselves. This is well illustrated in the case of female barrenness. This can be caused by Spirit-of-the-Above because this spirit promotes natural fertility and where it is given it can also be withheld; by dead kin, kinswomen especially; by the evil eye or witchcraft; by the woman concerned by her own acts. Physical symptoms, therefore, provide only some clues. An additional and more conclusive diagnosis is required and this is provided at divination. The theoretical classification by which the Mandari attempt to order pathological symptoms cannot, therefore, necessarily be applied in practice.

VI

If one asks a Mandari why mental and physical illness should be associated with Celestial Spirit, a usual answer is, 'it just is' (*kanaŋ*). This word is used—sometimes irritatingly I must confess —when Mandari cannot or do not wish to give a reason for something. 'It just is' may be accompanied by a shrug, dismissing the question as futile. More specifically the answer to the inquiry as to why a particular victim is chosen may be, 'It is Creator; no one knows why Ki makes people ill and destroys them.' This partly shows an acceptance of spiritual forces in general as outside man's understanding and control. But when Mandari refuse even to question the reason for the initial selection they are making an assumption regarding the peculiar arbitrariness of the Spirit-of-the-Above in *particular*, which they see to be exemplified in heavenly bodies with their free movements, the weather with its dangerous uncertainties, the separated cosmos governed by its own independent laws (once together now apart) pressing down upon the phenomenal world. There is no suggestion that the sick person in the initial situation is at fault, nor at this stage is there an established relationship between patient and spirit which needs recognition or extension as there is once a spirit is established by a shrine.

The assumption is that the Spirit seeks participation in the human group and that illness is the sign of this wish. 'The Above wishes for meat so it visits a family', the Mandari say. This comment should be considered in relation to all that eating together implies. People who do this are kin or friends, and no one eats with strangers or enemies. Eating therefore denotes kinship, or the wish to establish kinship. So a quasi-kin relationship is established between a family and the spirit and this is marked by the symbolic sharing of meat. Pieces of sacrificial meat are dropped on the ground for the spirit during the ritual meal and parts of the carcass are classified as the meat of Spirit-of-the-Above and these must only be eaten by elders of the family to which the spirit belongs. They symbolize the intimate relationship between it and those who eat them and to give away this meat indiscriminately to 'outsiders'— distant kin—implies rejection of the spirit and leads to illness.

The association with fatal disease is explained with reference to Celestial Spirit as an agent of Creator and expressed metaphorically, 'Ki kills people and consumes their bodies and their life can ascend to Creator.' This is consistent with the assumption that death does not occur without a cause, but that the instruments of death are Creator's agents and not Creator himself.

A more specific reason for celestial sickness is given if repeated outbreaks occur in the same family. An explanation along the lines that Spirit-of-the-Above 'now wishes for something more', will imply that the spirit desires the initial relationship to be reaffirmed with another offering or wishes to extend the relationship to other kinsmen. The sickness is no longer fortuitous; it has a history and is part of an anticipated, if unwanted, on-going pattern.

As in all cases of illness the course of action to be taken is laid down by the diviner who has revealed the original causal agent.

If celestial sickness is shown to be serious an ox or sheep is sacrificed; in minor indisposition, dedication may be sufficient. The sheep is the chosen animal for dedication to Spirit-of-the-Above because it belongs to the category 'cool' (*tato*), and 'Above is cool like the rain.' Anything which is classified 'hot' (*tomaka*), like goat's meat, must never be offered to the spirit, or 'the sun intensifies and drought follows'. Animals with neutral qualities like cattle are suitable—'they are neither hot nor cold'. Chickens, 'bird of the Above', can be substituted for these animals in sacrifice if the family is poor, but chickens are never used in dedication, because 'they are too small' (insignificant) and, moreover, they are not exclusively the offering of Spirit-of-the-Above. Dedicated sheep are described as 'sheep of the Above'. These cannot be given in bride-wealth or in compensation, nor can they be sold or exchanged. Whole flocks may be set aside and economically proscribed for this reason. Dedicated animals are always females, and their lambs enter the protected class, ewes awaiting further dedication and rams sacrificial killings. Exchanging or selling a proscribed animal, like giving away sacrificial meat, is equivalent to severing relationship with Spirit-of-the-Above, and destroys the protective element believed to reside in the dedicated animal itself, which turns away sickness—'Above comes to the homestead and sees its own (sheep) and leaves the people in peace.' To demonstrate the association between the animal and the sufferer, a small piece is cut from the animal's ear and hung on the sufferer's neck. If further illness breaks out the sheep is brought back, pegged down, and libations of beer are poured over the peg while the owning spirit is addressed.

When a doctor is able to link a series of illnesses to this one source, then 'Above has come to stay', and a shrine must be raised. This diagnosis may at first be rejected by a family because shrines are costly to raise, and once established require attention. If they were raised every time a celestial illness was diagnosed the majority of homesteads would have them, but this is far from being the case and they are, in fact, relatively rare; but they do tend to be found in clusters, for reasons which will be understood when I come to discuss the spread and inheritance of cult spirits.

The Mandari describe the raising of a shrine as 'planting a wood' (*ködi bobogga*), or 'planting an Above' (Ki *bobogga*); the shrine itself is spoken of as the ' "wood" or "pole" of the Above' (*ködi lo* Ki). After one has been raised, the relationship between family and spirit is regularized. The raising is marked by the slaughter of an ox, when the doctor addresses the spirit and explains its new relationship. Strips of hide from the sacrificial ox are hung on the branches of the shrine as protective talismans 'so that when Ki visits the homestead it may see that it has received an ox'. A shrine for this type of spirit is sited in the centre of the homestead yard, facing the front of the hut and 'open to the sky'. Correct positioning is important because this symbolizes the boundless nature of everything celestial ('of the outside'); free and open things must not be taken inside or enclosed.

A shrine becomes the site of all future sacrifice for Spirit-of-the-Above and of the monthly purification ritual offered to Creator. It must not, however, on any account be used in rites for

TABLE 1. *Free-Spirits-of-the-Above* (Kijin)

Mandari	Dinka or Atwot	Moru
1. Male	1. Male	1. Male
Garaŋ	Jombai	Böröju
Kuluŋ	Garaŋdit	
	Löi	
2. Female	2. Female	
Awuk	Ayak	
	Abuk	

Note. Kuluŋ is referred to as 'the black bird of the Above', and is, I would think, the raven.

ancestors; the latter are 'hot' phenomena (Spirit-of-the-Below) and 'have their own place at the hearth under the hut'. If an ancestor rite was offered at this shrine it would confuse the nature and object of the sacrifice and lead to further illness; the same goes for rites for phenomena known as *Jok*, which are also 'hot' and have their own place.

Individualized Free-Spirits-of-the-Above (*kijin*) also receive shrines in the form of plain or ornamented cattle pegs known as 'pegs of the Above' (*köluti na* Ki). Some of these spirits are picked up during a visit to the Dinka, others come through a marriage link; some are male, some female. They follow out an illness which is diagnosed as having something foreign about it and reflects contact across Mandari boundaries. A glance at the list above will show that 'foreign' spirits now outnumber indigenous Mandari ones. The former tend to be treated, and their shrines raised, by doctors who themselves have external kinship links, or who have been apprenticed in Aliab Dinka or Atwot.

While routine offerings are not made at shrines they must not be neglected. The wife of the owner of a shrine always pours

a little beer at it after brewing. Failure to do this shows indifference
and can result in sickness. The spirit is also remembered at certain
seasons, and beer is poured down, for instance, when the grass is
burnt off and the men begin to move out to cattle-camps. If anyone
has been ill before the move the family head may call the doctor
who raised the shrine and a sheep or chicken may be sacrificed.
Rites carried out before dry season migrations protect the family
while they are away; the spirit is told the reason for the offering
and asked to remain tranquil until they return. Libations are
also poured after harvest when the first brewings of the harvested
grain take place.

While Spirit-of-the-Above is not specifically a lineage spirit,
this impression is sometimes given because chains of celestial
ownership can become established within a lineage. This occurs
partly because once a spirit has been 'planted' in a shrine, it must
be inherited on its owner's death, and partly because of its tendency to spread through other kinship links. A current celestial
association has often passed through a grandfather to a father and
on to a son, or it has passed from a man to his brother or brothers,
and on to their child or children, or it may have been brought into
a line by a wife whom it has followed from her natal home. It then
passes to her children, and through a daughter it may be carried
out again into another line. Heritage follows through men or
women, to men or women, and ownership multiplies rather than
the reverse, a fact of which Mandari are very conscious, hence the
disinclination to establish the spirit in the first place.

While spread is theoretically between those closely related by
blood ties in fact this generally means between members of a small
agnatic kin group occupying one hamlet or village. If a man moves
away to relatives elsewhere, the spiritual links to his kin group
left behind will, after a time, be less regularly brought to mind,
while new 'causes' incidental to his new situation will feature
more prominently; within a close radius, on the other hand,
illness and death are likely to be attributed to an established cause
available to hand unless there is strong evidence for one of another
type.

It is important to stress that diagnosis is usually made by a
doctor who follows events in his locality, and the explanation he
gives will be influenced by his knowledge of the family's previous
illness history, their associated spiritual phenomena, and the social

situation existing between the individual members themselves
and between them and other persons in the community. Laymen
may also anticipate the professional diagnosis: 'Once Above has
established itself it looks round and finds close kinsmen with good
homesteads where it then wishes to be planted.' Even when a
spirit has not yet claimed a victim in the other homesteads of
a polygynous family their members are concerned directly in its
welfare, and receive meat from its sacrifices. Sacrifice is made
in the homestead of the wife where the sickness occurs; thus, if
a man has four wives, and if the initial sickness affects the wife
or children of homestead four, the sacrifice is carried out and the
shrine raised there; but members of homesteads one, two, and
three also attend and the meat is divided equally between all house-
holds. The intestines and stomach (the women's portion) are given
to all wives, chest meat and one leg go to the husband for division
between all wives and children, three legs and other unclassified
cuts to 'people of the outside', the male and female lineage elders
who attend the rite. Head and horns belong to the husband, the
'owner of the sacrifice', who hangs the horns for a short time on
the new shrine; the skin becomes a mat for the wife who 'owns the
sacrifice'. If a husband is ill, the rite takes place in his head wife's
homestead and the shrine is planted there; the meat is apportioned
as described. (A married doctor also sites the shrine for his spirit
in his head wife's homestead so that she can look after it and help
him collect herbal medicines.) When beer is brewed by one wife
a little is taken to the homesteads of co-wives to pour down. This
mutual shrine-tending depends on wives living near each other.
If a co-wife lives in another village—for convenience or because of
quarrelling—regular attention at other wives' shrines is difficult.
Distance, however, is said to inhibit effects from the spirit, though
I have heard diagnoses made attributing disease to a free Spirit-
of-the-Above, which has, in fact, 'followed' for a considerable
distance.

When a homestead head dies, his shrine falls to his eldest son,
'the one at the head' (*karo*), and if there are other sons, to the
youngest as well, the 'child of the end' (*nyiyo lo dutet*), provided
each is married and has a homestead of his own where the shrine
can be sited. If one of the other brothers falls ill, the eldest comes
and marks him with beer or cuts a ritual cucumber on his behalf.
When the eldest brother dies, the youngest, who already has a

shrine, takes over the ritual duties on behalf of other brothers and their families. Should a line of brothers and father's brothers' sons die out, the sister's son who can inherit the wife of either the eldest or youngest son takes over the shrine. If an inherited widow bears a son by her inheritor this son takes over the shrine when he is adult, bringing it back into the agnatic line. (The children of the inherited widow belong to the dead husband and not to the inheritor.) The inheritor only tends the shrine until the dead man has a son to take it over. Relationship with a spirit is never terminated by death, and if a shrine is left uninherited a remaining blood relative may fall ill. Failure to follow up inheritance will certainly be noted by a local diviner and used in due course as a cause in some later illness.

One family near whose homestead I lived showed typical shrine clustering. Its head, Chief Korondo of Dari, inherited a large shrine from his father. Korondo himself suffered from chronic but mild nocturnal convulsions, logically extending the link from the father. He had killed many oxen and sheep in attempts to deal with his own chronic condition, with the death of a brother, and with that of his senior wife whose hut was struck by lightning. This woman's eldest son now has a shrine in his senior wife's homestead. Korondo's youngest brother ('the child of the end') also inherited the father's shrine, while another brother, a doctor named Deŋdit, raised one independently after a reputed miracle which featured the fall of a bracelet from the sky. After this he began to suffer a nervous disorder.

Within this one family, therefore, gathered in one hamlet, there are four shrines and several associations, some inherited, others coming in incidentally to the initial attachment. Some represent physical illness, some nervous disorders and others intervention from the sky. Korondo would not allow me to photograph his shrines because of his illness and I had to be content with making sketches of them from memory (see Fig. 1).[1] The sketch shows that Korondo's family also has a *Jok* association.[2]

Because a family has an established spirit it does not necessarily mean that all illness will automatically be interpreted in these

---

[1] Many Mandari expressed apprehension about photography. As a rule, therefore, I refrained from taking photographs during ritual or other ceremonial occasions.

[2] *Jok*; see Chapter 3.

terms. Several causes may be implicated. However, the idea of spread from a single source is common, the spiritual relationship extending as the kinship group with which it is associated grows.

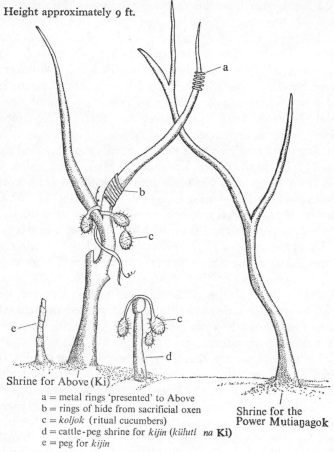

Height approximately 9 ft.

Shrine for Above (Ki)

a = metal rings 'presented' to Above
b = rings of hide from sacrificial oxen
c = *koljok* (ritual cucumbers)
d = cattle-peg shrine for *kijin* (*küluti na* **Ki**)
e = peg for *kijin*

Shrine for the
Power Mutiaɲagok

FIG. I. *Shrines in homestead of Chief Korondo*

Something must be said about the position of women in relation to an inherited spirit. The illness of unmarried daughters and sisters living in their natal homestead is logically related to its established spirits, and, even when women move away at marriage such spirits may follow them. Illness is sometimes diagnosed in terms of the spirit of the natal home even where the 'cutting-off' rite is performed. In such cases an attempt is made to return the spirit to its place of origin at a rite which takes place in the marital homestead, but is attended by the woman's father and kin. While the husband produces the sheep for dedication or sacrifice, the woman's father officiates at the ceremony because it is 'his Above', and not one associated with the line of the woman's husband. The father dedicates the animal and instructs his spirit to take it and leave the woman and any offspring she may bear. The sheep is also addressed by the husband, and the woman is anointed protectively with a mixture of sesame oil and millet seed. If the animal is a ewe, the father places it in his herd as a dedicated sheep and 'the Above returns with it'. A castrated ram is killed at his shrine after it has again been addressed, and the meat is eaten by closely related elders. If the woman shows no improvement, another sheep is found, 'the Above having refused the first'. Should this also fail, the doctor informs the woman's husband that 'the Above has come to stay; it likes the homestead where it found many possessions and much food'. A new shrine is then planted in her homestead and in time the spirit passes to her children as their illness is diagnosed in terms of its presence. Many families have associations established in this way through female links.

A wife can come under the influences of her marital homestead but she cannot pass those back to her natal kin. The implication here is that a married woman is affected as an *individual* in her role of wife. Similarly if a woman's children take on their father's Spirit-of-the-Above they cannot pass this back to their maternal kin. In the main, spiritual attachments tend to follow the general pattern of jural descent and property inheritance.

While a spirit can enter through women, women do not inherit in the same way as men and spread through women is generally less than it is through men. This is because women often move to another part of the country at marriage, and there is evidence to show that spiritual links with the natal home are then more likely to be forgotten. A distant move brings her within the influence of new practitioners, whereas if she remains near her home she will in all probability be treated by the same doctor as treats her own kin. However, in order to make his diagnosis a doctor needs to probe past history, and even if he knows nothing of the patient's background he will be skilled in extracting what is relevant from the patient. The following divination I attended shows how a doctor who had never been near a foreign patient's village obtained information not only about the patient's sicknesses and those occurring on his father's side, but those of his wife's father, as well.

CASE I. *The Atwot Chief and the Free-Spirit-of-the-Above Garaŋdit*

This case concerned a chief of the neighbouring Atwot tribe who had travelled to Mandari with his wife and sister to consult a Mandari doctor named Ako Akurukway who claims to work through association with the Dinka free-Spirit-of-the-Above Jombai.[1] Dinka and Atwot living near the Mandari border, cross fairly frequently to consult Mandari doctors. Ako Akurukway has Dinka maternal connections and Dinka affines through his sister, and a proportion of his patients come from this source.

The trouble was that the chief's wife, who appeared to me to be already in her middle twenties, was childless. The father's young widow whom the chief had inherited had also not conceived, although she had previously had a child by the deceased father; a baby born to the chief's sister had died.

Ako agreed to divine the case, and seated the patients on a mat under the raised veranda of the hut. This is the correct place for divination because it is an open space where the proceedings can be seen, and openness to the community is the hallmark of beneficial ritual as opposed to sorcery, which is performed in secret. Ako sat cross-legged facing the chief in the face-to-face position of divination, and asked for 50 piastres (about 50p) to 'open' the case. This payment allows the doctor to begin work. Ako was asking many times the usual opening fee which is normally a piece of tobacco or a small coin, because the patient was a foreigner and a chief. After a period of 'smelling out'—shaking the divining rattle up-and-down while facing the patient—Ako stopped and said that he must have a further 10 piastres for his assistant, indicating an impecunious Atwot tribesman who was living in his homestead and paying for his own treatment by cultivating Ako's fields. Ako explained that he himself could not understand the Atwot language, and throughout the session the Atwot acted as interpreter. Divination proceeded with Ako questioning the chief about his family history, about his wife's

---

[1] Dr. Lienhardt tells me that he believes 'Jombai' to be a Mandari rendering of 'Jong Bai' meaning in Dinka 'spirit of the village'.

background, and finally about their own troubles. He paused
every now and then for periods of silent concentration. During
these silences the doctor is described as 'working with his head'.

Ako eventually broke off, saying that the divination was going
badly because his 'spirit' was not satisfied with the payment, and
something more must be added. A wrangle began over whether
the chief should hand over his spear. A Mandari elder named
Awor, an affine of Ako's, eventually persuaded him that this was
unreasonable and that the chief could not travel back unarmed
and accompanied by two women.

After divining for about an hour, Ako made this diagnosis.
A Dinka spirit named Garaŋdit, belonging to her father, was
already planted in the natal homestead of the barren wife. This
spirit had for some time wished to extend its influence to the
marital homestead and the signs of this wish had been the infertility; then, as this failed to elicit any response, the killing of the
husband's sister's child. The chief should therefore raise a shrine
to Garaŋdit. Ako agreed to travel to Atwot to supervise this at
the beginning of the rains. In the meantime a chicken was to be
killed and the head hung in the doorway of the wife's hut to protect
the family while they were away in dry season camps.

After Ako had given this diagnosis, the chief presented him with
a neutered ram, which Ako agreed to kill as further protection
for the family. For this small rite, the patients were seated on
a mat in the open yard to the west side of the homestead and
facing west, while Ako led the ram up and down by its tethering
cord addressing Garaŋdit under his breath telling the spirit to
let the family be, because a shrine would be raised for it in due
course. The animal eventually urinated; an essential sign that
a sacrificial animal is acceptable, and Ako used some of the earth
mixed with urine to mark the supplicants on the chest, forehead,
and back of the neck. Marking gives protection and also formally
identifies the animal with the patient. As the Mandari explain,
'the marking shows the spirit whom the animal is being sacrificed
for, so that it does not make a mistake.' Awor also led the animal
round and invoked. Then he and Ako threw it on its side and the
patients were made to sit on it, while Ako addressed the ram
itself and explained that it was being sacrificed for Garaŋdit on
the patient's behalf. The statement to the animal is important,
since domestic animals killed arbitrarily may become dangerous

phenomena known as *nyök*. The animal's throat was then cut. The meat and skin belonged to Ako for, although he had killed it for his patient, it had been presented to him as a gift. When a patient produces his own animal for sacrifice on the instruction of the doctor, he keeps the meat, and the doctor only receives the customary portion.

Ako's fee for the divination was two Sudanese pounds, to be handed over at the shrine-raising. This sum represented 50 piastres a patient, together with 50 for the woman's father, the 'owner' of Garaŋdit. A cow and bull-calf would later be paid when the woman's fertility had been demonstrated. This costly treatment would be beyond the reach of an ordinary patient, and it might suggest that Ako was exploiting these people. But it must be borne in mind that doctors often have to treat poor patients or kin free and they cannot altogether be blamed for reimbursing themselves where they can. For the Mandari, the Dinka and the Atwot have something of the reputation American visitors have for the English and although the tendency to treat them as fair game may be regrettable it is understandable.

The form of simple divination just described is used in preliminary diagnoses, or where the patient comes from a distance. A full divination, rites for raising shrines and major sacrifices, must always be held in the patient's own homestead where his senior kin can address the sacrificial animal; a doctor travels to a patient's homestead to carry out such rites, staying a few days as a guest. Once a homestead has a shrine, routine divinations take place there. A doctor carries out divinations in connection with his own or his family's health at his own shrine and is called in by patients to carry out divinations concerned with their health at their own shrines.

CASE 2. *Ako Akurukway's Routine Divination*

The following is an example of a routine divination using a chicken, not a rattle, carried out by the doctor Ako for his family. Only the immediate family and a few close relatives attend such small affairs. Ako had just completed the construction of a new homestead, and during weeks of hard work he and his children had been unwell. Before the family took up residence, one of his first moves was to question his Dinka spirit, Jombai, to find out if circumstances would be favourable in the new home, and if the spirit was satisfied with its new site. (Spirits move with families; old shrines are left in abandoned homesteads and temporary ones put up pending the planting of permanent shrines with sacrifice.) Ako's wife, Muli, and her three children were the patients. A Cic Dinka elder named Monyel, who works in the hamlet as a smith and is related through Ako's mother, Ako's sister, who is married to a Dinka immigrant and occupies an

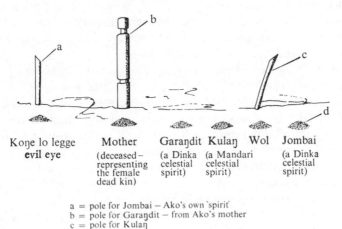

| Koŋe lo legge **evil eye** | Mother (deceased – representing the female dead kin) | Garaŋdit (a Dinka celestial spirit) | Kulaŋ (a Mandari celestial spirit) | Wol | Jombai (a Dinka celestial spirit) |

a = pole for Jombai – Ako's own 'spirit'
b = pole for Garaŋdit – from Ako's mother
c = pole for Kulaŋ
d = ash heaps

FIG. 2. *Divination by chicken and ashes*

adjacent homestead, and an old woman neighbour were present, besides myself.

The ceremony was held at sundown (like dawn, one of the two cool times of day); simple makeshift shrines of cattle-pegs replaced the large horned shrine and pegs. Three forms of Spirit-of-the-Above constitute Ako's spiritual heritage. The stage for the divination was set with six heaps of ash behind the pegs as shown in Fig. 2.

Each ash-heap represented a possible source of the illnesses.

Ako held a young chicken by the legs with the head upright and pointed it at the heap on the extreme right, addressing his own guide-spirit, Jombai:

You, Jombai, if it is you who are making me ill so that I am unable to cultivate and my fields run to weeds, here is your chicken. Let your heart be more favourable to us. If the ill-health has not come from you, let the chicken die outside [away from the pole].

At each heap he addressed the agency represented, at the same time tapping the chicken on the ground and spraying it with homestead dust to emphasize his words, then smoothing the ground round the appropriate ash heap with his hand.

Ako has a sense of humour and plays to his audience, particularly when the occasion is not too serious. He began to reprimand the spirits, jokingly giving an elaborate picture of his sufferings. When each heap had been addressed, he went round them again repeating their names so that they and the audience would be sure which heap stood for which agent, and there would be no misunderstanding.

His wife and children moved up and seated themselves to one side, facing the posts, and the four spectators assembled in a rough semicircle in front of the ash heaps. Ako handed the chicken to Monyel who passed it round the head and chest of the wife and of each child, round each post, and finally around each ash heap, at the same time addressing the agents and drawing their attention to the patients. Then Ako and Monyel squatted facing each other by the posts, holding the chicken between them while invocations were sung and spoken, in Dinka, because, as Ako explained, his spirit is a Dinka one. By these invocations, Mandari say, 'they [the spirits] are summoned and supplicated' (*Luluŋa ko momola*).

Ako then cut off the chicken's head and everyone began clapping and shouting, '*Miŋga, Miŋga, miŋga ta'yu*'. This chorus, in the Moru language, has been added on to the Mandari chicken divination, and as far as I know is the only instance of incorporation of a Moru formula. The chicken's headless body was pushed and prodded to make it rush about vigorously so that its final place of collapse could not be said to have been influenced.

Eventually it fell near the Garaŋdit ash-heap. Ako picked it up and laid it at the Garaŋdit pole; then he took the severed head, and holding the beak open made each patient spit into it to rid them of evil and sickness which are taken away in the head when it is thrown, full of contaminated spittle, towards sunset, the place of evil. Before throwing it, Ako walked a short distance along the path into the bush where he addressed the head telling it to take away evil and sickness. As he threw it into the undergrowth, everyone raised their hands towards the west, at the same time making the sound Wooooooooosssshh! miming the driving away of evil.

Water was then brought by Muli who splashed us all with a few drops and poured the remainder on to the ash heaps. The heaps were wetted because it was the time of the early rains (*ja'be*); if they were scattered dry, 'the Above might be angered and hold up the rain'. In the dry season wetting is unnecessary as there is no falling rain to injure, the ashes are simply swept up and thrown into the bush. This is a further example of behaviour manifesting belief in the sensitivity of rain to human action and to certain things used by people—in this case ashes, the residue of hot fire— at the time of the uncertain early rains. The participants are splashed with water before they disperse so that they may be 'cooled' from the endangering 'heat' released by the sickness and evil eliminated at the rite. The divination being over, we went into the hut and drank the beer left over from the libations poured at sunrise at the poles.

As a result of the divination Ako told me he would sacrifice an ox to Garaŋdit at the beginning of the dry season. Sacrifice was not possible at that moment because it was the lean time of early rains, and if an ox were killed without valid reason neigh-bours would suspect that Ako had killed 'in greed for meat', and he would be shamed. He pointed out that there was no serious sickness to warrant immediate sacrifice. In hunger or poverty, 'spirits must be reasonable and wait like men, who wait months or years for their dues.' When 'spirits show impatience'—the sickness is serious or recurrent—the Mandari sacrifice at once. The interim offering, such as that made by the Atwot chief, is typical of acceptable compromise.

I did not witness a shrine-raising ceremony, but the following description of one is typical of several given to me. Before the tree from which the pole is carved is felled, beer is brewed and drunk in the homestead. On the day of the raising, lineage elders together with the doctor treating the case assemble, and the sacrificial 'ox' (generally a sheep) is tethered in the homestead. The pole which has lain in readiness in the cultivations is then carried in by the bearer party who circle the hut with it three times before converging on the site. A hole is dug, and beer, tobacco, unground grain, and a ritual cucumber are placed in it, and then the pole is set. The doctor addresses Spirit-of-the-Above: 'You Above, behold your ox which is to be sacrificed for you. Take this food, together with this ox of yours, and let the family be in peace.'

If he uses this particular method the doctor then stands in the centre of the yard and sings praise-hymns. These are patterned on the praise-poems for favourite oxen, and now, like the poems, are often in the Dinka language although some traditional Mandari ones remain. The ox is led round the homestead three times, its droppings or urine used in the standard markings, its throat cut, and the meat divided up.

One rib-case is removed and a small back-rib is selected from it, this is the 'meat-of-the-Above' which is boiled and placed in the 'pot-of-the-Above' which is kept in the back of the hut on the right-hand side: this meat is eaten later by the owner of the sacrifice. Other ritual parts are cooked and eaten in the evening by the elders. The non-ritual portions (legs and part of the back) are divided out according to the attendance.[1]

Three days later the doctor returns for the sweeping-out of the homestead yard and the dwelling hut. The hut is swept inside (upstairs and downstairs) and underneath where people sit. The rubbish is taken to the waste-land and placed in a rain-pool (*sese*). If planting takes place in the dry season it will be laid in a shallow depression which will later fill with rain. The moistening of the rubbish, which is eliminated in the waste-land, ensures 'coolness' in the homestead and among its members. The latter are also splashed with water by the doctor who again addresses the spirit:

> You Above, let their bodies be cool:
> An ox has been sacrificed.

When a shrine eventually rots and falls, it must never be used as firewood. This applies to all shrines, including those raised for Dinka spirits and powers: should old shrines be burnt 'people would die'. At the same time that beer is brewed and the doctor is summoned to raise the new pole, the old one is laid in a rain-pool in the bush. If a family are poor, it is not unusual for the old pole to remain lying in the homestead for months, while grain for beer and the animal for the raising of the new one are sought. The old pole cannot be disposed of until the replacement is erected, and I frequently saw old poles lying around awaiting ceremonial disposal. It is also forbidden to cut, or use as firewood,

---

[1] The principles regarding the division of ritual meat are summarized in Appendix I at the end of the book where specific variations in division are also discussed.

the tree, or the remainder of it, from which a shrine has been carved.

VII

While the cult of Spirit-of-the-Above is practised throughout Mandari and most families have suffered sickness diagnosed as from this source, many never raise a shrine. Once, however, a family have accepted a permanent link by raising one, it is only a matter of time before the association spreads involving other kin and, over the years, a group of related families with their own shrines, based on one initial contact, becomes a new lineage. The comment, 'Your Above is making us ill', is laden with meaning in social terms. The spread is partly related to kinship rules and property inheritance and partly to Mandari assumptions about the ways in which a spirit reveals its presence—in mental and physical illness and in natural events—allowing a wide range of unavoidable casualties to be traced to this source.

The trend of an established cult, however, is broken up by the intervention of other agents, and families with Spirit-of-the-Above may also carry out rites for ghosts and sin cleansings in response to sickness. Some families 'own' more than one spirit; then diagnoses tends to point first to one and then to another, guided partly by the characteristics of the illness itself (and Mandari have quite a sophisticated symptom aetiology), and partly by the result of divination, which, in turn, depends on the doctor's knowledge and assessment of the patient's situation and history.

At the present time a new confusion has arisen in the diagnostic field because of what has now become a fairly widespread adherence to a foreign cult. This I describe in the following chapter.

3

JOK: A FOREIGN POSSESSION CULT

I

THE Mandari claim that during the last few decades new forces affecting health and well-being have made an appearance in their country. The Mandari category designation for these forces which are manifest in a multiple form is *Jok* (sing. *Joksho*, plural *Jok* or *Jokan*). I shall refer to them as 'Powers'.[1]

It seems appropriate to consider the cult relating to Powers at this point since it bears some correspondence to the traditional cult of Spirit-of-the-Above. The notion of arbitrary attachment to persons, the spread and inheritance, the raising of shrines by those pervaded by Powers, the use of 'possession'—though in a new and extreme form—by doctors treating patients, shows a striking superficial resemblance to the cult described in the previous chapter, although important differences exist.

Mandari express the view that Powers have streamed into their country over a period from the neighbouring Aliab Dinka and Atwot. In making this assessment, Mandari are in fact making a statement about certain new and real cultural influences, and about processes of change by which they have been affected. From evidence given by Mandari themselves, the history of the origin of Powers and their gradual pervasion of the Mandari scene is as follows. Mandari say they first appeared around the turn of the century in scattered areas, but became a force to be reckoned with about the 1920s. Significantly, this was the period during which, after sporadic attempts to subdue the Dinka tribes and bring them under control, the Sudan Administration succeeded in controlling the fighting and raiding, the traditional Mandari–Dinka relationship, and established relatively effective administrative control.

[1] Dr. Lienhardt has used the word 'Powers' (or 'a Power') to describe all Dinka categories of 'Spirit'. I use it here in a rather different sense since I reserve it as a descriptive term for specifically *foreign* agents, typically seen to have originated from the Dinka. There may therefore be a rough correspondence between *some* of the minor Dinka Powers and the Powers now claimed to have infiltrated Mandari-land. See *Divinity and Experience*, part i, pp. 28–32.

From the beginning of the century, however, social contacts of a non-aggressive kind had already begun to form between the Dinka and Atwot on the one side, and the Mandari on the other. With the measure of public security which followed Administration, these contacts, which were primarily of an economic kind, were greatly extended. Eventually a system was established, whereby the three peoples agreed to share their different types of seasonal grazing on an exchange basis, with the aim of solving their common problem of grazing shortage. Mandari cattle now graze Aliab sedgeswamp in the dry season, and the Aliab and the Atwot use Mandari woodland during the rains. Grazing contacts led to intermarriage between the young people of the different tribes who met in the camps.

To understand the effect of these new social contacts it must be remembered that the Mandari number around 15,000 souls and occupy a narrow strip of country. Among so small a population, spread thinly over a limited area, ideas penetrate and circulate quickly, and Mandari have been more radically affected by their Dinka neighbours than the latter have been by Mandari. The Aliab Dinka alone have a population at least five times that of Mandari, and they are backed by the main body of the other Dinka tribes numbering about 900,000 souls in all, and occupying an enormous area.[1]

At a rather superficial level some Dinka-ization of Mandari culture has resulted,[2] which has spread fastest among the young and among those richest in cattle, since apart from cattle the Mandari and the Dinka have few interests in common. But although the new Dinka influences appear rather striking, the structure of Mandari social groups, customary modes of behaviour, and what might loosely be described as the Mandari system of values, have not been modified or superseded. Further, traditional hostilities between the Mandari and the Dinka remain masked rather than eliminated, and thinly veiled animosity is implicit in the bitter way the Mandari speak about these neighbours— particularly the Aliab who belong to the vast, aggressive, Dinka masses which stretch away to the north and west. The Atwot, less numerous and perhaps more peaceable, are generally described as reasonable and easy to get on with.

[1] Lienhardt, *Divinity and Experience*, Introduction p. i.
[2] The 'Americanization' of our Western world could offer some analogy.

Tensions inherent in the new contacts have found ritualized expression in the *Jok* cult. It was inevitable that new conceptual categories would be needed to contain the new social relationships and particularly to explain those features of them which were disagreeable. The new conceptions also fit and explain random happenings of a disturbing nature, such as a Mandari falling ill while away in the Aliab.

Spread by contagion was already assumed to be a characteristic of traditional spirits. This notion has simply been extended in relation to Powers, which are said to pass in cattle, goats, and property as well as through persons. At first Mandari women passed *out* to Dinka in marriage and it was the incoming bride-wealth cattle which were seen to bring the Powers; later, as maternal kinship grew out of marriage, kinship links became the channel. The Mandari also associate the entry of Powers with the arrival of alien forces of law and order and, particularly, with efforts to subdue the hostile Aliab. Certain punitive expeditions carried out against Aliab and Atwot are seen as directly instrumental in bringing Powers into Mandari country.

One of these armed forays was against a group of Atwot who were camping in open bush on Mokido land; a number of Atwot were killed and wounded. The Mandari constantly return to this incident, declaring, 'The blood of people with *Jok* was spilt on our soil, so the angry *Jok* belonging to the dead and dying Atwot were loosed in Mandari.'

After this, the spread of Powers was assured. The belief that Powers can be associated with, and pass on in, objects and animals belonging to their 'owners', meant that they were now seen as likely to accompany homicide compensation awarded to Mandari against Atwot and Aliab: '*Jok* came with the cattle and goats continually being handed over in fines.' Fines are forced payments made by resentful and angry owners and Powers associated with them are seen as particularly malevolent.

Powers can also spread through agreed economic exchanges and marriage payments—'*Jok* may come with any sheep or goat'—although in such transactions this is less likely, since *kurkur* takes place, an act which ensures that the animal 'goes happily' and that the owner parts with it willingly.[1] Those who buy or receive

---

[1] When acquiring an animal, particularly a female, the buyer makes a small gift over and above the actual payment (for instance, 10 piastres (10p) or

animals from families with Powers may, in time, find the Power attached to them even if a rite of severance has been performed, since, the Mandari explain, rites are not always effective. Sometimes neither party is aware of the Power in the seller's family because it belongs to a distant relative. The ownership may be revealed later by a doctor who knows the backgrounds of both families.

Mandari recognize that exchanging property or receiving bridewealth where persons are of different tribes and of unknown backgrounds is potentially dangerous, but it has become an unavoidable part of social life. They remain suspicious about dealings with Dinka whom they believe in any case to be tricky and unreliable.

Having been assimilated through channels of economic co-operation, Powers spread within Mandari itself through exchange, through marriage, and through blood ties. The revelations of diviners, whose business it is to watch events and follow the ramifications of marriage and kinship, ensure the onward transmission.

Even during the short period from 1950 to 1958 it was clear to me that an increasing number of shrines to Powers were being set up in Mandari. In those areas most consistently infiltrated by Atwot and Aliab Dinka (the west and north-west) where intermarriage with Atwot and Aliab is most frequent, shrines are most numerous. Towards the Nyangwara border, where hostility inhibits intermarriage, shrines for Powers are rare. The Mandari say that Powers are now spreading eastwards, into the neighbouring Bari-speaking Nyangwara tribe and beyond; however, two itinerant Aliab doctors whom I met among the Nile-dwelling Köbora, reported a resistance to Powers in that area and said that they had had little success in getting people to accept their shrines.

The word '*jok*' is now used to describe any illness thought to have spread or to have been picked up from a neighbouring tribe. Wöli, for example, a sickness said to cover the body with sores, is said to have come from the Moru on the western boundary.

tobacco). If this is omitted the animal may be barren or sickly. Then the buyer remembers his omission and invites the former owner to a beer drink or makes him a small present. Tokens are also handed over for bride-wealth animals when the cattle are delivered by the bridegroom's kin; the bride's people give bracelets, spears, or arrows—'then their [the former owners'] hearts are content.'

The Moru are not Nilotic and are without cattle, and the Mandari maintain 'we reject the *Jok* of the Moru'. However, Powers are seen to pass in beads and artefacts exchanged for grain and tobacco in sporadic trade carried on at the Moru border. Despite the impossibility of direct contact with the distant Azande I have heard of illness being diagnosed as an Azande *Joksho* named Quirra. While the tendency is growing to refer to any sickness diagnosed as stemming from a non-Mandari source as *jok*, such illnesses are not necessarily described as *jok* in their country of supposed origin, and the term means little more than 'illness from a foreign source'.

II

The conceptual placing of Powers is very important to Mandari and attempts are constantly made to define this. Such statements as 'they (Powers) are not Dun', implies that they are not part of traditional religion. On the other hand Powers are invisible—at least to ordinary untrained persons—their being is therefore not of the purely physical world. Between the spiritual and the human categories their place is somewhat uncertain. They seem to belong to that third grouping, implied by the Mandari though not differentiated by name, to which forces such as witchcraft and sorcery and the psychic forces embodied in certain animals belong, and which I describe as the para-normal.[1] It is logical to place Powers among those things that have a closer connection with the material world than with religious agents because, as I shall explain, they are based on human stereotypes.

Ultimately, however, the Mandari are uncertain how to explain them and are therefore evasive when questioned about them: 'We do not know, they come from Dinka, so no one can know for certain.' A layman may suggest that one consult a specialist of Powers. The fact that ordinary people are confused, and only trained specialists are thought to understand them, is one of the reasons for the contradictions and the success of the cult. Control is concentrated in the hands of specialists who can exploit its possibilities without check, because unlike traditional cults it is

---

[1] I use this term in the sense of 'pertaining to phenomena and conditions which appear to lie outside the domain of physical law' or 'pertaining to some hyper-physical agency'. This is in accordance with the Mandari view of the phenomena as 'beyond' or 'alongside' the material.

not open to informed comment by intelligent older laymen. Powers are considered unacceptable and dangerous partly because people do not know what they are dealing with; they are particularly rejected by the older generation, the upholders of tradition, and there is often scarcely veiled antagonism between older doctors treating conventional cases with Mandari methods, and younger, often Dinka-trained doctors of Powers. As an older practitioner complained to me, 'in the old days we only knew Creator, the Above, and the ghosts of the dead.'

Those doctors who have specialized in the treatment of Powers are active in defending and promoting the cult. They claim that they have to help those who come under the influence of Powers and that they are trying to perfect techniques of treatment in the face of unwarranted opposition.

The Mandari are forced to take note of Powers because they are now put forward as causes in illness and death and, when people are ill, their overriding concern is to be cured. Many, who would like to reject the whole notion of Powers may employ *Jok* practitioners when they have tried traditional methods and failed to find a cure. It seems a possibility that the new agents could eventually take a dominant place in explanations of sickness partly, perhaps, because of the spectacular treatments developed by the ambitious younger-generation *Jok* doctors.

These doctors assiduously build up explanatory theories which have considerable plausibility. One of them gave me a different explanation for the presence of Powers from the one usually put forward (that they came by contagion from the Dinka), maintaining that they had always existed in Mandari but that when people suffered from them the true cause of the symptoms was not recognized. The illnesses were wrongly diagnosed, 'as Above or ghost-sickness', so the wrong treatment was given and the patients never got well. It was the *training*, the power to diagnose and to cure, that had been recently introduced from the Aliab. I encountered a similar attempt to authenticate a new agent and its treatment during a visit to the Nile Köbora. A Mandari doctor living and practising there told me that he had tried to introduce both Powers and Spirit-of-the-Above as agents in illness but without as yet any success. He said to me, 'Here [in Köbora] their doctors are useless because they put everything down to ancestors and so people never recover.' He suggested that in time the new agents might be accepted, and pointed out that the Mandari originally 'refused Powers when they were first brought from Dinka', but that 'now all the Mandari know about them'. Doctors often complained to me about the slowness, stubbornness, and stupidity of people in the face of indisputable new evidence.

The varying attitudes expressed exemplify attempts by the layman, the traditional doctor, and the new-style practitioner, to account for phenomena which do not belong to accepted experience. In a wider sense this controversy represents an attempt in common to come to terms with new and disturbing social trends and to categorize them in a viable manner.

III

Two accounts of the origin of Powers give a vivid insight into their supposed nature and explain many features of the doctor's treatment. The first was recounted by Kok (also called Ajayich), who is an Atwot by birth, but domiciled since childhood with maternal kin in Mandari, where he practises. He claimed to know the Atwot version:

In the old days *Jokan* were people like men and walked about the earth. When the people went to camps in the dry season, they went too and had separate camps. The people were always quarrelling with them and the *Jokan* got the worst of it and were continually harried. So they approached Creator and asked him to help; Creator listened and said he would send a whirlwind into the men's camp. And there was a dog who could speak like a person, and he went to the people and warned them saying 'a whirlwind is about to come and you must all cover your eyes!' But the people would not listen and beat the dog saying 'What are you talking about?' Then the wind came. But one man listened to the dog and threw himself on the ground and covered his eyes. The eyes of all the others were pierced with dust, so they were blinded and could no longer see the *Jokan*. The man whose eyes were whole could see them and he became the first *Jok* doctor.

After that, when the *Jokan* came to attack men, the dogs began to bark, but the men could not see them and did not know from which side they were being attacked. Then a *Joksho* called Abiyel threw a spear at a man and hit him in the side of the chest. Then all the *Jokan* came and sat down with the people by the cattle fires. They caught people, who began to suffer pains, swellings and fevers and to die. Then the man who became the doctor came to the *Jokan* and said 'Do not kill the men, but let them give you a cow, and leave them in peace.' This man became the intermediary between men and *Jokan*.[1]

In this story *Jok* are represented as beings, living a pastoral life in conflict with humans. Divine intervention veils them from sight but one man retains the power to see what has now become the invisible, and he emerges as the prototype *Jok* doctor. His ability to see Powers supports the contemporary doctor's claim that he also may actually see them—'the *Jok* appear to the doctor like the shadow of a man with teeth and eyes'. Mutianagok and Munork are said to be visible in shadowy form in trees.

This story reveals an extra-sensory plane, behind but impinging on the material world. In the face of attacks from it, man becomes impotent and dies, because he cannot control it or establish a *modus vivendi* with it. Eventually, through the doctor, the human mediator, a system of exchange is established and sickness is averted by giving an ox in place of the victim.

The Aliab Dinka version was told to me by Ako Akurukway.

Jokan came from the people of the underworld. Long ago the only son of a man died. The father was desolate and wanted to follow his son to the underworld. So he dug a hole into the earth and followed the path his son had taken. After a while he came to the house of the chief of the underworld where a dance was in progress. The chief asked him what he wanted, so he replied, 'I want my child.' The chief replied, 'All right, sit down and he will come.' Then all the people assembled to dance, and the man said, 'There is my child with the big feather.' But the boy remonstrated with his father, 'Why have you come after me here?' And his father replied, 'I have only one son.' The chief told the father he could leave with the boy, but warned him that he must never reveal anything about the underworld, or sing the songs he had heard because they were the songs of the underworld and the *Jokan*.

The man and his son went home and on arrival the man killed three oxen and all the people came together and feasted, and questioned the man about his journey. And during the feasting and drinking the man began to sing the songs he had heard in the underworld, and as he sang, the *Jokan* heard, and came among men, and began to trouble those on Earth.

And they seized (*moka*) people, who fell ill. And the man who had visited the underworld became the first doctor because he knew the

---

[1] A Dinka law student from Khartoum University confirmed that this story is known in Dinka.

songs. After that all the *Jokan* came: Mutiaŋagok, Adwegdwor, Mayom, Magok, Wel, and others.

Powers again feature as earthly phenomena, keepers of the underworld associated with the dead. The songs by which they are 'called' by doctors during mediumistic seances are mentioned.

Both accounts emphasize the doctors' ability to see and communicate with Powers and to act as mediators. The very fact that such stories exist at all illustrates the mundane nature of Powers. The Mandari never attempt to speculate about the origin of Creator or his agents, or represent them in material form. No one has seen Creator or Spirit-of-the-Above, and Mandari do not 'see' the ghosts of dead kin in this immediate sense, though they may see them as dream images.

IV

The relationship between a man and a Power which has seized his family and been established by the raising of a shrine, is described in kinship terms: 'The Power becomes a relative, a person of the homestead' (*Joksho ge ayuŋi, ŋutu lo baŋ*). As a kinsman it may pass on to a close blood relative, and it has a greater range of spread than Spirit-of-the-Above in that a Power may pass to anyone living in the homestead, including a retainer or affine.

The relationship between a Power and its owner is seen to be highly ambivalent. It is a protector and a destroyer, a friend and a greedy parasite. It involves its owner in expense by constant demands for food and Mandari seldom feel that the protection it is said to afford compensates for disadvantages of ownership—'*Jok* are malignant and never benevolent like the ancestors who help a man.' Powers are not active guardians, and their protective element lies purely in their potential threat to others. If, for instance, a man steals from a homestead which owns a Power, he may fall ill, because it pervades the possessions of its adopted owner making their removal dangerous. A Power can be sent out after a thief, and if someone angers its owner, or a night-witch approaches to harm him, they may fall ill. The non-related person affected by it can only placate it in the last resort by planting a shrine himself. Thus it is said, 'while a *Joksho* is a hard master, it has its price, it is a man's friend and one of his homestead so it protects his possession and must be paid accordingly'.

An incident involving Ako Akurukway illustrates this assumed protective element, but before recounting it I should explain the supposed nature of Dinka Celestial Spirits, since Ako's association with Jombai, one of such spirits, explains his ability to treat Powers and was also said to account for the return of his property. A Dinka Celestial Spirit is treated and worked exactly as a Power, and laymen make no distinction between the two. I challenged Ako on this point and he stated that 'those possessed by a Dinka spirit can treat Powers, for such a purpose they are all the same'. He insisted, none the less, that there was what might be described as a theoretical difference—'one that only doctors can appreciate'.

Ako's property was returned to him in the following manner. While travelling on a sickness case, he mislaid his pipe. At once he announced this, saying 'The pipe of Jombai has been lost.' He told me that it would certainly be returned since no one would dare to use it. As he predicted, a man who had picked it up some fifteen miles away returned it. Here the personal property of a well-known practitioner of a Dinka spirit was concerned; in the case of the property of laymen who own Powers, return might not have been assured.

The Mandari attempt to avoid the consequences of diagnosis involving Powers because they fear them and the economic demands involved in ownership. A *Jok* doctor told me, however, that once a family had had repeated illness attributed to a Power, it is compelled eventually to accept 'because Powers are tenacious'. Eventual capitulation, of course, turns on the tactics of the doctor, who follows up incidences of sickness. Even a change of doctor may not release a patient because the diagnosis may have become common knowledge and be supported by the next one. The diligent watchfulness of the doctor of Powers is an important feature in the spread and maintenance of the cult, as, indeed, is that of the traditional doctor in relation to traditional religious cults.

The persistence with which Powers are thought to seek out avenues for attachment within a kinship group was described as follows:

A Power is planted in the homestead of one wife and then a man marries a second wife who cooks very well and makes good sauces and beer, and it wants to become a member of her homestead too so that it can eat. So the new wife falls ill. The doctor comes and says 'you have Mutiaŋagok in your homestead, now Mutiaŋagok wishes to be planted here as well because this is a very good site with a lot to eat.' Then the man plants a pole in his homestead as well. In time the Power sees that the wife of the man's brother is always brewing beer . . .

Here the Power follows in the track of good food and beer, which shows that the very human characteristic of greed is part of its nature.

V

Specialists have evolved a classification of sickness, said to be caused by Powers, along the lines of traditional medicine grouping together a number of symptoms and naming them after a particular Power. Much the same terminology is also used to describe the onset of the symptoms—'He has a Power' (*gwa ko Joksho*), or 'he has Mutiaŋagok' (*gwa ko Mutiaŋagok*). The distinctive pole shrines make it possible to tell, immediately, which Power is involved. Powers have their own medicines, though some are interchangeable between them. The most important Powers and the pole shrines planted for them are as follows:[1]

1. *Mutiaŋagok.* This is a killer, its symptoms violent, although a patient may recover from a mild atttack. Symptoms are severe pains in the head, back, or chest; the body is hot and the patient may be panting or delirious. A root medicine is pounded, mixed in water and administered by mouth. In a mild attack an animal is tied up for a few days 'for the Power to see', while people wait for the sickness to pass, then it is released; but if a victim continues seriously ill, it is killed and a shrine planted. A bull calf or two large neutered goats may be demanded.

2. *Mayom.* Mayom is a swelling illness; if the whole body swells death follows rapidly. In a mild, or partial form, one limb for instance, being affected, the patient may be ill for a long time but there is a chance of recovery. An ox may be killed for Mayom

---

[1] For details of plants used as medicines and shrines see Appendices. In Appendix II I give drawings of shrines. The larger ones are sections cut from branches and may stand 6–7 feet high. Medicines are listed in Appendix III.

and a shrine raised. Cuts are sometimes made in a swollen limb or part of the body and a pounded medicine rubbed in.[1]

3. Two Powers, *Adwegdwor* and *Agok*, have similar characteristics; head and chest are hot, there is severe headache and pain across the eyes often accompanied by diarrhoea and vomiting. Like Mayom, they can cause swelling, although this is not typical. Patients are said often to die in the early morning. Treatment is by medicine, and the raising of a shrine with a goat.

4. *Ukor* affects the bowel causing diarrhoea and the passing of blood. Medicine is administered, and a small shrine without a pole is made. Ukor is seldom fatal, unless occurring in association with other causes.

5. *Weltoc*. This causes 'wasting'. The victim 'sits in one place', depressed, debilitated, or lethargic; 'his eyes fail and his body wastes away.' A chicken is killed and cooked and eaten by the elders in the bush; a small pole may be raised.

6. *Abyel*. Pain in the side near the heart; a goat is killed; no shrine is planted.

7. *Mayar* and *Woŋkoro*. These are chest illnesses. Mayar is a slow killer; the patient coughs, his body becomes thin and wasted and there may be blood in the sputum. Mandari say Mayar is only curable in the very early stages and its fatal character is recognized. An element of physical contagion is said to be involved, and patients use their own drinking vessels and dishes and have separate sleeping mats. A diet of milk and other special delicacies is recommended to maintain strength. Mandari explain the rules for separating the utensils, by saying that this 'Jok has great potency' and can easily pass through a sick person's possessions. The Mandari see this Power as tending 'to kill over a group'; they also consider it may 'come out' in the offspring of a sufferer.[2] Woŋkoro is a violent and quick-killing chest illness; the symptoms are chest pains, difficulty in breathing, coughing, feverishness, heat, and delirium. If the patient does recover there is a long convalescence. Spirit-of-the-Above also causes symptoms similar to Woŋkoro, but in the former the body is 'cold and shaking', while in the latter—as in all illness from Powers—it is 'hot'.

---

[1] Mandari say Mayom occurs fairly frequently, and I saw a case of a sudden illness where the man's body appeared to swell and death followed; local opinion assumed a Power was involved.

[2] I think the Mandari may be describing pulmonary tuberculosis, which would appear to be fairly common. Woŋkoro is, I think, pneumonia.

Woŋkoro follows from the touching or picking up of a feather of a black bird (perhaps the raven?) or from drinking from a pool from which the bird drinks. Woŋkoro and Mayar are said to have 'come from the Moru' and are not '*jok*' in the strict sense, but they are examples of those diseases with a foreign source which are loosely called '*jok*'. No shrines are made.

While doctors believe that they can recognize specific Powers in such symptoms as described, diagnosis is not made on physical evidence alone. Background social circumstances and existing associations with other spiritual agents must be taken into account. It will be apparent that many symptoms are also typical of sickness caused by Celestial Spirits, and some could also be interpreted as ghost-sickness. Others, however, are essentially typical of Powers, and, if these should occur in a patient in whose history such a contact is traced, they constitute proof; even a layman can guess that a man is suffering from Mayom, for instance, if he already has this Power in the family. It is always, however, on the result of the doctor's divination that final decision and treatment depend.

Powers, like religious agents, receive animal sacrifice, and animals killed for Powers must be selected from the correct class. They must not be given sheep because their meat is 'cool'. The typical offering for a Power is the 'hot' goat, coloured black or red rather than pure white, and they also receive chickens and beer.

Property allocations are made for Powers and these are jealously guarded. The gourds and pots in which their food is presented, or in which their sacrificial meat is cooked, are kept strictly apart from pots used for cooking offerings to other agents. One common pot is 'the black pot of Mutiaŋagok', (*isa lura na Mutiaŋagok*). These pots are used for homestead meals, but in the context of a rite the Power's meat must be cooked in it. A mistake is very dangerous.[1] The view that Powers are touchy accords with the characteristics they share with persons. As the Mandari put it, 'if elders are not treated with respect, or do not receive their appropriate meat at ceremonies, they become petulant and com-

---

[1] A doctor once suggested to me that Powers and Ghosts are 'friends', whereas Powers and Celestial Spirits 'hate each other', stressing the assumed neutrality of phenomena which are of a similar order—thus both Powers and Ghosts are terrestrial, but Powers and Celestial Spirits belong to antipathetic conceptual divisions.

plain. Powers react dangerously in a similar way if their wants are ignored.'

Regular sacrifices are not made to Powers and it is the occurrence of illness which elicits action. But beer libations are always poured at shrines after brewing. The special pot set out by the hut supports for the Power Ukor is also kept filled because if it lies empty someone may have a minor accident—suffer a scorpion bite or fall and break a limb. Those who can afford to do so will brew beer for their Power when they perform the routine rite at the beginning of each lunar month and if they have reason for apprehension they will also kill a chicken. Offerings are curtailed in poverty or in times of food shortage. When sickness is attributed to an established Power, more valuable offerings must be made, and the type of food or meat required is revealed by the doctor either by divination or by the new practice of mediumistic seance. Wealth and status and severity of illness are factors determining the value of the offerings.

It is important that a Power should share in the possessions and crops of its owner's homestead; thus a grain-bearing seedling, symbolizing the crops in general, may be presented at a shrine. As the grain heads begin to swell, a root of the small millet *laly* is transplanted to the foot of the shrine to ripen there, or a ground-nut plant is hung on the pole when this crop is dug. The grain can then be harvested and eaten without the family having colds or indigestion. Before newly harvested grain is pounded, cooked, and eaten as porridge, beer is brewed from the new crop and drunk by every household, and some of this is always poured down at shrines, 'so that the Power may see and drink'. These presentations encourage the Power to protect the crops from thieves and witches: 'the Power can see and keep watch'; the seedlings also 'show' the Power what it can expect in the form of beer or food if the harvest is abundant.

VI

Before I describe and comment on a number of treatments I attended for patients suffering from disorders claimed to be caused by Powers, I should draw attention to the new type of diagnostic investigation which I call the seance. At a seance a number of new techniques of mediumship are used either alone or in succession. The first of these involves a violent form of induced possession (*molja*) under which the Power is said to 'speak' directly through the doctor as the medium. In the second method no utterances may be made under the induced possession (the Power does not 'speak'), but after the possession has run its course the doctor holds a dialogue with it. In the latter case the doctor acts as a medium when he is in a normal condition. I describe this latter technique as the 'question and answer' method.

SEANCE NO. I. *Treatment of Asek of Jarra clan*

Ako Akurukway asked me whether I would like to go with him to 'question' a Power in the homestead of a man named Asek. Asek's father had died some time before; Asek and his brothers, who were unmarried, had continued to live with their widowed mother. Then Asek's elder brother married, but the family still kept together. Later two other brothers died, and in due course Asek himself became sick. Several doctors had been summoned to give treatment at various times but it was evident from the continuing sicknesses that none had found the correct cause. Some months before my arrival Ako was called in. He diagnosed the sickness series as deriving from the Power Mutiaŋagok which had 'followed' Asek's mother, a Dinka woman, from Agar. He therefore prescribed the sacrifice of a bull and the raising of a shrine. This was done and Asek recovered. Having the inclination, and the necessary aptitude, Asek became apprenticed to Ako. His tuition, for which he paid ten goats, had continued since his cure and at the time of our visit he was beginning independent practice. Asek had asked Ako to return and 'question' the Power which he had originally planted, to confirm that all was well. Follow-up questioning after a shrine has been planted is routine and precautionary; it also provides an occasion for probing the Power about current indispositions. In this instance, Asek's mother and his surviving brother's wife had been unwell and the latter's child had fallen on to the fire and suffered minor burns.

On arrival in Jarra we found that Asek was away treating a patient. When, at dusk, there was no sign of Asek, Ako decided to have a preliminary 'questioning' of his own spirit, Jombai, to obtain guidance for the main session which would be held the following day.

2. Ako Akurukway pours a libation at the shrine for Mutiaŋagok. At rear, the hut in which the seance took place

At his suggestion, therefore, those present went into the hut. In addition to Asek's mother, brother, sister-in-law, and her child, they included a number of closely related elders who had drifted in during the day. The latter were entitled to attend to hear the diagnoses, to lend support, and possibly to benefit themselves.

The seance began, as is customary, with the singing of songs which are said to summon the Powers so that communication may be established. Ako was assisted by Asek's brother, while the audience joined in the chorus: rhythmic clapping accompanied the singing. After a while, Ako took up his diviner's rattle and began to rub the back of the hut with a circular motion in a clockwise direction. The audience stopped singing and clapping and there was silence except for the scraping of the rattle on the clay wall. Then a voice began to come through the darkness from a point low down at the back of the hut. Dinka words were eventually distinguishable. The speaker was disclosed as Jombai; as is usual with Dinka spirits it was speaking in its own language. The seance then continued, interrupted periodically by interludes of singing and clapping led by Ako. A seance has the following pattern:

Vernacular	*English translation*
Ako—'Kudwal[1] Jombai'	'Salutations Jombai'
Voice said to be	
Jombai—'Kudwal Ako;	'Salutations Ako;
Kudwal Taliŋ', etc.	Salutations All', etc.
Chorus of people—'Kudwal	'Greetings Jombai, greetings
Jombai, Kudwal Mar,	Chief' (in Mandari, then in
Kudwal Beny, Aba', etc.	Dinka), 'Greetings father', etc.

After exchanges of courtesies and inquiries after the welfare of individuals to which all present replied suitably, Ako confirmed that it was really Jombai speaking. Then he put questions in Dinka, translating the replies into Mandari. Questions related to health and sickness and were posed along the following lines: '*Beny* (Chief), my wife is always suffering from pains and aches in the joints, and my small son is ailing, what shall I do?' After the spirit had answered each question in turn, Ako inquired about the main seance at which the Power of the shrine would be questioned, and Jombai affirmed that the occasion would be propitious. Ako

---

[1] *Kudwal*, a Dinka greeting, is now used over much of Mandari in preference to the traditional *mötö*.

then said Jombai wished us all to go home and reassemble at dawn for the main seance when Jombai would be answering, together with the Power Mutiaŋagok. Throughout this seance Jombai had spoken very faintly and had had to be encouraged frequently by Ako. The company then dispersed.

Next morning at dawn we walked to the homestead from a neighbouring hamlet and in the course of the walk Ako lost his pipe with the results already described. We arrived about 7 a.m. and found no sign of Asek so the session was again postponed. We passed another idle day, during which members of the hamlet began to assemble for what would by this time be an evening event. About noon, Ako began to blow a whistle. Shortly afterwards we saw Asek approaching. Ako and Asek greeted each other and Asek observed that he had come from treating a case but offered no apology for the delay which was not considered of importance. At this point it was found that the elder brother, the owner of the homestead, had disappeared, and the session was again postponed.

Ako then performed a preliminary rite. Asek's mother, who had been indisposed, was seated by the shrine and Ako passed a gourd of beer, brewed for the occasion, round her head and then poured a libation by the base of the shrine. He addressed Mutiaŋagok, drawing attention to the old woman, her daughters-in-law, and the latter's children.

Ako and I were then given food; groundnuts, honey, beer, sweet millet, and dried meat with a vegetable sauce—prized delicacies, only produced for important guests. In the late afternoon Asek's brother arrived, accompanied by two youths carrying a large basketwork container of groundnuts and pots of honey which were presented to Ako. Asek expressed regret that the gifts were not more lavish, but blamed the poor harvest and widespread hunger. Five piastres were handed to me as a 'person' of Ako's entourage.

We then entered the hut. In addition to the family about ten people, mostly older lineage males, were present. The men sat in a semicircle in the centre of the floor, the women grouped themselves near the door. I was given a place directly behind Ako, 'so that the Awuk can see my work'. Asek also sat at the back by Ako's side facing the audience and assisted by shaking his rattle and leading the singing.

Ako, his back to the audience, sat cross-legged facing the back
wall and led the opening phrases of the song, while the audience,
clapping rhythmically, sang the chorus. Singing goes on repeti-
tively, with the leader now and then introducing a theme on his
own, the audience then taking up the chorus. The songs are
typical Aliab Dinka dance songs, described as 'the dance of the
Powers (*löri lo Jok*), which calls them near, so that they can be
questioned. Without the singing they would remain far away.'
Ako occasionally paused to compliment the singers or encourage
greater effort—'Sing well, so that Mutiaŋagok can hear.' During the
singing he and Asek shook divining rattles, and old women ululated.

The hut soon became stifling; by this time it was full of close
Jarra kin and more distant neighbours who, hearing a session was
in progress, tried to press in through the entrance. The mood was
one of excitement and anticipation. Sweat poured down the faces
and bodies of Ako and his assistants and their movements and
rattlings became more frenetic.

Ako eventually showed signs of possession. His body began to
twitch and then to jerk violently up and down and from side to
side, his eyes were closed, and sweat streamed down his face,
back, and chest. The chorus swelled as the audience urged the
spirit to manifest itself. Ako's movements became increasingly
convulsed and he appeared to be disassociated. At this point the
spirits are said to have 'taken over' the doctor's body. This was
the climax of the possession, and the contortions began to lessen
until they stopped altogether. The clapping and singing continued,
and after a moment the hut began to sway. The Mandari had
already told me that Powers made huts move during seances but
I had not taken this too seriously. However, I felt a movement,
which began gently and grew quite pronounced. The hut seemed
to tremble and then to sway from side to side. For perhaps half a
minute we rocked backwards and forwards, the contents of a beer-
pot slopping over, then the movements stopped and the audience
ceased to clap and sing. The swaying of the hut is said to be 'the
dance of the *Jokan*, who, at that point, are in the hut in numbers'.

Ako took up his rattle again and began to rub the back wall with
the same circular movement as before, producing a harsh rasping
and a sharp rattling from the seeds in the rattle. A voice began to
'speak', this time from the centre of the circle described by the
rattle.

The Power which 'spoke' was identified as Mutianagok, the owner of the shrine. Like Jombai the previous evening, Mutianagok made a low murmuring sound, little more than a hollow sighing. Ako greeted it in Dinka, then explained to the audience that they were to listen carefully as Mutianagok was speaking to them. The Power characteristically greeted those present, important personages being addressed by name. Its voice was very faint and Ako repeated its words. He would confirm after some muffled moanings: 'Mutianagok says, *Kudwal* Asek', to which Asek replied, '*Kudwal Beny*'; 'Mutianagok says, *Kudwal* to the white person', to which I answered, '*Kudwal Beny*.' The 'voice' gained strength, but still remained rather erratic, occasionally falling to a whisper or dying away altogether.

Elders and family heads began asking questions, which Ako relayed to the Power in Dinka, also translating the replies. A man told me afterwards that he had easily been able to understand the Power, although not everybody there would be able to do so because Dinka is not widely spoken in this part of Mandari. Before putting a question, a petitioner placed a payment, 'for the asking', into 'the black pot of Mutianagok' which had been taken down and placed on Ako's left. Payments were described to me afterwards by Ako as being 'for the wife of the Power in the doctor's body'. They differ from the fees paid to the doctor by the person calling the session, in that they make it possible for the Power to answer a specific inquiry. If it were not paid its 'owner' might fall ill because he is responsible for extracting payments.

Questions centred round indisposition, barrenness, and bewitching. Answers can be obtained even though the Power is not itself concerned in the problem, since it can transcend the limitations of human knowledge. Asek's brother inquired about the illness of his wife and mother and offered to sacrifice an ox if this would prevent more illness. After making his petition he deposited 5 piastres in the Power's pot.

The following are examples of questions asked:

Beny, if it is you who are causing us to suffer in such and such a way so that we are unable to cultivate and there is no one left to herd the cattle, stop plaguing us, let us remain in peace. If you kill us, our cattle will also die and then how do you expect us to kill oxen for you? Let us know if the illness is from you!

Tell us Beny, why people are always bewitching us—so and so is crippled with pains in the joints, my wife is also ailing and laid up. Tell us where these misfortunes come from.

Or, assuming the Power knows already, simply:

Beny, what about so and so?

The Power replied through Ako saying, for instance:

It is all right, so and so, your wife will get well, the illness is only an indisposition [a 'small thing'].

Or, in a case of supposed bewitching:

It is not I, Mutianagok, who am causing this illness, but someone from outside! [Meaning a hostile person from another village.]

Sometimes the direction of the witchcraft was indicated:

It comes from the East!

In one case the Power warned a man:

Look out for people among you who are envious of you!

In another:

You must call a doctor and kill a chicken for the Above.

Again:

The people of your line [ancestors] want meat; go and kill a cow for them and you will recover!

One man attempted a question which Ako ruled invalid, telling him to: 'Go out and call the father of your homestead and ask through him.' It appears the man was an 'outsider' (possibly an affine living in the hamlet); such a person should approach the Power of the agnatic line through a senior man related to the 'owner' of the Power. Finally Mutianagok asked about my health, my activities in Mandari and what I sought. I was informed, after Ako had explained my position, that I would come to no harm, but would remain in peace and return safely to my own people— 'Awuk na Ki, who came from the sky, will return by the sky.'[1]

The momentum of the seance was slowing down, interested parties having received answers to their problems, so Ako asked Mutianagok whether it was contented with its new homestead or had further requirements. The Power appeared reasonably satisfied, but it showed its disposition to move on by saying that, if a

---

[1] Ako had explained to the Power my arrival in the Sudan by aeroplane.

bull calf were available later in the year, this should be killed by Asek's brother for his wife and child and a shrine erected in his own homestead. Beer should also be poured down in the homestead of Asek and his old mother for continued 'safe sleep'.

Ako wound up the proceedings by announcing that Mutiaŋagok had nothing further to say and everyone could go home; an unceremonious scramble from the hut followed. Before leaving everyone was gathered into a semicircle in the yard and marked protectively by Ako who picked a branch of the rain creeper *Tirioti*, dipped it in a gourd of water and, beginning at the righthand person, splashed each in turn on the head, chest, and legs. Ako then spat on our heads.

He and I and lineage elders finished the beer. Before we finally left, Asek's mother spat on our heads and prayed to Creator for our safety; 'Go well, and Creator be with you, and let all evil depart away into the bush.' Ako promised that he would return in the wet season for the raising of the brother's pole.[1]

COMMENT

At the seance the doctor used a technique of spirit mediumship new to the Mandari and involving interrogation of the Power. During the main seance he first experienced an induced possession in which the Power is said to 'take over' his body. Later he summoned the Power without being possessed and 'questioned' it. In these questions and answers, the doctor uses a ventriloquial technique (reported also from neighbouring areas, including Nuer and Bunyoro), which is unique to *Jok* doctors.

While induced possession is also new, possession as such is already known and understood in the spontaneous Celestial possession. Induced possessions take a characteristic form, although each doctor will employ his own perfected methods, and some achieve a more violent convulsion than others.

In the main seance the doctor practised another technique, hut-moving, or 'dancing' as the Mandari put it, which followed a considerable period—perhaps an hour—of rhythmical clapping

---

[1] Ako returned in October, but I was due to leave Mandari and could not accompany him. As I passed through Tali Post, his brother intercepted me and told me Ako had been taken seriously ill in Jarra. I was very pressed for time and did not stop. When I returned to Mandari six years later I learned that he had died in Juba Hospital. I would like to pay tribute to a friend who gave me valuable help and an insight into the doctor's profession.

and singing. Huts are solidly built structures raised from the ground on stout tree trunks sunk into the earth, a log platform lies on these supports and makes the floor of the hut, a platform extends outwards from the doorway (Plate 7). A hut holds about fifteen to twenty people closely crowded. The hut in question was smaller than others in which I have attended seances where there was no movement and perhaps it was structurally unstable. Another explanation for the motion that I felt would be that I was, myself, subject, like others present, to some form of suggestion. But I think this unlikely, as my object in attending was to observe carefully what was taking place and I was emotionally detached. Further, the slopping over of the beer would seem to confirm the movement.

I found audience reaction to the seances very mixed. Some people were prepared to take them at face value, others were openly sceptical. A wide range of contradictory opinion emerges in response to questions about seances which would never be expressed in a discussion of traditional methods, the validity of which is never at issue, although the activities of certain doctors may be. Those who repudiate Powers see the whole process as fraudulent; others who allow that they exist, or who have received a successful treatment at the hands of a *Jok* doctor, think that something of real value is involved. Because Powers are from 'outside' people cannot easily judge the action of their doctors; rules of conventional ritual cannot be contravened. I was, however, told several times that it is not a Power that speaks but the doctor— 'He talks in a disguised voice in his chest.' No one could tell me how he did this, and it is recognized that these doctors have carefully guarded trade secrets, passed on to a closed circle of vetted pupils.

It is not perhaps surprising that the audience cannot easily explain the voices in view of the gloom and congestion in the hut and the fact that the doctor sits with his back to the audience for this part of the performance. Those closest to him are accomplices— in this case Asek and his elder brother. I myself, sitting close by, could not see anything obvious which would have made me guess what he was doing. The audience is also in a highly receptive state and the whole atmosphere is unconducive to critical observation.

A parallel could perhaps be drawn between the new style doctor in Mandari society and faith healers and others who practise 'fringe' medicine in our own society, some of whom appear to effect cures by unorthodox methods. In the same way that the fringe healer is unacceptable to the main stream of medical practice here, the *Jok* doctor tends to be regarded as a charlatan by traditional Mandari practitioners. In both cases, however, it may be cautiously allowed that patients appear to derive some benefit. Faith-healers, in our society, of course, offer little challenge to established medicine, whereas *Jok* doctors do appear to present a challenge to Mandari traditional methods. The greater success in gaining acceptance by the *Jok* doctor over the faith-healer is due to the fact that he works within the same range of ideas as the traditional doctor; confidence in supernatural healing agents is the basis of both types of treatment and the methods are not fundamentally opposed. Faith healing, on the other hand, with its reliance on the spiritual, is seen to contradict the laws of science.

In the next seance, induced possession is the means by which the doctor becomes the direct channel of communication for the Power. It also illustrates the incorporation of a traditional treatment known as *möröröju* in the seance.

SEANCE NO. 2. *Treatment in the homestead of Nyökeru*

A young widower, Ajak Patis, of Mandiye lineage attached to Dari clan, had previously raised a pole for the *Jok* Mayom. During the current year, members of the family of his father's brother, an elder named Nyökeru, had been troubled by ailments. Nyöki Bero, who specializes in treatments of disorders caused by Spirit-of-the-Above had been called in, and his preliminary diagnosis indicated that it was not the latter, but the Power Mayom from the nephew's homestead, which was responsible. I was told that in the past Nyökeru had refused to raise a shrine to Mayom although he had been warned that he should do so by the doctor who raised that of Ajak Patis. Nyökeru's unmarried son, Alinakway, was, at that very moment, temporarily crippled by festering guinea-worm sores and swellings.

After the family had heard Nyöki's diagnosis they agreed that Mayom should be planted in Nyökeru's homestead, but first Mayom, planted in the homestead of Ajak Patis, would be questioned as to whether it was, indeed, the agent of illness, or whether there were other, or contributory ones at work.

This session lasted three days. Part of the proceedings was

held in the homestead of Ajak Patis, part in that of Nyökeru. Three practitioners attended. Nyöki Bero, a doctor who is possessed by the Dinka Celestial Spirit Löi, and treats celestial illness with a form of possession generally typical of Dinka-trained doctors, was consulted because as well as being a rising younger practitioner, he is an affine of Mandiye and lives in the hamlet with his wife's people. He had given the preliminary diagnosis but, as he does not treat or 'question' Powers he called in Kok (Ajayich), who lives in the hamlet adjacent to Mandiye, and who, as a *Jok* specialist, would lead the case. Ako Akurukway was also present for part of the time and gave advice as a neighbour and affine. He told me that he had only come to help his relatives and would take no fee. He and Nyöki Bero are paternal first cousins.

Mandiye lineage has segmented into two well-defined hamlets under extended family heads and separated by about a mile of bush. Men and women elders of the senior segment (that of Nyökeru) who were at home, came to the seance, but members of the junior segment, living in Agwadyir under Butis Agworoŋ, did not come because the segments are growing apart, each performing separate rites and acting independently in day-to-day affairs, although the whole lineage is represented at the Chief of Dari's meeting tree by the younger of the two hamlet heads, the Government headman Butis Agworoŋ.

On the first day, about thirty or forty people assembled. Beer had been brewed, for those who come and give support to a large session expect to drink at different points in the proceedings, and libations must be poured down for Powers and other spirits and at the edge of the homestead and the openings of paths to ward off witches and other evil influences. Those present were Mandiye, together with members of small outsider and client groups attached to them as proto-agnates or affines. The latter only came to look on and drink. A few prominent elders of Dari lineage whose homesteads border those of Mandiye and who are their affines came to drink for a short period.[1] Among them was the Dari Chief. Non-related visitors and affines do not enter the hut for the

---

[1] Dari and Mandiye have a special relationship through the marriage of a woman five generations back with Mar Are of Dari. The woman 'came with a baby boy by an unknown man' and Mar Are paid bride-wealth for her and became the boy's pater. This boy founded Mandiye. Any marriages between Dari chiefly line and Mandiye are with people *attached* to Mandiye and not with the direct line of Mandiye.

questioning, but social etiquette does not exclude even casual spectators from important ritual gatherings which provide an occasion for social entertainment. A large crowd enhances the prestige of the man calling the session and is good publicity for the doctor. Anyone crossing the hamlet may stop for a moment to watch or drink beer, but those without social or residential ties do not make a point of attending each other's rites. If some misfortune followed, people might associate it with them and begin to ask why they were there in the first place, so well-intentioned people are careful not to arouse suspicion.

On the appointed morning I arrived at Nyökeru's homestead and found a large gathering assembled. Important men and women elders taking part were seated under the hut and veranda while neighbours and related spectators sat under nearby trees. Almost at once it was announced that the seance would begin, and men of the family and lineage elders climbed into the hut. The women and those not directly concerned gathered on the raised veranda outside the entrance. Aliŋakway's mother and sister sat inside the hut near the door but, as usual on these occasions, the rest of the audience was predominantly male. I speak of Aliŋakway as the patient, because he was at that time a sufferer about to receive treatment, but in a case of this kind where a family has had intermittent trouble, it is the whole family which is being treated.

Kok and Nyöki (the two doctors) sat at the back of the hut facing the audience; Ako arrived on the second day. The purpose of the seance was a preliminary exploration of causal factors so that the questioning of the relevant Powers could be held the next day, and to give some immediate treatment to Aliŋakway. The first divination was carried out under possession, and the question and answer method was not employed.

Kok led the preliminary singing and the rattle shaking. After about three-quarters of an hour of preparatory singing and rattling Nyöki, possessed by the Dinka spirit, Löi, began to shake, showing imminent dissociation. This doctor's movements are particularly violent and sometimes have to be controlled by assistants. As he became convulsed, the clapping and singing increased in volume, the audience striving to urge the spirit into his body. Nyöki began to speak in an incoherent stream of words, while Kok, sitting beside him, rapidly translated. A spate of utterance was followed by a period of singing and clapping.

As the convulsion advanced Nyöki became less and less intelligible, and his movements so uncontrolled that assistants leant forward to hold him down. A final spasm heaved his rigid body off the floor and against the wall of the hut. Then he sank slowly forward and rested limply. Almost at once he collected himself, sat up, wiped his face and mouth and leaned in a dazed fashion against the wall. Someone handed him a pipe filled with tobacco, and a piece of smouldering charcoal.

During this possession the spirit had spoken in Mandari, but only those close by could distinguish the words. Nyöki's voice under possession is high and hiccuping and seems to be forced explosively from his mouth in a never-ending stream of words. Clear translation for the audience depends on the translator who only relays important points while the 'voice' rattles on uninterrupted.

After Nyöki had pronounced, Kok took over. Seated cross-legged in the centre of the hut, directly facing Aliŋakway (the patient), he began shaking his divining rattle in time to the singing, keeping his eyes steadily fixed on Aliŋakway's face. By now, audience and doctors were in a highly prepared state, and Kok was possessed almost immediately. Simultaneously, Aliŋakway's sister, who was sitting near me, had an hysterical fit. As she began to twitch and shake rhythmically in time to the rattling, two men leant over and seized her wrists to hold her down to the floor until the convulsions passed. This girl is a known chronic sufferer from girlhood convulsions and it is not unusual for girls who have this susceptibility to have such attacks at a seance. As she shook and twitched, Kok threw aside his rattle and began speaking rapidly in Dinka, while a man on his right translated.

After a short pronouncement Kok began to ride forward on his knees towards Aliŋakway and, with a sudden jerk, fell on to him and fixed his mouth on his leg. He crouched over the limb for a moment, then swayed back on to his haunches with his hands clapped over his mouth and groped his way to a far corner of the hut, trampling those in his way, and spat violently. Swaying back to his position opposite Aliŋakway he repeated the sucking operation on his chest. This time on releasing his hold, he made for the hut entrance, the audience drawing away to enable him to spit through it. He repeated the sucking and spitting four times, on different parts of Aliŋakway's limbs and body; once he spat out what looked like a thin stream of bloody saliva. As he worked, those sitting by helped him by kneading and pressing the flesh around the painful places in Aliŋakway's flesh towards Kok's mouth. Finally Kok shot forward and fastened on Aliŋakway's chest where he hung for so long that attempts were made to pull him away. He held on writhing, sweat pouring down his face, until what he wrestled with appeared to come away and he fell backwards with his hands over his mouth and groped to the side of the hut to spit, scattering gourds in all directions. He returned, sat down again and continued to jerk weakly for a few moments, then he released limply. He opened his eyes, which had been half closed, or open and staring, and looked round in a dazed manner.

When a possession has run its course, a doctor cannot prolong it, nor does he follow it up with another. The climax of the fit only lasts for about five or at the most ten minutes, although the period of preparatory stimulation and jerking about may continue for an hour or more. The point at which the Mandari say 'the spirit leaves the body' is so clear to everyone that they immediately begin clambering out of the stifling darkness and retire to nearby shade trees to smoke and discuss. Those who have work nearby go home. Most of the audience would, on this occasion, be spending the day in or around the patient's homestead in anticipation of the main questioning during the evening.

I could not follow what was said during the seance but was told afterwards that the doctors had been possessed by their own spirits: Nyöki by Löi, and Kok by Gurumbek, a Dinka Spirit-of-the-Above. The spirits had told the audience to return in the evening when the Power causing the illness would speak. They had ruled that the questioning should begin in the homestead of Ajak Patis where the *Jok* Mayom was planted and continue in that of Nyökeru. Mayom would require a black goat to be brought to the homestead for slaughter.

Kok had performed an operation known as *mömöröju* to remove from Aliŋakway's body contaminated blood put there by someone with the evil eye. The blood had inflamed the guinea-worm swellings and prevented healing. When I asked Aliŋakway about his sensations during the operation, he told me that it was uncomfortable but not painful—'The doctor only sucks with his gums and tongue.' What Kok produced appeared to be blood and saliva. Mandari say that the difference between a genuine doctor and a fake is that the latter, if they sucked, could not bring out anything. The doctor spits to one side or out of the door to avoid dropping contaminated spittle on the spectators.

When the audience reassembled it was full moon, and there was a very large crowd. As instructed, the session was opened in the homestead of Ajak Patis. Ako Akurukway was now present. When I arrived, beer drinking was in full swing; the elders had grouped themselves round the yard on mats in accordance with their sex and type of relationship to the family and to each other. Some Dari elders and the Chief were present, but the latter left before the questioning.

While the audience sat about smoking and drinking, Nyöki and Kok began some boisterous gymnastics, turning somersaults, performing acrobatics, and simulating possession. Exhibitionism untypical of traditional practitioners is a technique employed by doctors of Powers who seem to challenge convention by their outrageous poses. With the exception of a few recognized individual 'jokers', the Mandari are not *outré* in their behaviour, but doctors of Powers seem to aim at eccentricity, perhaps to differentiate themselves from the traditional stream of medical practice, to impress, and to enhance their reputation for dynamism. By doing so they can also attract adverse criticism.

After jumping about and performing contortions, Nyöki picked up a clod of earth and hurled it at the shrine abusing and up-braiding the Power. This attack aroused mutterings of disapproval from some elders who obviously felt that Nyöki was going too far. I have seen him overplay his hand on other occasions, and his eccentric behaviour and outspokenness arouses criticism. After attacking the Power, Nyöki knelt shaking in the centre of the mat, then began to bound along on his knees, spinging into the air with his legs doubled under him. It was clear that the spirit was immi-nent and people gathered round clapping and singing. Words streamed from Nyöki's lips; then Kok fell into a convulsion. The excited audience pressed around, the women ululating. After a short interval of 'pronouncing', the translators told us to enter the hut so that Mayom could speak. Thereupon everyone con-cerned, and such lineage hangers-on as could be squeezed in, entered the hut.

Kok began the session using the question and answer technique, and calling up Mayom from the back of the hut with his rattle.

A hollow moaning sound came forth, then a weak, rapid voice. Kok posed the questions and relayed the faint replies. A number of people petitioned along the lines described at the Jarra session and, after answering, the Power announced that it had nothing more to say. I was told later that the need for the killing of a black goat and the raising of a pole in the homestead of Aliŋakway had been confirmed, and that a chicken was also to be killed at Mayom's pole in Ajak Patis's homestead. After prevarication on the part of the elders, who wished to make sure that the offerings were really necessary and, if made, would grant freedom from illness, the Power was told that its demands would be met.

It was then Ako Akurukway's turn to become possessed. His spirit, Jombai, spoke directly through him, informing the people that the first part of the proceedings was now over and that, having heard the wishes of Mayom, they should go to Aliŋakway's homestead and again question the Power about the kind of offering and shrine required in its homestead.

At this point I went home exhausted; it was late, and the questioning could well continue in the other hut all night.

At dawn, the black goat, earmarked and brought to the homestead after the revelations of the morning session, was killed and the new pole raised. I missed this having misunderstood the time, but Kok and Nyöki gave me details. The shrine was a replica of that planted for Mayom by Ajak Patis—a large notched pole without 'horns', positioned against the hut's supports on the right side of the ascent ladder in the area of the veranda known as bor.

When I returned to the homestead that evening hoping to see the goat being sacrificed, the women were already dividing out the remainder of its meat and cooking a sacrificial chicken. Kok and Nyöki were waiting for their portions. Each would receive a leg, and cuts from the neck and shoulder. Each had asked a fee of one Sudanese pound, the payment to be made over a period. Before leaving, Nyöki took 25 piastres from the gifts of coins left by those attending the pole raising, and Kok, as the chief consultant, took 35 piastres. Nyöki, who was related to the patient would, in all probability, forgo the balance due to him, a normal practice when a doctor is a kinsman or affine.

A collection of objects and equipment, the property of Aliŋakway and his father, had been placed by the new pole, including two hunting spears, head-rests, a squatting seat, and a bow and arrows.

There were also beads, coiled copper wire, money, and knobs of tobacco. The patient's personal possessions are laid at the shrine so that the Power can observe them and take them and their owner under its protection; the other things are gifts given to the Power by those attending the sessions and eating the meat of its goat. Three heaps of cow dung were smouldering round the shrine, in order, I was informed, 'that the smoke may go up and the Power and other spirits see and take note of it'. (Smoking cow dung symbolizes cattle fires and hence the owner's animals.) A gourd of millet porridge had been placed, to which one of the chicken stock was added.

The food offerings are left at the pole for a short time and then eaten by homestead elders. The gifts and personal effects would remain until the family left for the dry season cattle-camps in a month's time, when the possessions would be put away or taken to the camp. While they are at the shrine, they may be used but, after use, must be returned to it. The first hunting spear, used for digging the hole for the shrine, is taken by the doctor as part fee. The second, with which the animal is killed, is retained by the owner. The beads, tobacco, and money are eventually divided out among members of the homestead. Those who pass by may pick up a piece of tobacco and smoke it; 'there is no harm in this, the Power laughs.'

At the cutting of the ritual cucumber at the end of the month during which the shrine is raised, grain is mixed with sesame oil and the family are marked protectively to remove potential sickness which may follow from the planting. This can come from many sources; some part of the ceremony might have been neglected or wrongly performed for instance, witches or people with the evil eye might have attended, and finally, close contact with the Power is in itself dangerous.

At this last seance Nyöki acted as a medium through possession by his Dinka spirit, Löi. Kok also used this method when working with Gurumbek, but later used the question and answer technique when he interrogated Mayom. When acting as a possessed medium, a doctor sits facing the audience and not with his back to them as in the question and answer position. 'His body and mouth are used by the spirit', he is in a convulsion, he foams at the mouth, his speech is rapid, jerky, high pitched, and interspersed with grunts and hiccups. His translator speaks descriptively, saying for instance, 'So and so spirit says a black goat must be cut'; 'The spirit says the illness is from so and so'; 'The spirit says you must return in the evening.'

The songs which are essential to the induced possession are in the Aliab Dinka language and some of the audience do not know them, although they follow the chorus and clap. Songs are part of the foreign background of the ritual and never feature in traditional rites, although intoned prayers have a place in some rain cere-monies. Mandari say that if no one present knew the songs the session could not take place, but that this never happens because the doctor has 'friends' or relatives who accompany him, or there will be people in the audience who have heard the songs on previous occasions. Chorus leaders and translators are very important: 'They are the assistants who help to summon the Power, and without the songs, *Jok* remain far away; it is only when they hear their songs they come near.' The singing, clapping, and rattling provide the stimulus for possession which explains why some sessions are more successful than others—'The Power speaks well'— while on other occasions 'The Power will not come.' Excuses are then made: 'The singing was bad so the Power did not hear', or, 'It refused.' These comments seem to indicate that the possession is genuine, though induced, for if the doctor were acting a part, he need not fail to manifest symptoms and have to seek excuses.

Chorus leaders and translators are often ex-patients, who help the doctor as they feel inclined. They receive a small fee from the doctor, described as *'taban l'yit'*, 'for his tiredness'—as we would say, 'for his trouble'.[1]

The comments of Ako and Kok on their sensations during possession may be of interest. Both claimed that during possession they were not conscious of what was taking place—'My body is taken over by the Power: it is the Power who acts and speaks.' Kok told me that after possession he felt exhausted and drained; that his body 'ached all over and was tired as if I have done hard and painful work'. Ako, on the contrary stressed a feeling of exhilaration, saying that his body 'felt strong' and that he had a sense of well-being.

In the seance and, indeed in relation to Powers in general, man takes the initiative in establishing a reputed communication with

---

[1] *Taban* is an Arabic word now in common use. The Mandari word for tired is *akanya*.

para-normal forces, reversing the order of traditional man–spirit communication. Spiritual agents make contact with man. Spontaneity is the hallmark of orthodox possession: 'Above falls upon a man arbitrarily.' To attempt to summon the spirit would be unthinkable, whereas the *Jok* doctor deliberately sets out to call his Power, to question it and to discover its needs.

Another feature of the seance which contrasts with traditional ritual, is the atmosphere of levity and entertainment. Seances lack the formal gravity of traditional rites. They also allow a much greater freedom of individual action on the part of the doctor than the conventional ritual which is not under the control of a single officiant but is open to immediate criticism by the informed audience of elders. Traditional ritual has, indeed, a background of social entertainment—the beer drinking or the ceremonial dance which may follow it—but the rite itself is formalized and never marked by the uninhibited self-expression of the seance.

A seance is not held when a patient is seriously ill, but either when recovery is well advanced or much later on as the follow-up which forges a permanent link with the Power. A seance may be exploratory, seeking to discover the future tenor of an existing relationship, or it may establish a new relationship. When a patient is seriously ill, the treatment is by medicine and sacrifice, and seriously ill patients are not the centre of long-drawn-out seances. The seance is, in a way, an appendage which serves other purposes than those strictly related to the cure of the illness itself.

It has frequently been pointed out that meeting for ritual is psychologically therapeutic, providing an element of reassurance and relief from anxiety; that during ritual a patient and his relatives can assemble and express their problems and anxieties and, together, receive reassurances and guidance. This element is particularly marked at seances, when individuals openly express worries and seek guidance; the individual in the audience puts his problem himself—the reverse of the process of traditional divination, where the doctor asks the questions and the patient only supplies the answers.

Mandari are quick to stress the undesirability of permitting sick or worried people to feel lonely or isolated. If someone is ill the family and kin gather round. In all crises people unite to solve problems. Those who isolate themselves are considered mad, those who are shunned for suspicion of witchcraft, as evil. Mandari disapproved of the way I refused to have visitors to sit at my side on the few occasions when I was sick, and they would say, 'Awuk, it is not good to lie alone and think too much.' Their advice appeared to show a perception of the psychological value of communication and perhaps also of a recognition that illness may lead to anxiety and depression, so that the patient is helped and his recovery even hastened, by the actively demonstrated support given by his kin. This aspect of the Mandari care of the sick struck me forcefully time and again. Its value in some instances should not be under-rated.

The other departure from tradition in the seance is the method of assembling persons in a hut and the exercise of audience control. The formless and to some extent random collection of people which spreads over a courtyard and its surroundings for traditional ritual is never a controlled group, although individuals who actually officiate co-operate with one another. Traditional ritual is held out of doors, but it is clear that a much greater control can be exercised *inside* a building because the audience is physically contained. The seance audience is deliberately manipulated by the doctor who encourages participation, urging the audience to sing and to give their utmost. Such group participation and control is something quite new in Mandari ritual.

Finally, a big seance with several doctors and lavish beer is expensive, but once one of the families of a lineage has a Power, others can make use of it to gain information.

The last case described provides an example of co-operation between kin and between one doctor and another. The main part of the work was done by Kok, supported by Nyöki, and so the former took the larger payment. For a number of reasons, doctors may decide to share a treatment, either to reciprocate a previous favour, or because there is a strong pointer in the case to a cause some do not wish to, or cannot, treat. They may choose to act on suggestions by the family concerned, who know about sickness and other happenings which have affected them over a period. As the doctor discusses the patient's problems a line of action may begin to present itself to him, but it must always convince his patients and be agreed to by them.

Doctors who specialize in the treatment of Powers have the reputation, whether deserved or not, of resenting poor patients likely to run up long-term debts, unless they are relatives. They certainly tend to charge more than traditional doctors, justifying the high fees by stressing that it is more tiring to use possession and to question spirits than to divine with a rattle, and one doctor told me that he himself would be harmed if payment were meagre because his Power would 'be angered and turn on him'. He also said that if payment were poor or the food and drink inappropriate, 'the *Jok* may not speak well. It likes a rich homestead where there is food and drink.'

VII

I have described two seances to illustrate varying techniques, but in neither case has the complete sequence of the sickness from its onset, through divination, preliminary questioning and shrine planting been shown. This is due both to the difficulty of finding out about the stages in a treatment, and to the fact that treatments tend to spread over a long period. Ako and Kok were most helpful in allowing me to travel with them and in warning me when rites would take place; but the cure sequence often covers several months, and I found that I came in either for the end rites of a case already begun or for the beginning of a treatment which would be completed after I had left.

Sickness treatments, particularly perhaps those for Powers, are often interrupted and protracted affairs. The necessity for haste depends on the severity of the sickness, factors of recurrence, or the presence of more than one spiritual agent. If, after a preliminary diagnosis and treatment, the patient remains reasonably trouble-free and if he is poor, a radical step like raising a shrine may be delayed for years, or a shrine may not be raised at all. But if following sickness is diagnosed, then people feel that more immediate action is necessary. A completely different reason may also be advanced by the same doctor for the illness, and then a number of agents, any of which may be turned up at any future divination, are known to be present in the family. Responsibility for delay in carrying through a treatment to its final conclusion of pole-raising may also rest with the doctor, who may be attending to his own affairs, or with the patient, who may have no animal for sacrifice or lack millet for beer.

Because of the unavoidable omissions in the sequence of the rites described, I shall summarize the procedure for an illness from the initial diagnosis to shrine planting. Much of what I describe is also standard procedure in raising a shrine to a Celestial Spirit.

When a doctor of Powers is called in, he examines the patient for external symptoms in the traditional manner, notes any information that the family can give about events leading up to the sickness and then asks for a payment (*ropet*). The payment, usually a piece of tobacco or a small coin, allows treatment to begin, showing that the doctor accepts the case. If the doctor, with some previous knowledge of the family's troubles, warns them that a seance is likely to be held, the payment is the sign for grain to be prepared for brewing.

At this first visit the doctor gives medicine for the physical symptoms; this is a very important part of the treatment, and when a doctor is called he always takes his medicine string with him.[1] After dosing the sufferer, the doctor uses rattle divination to determine agents and preliminary action. Since a Power can only be questioned in the homestead where it originates or where it is about to be planted, rattle divination is always used when the patient travels to the doctor. For other cases he may decide to divine again in the evening under possession or, if the illness is slight, he may postpone this and wait to see if the patient recovers after perhaps a beer libation. If a seance is held it takes place as described, and the doctor may give additional treatment during it. If the patient dies, the Power may be questioned after the burial.

It is believed to be essential that a Power should be properly established, particularly if it has been 'drawn out' of a sick man by the diviner's rattle, otherwise it is dispossessed and wanders about doing indiscriminate harm. If the doctor's verdict is accepted, which is not always the case, people wait to see how the patient progresses before raising the shrine. Meanwhile an interim offering is made. After a good recovery, confirming the correctness of the diagnosis, the family earmarks an animal and the prepared grain is put on to brew.

If the patient dies, no fee is charged, although the payment for the divination stands. The family may suspect a wrong diagnosis, and the doctor must excuse himself as best he can on the grounds that he was called too late, that the Power 'refused', or other agents intervened. A lot depends upon the doctor's personality and

---

[1] Medicines are small sections cut from the roots of different species of tree and plant, threaded on a narrow thong or plaited grass.

reputation. If a patient dies under treatment by a doctor thought to have the evil eye or to be a witch, the doctor may be accused of a deliberate killing. This has been the misfortune of one doctor who is regularly consulted and thought to be clever; some people also believe him to be responsible for deaths, and he faces a section of public opinion which is very hostile.

THE SHRINE PLANTING

The elders reassemble with the doctor for the raising of the shrine and beer is circulated. The earmarked sacrificial animal is meanwhile fetched from the cattle-camp and, at dusk, the doctor may be possessed again to confirm the spirit is satisfied. Other gifts may then be demanded—a chicken or further payment for the doctor.

The homestead owner addresses the Power, drawing attention to the ox:

You, so and so power. You are killing and making our people ill. Here is your ox, we are to become related. Here is your meat, and oil which will be placed in a pot for you and you will find food here. You must let us sleep in peace and not make us ill.

The ox is thrown and the throat cut. The meat is divided up and the animal's head is put aside for cooking in the early morning or the evening, depending on the time of the rite. The remaining meat and the beer for the 'planting' are placed in the hut.

The new pole shrine, roughly shaped, is lying in readiness in the nearby scrubland; it is now completed and any decorative carving added. Then it is left in the bush overnight—'It is still only wood.'

At dawn the ox head is put on to boil, while the doctor, who has usually slept in the homestead, digs the hole for the pole: a gourd of beer is put beside this, together with a ladle of sesame oil and a live chicken with the legs tied. The men of the family and lineage then carry in the pole bearing it level and handling it gently. The procession moves slowly, circling the homestead and the edge of the cultivation; the men chant songs, the women follow ululating. The songs are said to 'belong to the Power' and 'call it to its new home'. When the homestead has been circled, the pole is laid beside the hole; the bearers, still singing, stand back in a circle round it. The pole is taken twice round the hut itself and, on the third circuit, the bearer party converges on the hole again holding the pole poised above it, while the doctor grasps the end and makes a feint of dropping it into position but, at the last moment, withdraws it. He does this three times, addressing the Power, saying, 'This is your position, enter here and do not harm the people.'

While the pole is supported over the hole, beer is poured in, then oil; a halved ritual cucumber (*kol jok*) is added, 'to make the Power potent so that it can guard its new home'. The pole is lowered while the doctor steadies it by the 'horns', then the new owner gently pushes in the earth with his knuckles 'so that the Power's eyes are not scratched'. Those assisting place their hands, one on top of the other, in the centre of the pole and the doctor splashes them with sesame oil—'so that they may be cool after handling the Power and their owners may suffer no ill effects'. The bearers stand back and the owner treads the earth down firmly. Members of the homestead, including women and children, then sit in a circle round the pole, the chicken is passed round their heads and the Power is addressed: 'Here is your meat and oil and beer, and here also is your chicken.'

The doctor steps back a few paces and severs the chicken's head; its jerking body must fall on its *side* at the back of the pole. Chickens killed for Spirit-of-the-Above must die 'spread on their backs' (*bata*), facing upwards and symbolizing 'the taking of the Celestial spirit back to the sky'; those for Powers die 'on their sides (*a maratat*), taking the Power down into the ground'.

The fall of the chicken is crucial; if the body jumps *away* from the pole, there may be unpleasant repercussions for the doctor, because rejection of sacrifice and pole is signified. Accusations that the whole performance has been fraudulent may follow. Another doctor may be called, the first receiving nominal payment. When discussing this, Kok told me that fortunately it had never happened to him, but at this point, the success or failure of the doctor's performance is determined by chance.

If the chicken is accepted, the doctor again instructs the Power to protect in exchange for 'meat'. The dead chicken is laid at the shrine till evening when it is cooked, and eaten by the doctor, homestead elders, and others entitled to eat chicken.[1] People eat sitting round the pole, and afterwards, wash their hands. The doctor then splashes them with water.

[1] See pp. 272–3.

After the killing of the chicken, the ox head, which has been simmering on a specially built fire in the centre of the yard, is eaten at the pole by all members of the family including women and children. The meat of a Power is never cooked at the homestead hearth since this is reserved for cooking the meat of the dead kin. Hand washing follows and people flick drops of water from their fingertips over each other. One leg and sometimes parts of the chest meat are taken by the doctor; the cuts with ritual significance belong to the homestead and are divided between its members according to their age and sex. Non-classified cuts are given to more distant kin. The hide is divided between the doctor and the owner, each taking one side.

In killings for shrine plantings, strips of skin from the animal's penis are not put round the wrists of the family as amulets because the animal is simply a 'cow [ox] of the planting' (*teŋ na boket*)— a mechanism which establishes the shrine—and not a sacrifice, so its parts have no potency as talismans. If people wish they can make them into tobacco pouches—mere articles of dress (*jupusi*). An ox-of-the-planting belongs in a different class from the animal sacrificed for illness. By the time a pole is raised the illness is usually over, and, anyhow this animal is not to effect a cure but to establish a Power in a permanent relationship. If further illness breaks out and an ox is killed, then the parts are used as amulets.

Certain gifts, together with weapons, implements, and food are placed at new shrines. People passing by may stop and place a small gift and, in return, are splashed with water so that 'contact with the newly planted Power will not make them trip or stub their toes'.

The cost of the shrine raising, like the doctor's fee, is always adjusted to the patient's economic circumstances. One in straitened circumstances will be allowed to plant with a goat or chicken. Kok admitted to me that his own shrine was raised for him by his mother's brother with a chicken. It is then usual for the owner, should he acquire property, to kill an ox later. However, a doctor may sometimes decide to refuse a poor patient, making excuses that the Power will only accept the offering specified and that he cannot treat unless this is forthcoming.

Once established a Power begins to circulate among its owner's close relatives as sickness breaks out. The on-going element tends to be most pronounced through sons, all of whom eventually inherit the Power. Daughters do not inherit, and they marry out and go off to other villages where their illnesses tend to be attributed to different agents. Although contact with the woman's natal family continues, distance lessens its effects. As a precaution, however, a newly wed husband can provide an animal for killing at his wife's natal shrine. This separates off the Power. Needless to say, this rite is often omitted, leaving a convenient explanation of future illness. Even when it is performed, the Mandari maintain 'a Power may still follow a woman.' I give an example of this in the next case, which also provides an illustration of the use a doctor makes of a previous case history in a new diagnosis, as also shown in Chapter 2.

CASE 1. *A Rek Dinka Woman Domiciled in Atwot*

This woman was the wife of a Rek Dinka domiciled in Atwot country who accompanied her. After bearing three children, all of whom died soon after birth, she was barren. Ako had treated her and she then bore a child. The couple were visiting Ako to show him the child (then a year old) and to hand over an ox in payment. The woman had also been unwell since her confinement and was to be treated.

Ako seated the couple and worked with his divining-rattle for about half an hour, pausing at intervals to place the rattle to his nose and meditate. Then he began a systematic interrogation. Each question and answer was followed by further shaking and 'smelling-out'. Ako sometimes paused to pass the rattle round the patient's head or rub it against his chest. He told me afterwards that this was done because the payment offered was insufficient— 'a Power resents being used for a trifle.' The protective passes with the rattle ensured that the patient remained 'cool', in spite of 'the displeasure of the Power at the poor fee'.

Throughout the divination, Ako placed sticks on the ground to record relevant points. The sticks lying horizontally represented the patient and members of his family; those lying at right angles represented former diagnoses Ako had to contend with. Thus:

Across. Stick 1 was for the husband and his father (cause or agencies associated with the man's descent line).

Stick 2 was for the wife and her father (background of the woman's line).

Sticks 3, 4, and 5 were for each child.
Down. 1 and 2 referred to former diagnoses relating to the Power Mutiaŋagok (on the man's side). 3 to 5 were for attacks of Wel (on the woman's side).

Ako had learned during divination, that the man had already planted Mutiaŋagok on the advice of an Atwot doctor: this Power was also planted in his father's homestead, the patient's link with it originating there. His wife's father had the Power Wel. Two possible sources suggested themselves; either Mutiaŋagok, already planted, needed further attention, or Wel from the woman's natal homestead was seeking to pass on to her conjugal home.

Ako decided that Wel must be planted in the wife's homestead and agreed to go to Atwot during the rainy season to raise the pole. Meanwhile, as it was the dry season, a black chicken should be killed to pacify the Power. Ako explained to me that it must be black 'for the eyes of the Power—to make them dark so that they do not spoil the man'.[1] The chicken is also 'meat to tie the mouth of the Power, so that it will not want a cow'. Unable to 'see' and satiated with meat, the Power is rendered harmless, and Ako's explanation reminds us that it has 'eyes and teeth like a man'.

The chicken would be decapitated by the patient on the homestead path; the head tied to the hut, the body thrown away in the bush. If it were eaten the sickness (*Jok*) would be consumed with it. When the head is tied up, the Power is told 'Do not kill, but wait for your cow, and in the meantime be contented with your chicken.' Ako told me that the pole could not be raised in the dry season since Powers must be planted 'when the earth is cool' during the rains. Important principles are involved here, and lethal danger may be released if they are ignored. There are also practical considerations like dry season grain shortage; rites also do not take place in drought except in emergencies, because people are away on the grassland. During the rains they come back to villages, particularly at harvest, a time of plenty, when millet is available for beer.

At the divination the Rek Dinka paid 20 piastres which Ako considered insufficient, and the patient agreed to thatch the roof of Ako's new hut. Ako gave the verdict only when this was agreed. Doctors may accept labour instead of payment from poor

---

[1] Black has the qualities of masking and darkening.

patients. Ako often employed poor Dinka patients, some of whom were affines introduced through his sister's Aliab Dinka husband.

I asked Ako what questions he had put during the divination (they had spoken in Dinka). At first he was evasive and said he had not asked questions but had been told everything by his Power: 'The Power smelt-out the case.' Later he admitted that he asked about the patient's background, but emphasized that the questions and the course of action were prompted by the Power and not by him: 'All the time I work with my rattle, the answers are put in my head by the Power.'[1]

In the next case exorcism removes symptoms, and a follow-up offering is also required to return the Power to its original owner.

CASE 2. *The Exorcism of a Power: the Illness of the Son of Magok of Dakotiaŋ Lineage*

The little son of Magok of Dakotiaŋ lineage, aged about five, was vomiting and had diarrhoea. Kok diagnosed the Power Muŋork. The child also had convulsions which Kok diagnosed as the *nyök* of a dead baby sister. (For further details of this see pp. 175–6.)

Kok treated the Power by ordering the child to be taken to the scrub outside the homestead, and laid at the back of a tree which was still in leaf. A small smoky fire (not a hot cooking one) was kindled with sticks and fresh green leaves. Kok beheaded a baby chick beside the fire and commanded the Power to leave the child: 'Here is your chicken, leave the child; take the chicken and leave it in health.' The residue of brewing (*fada*) was rubbed on the child's head and chest and the remainder left with the chicken, 'for the Power'. The child was then taken home.

Kok explained that the child is held over the fire so that the smoke drives out the Power. 'It is irritated by smoke and leaves its victim, as a person moves away from a smoking fire.' The chick and the food compensate it for the disagreeable smoke and for being driven out; 'If it were not appeased, it would be angry and harm indiscriminately.'

The family were told to find a goat for the grandmother from whom the Power had originated, 'because it must be taken back to its own home; if it is not returned it lingers in the homestead'. The goat is, in fact, killed and eaten by the child's close kin. Only

---

[1] Evans-Pritchard records the same kind of statement from an Azande doctor. Cf. *Witchcraft, Oracles, and Magic*, pp. 175–6.

the head and skin are given to the grandmother, and in these 'the Power goes back.' The head and skin of any animal symbolize its totality, and these are always retained by the owner of the sacrifice— in this case the grandmother.[1] Head and skin also legally identify an animal, and must be produced if a loaned animal is killed by the person who borrows.

VIII

The Powers said to cause sickness, such as Mutiaŋagok and Mayom, invoked at the seances described above, can readily be seen to be models or stereotypes of a generalized idea of the Dinka held by the Mandari. Particular aspects of 'Dinkaness' are further represented by the particular Powers.

It is clear, I hope, from the evidence offered, that sickness is attributed to a Power where there is, or has been, a real experience of contact with Dinka or Atwot. Each new pole shrine makes a link back to such a connection, either directly or through a Mandari contact, as in the case of a Mandari–Mandari marriage, where one side already has a hereditary Power and has infected the other.

A Power is only one among a number of other models which the Mandari use to represent foreign connections of one kind or another; others are the client–witch stereotype and the man–animal metamorphosis.[2] Such models stress real or supposed adverse characteristics of the persons or group who act as the prototype of the model.

There are plenty of rational reasons why the Mandari may view the Dinka as a threat to their autonomy and separate identity and why emotive images should play an important part in their responses to Dinka. In the affinal relationship—at the very core of the problem—Dinka tend to be dominant because most mixed marriages have, in the past, represented a step down on the part of rich Dinka who have married high-status Mandari girls as second and third wives. The bride-wealth payments, which were exceptional for the Mandari, were not above the average for Dinka, with their greater wealth in cattle. The superior wealth of the Dinka has tended to make the Mandari feel that they are patronizing in their personal dealings and it does appear, perhaps as a consequence of

[1] Sometimes the doctor treating the case may take half the hide, particularly when a Power is involved.   [2] pp. 255 ff.

their numerical and territorial superiority, that Dinka display a more arrogant and aggressive character than Mandari. In addition to these irritants, Mandari suspect the Dinka of coveting their northern territory. There have, indeed, been unsuccessful attempts in the past to penetrate this area.

The way in which the Mandari react towards Powers, and the way in which they describe them, suggest that they represent selected characteristics which Mandari not only assume to be typical of Dinka, but which they most dislike. Powers are described as 'greedy', 'capricious', and 'tenacious'—'hard masters having their price'. They have 'eyes' and 'teeth'—the ability to see where the good thing is and devour it. The Mandari already have a conventional image of the Dinka themselves as greedy, pushing, arrogant, tricky, and demanding; now more than ever they see them as bent on swallowing up their best women and material resources, as swarming in great numbers and spreading arrogantly over their country. Although Mandari say that they like and respect individual Dinka, and may get on well with their own Dinka in-laws, the idea of the 'foreigner' who arouses apprehension and perhaps jealousy is always present.

The Mandari cannot help but be aware, as they look around them, that the Dinka have now penetrated their country as they never had formerly and that they only have themselves to blame. They have been trapped by their readiness to absorb foreigners and foreign contacts, because their society is based on principles of openness. As I have shown elsewhere, Mandari clients can also present a threat to their patrons, but control can more easily be exercised over a client than over the Dinka. The example of what has happened in Mandari may partly account for the total rejection of all Dinka contacts by the neighbouring Köbora and Tsera.

The Mandari are facing the problem of how to contain the disruptive Dinka presence while deriving benefits from it. They know that it cannot be repudiated without destroying valuable economic contracts and from this dilemma springs their ambivalent attitude, and their anxiety and bitterness. Ambivalence is also manifested towards Dinka Powers, which Mandari would like to repudiate but cannot, because they cannot bring themselves to repudiate the prototype—the living Dinka contact. The sickness diagnoses given by doctors, many with vested interests, limit their chance of disengagement still further.

An observer cannot help feeling that, in spite of their complaints, in the final analysis the Mandari have gained more than they have lost by their new relationships, certainly in the vital field of cattle husbandry. But it is true that in the day-to-day situation, new conflicts and irritants have been introduced. These include an influx of Dinka in-laws demanding hospitality when there is a food-shortage in the Aliab (usually coinciding with a shortage in Mandari), and incessant demands for gifts of one kind or another. Mandari youths with few cattle but living in areas infiltrated by Dinka complain with some reason that fathers prefer Dinka suitors for their most attractive daughters. Problems have also arisen for the few Mandari men who have married Dinka wives; they complain that their wives are sometimes abruptly taken back by their Dinka kin on what seem to the Mandari to be bogus pretexts and often without the return of the bride-wealth. This still happens in spite of the newly convened Dinka–Mandari courts which meet periodically to deal with such cases.

Mandari are gradually adjusting to these inevitable tribulations, as they are also coming to accept diagnosis in terms of Dinka Powers. The rituals are even perhaps useful in providing emotional rallying points for the expression of feelings about the new relationships in general, and for explaining special features of actual contacts. Shrines to Powers are always more numerous where Dinka–Mandari contact is highest—in those areas, that is to say, where stress arising from the foreign connection is greatest. Diagnosis in these terms is acceptable because it develops automatically out of the situation of involvement and because the agents of sickness are seen to embody characteristics belonging to those who initiate the stress. The spread is most rapid across areas where the stressful contact is most keenly felt.[1]

The fact that highly mobile aggressive and free-moving forms of 'spirit' or para-normal agent are also reported from other Nilotic areas does not, I think, detract from this hypothesis. On the contrary, I believe that the evidence of foreign ideas and influences available on such free-circulating models is sufficient to confirm my argument, in that while the source idea has much in common in all areas it has been differently applied. The differences

---

[1] On this subject, J. Beattie's material on the Nyoro provides a similar example from East Africa. See his *Bunyoro: an African Kingdom* (New York, 1960), p. 78.

appear to be directly related to the different situations of the peoples who have been affected by the foreign contacts.

A glance at the comparative evidence will make this clear. In a number of Nilotic areas phenomena are found, sometimes called '*Jok*' and sometimes known by other names, which are claimed to be of foreign origin. In the Mandari case the claim is, categorically, that *Jok* 'come from Dinka' which includes the Atwot (for general purposes described as 'Juŋo'—'Dinka'). The seance as I describe it for Mandari appears, however, to resemble more closely a Nuer phenomenon (see below) and this would suggest perhaps a stronger Atwot influence since the Atwot are of Nuer extraction.

The fact that the Mandari themselves are unsure of the origin of the specific Powers adds to the confusion. One doctor, however, told me that all the main Powers—Mutiaŋagok, Agok, Wel, Ukor, Malual, Adwegdwor, Teŋberiok, and Jombai—were from the Atwot, and that only Löi and Möjut (two forms of 'Dinka Spirit-of-the-Above') were from the Aliab Dinka.

Borrowed words or names used to distinguish a particular cult-fragment clearly reflect a particular contact. The specific name becomes a sub-stereotype of the more general one of free-ranging 'foreignness'. Certain evidence exists for the provenance of the words used as names for Powers. Thus the Mandari word '*Jok*' is the generic word for 'spirit' in Dinka—the category referred to by Lienhardt as 'Powers'.[1] Lienhardt also describes a fetish bundle called 'Mathiang gok' which may be owned by one of a class of magical practitioners and which has attributes which bring it within the class of Powers (*Jok*) but as a Power of a low order.[2] He confirmed that Malual and Muŋork are Dinka names.

From the Nuer, Evans-Pritchard reports a fetish called 'Ku-langni' embodied in a root medicine with a special dynamic. Fetishes are unanimously agreed to be foreign.[3] He comments that the Nuer have tried, not entirely successfully, to assimilate these Sudanic 'medicines' to their refracted religious model of spirit, by referring to them as '*gaatnyadeang*', 'children or daughters of Deŋ'—Deŋ being an assimilated Dinka spirit. Among the names of fetishes given by Evans-Pritchard are 'Mathiang' and 'Malual'.[4]

---

[1] *Divinity and Experience*, p. 29.   [2] Ibid., pp. 64–5.
[3] *Nuer Religion*, pp. 100–3.
[4] See also *Divinity and Experience*, p. 65 n. 2, for another account of this fetish.

Millais, who visited the Southern Sudan in 1923, commenting on what he

Nuer fetishes have a superficial similarity to Mandari Powers in that they are 'owned' and cause sickness; but the Nuer, like the Dinka, seem to use them chiefly as a means of injuring enemies. Fetishes belong to the sphere of individual control over occult powers and there is no elaborate cult. The Nuer show some of the dislike and rejection that I found in the Mandari in relation to Powers, and Evans-Pritchard suggests that the fetishes have only been placed in the category of spirit, 'by the logical necessity of assimilating the powers attributed to them to some model Nuer already possessed'.[1] Fetishes have, however, been appended at a very low conceptual level.

Howell gives a more detailed description of the Nuer phenomena which he prefers to describe as 'spirits'; he includes a brief summary of something very like a Mandari seance, with details of a song.[2] The reports of Howell and Evans-Pritchard come from different parts of Nuer-land and Howell's visit was made a decade later, which may account for the difference in emphasis. The influence of their 'Spirits' may be stronger in certain parts of Nuer-land, just as the influence of Powers is greater in some areas of Mandari than in others. Local circumstances in different regions may control the spread of the cults. Howell and Evans-Pritchard both encountered the problem of classifying these phenomena which are seen to operate at a non-material level but are not a part of the accepted religious categories. To overcome this problem I have used the designation 'para-normal' since in the Mandari case there is a stated rejection of them as 'religious'. 'Theological'

calls the 'purging of witchcraft', gives the following account of a form of witch-craft called 'Mattiang Goh', which confirms Evans-Pritchard's view that Nuer fetishes originate among the Sudanic peoples known as Jur, who live south of Rumbek: 'Major Kidd commenced operations in Rembeck district by catching a witch doctor named Amai who practised two forms of witchcraft, known through Dinkaland as Mattiang Goh and Toot Bwong. . . . Mattiah Goh has been known in Bahr-el-Ghazal . . . for some 40 years, since a certain Juer named Gash warned people that he was master of a spirit which entered the bodies of his enemies through a certain root of which he alone knew the secret. This man made his secret known to the Agar Dinkas of Rumbek, and afterwards to the Atuot and Cheesch Dinkas of the Lao region.' J. G. Millais, *Far Away up the Nile* (London, 1924), p. 167.

[1] *Nuer Religion*, p. 104.
[2] P. P. Howell, 'Some Observations on "Earthly Spirits" among the Nuer', *Man*, vol. liii (1953), pp. 85–8. For a wider comparison see also Beattie's description of spirit possession among the Bunyoro, 'Group Aspects of the Nyoro Spirit Mediumship Cult', *Rhodes–Livingstone Journal*, vol. xxx (1963), and 'The Ghost Cult in Bunyoro', *Ethnology*, vol. iii (1964).

rejection does not, in the Nuer case at least, appear to be so overtly stressed.

From the evidence available it seems that a common stereotype may indeed be involved, which has as its two basic ingredients 'foreignness' and an aggressive quality which mirrors the clash of interests inherent in a widening of communication at all levels. Given this basic model, each culture has developed it in the light of its own situation.

The Mandari seem to have made much more of it than either the Nuer or the Dinka, as one would expect in view of their particular vulnerability. The huge Dinka populations have assimilated foreign ideas and foreign groups, which offer little challenge, relatively easily—although any new impression which requires explanation and some re-thinking will require a new, if minor, category for expression. For the Nuer, foreign contacts present even less of a threat; the Nuer are the most powerful of the Southern Sudan Nilotics and have already absorbed large numbers of Dinka. Indigenous foreign contacts are quite unimportant for the Nuer. It is of interest that the European Administration has been the only external influence that has had any real effect on them. In his description of the rise of the Nuer prophets Evans-Pritchard has made it clear that the Administration was a sufficiently organized and powerful force to be a threat that could not be contained.[1]

The problem is a very different one for the Mandari who are vulnerably placed on the periphery of large blocks of Nilotics. Their small country can easily be overrun both in the physical sense and by ideas and influences. They are already mixed, having absorbed numbers of non-Mandari, over a period and granted to them special status. A new confrontation of the magnitude of the Dinka presence represents a serious problem since it is both socially disruptive and emotionally traumatic. The Mandari have been required to make a much greater adjustment than either of the other two Nilotic peoples.

The influence of Mandari doctors with foreign contacts in the spread of the new rituals must not be underestimated. While the older-established population tends to resist new ideas, vested interests promulgate them. Ordinary people, by apathy and passive acceptance, inadvertently help to circulate them. The

---

[1] Evans-Pritchard, *The Nuer*, pp. 188–9.

potential exists in the new social forces at work, ready to be exploited by the doctors, for it seems that the human psyche needs to create stereotypes to explain and reflect events that are fundamentally disturbing. Doctors have acted as channels for focusing diffused anxieties and giving them outlet, but they have also tended to promote and spread these anxieties by drawing attention to past links and contacts which might otherwise have lain forgotten. The cult has gathered momentum through their spectacular cures; they have embellished and developed, adding arbitrary borrowings made from traditional rituals. Nevertheless, Mandari have been unable to accept Powers into their religious order in spite of the acceptance at the pragmatic level of disease and cure, because this would be tantamount to embracing the notion of 'Dinkaness', of 'foreignness', into the very core of their ideological system; something which at the present time, at any rate, is unthinkable.

Inasmuch as the stereotypes in which Powers are presented and the rejection and ambivalence they provoke, reflect the threat—real or imaginary—to exclusive identity which arises in a changing social situation, the Mandari cult invites comparison with a phenomenon reported from other parts of the world, most notably from Oceania. In those other areas, cults have arisen where there has been a radical breakdown in the traditional culture typically precipitated by the impact of a Western-type open society upon a relatively closed, indigenous one.[1] The situation in Mandari is, however, somewhat different in fact, and apparent similarities should be interpreted with caution.

In the first place, no real deprivation of a material or spiritual kind is involved for the Mandari. There is little evidence to suggest that the Mandari have suffered much because of their new Dinka contacts; in fact, at the material level, the reverse may be true. Secondly, the Dinka are not, in the full sense, a foreign power but rather traditional neighbours with a similar culture and many identical interests. Moreover they do not settle and take over. Thirdly, Mandari has never been a closed society, quite the reverse. None the less, Dinka-ization differs from the traditional idiom of absorbing foreigners (clients and settlers) in that the

---

[1] I refer to those movements which have been described as millenarian, syncretistic, and cargo cults. From a large body of literature the reader may refer to *New Heaven New Earth* by Kenelm Burridge (Oxford, 1969).

Dinka are not assimilated. They are so numerous that, on the contrary, the Mandari fear that they themselves may be assimilated.

While the new Dinka–Mandari involvement cannot be isolated from the involvement of the whole of the Southern Sudan with the Anglo-Egyptian Administration which has gradually been extending its role since around the 1920s, it would be wrong to suggest that the new cult is, in any way, simply a response to Administrative pressures. The Administration has only indirectly been responsible for its rise in that it provided the background of social security against which new indigenous contacts could develop; mutual cattle interests then made it meaningful for the two peoples to have such contacts. The Mandari have established no comparable relations with their cattleless Moru neighbours.

The Administration has indeed been another source of apprehension and of challenge and has had to be reckoned with simultaneously. But the Administration is accepted with resignation as unalterable and uncontrollable, as something altogether remote in a way that the Dinka can never be. At the present time, Dinka are more directly a part of the problems of daily life for many people than is the Administration. Mandari have not been subjected to anything approaching the persistent European or Arab influence that has affected peoples living in more accessible areas or around towns, and the proliferation of Powers does not appear to reflect in any direct way a breakdown in the social order due to such influences.

It is significant that the powerful Köbora living on the river Nile and much more open to external influences through the staging-post of Terekeka, have consistently refused to accept Powers and have also rejected Dinka advances for the simple reason that they have ample dry-season grazing and large herds. The Dinka have nothing to offer them; these peoples have also rejected Mandari cults.

A widening of communication, deliberately sought, with its accompanying stresses, rather than internal breakdown or disintegration is involved. This is not to deny that breakdown of cultural self-consciousness may well occur in the future, but this will be of a different order and in response to different influences.

A further feature which may seem to indicate a basis for comparison with millenarian movements is the fact that such movements have been marked by an increase in, or the appearance of, varying forms of spirit possession. Possession of a special kind is also central to the cult of Powers. However, in those other areas possession has tended to be random and uncontrolled, widespread among cult adherents who represent the more deprived element of the society. It has often been just those very categories least able to benefit from the changes which have expressed their frustrations in the compensation of possession.

The Mandari phenomenon represents, on the contrary, control, discipline, and selectivity. It is only used by the few, and then to their considerable advantage. Mandari society lacks favoured classes to take advantage of new material benefits and such benefits are as yet hardly available. Possession is not the hallmark of the deprived, but of the carefully trained. It is true that many doctors who use the induced form are persons of non-Mandari origin or their descendants, none the less, it would be inaccurate to regard the new class of doctor as being a deprived category.

It seems clear that while the Mandari accept with some tolerance the presence of outsiders in small numbers, they do not so easily accept them when their numbers and the mode of their entry precludes the exercise of control over them. They also appear to react strongly to new ideas. Foreign ideologies are not acquired and accepted passively; their nature is scrutinized, discussed, weighed against traditional beliefs, and, on balance, rejected. A time factor may operate here; perhaps I worked in Mandari during an era of heightened controversy—during the period when the mature generation who were involved in the forging of the new associations and were most directly affected by them, remained a force. There is some evidence, I think, that younger people are less concerned and it may well be that in the future, provided the material benefits from the Dinka connection are maintained, foreign agents of all kinds will meet with less resistance and that in time the foreign origin of Powers becoming remote, it will cease to be of consequence.

4

DEATH AND BURIAL RITES

As Professor Evans-Pritchard has pointed out, burial and mortuary rites are part of a continuum which begins at the moment of death and culminates in the rites for the dead as ancestor, and no part of this sequence can meaningfully be considered in isolation.[1] It will become clear as the ritual states are described that significant time periods are used by the Mandari to help to channel and resolve the emotions which are engendered by death, and to bring about the harmonious re-allocation of roles. These ritual time periods are also an expression of Mandari ideas about time as a factor in human experience.

I

A death is announced by the wailing of the bereaved women, who lament again at each sundown and dawn until after the burial. Interment takes place as soon as possible, but conforms to the rule that it must take place at one of the physically and conceptually cool times of day, the early morning or late afternoon, and also allow for important kin to be assembled. Burial concerns the immediate family which includes the grandparents, the parents' siblings, and the brothers and sisters of the deceased; it is not the affair of remoter lineage kin, maternal relatives, or affines, who come later. The parents and siblings of a dead married woman go to mourn at her grave immediately after burial if they live at a distance, and her husband and his kin are responsible for the burial itself.

The grave is sited in the homestead yard, opposite the doorway of the dwelling hut. Young unmarried persons are sometimes buried in the family's domestic goat-kraal which is then abandoned.[2] People are never buried in cattle-camps unless it is

[1] R. Hertz, *Death and the Right Hand* (London, 1960), Introduction by E. E. Evans-Pritchard.
[2] Several members of the Dari chiefly family who died in rapid succession have been buried in the chief's domestic goat-kraal, including married persons.

impossible for the body to be transported home. The correct procedure, important for the repose of the dead and the health of
the living, is burial in the homestead, and there is concern when
burial is elsewhere because the correct rites may not be carried
out and the grave cannot be tended.

Senior married women of the extended family wash the corpse
and anoint it with shea-butter oil, a 'black' oil described as ritually
'hot', which must therefore not be used for the ritual cleansing of the
living. The blackness of the oil makes it correct for use on the
dead by colour analogy. A new-born baby may also be oiled with
shea oil, which here is simply said to be beneficial for its skin;
it may also be that the obscuring qualities of the 'blackness' (which
can have protective significance) make it positively beneficial.

The head of a corpse is shaved and beads and ornaments are
removed, 'so that the dead may enter the grave black and nude
as they came into life'. A married woman must be buried in her
goat-skin loin covering—the symbol of her full maturity—but,
like a man, she is stripped of decorations and shaved. Before it is
placed in the grave a corpse is wrapped in a mat, or if the deceased
is a chief, sewn up in the hide of an ox killed for this purpose.
Washed and anointed, the body is laid out under the raised
veranda. The family sit round it taking care to leave a space, since
to press close is disrespectful. Grave-diggers work quietly and older
people are restrained, only children giving vent to their sorrow.

Closely related males dig the grave, but a father's sister who
is over the menopause may help if necessary. Unmarried girls or
young married women must never dig graves or they may damage
their fertility, and the widow herself is also forbidden to do so.
The square grave-hole, about the length of the corpse and in
depth reaching to the chest of a standing adult, is lined with wood
slats similar to those used in hut-flooring and the body, rolled in
the mat, rests on these. Another mat covers it, then more wooden
slats, sloped to form a roof and prevent the earth touching it.

The body is laid on its right side (a woman is laid on her left
side) with the head pointing towards the east—'the place from
which Logobong came'—and the feet pointing to the west—'the
direction to which Logobong travelled'. If the corpse is wrongly
placed illness may follow. The east–west orientation symbolizes
the passage of human life, from youth, through maturity to age
and death, 'as the sun rises in the east, crosses the sky, and sets

in the west'; it also calls to mind the journey of Logobong as the dead faces the good, his feet pointing towards evil and sin which are behind him.

Last addresses are now made. At the burial of Awor, a friend and neighbour, at which I was present, each grave-digger picked up a little earth or a small stone, spat on it, passed it round his head and dropped it into the grave, at the same time making a short address. Awor's daughters followed in turn and then his widow. After her address the widow stretched out her arms with a cry and sank to the ground. The women carried her from the grave and seated her. She is now free to express her sorrow and indeed is expected to do so. A deeply distressed widow may have to be prevented from injuring herself or throwing herself into the grave.

The senior elder then made the formal dedication throwing a handful of dust into the grave as he spoke:

You death (*do twan*), you have finally killed. Now leave us alone: you also have come to an end in the grave with your dead.

Now my son [addressing the dead man], Creator has come and taken you from among us. This is Creator's affair who made men. You must let us remain without sickness and free from trouble.

In the first prayer the assertion that death has 'come to an end in the grave' proclaims that death will not strike again; it also states the elimination of death as an abstract idea, a recurrent theme throughout death rites. The implication of the second prayer is that the man is ultimately taken by Creator, notwithstanding that the death will later be attributed to a specific cause which may demand action by the kin.

At Awor's burial a frond of the rain creeper called *dölöŋi* was tied to his left hand little finger and brought up through the mounded earth and left to trail over the outside. The creeper was essential because death occurred in the early rainy season (*ja'be*); if it is omitted Mandari say the new rain is taken into the ground and a drought follows. It is not used in the dry season.

The symbolism of the creeper relates to the duality in the universe and its counterpart in man who belongs to both the celestial and the terrestrial and whose body consists of both matter and moisture. The moist part, which is 'of the celestial' and rain-associated, buried in the earth—the terrestrial—is symbolically raised up into the open again by the sappy creeper. After the mound has been smoothed over leaving the creeper trailing outside, a miniature hut of grain stalks or a simple grass roof a few feet high, is built over it as protection against the weather and wild animals.

Close neighbours and kin living nearby now begin to arrive to express formal sympathy. Women approach wailing, throwing themselves in the dust and beating their heads on the ground. The grave-diggers dash out to prevent serious injuries. The violence with which some old women throw themselves full length makes one wonder how they avoid breaking bones. After this demonstration of grief they are led into the homestead. Men, who always mourn with restraint, approach quietly with bowed heads. All are then seated in orderly fashion. Gourds of water are carried to the grave by an old female relative (never the widow), so that the grave-diggers can wash away the earth and clay from their limbs, a washing which also removes the pollution of grave-digging, said to cause guinea-worm sores. The vigil begins. Close relatives sit with the widow until after the killing of the burial ox.

At Awor's burial, his father's brother's son arrived from the cattle-camp at this point. This man had raised a shrine to a Power and it was felt by Awor's family that this Power might have caused his death. Bitter recriminations began; it seemed to be implied that if the man had come sooner and brought certain medicines he had been given for the treatment of the Power, Awor might not have died. The unfortunate man protested that he had come immediately he received news of the illness. As a family quarrel was evidently breaking out, I left.

Purifications, which it would not be appropriate for a stranger to watch, must now be carried out to allow the bereaved family to eat and drink and use essential possessions; neglect of purifications is a cause of illness and death. There are two elements in the cleansings; first, the pollution of death must be removed from the family and their possessions, and secondly, death places the family in a liminal state, and in order to allow them to take up the thread of living again they must be gradually re-introduced to fundamentals like eating and drinking.

To 'make drinking safe for them', a family elder dips a blade of grass three times into a gourd of water and places it each time in the mouths of the members of the family, in turn; each time the recipient spits out grass and water. The giving of the grass is accompanied by such words as 'Your father has completed his life and is dead, drink and forget him.' To make the food safe for the family the remains of durrah porridge, sauce, oil, or vegetables which were prepared for the dead, are collected in pots and given to old women neighbours to eat outside in the bush. These are polluted and dangerous to the kin and must be consumed by outsiders away from the homestead, or a condition known as *bur* (swelling of the belly as in ruptured hernia) results.[1] Tobacco is also given to visitors, after which the family may smoke.

The disposal of food remains and tobacco by giving them to neighbours, emphasizes that death pollutes the food for the family of the dead only, but does not affect it for non-related persons. The food was prepared for the dead who can no longer eat it and, through identification, his close kin do not eat it either. Only the small quantity of food already prepared is involved, and not the whole contents of storage utensils or grain-stores; these are not disposed of, although they must be cleansed together with hut utensils, at the more general cleansing carried out either by an elder or by the doctor who treated the dead. For this cleansing of the homestead a medicine-root named *chuluk* is crushed in water and the cooking and household utensils washed in it. To purify the grain-store a small quantity of grain representative of each plant—millets, maize, sesame, groundnuts, and pulses—is placed in a pot and given to old female neighbours who cook and eat it in the bush. Other food remains are simply thrown away, together with the ashes of the fires by which the mourners have sat. The family can eat them and drink freely and, with the exception of the widow, can carry out essential household tasks.

II

An ox is speared in the evening following burial. (Because of poverty a goat was killed by clubbing at Awor's burial.) The animal killed at this point is not a sacrificial offering but 'the thing by which a person is buried (*nokösi*)'. First, it is part of

---

[1] If persons unwittingly break the prohibition they are taken to an ant-hill of a small biting red ant, where ants are placed on their bodies to suck out the contaminated blood and with it the danger of sickness. This is described as 'destroying the prohibition' (*bönöju na dunye*). Hernia, *buru na ɲuta tulu*, is also recognized to be caused by strain.

the equipment necessary for burial. Secondly, it has a protective element for everyone taking part, and to fail to kill an animal would be to take a risk even the poorest would avoid. Thirdly, the ox is killed in vengeance; this killing also represents at a deeper level an attack on death itself. It is the first of a series of such attacks, which are a recurring feature of the death-rites sequence. Apart from its symbolic significance the animal also provides meat for the visiting mourners. At Awor's burial his cousin Nyöki who provided the goat, struck it first, followed by Ako Akurukway; other relatives then strike it to associate themselves with its killing; similarly when an ox is speared people come and press on the spear in turn.

The meat of the burial ox is divided between the lineage elders and neighbours who come to mourn, but it is forbidden to the bereaved family. The Mandari explain this saying, 'It is not eaten by the family because it is the ox-of-the-burial and is not an ox for the dead man himself or for his ghost.' They are stressing that at this point the deceased is in a liminal position; and not as yet wholly separated from the living. Both his and their positions will change with time and later killings offered to him as a ghost will be eaten by all. The object will then be to bridge another kind of separation by eating together, rather than to show solidarity in separation by abstaining. Burial killings are primarily rites of separation and in any rite of this kind, for example to cleanse homicides or other sinners, the central party cannot eat. It is consistent therefore that the ox killed to provide the skin shroud for a dead chief is also not eaten by his family, but only by members of his lineage. The horns of burial animals, together with those of any animals killed earlier to treat the illness, are placed on the roof of the grave shelter as markers.

The age-mates of a deceased are subject to the same food prohibitions as members of the family and must not eat the meat of the mortuary killings or drink beer at any age-mate's death ceremonies. A degree of identification similar to that of blood relationship is assumed to link those born during the same year (one wet and one dry season), and this link, like that of kinship, is not automatically broken by death. The age-mate, like the kinsmen, must gradually be adjusted to his severed relationship. Final separation between living and dead is not completed for at least a year after death, and soon after death, particularly, both age-mates and kin are still intimately linked with the dead. The burial ox stands for all those who are identified with the dead and Mandari say that to eat its meat would be like eating the meat of one's own burial. Solidarity between age-mates is more permanent for men than women, but even women, who separate at marriage, retain the knowledge of being age-mates and attend each other's burials if they married within the same village; they are unlikely to make the journey if living elsewhere.

Death breaks the link between age-mates, forged by a life of common experience and, when they attend each other's death rites, their behaviour defines and emphasizes the link and its breaking. Solidarity is shown and identification marked in two opposite ways, either by abstaining from something or by deliberately indulging in it. Since eating together is the clearest way of stressing identification and particularly is a mark of the bond between age-mates, when these deliberately abstain from eating at burial, grave-sweeping, and mortuary rites, they are sharply differentiating themselves from other less closely linked mourners, who are eating.[1]

III

Strict vigil now begins for the close kin of a dead adult—the spouses, parents, or siblings—all of whom mourn in the homestead for four days. The wife if the husband has died, the mother in the case of an offspring, or the daughters on the death of a parent, must not engage in any domestic tasks. Women from nearby homesteads who spend the day with the widow bring food. Lacking women kin or neighbours a daughter may cook, but never the widow, who must sit in silence under the hut, only accepting food and drink after persuasion. Men, who never perform household tasks, are not affected by these prohibitions. After four days, marked by the cessation of all homestead activities, the general cleansing of the family and homestead known as 'the taking of the ashes to the waste-land' (phulö joŋa mudiŋ) takes place .

The homestead and yard are now thoroughly swept by an old woman. The hearth ashes and the ash heaps, by which visiting mourners have slept, are put in baskets together with the hair

---

[1] Others may be abstaining because unmarried courtable girls are present, or affines who must be 'respected'.

shaved from the head of the dead and the shaft of the hoe with which the grave was dug, and are thrown away in an isolated place in the scrubland. The widow or widower, who accompanies this disposal, addresses the hoe and ashes, placing the following curse:

You hoe (*do dogule*), and you ashes (*do phulö*), you listen now. If my husband has died and the death is sent by Creator only, well and good; but if it is through witches, or evil people, may they be buried too. If those who hated my man 'trip over this place' (*ryok pit ana*) let them die.

Members of the family then shave their heads and remove beads and ornaments which are placed in a pot under the grave shelter. Bands of hide cut from the skin of the burial ox are placed round the wrists, foreheads, and waists of widows and mother and ashes are smeared on their faces and bodies. A husband or father places a hide band on his forehead and a fibre round his waist; siblings only wear hide neck bands. Lineage relatives shave their heads in their own homes, take off their beads and place these in a container in the roof thatch.

Certain possessions which represent the social personality of the dead are now destroyed; a dead woman's cooking pot, her food gourd, spoon, and head-rest. A husband's 'pot-of-the-back-of-the-hut' (*ise na kadi bot*), a ritual pot which is always kept filled by the wife with delicacies such as dried meat, groundnut paste, or relish, and is for the husband's exclusive use. All these are smashed in the path where the ashes are placed and are all personal possessions used exclusively by the dead, none of them is a general household possessions which can continue to be used by members of the homestead. A wife's special cooking pot represents her position as a wife and mother and she brings it with her when she marries. A girl will seek to acquire a good pot and put it aside against her future marriage. The husband's pot-of-the-back-of-the-hut represents his personal marital relationship with his wife.

Other equipment belonging to a dead woman, or a man's weapons, is divided up in customary manner, and so also, after the required period, are ornaments or garments.

After the ashes have been disposed of a chicken is killed for the dead man himself, for 'his life' (*ködörö ny'it*). An elder (or the doctor who attended the dead during his sickness) passes the chicken round the heads of all members of the family and tells the dead not to do harm but to rest quietly. This killing relates to the potentiality of becoming *nyök*.[1]

The dead chicken is held over the fire and the singed feathers are rubbed on the noses and faces of members of the family to prevent the sickness returning to them or their being troubled by bad dreams. If the dead man was rich a goat is killed, the head cut off, and the hair singed and used in the same way. The flesh of these killings is eaten by lineage elders and neighbours; again the family abstain. The Mandari describe this killing as the act 'whereby the living and the dead take final farewell of each other' (*yutu seser bok a diton*). It is also known as 'the washing of the face' (*puriel*).

On the fifth day the ox for the ritual vengeance is led round the grave, addressed by an elder who charges it to 'follow the death and seek out the killer', and then speared in order to make the blood 'hot'. Its meat is eaten by everyone, including members of the dead man's family and his widow because, by eating it, they participate in the act of vengeance. Strips of the hide are hung round the necks of members of the family and round the waists of the widow or mother, the horns are placed on the top of the grave-hut. At the same time certain possessions of the dead are hung up inside the grave-hut, including, for a man, his bow, quiver and arrows, spears, dance-tails, and beads, and for a woman, her beads and other ornaments (Fig. 3). The pith-helmet of an administrative chief is sometimes hung up with his weapons. These helmets, similar to those worn by District Commissioners, have become symbols of administrative chieftainship. The drum of the chiefdom, where such exists, may also be placed on a chief's grave. Clothing and utensils are never placed in grave-huts, but certain identifying possessions are placed there for a time, particularly those which stand for masculinity (weapons), for femininity (decorations), and for office. These are later removed at the grave-sweeping ceremony, when the grave-hut is dismantled.

The close relatives stay the four days and nights before the slaughter of the ox, to watch 'in the place of death'. They carry out their vigil in silence, avoiding unnecessary movement and, above all, angry words or quarrelling. Ill-mannered behaviour in the place of death insults the dead and his relatives and may cause sickness. When the ashes have been disposed of on the fourth

[1] *nyök*: see pp. 226 ff.

day, people go home, perhaps one or two old women staying to cook and care for young children. But even when close relatives no longer spend the daytime in the homestead, they may return there to sleep to prevent the family from trying to harm themselves

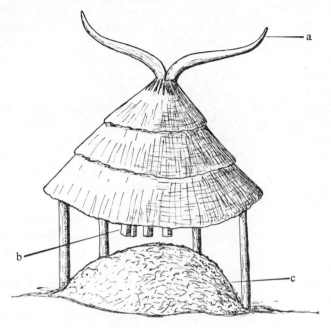

a = horns of ox slaughtered at burial
b = possessions hanging under roof
c = grave mound

FIG. 3. *Grave-hut*

during the night; they also watch the grave to drive off scavenging animals.

Close kin may sleep at a grave for up to three months, and the immediate family until the grave-sweeping. They stay not only to comfort the bereaved, but because it is considered wrong for the recently dead to be left alone. When the grave-sweeping is completed they are free to follow the cattle to the grasslands. Before this time, a widow or widower tries to walk back to sleep at the grave while spending the day in the camp. If the cattle are away on distant grasslands mourners put their animals in charge of relatives and stay behind.

IV

When news reaches a mother's brother that his sister's son is dead he comes to his nephew's homestead and makes a formal display of grief. He may rush into the homestead shouting, leaping about, and making aggressive passes with his spear. He runs round the huts and grain-stores and attacks buildings with spear or stick, breaking any pots which have been left outside and throwing cooking utensils into the scrub. The Mandari say this is like 'war' (*gor*). Men of the homestead withdraw when they see him coming and women stay in the hut.

This display of hostility dramatizes the conflict of interests between blood-relationship and affinity. The initial basis for it is the fact that, on marriage, a woman is taken away from her kin. The dead man's father is the mother's brother's affine, and the nephew belongs to a different descent line from his maternal uncle but, in blood-relationship, he is a member of his line. Hostility is directed against the father-in-law and his lineage, not against the sister and her children. In the reverse situation—the death of a mother's brother—there are no conventional patterns of hostility to play out. The nephew comes respectfully to mourn and, later, takes an ox to the mortuary ceremony.

Because of the bond between a man and his sister's son, the mother's brother is entitled to compensation for the death.[1] Payment 'for the blood of the dead' is demanded when the mother's brother has finished his demonstration. Everyone reassembles and he threatens his affines saying that unless he receives his entitlement of a cow and calf he will prevent the burial—a formal threat, as this may already be completed. He is promised a goat, or if his affines are rich, a cow and calf, to be handed over at the mortuary rite. At this ceremony the maternal uncle demands 'the bow of my nephew' (a circumlocution for these animals) and he himself hands over an ox or goat. (The handing over takes the form of an exchange.) When the compensation has been agreed he splashes water on the homestead to signify that his anger is not directed towards the family itself and to ensure that they do not suffer indispositions because of his sorrow.

[1] This is not the only situation in which a mother's brother receives compensation. In the case of a wife's adultery with a member of her husband's lineage—a form of incest—the husband cannot receive compensation, but it may be felt that compensation is due and the mother's brother receives an animal.

The mother's brother never attends the burial or the grave-sweeping, and if he should arrive while burial is taking place he walks round in the bush outside: 'He stays outside and makes a demonstration because he is grief-stricken. He waits to come and pay his respects later at the raising of the grave poles when he will bring an ox or goat to mourn and in return receive his dues.' On no account can the mother's brother dig the nephew's grave. The Mandari say, 'He is very important (*a duŋ*), and if he buries the "bowels" (*moynettes*) of his sister's son her descendants will die out.' If, however, the nephew is the last of his line the mother's brother can bury him. A sister's son, on the other hand, can bury the mother's brother or the mother's brother's wife, without ill effects; a sister's son can also inherit the mother's brother's widow, but the mother's brother cannot take the widow of the dead sister's son.

There are also restrictions on a man burying certain affines. Under no circumstances can he bury his mother-in-law, or his wife and children may sicken or die. The prohibition applies also to his father-in-law, although the latter is less powerful and dangerous than the mother-in-law. Burial prohibitions are part of the avoidance rules which regulate the behaviour of a man to his affines, especially to his mother-in-law, who is very 'potent' (*pötö*), and must not be touched.[1] A man can bury a brother-in-law or other in-law relative in the category of *lutu* or *detayit*.[2]

While homestead burial is the ideal there are unavoidable exceptions. A person may die in a distant dry season camp, say among the Aliab; then burial is carried out in the camp. An ox is killed over the grave, but no grave-shelter or pole is raised; the grave-mound is simply smoothed over and a stone or piece of laterite, if available, is set up to mark the spot. The camp is then abandoned. Burial in the bush on a journey or in a camp is simply a means of disposing of the physical remains, and rites for the dead cannot be carried out at the spot. Grave poles are, however, raised in the dead person's homestead, accompanied by the appropriate rites. Thus, on the grave of a girl who had died after eloping, I saw her beads and ornaments returned by her lover. The body had been buried by his kin elsewhere.

[1] I discuss this further on pp. 219–20.
[2] A man calls his wife's brother and all men she calls 'brother', *lutu*. This is repeated in the next descending generation. A man calls his wife's sister and all those she calls 'sister', *detayit*.

The fact that homestead mortuary rites are performed even when the body lies elsewhere, shows that the disposal of the physical remains, although important, is not the overriding factor. The dead personality is thought of in association with the homestead; it is there that contact will be maintained because it is *there* that the effects of the continuing personality will be felt. However, this kind of mischance disturbs people; it may be shown later to have had harmful effects in that some future sickness may be attributed to it by a diviner.

v

After burial a marginal period of one year should elapse before the mortuary ceremony. This may, in fact, be anything from nine months to eighteen months or two years. During this marginal period an interim ceremony takes place, which is known variously as 'the smoothing of the grave with clay' (*borowa na kwe na ŋutu*), 'the pouring over of the grave with beer' (*bukusi kwe ny'it ko yawa*), or 'the sweeping of the grave' (*rere kwe*). *Kwe*, the word for grave, is also the word for 'head'.

The grave-sweeping takes place six months after burial, although the time at which it is held varies according to the season in which the person dies; it may take place after three or four months if death occurred at the end of the rains and the family must move to dry season pastures but wish to complete this stage of the death rites before they leave. Sweeping also depends on economic considerations; in famine or poverty it may be postponed, in extreme cases for a year. This is undesirable because the mortuary rite will then be delayed into a second year, the dead may feel neglected, and his aggrieved disposition cause illness.

Unlike the burial, which is a closed ritual attended only by the family, a grave-sweeping is the concern of all kin. If the dead was from a landowning clan, the elders of each collateral lineage must attend. Women of the agnatic line who have married out—sisters and father's sisters—travel back for the rite, accompanied by their husbands, and even more remotely related lineage women return for the 'grave-sweeping' of an important adult. Maternal kin and affines send representatives. Neighbours and friends attend the beer drinking, and local young people attend the evening dancing, but none of these latter attend the rites. The status and reputation of the dead determine the outside attendance. At a chief's grave-sweeping, chiefs of neighbouring territories send representatives to show good-will, sympathy, and respect.

The Mandari say that on such an occasion 'one goes to mourn the one who has died' (*ŋutu wörö gween ŋutu luga ŋutwan*). People mourn with gifts; if they attend individually they bring tobacco, grain, groundnuts, or small coins; a whole lineage sends a goat or the equivalent in money. All those who pay their respects receive hospitality.

A typical ceremony which I attended, was the grave-sweeping of Majaka, a young man of Mandiye lineage, whose burial had taken place five months previously. The ceremony began just after dawn and was attended by close kin only, other kin arriving for the celebrations which followed. When I arrived the family were clustered in groups in and around the homestead. Those not actively participating were sitting under the hut or on mats in the yard, one or two early arrivals who had journeyed during the night, were seated outside under shady trees.

This rite is described as being for the family and for the old people, particularly the women. It is unusual for outsiders to watch it, and an old woman asked when she saw me, 'Why has she come now? Does she not know the beer drinking is not until later?' When I presented a mourning gift and explained I had come to mourn for my brother, she was mollified.[1] The bereaved women were seated in a group facing the entrance to the grave-hut, which in this case had walls and a doorway. All were smeared with ashes, their hair long and unkempt or shaven. Among them were the mother's co-wives, the father's sisters, the wives of the father's brothers, and the dead man's sisters. The dead youth's own mother sat in the front of this cluster and kept up a continuous high pitched lament in which she reiterated the circumstances of the death and praised her son's character. Inside the grave-hut four old women, grandmothers and paternal aunts, were smoothing the surface of the grave mound with wet clay. From time to time, the dead man's sister and mother's co-wives beat their heads on the ground, threw themselves about, or made attempts to rush

---

[1] I had a personal link with this family, because the youth's sister gave me my Mandari name on my arrival.

off into the bush, a demonstration of grief socially enjoined on female mourners.

The smoothing was completed around mid-morning and everyone sat down to rest. Neighbours and relatives began to arrive, and gifts were handed to the father's brother, the master of the ceremonies, who had inherited the dead man's mother, the father being dead. Amongst the gifts was a nanny-goat brought by the mother's brother's lineage—'for the dead man's ghost'. This joins the family herd, since animals are seldom killed at grave-sweepings, which require only beer offerings.

Beer was circulated among the men and women elders, and the father's brother poured libations on the hearth for the ancestors, on the grave for the dead man, and at the junctions of paths to protect the homestead against those with the evil eye who might attend the rite. At each pouring he offered a short prayer under his breath for safe keeping and health. Other elders also poured and prayed. Grave-sweepings are never occasions for long invocations and the statements (*deŋgu*) which characterize sickness rites, when causes are sought and approaches made to spirits. 'The grave is simply swept', as the Mandari put it, 'with beer.'

The ceremonial dance, *damaya*, 'the great dance of tradition' (*löri duŋ lo beron*) which terminates important rites, begins in the evening. Beer is again drunk by old men and women who take a prominent part in ceremonial dances. Members of different chiefdoms dance in separate formations within the main configuration of the dance. A group leads in singing one of its chiefdom's own songs and other people gradually join in. Some songs are deliberate attacks upon members of other chiefdoms who may be present, and then the singing can lead to angry outbursts or brawling. I saw an instance of this during Majaka's grave-sweeping when representatives from Mokido sang a song attacking persons attached to Dari, the owners of the land, enraging a Dari man who threatened the Mokido song-leader with a spear and had to be disarmed.[1]

The grave-sweeping ends the mourning obligations of lineage relatives who resume normal dress. Beads and other decorations which have been put aside in the roof are splashed with sesame

---

[1] For examples of 'attacking songs', see my *Chiefs and Strangers*, pp. 149–52, and 'Mandari Witchcraft' in *Witchcraft and Sorcery in East Africa*, ed. J. Middleton and E. H. Winter (London, 1963), pp. 113–17.

oil for 'coolness' and then re-threaded. Their owners are then free to dance in other villages. Close kin continue mourning.

Although the Mandari do not comment directly on the changes which are effected by the burial and the progression through the periods leading up to the grave-sweeping and the mortuary rites, certain changes are implicit by the nature of the ritual acts. The burial marks the end of the physical human being. The immediate alienation of the family from normal living because of their identification with the dead, the cleansing of the homestead and persons, and the killing of the vengeance ox on the fifth day all emphasize this aspect of death.

The grave-sweeping marks a further change. The living look back to mourn the human being and forward to give recognition to the new ghost. The widow and the women of the family still make public lamentation but the grave-hut is dismantled, the possessions of the dead are removed from the grave and after being purified are used again or distributed; the grave is smoothed over for the last time. The pouring of libations for the dead begins, showing that the dead is now able to receive offerings—the first of many received as an individual ghost, or shared in, as one of the ancestral collectivity. The dead is now orientated towards the ancestors rather than towards the living. But the kinship personality and roles occupied during life remain operative and binding, as is shown by the fact that a widower cannot yet remarry, nor can a widow be inherited.

VI

The mortuary ceremonies are described as the closing over of a person's head (*togomo na ŋutu kwe*). Closing over is effected by raising wooden poles which are referred to as 'memorials'— 'a thing for calling to mind' (*deŋit*).

The mortuary rite is the climax of the death sequence and requires the killing of at least one ox. A person cannot be 'closed up' (*gomo*) with beer or small stock, so a poor family may contract a long-standing debt in order to provide this ox. When a powerful landowning family head dies oxen are slaughtered by brothers, adult sons, and heads of collateral lineages.[1]

---

[1] At the mortuary ceremony of Chief Korondo of Dari, his son told me that ten animals, cattle and goats, had been killed.

Senior relatives who live at a distance make every effort to attend in order to give recognition to common blood ties (*töyuŋi*). This may be the only time that dispersed agnates of large clans can show that they are still '*baŋ lo Aba*', 'homestead of our father'. Representatives of lines of mother's brothers (true and classificatory) and affines also attend together with father's sisters and sisters with their husbands and representative elders of the husband's lineage. It is claimed that 'the whole country will come' to a chief's mortuary rite. In fact, representatives from surrounding chiefdoms are expected but, unless people are related, those from remote areas do not attend. At a powerful chief's mortuary rite, however, representatives of 'the whole country' is not far from the truth.

A doctor, often the one who attended the deceased, is called before the day is fixed, to determine whether it will be auspicious. His divination also decides the type of pole, known as *togomet*, to be raised, for it is the doctor who reveals whether the dead is contented or disturbed. If he reveals, 'His heart is ill-disposed; you must seek a large ox and give him a lot of wood', the grave will be covered with a heap of logs to make dense shade to 'cool' it. It is the disposition of the heart which determines the kind of pole, not the sex or age of the deceased. Age and status, however, have relevance, in that young unmarried persons or those of low status are rarely covered with a large pile, because they are seldom the source of serious mystical trouble. The unmarried have no descendants, the people generally affected, and few social and economic obligations, so consequently the range of their influence is limited.

A dead chief or important elder often, though not inevitably, receives a quantity of wood. The Mandari observe that people die in varying ways for different reasons and in different moods; these factors determine their influence on the living: 'Some have a resentful heart, they die angry; others die with a peaceful heart and are satisfied.' Those who die violently or are killed by witchcraft are particularly dangerous. It is their kin who will bear the brunt of this, but they can protect themselves to some extent by taking one of the recognized actions against a witch or killer or, at least, by seeing that the death rites are carried out in a manner which helps adjustment.

Single poles are ornamented with simple carving and stained

dark red with a paste of ochre and sesame oil which is absorbed
into the wood and acts as a preservative. In addition to purely
decorative ornamentation the top of the pole may be carved to
represent a woman's hair, or a stump may be left half way down
on a male or female pole, incised with a grid pattern, to represent
the umbilicus. When a pile of logs is assembled, or three or four

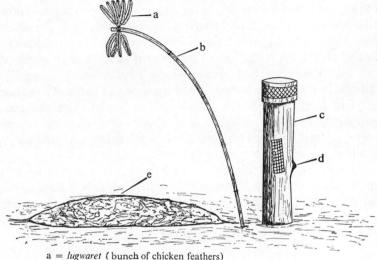

a = *lugwaret* (bunch of chicken feathers)
b = *kiriti* (bamboo)
c = grave pole, decorated with carving and red ochre
d = *kapulet* (umbilicus)
e = grave mound

FIG. 4. *Mortuary talisman*

are linked, abstract designs from the human form and decorative
staining are not used.

Since mortuary rites bring large crowds, the doctor is called
to show by divination the ritual precautions required. He may
order a chicken to be killed and eaten at the grave by lineage
elders. The head and feathers, or the whole bird, are tied to
a bamboo erected over it, so that as the wind blows the bamboo
bends over the grave and the chicken remains swaying backwards
and forwards carrying away dangerous influences (Fig. 4). Cooling
water is also sprinkled. The doctor who advises here is not paid,
but receives a leg of the sacrificial ox.

During the ceremony and the daytime dancing round the grave, ashes are thrown at those approaching it and water is flicked on the dancers to cool harmful dispositions. The Mandari recognize the danger of quarrels breaking out where large crowds congregate. Acts of violence are dangerous to the bereaved in their sensitive state and may also lead to lasting enmity. Fighting at the mortuary rites of a chief can spoil the rain and lead to famine. Dari quoted to me the case of the last installed chief of Jungwa, Garaŋ Aputu, to illustrate the far-reaching consequences of such violence. Garaŋ was speared in the foot as he ran forward to make a symbolic pass at a mortuary rite. Some said the wounding was deliberate, but whatever the truth, Garaŋ died a year later, divination revealing that a sorcerer had prevented the wound from healing. The Administration then amalgamated Jungwa with Dari, and Korondo, chief of Dari, who visited Jungwa in connection with the amalgamation, claims that the illness which led eventually to his retirement showed itself on his return. He attributed it, he told me, to the hostility of the Jungwa to his visit.

As mortuary rites are known to be potentially explosive occasions, those who know that others with whom they are carrying on active hostilities will be present, keep away. At the mortuary ceremony of the late chief Mar Pilari of Dari, for instance, Mokido were absent because of their affray with Dari.

VII

The mortuary rite of Mar Alinya of Jokari clan is an illustration of certain features omitted in rites for ordinary people. The Jokari are an important segment of Bora stock, and formerly held an independent chieftainship. Recently their decrease in numbers led to administrative amalgamation with the Mokido, when they lost their independent political status to the more numerous Mokido who were given the administrative chieftainship. The Jokari, however, continued to accord their clan head chiefly status and carried out appropriate rituals at his death.

The ceremony took place in April, at the beginning of the early rains. Alinya had been dead for two years, a longer period than usual having elapsed to allow for the accumulation of grain for beer, after bad harvests.

On the evening before the rite the Jokari drum, silenced by the death, was beaten. This is the preliminary announcement and

normally people dance, but this dancing is not part of the ceremony and on this occasion a bad thunderstorm prevented it.

The ceremony on the following day was divided into roughly
three parts:

1. The bringing in and raising of the grave poles.
2. The sacrificing of oxen and the addresses to the dead man
   and the ancestors.
3. The ceremonial dance (*damaya*).

The mortuary rite took place in the homestead of the senior
wife, and the dance was held on the cleared dance ground which
is a feature of the homes of prominent men. The chief's eldest
son, a married man of about forty, acted as master of ceremonies.

At dawn members of the extended family and close kin assembled. At about seven o'clock the grave poles, which had been cut
and shaped, were carried in ceremonially from the bush where
they had been lying during the night.[1] Each pole was carried
separately, laid across stout boughs borne on the shoulders of
eight or ten men. The bearers were followed by others shouting
and gesticulating, and women ululating. Each pole was laid by
the grave with the end which goes into the ground facing inwards
and the fork ends, which notch together, facing outwards; then
the bearers ran off jumping and shouting into the bush to fetch
the next. When all the poles were positioned they formed a circle
radiating out from the central grave-mound.

The bearer party dug holes for the poles and raised them in
pairs, each linked with its opposite number by the forked end.
Their adjustment took time, and was accompanied by argument
and shouted instructions. A man climbed on to the top, and sat
on the forks to test their stability; then the holes were filled in and
the earth pressed firmly down.

Senior men and women who, though related as lineage, maternal,
or affinal kin, were living at some distance, began to arrive and
were seated by the master of ceremonies under trees round the
homestead. Those of different political units sat apart, and any
between whom feelings were strained because of unsettled disputes

---

[1] Poles are cut from the trunks or the larger branches of trees which have
previously been burnt off and then left until the wood has seasoned. Before
a tree is felled a goat may be tied up under it for a few moments and a short
address made by a senior person to protect those felling it, or a little beer may
be brewed and drunk.

were carefully separated by members of friendly groups. Close relatives entered the homestead or joined the general mêlée round the grave.

When the poles were sited, the bearers stood back from the grave and were marked on the brow, chest, and back of the neck by a senior woman, with water mixed with seeds of the *kitöli* tree. Marking removes the danger of indisposition following contact with the grave. The bearer party then fanned out into the bush in mock defence formation, the men snatching up grain stalks to represent spears and charging round the homestead and cultivations, dodging and sparring and imitating the successful routing of an enemy. Women raced after them waving leafy branches and grain stalks and ululating.

This miming of defence of the homestead and the rout of the enemy is said by the Mandari to be 'like the wars of the old days', and to represent the dangerous position of the country, left without a leader. It is also explained as an attack on witches and sorcerers who may come to exult at or harm the grave; and finally, as another attack on death itself. It represents a statement on three levels— political, ritual, and ideological—against forces which threaten the life of the community. Under pre-Administration conditions a chiefdom was, in fact, vulnerable to attack at such a time from rivals who were waiting an opportunity to weaken or overthrow it. Even now, when violent political action is inhibited, the chiefdom is weakened and its people deprived of moral leadership when a good chief dies and his successor is, as yet, of unknown quality. The symbolic defence is not a feature of the mortuary ceremonies of ordinary people.

When scrub and homestead had been circled, the bearers ran back and began to dance round the grave with the usual shuffling step, singing their respective chiefdom's songs and songs composed for the occasion, including *mudu*, a song which solicits gifts from a chief; an honouring song composed by the son; and a Dinka song praising a chief possessed by Celestial Spirit—particularly appropriate because of the hereditary rain power (Ki) of chiefs of Jokari.

Dancing was punctuated by pauses when people stood for the singing of a verse. Spectators filtered in and there was stylized sparring and dodging with spears and shooting with bows and arrows. Girls fell down in convulsions or staggered round shaking

3. Memorial with heaped logs: grave of Bushe, chief of Mokido. Horns of sacrificial oxen lie on top, the horns of a display-ox at left

4. Ornamented memorial. The spiny Euphorbia cutting 'protects' the newly made grave from scavenging animals

5. Memorial with four notched poles: grave of the senior wife of Chief Korondo. Incised markings at the head of the pole represent the hair; those on the knot half-way down, the navel. At right a dispute is heard at the Dari meeting-tree

and twitching, a sign that Spirit-of-the-Above was present. The bereaved women again lamented, beating their heads on the ground, trying to run off into the bush, or throwing themselves on to the grave, while others restrained them. The Mandari recognize that this is a traumatic day, particularly for widows, because, with the completion of the mortuary rites, their conjugal ties with the head are severed. They have removed their mourning and selected their inheritors.

Procession round the grave and later, as the crowd swelled, round the dance-space, continued until midday. Women walked round assiduously sprinkling water on the dancers to cool those with quarrelsome dispositions or grievances. At midday beer was circulated for the bearers and for new arrivals. The beer is carried into the bush and drunk unobserved as a precaution against being overlooked by the evil eye, and because persons are present with whom eating and drinking are forbidden (in-law relatives of a man and unrelated girls; also persons avoiding one another because of bloodshed). Lineages of affines and lineages classified as mother's brothers arrived with mourning gifts. The Bora lineage of Mokido (classificatory mother's brother) brought a white nanny-goat for the dead man's herd as a 'goat of the ancestors'; the Dari (affines) brought 50 piastres; the Nyayo (linked by former marriages) brought hoe. The Jabour who are related and would have brought a gift, were absent because of a dispute between them and the Jokari.

At noon the sacrificial ox of the Jokari, tied up outside, was pegged near the grave. A lineage elder stood up holding a calabash of flour and made a brief address to Creator (*Dun*) and the Jokari ancestors, calling on the grandfathers collectively, then calling by name on the grandfather, father, and finally on the dead man himself:

You, Oh our grandfathers and you so-and-so [naming the true grandfather], and you, Oh our father, today poles are being raised for you and your grave is completed. After this we do not want any more illness, misfortune, or death. These cows are for you [addressing the dead man]. Do not become a bad influence, but only one for good; be benevolent towards us and help us.

He threw a handful of flour into the air and continued: 'All those with the evil eye, all illness and wrong-doing, all evil talk and quarrelling be far away from us today; let them go away to the west.' He then threw the flour for the second time towards the west, where the sun sets. Finally he asked: 'That the people may receive health and peace from the north-east where the sun rises; from Logobong in the east' and he threw the flour for the third time towards the north-east.

Another elder led the ox round the grave: eventually it urinated. The elder scraped up earth and urine, threw them outwards from himself three times, and prayed: 'You Creator (*do Dun*) and you also the below (*do Kak*) and the grandfathers who have died; bless the people, remove all sin and evil, do not ordain that anyone shall fall sick.'

Addresses at mortuary ceremonies are brief. 'In death there is nothing to say, people simply "take farewell" (*seser bok*)', with such words: 'Now you have been buried and your grave poles raised; here are your cows; let us salute each other and part.'

After the commitment the elder ordered the ox to be killed. The carcass was skinned immediately and the meat divided into heaps for later allocation. The breast meat (*kido*), the ritual portions, would be boiled and eaten in the afternoon by the homestead owner, the doctor, and closely related elders. This meat is 'potent' (*töpötö*) and can only be eaten by the deceased's closest kin. Kidneys and liver are also ritual portions eaten by the related male elders, the stomach lining and intestines are the portion of related female elders. The skin is kept by the owner to be made into a drum-cover or sleeping-mat. The head is also his. Ritual portions are boiled in the blood. The blood is described as pleasing to the dead and if a breeze stirs momentarily during the ritual meal it is a sign that the deceased has come to feast.

Immediately after the killing all the meat (except the ritual parts which were taken straight into the hut) was displayed on the top of the grave poles, including the head which was laid on the grave itself (Fig. 5). Later in the day the non-ritual meat, legs, back shoulders, etc., was allocated to the visitors, who included non-agnatic relatives of various categories. This meat is carried home and re-divided on arrival, part of it may be roasted in the bush and eaten before departure.

In the late afternoon the 'whole country' arrived to honour the chief. This formal tribute is paid by neighbouring chiefdoms as political rivals and not as relatives, although kin of different kinds are within each delegation.

The representatives of chiefdoms or clans approached the homestead in a series of waves, each following a few hundred yards behind the one in front. The Dari and their chief arrived first, followed immediately by the Mokido, then by lineages of the Nyayo with small neighbouring clans. The columns were led by young men armed with spears and bows and carrying war shields:

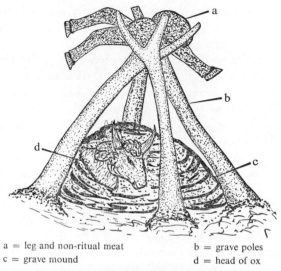

a = leg and non-ritual meat   b = grave poles
c = grave mound   d = head of ox

FIG. 5. *Display of mortuary meat*

behind them followed the visiting chief and notables, then important clients and female elders. Within sight of the homestead the young men broke into a run and fanned out in front of the columns shaking their spears threateningly towards the homestead, and shouting out ox-names and dodging and sparring. Every few yards two or three knelt on one knee side by side to sing praise-songs.[1] As the attackers circled the homestead Jokari women showered them with ashes to prevent wounding. Prominent women accompanying the delegations who threw themselves down, beating their heads on the ground, were raised by members of the homestead and led forward. Jokari women ran out snatching up grain stalks and mingled with the attackers who began to mill

---

[1] The shouting of ox-names and praise-songs relates in this context to the simulated 'war' situation.

round the grave making threatening passes at it with their spears while the Jokari ringed it round to protect it. A Jokari man climbed on to the top of the grave poles and sat in the forks armed with a bow and arrow made of a bent twig strung with plaited grass with a grain-stalk arrow-shaft. Each time the attackers surged forward he bent the bow towards them but without releasing the 'arrow'. He was positioned on the poles under the doctor's direction to symbolize the defence of the grave. The demonstrators then knelt in a circle round the grave several ranks deep, with their spears raised towards it, and sang a mortuary song.

The leader (Garaŋ Adulla, the representative of the Dari chief) then leapt up and began to sing the Dari clan song, 'Miri na Tali', processing around the grave in the standard mortuary dance, visitors and members of the homestead gradually joining in. The widow stood by the grave sprinkling water. The visiting parties then broke up and entered the homestead, mats were spread, greetings exchanged, and beer provided.

The symbolic attack represents a formal display of respect for a deceased chiefly rival. The repulse signifies the integrity of the chiefdom whose people unite to defend the grave of their dead ruler. Certain truths of the situation of a chief's death and essentials of chieftainship are here enacted, and much of the symbolism is obvious, the Mandari themselves readily giving explanations. They suggest that staging a mock attack averts a real one. This was a serious danger on the death of a chief in pre-Administration times, as they pointed out when discussing the mock defence of the pole-bearers, and it is still theoretically possible. At another level the attack is one of the attacks on death like the pole-bearers' mock fight, the mother's brother's hostile demonstration, and the killing of the vengeance ox.

The attackers are also represented as trying to take away the 'potency of chieftainship' (*töpötö na tomatatan*)—the essence and potency of office—which would be diminished if they speared the grave. As they are repulsed the virtue is retained. Furthermore, the hereditary 'power of the Above' (Ki) in the Jokari chiefly line, already temporarily weakened by death, is further decreased if the grave is touched. Its preservation is one of the explanations given for the posting of the guardian with the bow and arrows. In the ultimate sense, of course, this virtue is a religious power and cannot be alienated.

After the central demonstration, smaller groups who continued to arrive throughout the day moved off to the open dancing space where dancing went on intermittently. The elders drank beer and the sacrificial meat was allocated. At sundown neighbours went home to eat, visitors dispersed to the homesteads of neighbourhood relatives, while close kin ate in the bereaved homestead.

At nightfall the Jokari drum was beaten for the dancing which celebrates the end of mourning. Family mourners now took part including the widows, dressed in new skins or cloths and with freshly shaven heads. This is an open dance, attended by everyone. For protection and to show themselves off, the young people of different chiefdoms danced together, fully armed, within the main body of the dance. Each group is recognized and their appearance and performance noted. After each of the rest pauses which punctuated dances, a group of dancers from a chiefdom came forward with their own dance-song, which others knew and sang, and when a group was tired they moved out and sat down. Sheaves of dry grass were lighted and carried as torches. Before dawn people dispersed to their homes, slept round the dance place, or went to the girls' courting huts.

In the morning the remaining visitors leave. This is the point at which the mother's brother claims his dues from his nephew's kin, saying: 'I seek the bow of my nephew.'

On the completion of the mortuary ceremonies the homestead may be abandoned. Whether or not people move depends on many factors. Mature widows often live on in their homesteads, but young ones may move to their inheritor's homestead, or he may build a new one for them. The death of young people or children rarely leads to a move. Daughters may keep their dead mother's homestead going under the supervision of a brother or relatives. If the family move they return each year after the rains to weed the grave and cut the grass round it; neglect of the grave, particularly in the years following the death, can lay up trouble.

VIII

I now give some details from the mortuary rites of two ordinary men—both, as it happens, members of the same lineage—to illustrate certain general features of mortuary rites.

(i) *Mortuary Rite for a Young Man of Nyayo Clan*

The youth had been buried in the domestic goat-kraal. The four grave poles were carried on by Nyayo men, and the bereaved family assembled at the grave and everyone was protectively splashed with water by the doctor. As kinsmen began to raise the poles, argument and recrimination broke out. It appeared that the poles were being raised after five months, at the time when a grave-sweeping is usually held. The dead man's family and lineage had decided on this because they were poor, and the death had followed another death and two years of bad harvests. A combined sweeping and mortuary rite was therefore to be held. The dead man's married sisters who had come from their husbands' homes in the east of Mandari, however, expressed strong disapproval and made determined efforts to prevent the pole-raising; eventually after discussion it was allowed to proceed.

There was no dancing because Nyayo were already in mourning, but beer was distributed to the family and lineage elders and drunk at the graveside. Libations were first poured down at the grave and prayers offered for safety.

Ajak Patis of Mandiye lineage, the mother's brother, then arrived, bringing a goat for sacrifice. Everyone was waiting around for the killing of the mortuary ox but as Nyjok, the head of Nyayo clan could not be found, by sunset people had dispersed to their homes.[1]

At dawn we reassembled for the questioning of the widow about her inheritor, which must be completed before the ox is killed. The family had now put aside their mourning, the heads of all who had grown their hair had been shaved, and the widow had put on a new goat-skin. Old men and women of the lineage grouped on mats with the widow in their midst were about to explain formally to her how she must choose an inheritor, when the married sisters again intervened and adamantly refused to allow the matter to be discussed. They said that the whole sequence of rites had been rushed in a most unseemly manner, and that everyone should have been attending a grave-sweeping and not a mortuary ceremony. After argument, it was agreed that the widow should go back with the women to their homes near Mount Tindolu until the following year when the question of inheritance would again

---

[1] Nyjok is a busy doctor and no one was surprised that he should be late.

be brought up. As she was breast-feeding, there could be no question of her sleeping with an inheritor at that time. This incident underlines the power of a sister in a brother's affairs. Her opinion, particularly as an adult married woman, carries weight and cannot be ignored. Since a man marries with his sister's cattle, her favourable disposition is essential to the health of his children.

Nyjok now being present, the family and elders with Ajak Patis went to the graveside and the ox was killed. I did not watch this as I was attending with Dari representatives and so remained seated with them outside the homestead. Visitors, distant kin, and affines do not watch the actual rites but wait quietly to receive their meat. The Dari received a leg and myself half a leg as 'a person of Dari'.

Because of the ambiguous nature of the ceremony—neither a grave-sweeping nor a mortuary rite—there was disagreement on how the animal should be killed. Eventually it was speared, as for a grave-sweeping, the elders deciding that the family should later try to find another ox for the dead man's ghost. The division of the meat was therefore *koret* (the word for any meat division including that of game animals). A ritual division is *tupi*.

Throughout the day visitors bring presents to the grave, which are later given to the widow. Anyone receiving beer hands over a token which in theory secures a portion of the sacrificial meat. A lineage which brings a goat receives a large cut such as a leg; individuals receive cuts which vary in size and type according to their gift and to their social and kinship status. At one mortuary ceremony which I attended I did not receive any meat although I had given 10 piastres and several people commiserated with me. Many kin were present and, although two oxen were killed, the meat was insufficient to go round. A neighbour raised this point and was told regretfully, 'How else can I act when there are so many important elders and kinsmen who must not be offended?' In fact the Mandari were most generous in giving me meat.

(ii) *Mortuary Rite for a Man of Nyayo Lineage of Böndöri-Nyayo Clan*

At this rite two oxen were killed, one provided by the mother's brothers, the other by Nyayo. When more than one animal is killed, the hosts eat the guests' animal and the visitors eat the hosts', with the exception of the ritual parts.

On this occasion argument broke out about the method of killing. A brother of the deceased who runs a small bush shop in Eastern Mandari was about to spear the mother's brother's ox, when a Nyayo elder rushed up and insisted angrily that it must have its throat cut, 'otherwise everyone will be ill!' Eventually the throat was cut.

Disagreement over the widow's inheritor followed. The elders who hear a widow's views are never members of the dead husband's own family, who take no part, but important men and women of her natal clan and of clans who do not have an interest in the matter, in this case Koreŋ and Bari Kujutat. On this occasion the young woman stubbornly refused to accept any relative of her dead husband, maintaining that she had only been married a short time, her baby had died, and she preferred to return to her parent's home from which she would later marry by her own choice. She eventually began to cry, repeating her refusal. Someone whispered to me that she seemed to be rather a stubborn girl. However, it is theoretically accepted that the widow can elect to go home and later marry independently. Such a decision raises the problem of the return of bride-wealth and every effort is therefore made to persuade a widow to stay. After a while a Bari Kujutat elder led her away to an empty homestead nearby and reasoned with her alone. When they returned the elder intimated that she had accepted a younger brother of the dead husband. When he heard the decision he also complained forcefully that he was too young to support her and was, in any case, engaged in trade which necessitated his constant travel. (A spectator told me that he was courting a girl and did not wish to jeopardize his own marriage chances.) There was a delay while he put his case but, like the girl, he eventually acquiesced. The Nyayo ox was then slaughtered. This ox, which is for the dead man's ghost, cannot be killed until the widow's future has been decided; if no agreement is reached the mortuary rites cannot be completed.

The accounts of the Nyayo rites show that they can be occasions for quarrelling and disagreement. Three factors account for the disharmony. First, people may simply make mistakes; secondly, there may be a difference of opinion about what is correct, and thirdly, circumstances may force a compromise.

The significance of mistakes, differences of opinion which lead to quarrels, and compromises, is that these provide the case material for doctors, who take careful note of divergencies from correct practice and interpret future events in the light of these. There is inevitably a doctor present at a major ritual, either the one who had treated the deceased, or one who is there in the capacity of a neighbour or relative. At the first of the Nyayo rites Ako Akurukway, with whom I attended, pointed out to me that the way they were doing things would certainly lead to trouble, and in this case he was suggesting mystical trouble, not simply family quarrelling.

The ordinary person is under constant pressure to meet the many demands on cattle and other resources which stem from illness, death, marriage payments, and other social obligations. People do their best and if they perform one rite instead of the required two, they explain the situation to the dead man. If subsequent misfortunes prove their compromise efforts to have been vain, they try to rectify the situation with further offerings. Since illness does not necessarily follow after compromise, this observed fact makes compromise action worth while. A certain risk is often unavoidable in ritual situations, as it must be in daily life, and this is recognized. But there may be disagreement about the degree of departure from the ideal which can be allowed in practice.

IX

The way in which the animals are killed in the stages of the death rites is of the utmost importance. The burial ox, 'the thing by which burial is affected' (*nokosi*), must be speared and likewise the animal killed on the fifth day after burial. Should an animal be killed at the grave-sweeping, which rarely happens, this, too, is speared. Spearing is said to make the blood 'hot' so that it will seek out the cause of the death. To kill by spearing (*rembu*) is an act of aggression, like fighting and vengeance, and a human homicide must always be purified to protect him from the shed blood. The blood of the speared burial ox has analogous dangerous qualities, and for this reason the animal is first addressed by an elder and its blood instructed to seek out the killer and destroy him. By addressing the blood and giving it direction the elder ensures that 'it does not return to the dead man's homestead'. The Mandari say that 'The ox is killed in this way because a man has just died; it is blood for his blood.' Death is also described as 'the first spear', and the spearing of the ox as 'the second spear', implying retaliation. The spearing of this animal is also said to be 'like the action of death'.

The killing of the mortuary ox involves quite different principles. It is no longer a vengeance killing for a dead man, but a sacrifice for a new ancestor, for by the time the mortuary ceremonies are reached, the dead man is able to receive the first of a series of offerings from his kin. In conformity with all sacrificial killings, the animal's throat is cut (*duŋgu*).[1] Before the killing an elder addresses the dead and asks for safe sleep, instructing him to be benevolent and watch over his kin. He is reminded that as a ghost he may receive oxen and beer and share in animals killed for the ancestors on the marriages of daughters. Such addresses are brief, and the animal may not even be led round the grave. The sacrifice is simply a confirmation of the dead man's change of state and his changed relationship with the kin who are left behind. If the mortuary ox were speared its blood would be hot and dangerous— 'because the blood goes forth to seek a killer and finding none returns to the homestead of the man who speared it'. The wrong kind of situation is created and illness might follow. Such a killing is inappropriate for a man who had been dead for a year and whose death had already been avenged.

There is, however, some local variation in method. For clans around central and western Mandari the principles just described are in force; but in the south-east, towards Nyangwara, the Mandari follow the Nyangwara custom (as do the Nile-dwelling Tsera and Köbora) of spearing mortuary animals. Thus Mijiki clan towards Tindalu spear mortuary oxen, and a man of this clan described how on the death of his father, the Mijiki chief, all the oxen were speared.[2]

Goats are often killed at mortuary rites; a married sister, particularly, brings a goat for a sibling of either sex. Mortuary goats must

---

[1] *Duŋgu* also means 'to sacrifice'.

[2] General principles regarding the killing of cattle are:

(*a*) In sacrifice, including sacrifice for illness and sin cleansing, the throat is cut whether the rite is held in the homestead or the cattle-camp.

(*b*) In killing for celebration or entertainment the killing is irrelevant and the animal may be speared. In killings of cattle in connection with young people's activities this is the method used; as when a new cattle-camp is set up. In connection with display-oxen and initiation, cattle are speared. Only in the *ritual* situation must the two methods be kept distinct.

be clubbed to death since their blood is 'hot', releasing sickness if spilt at a grave.

X

Full death rites are performed for adults and for children over the age of about eight, but the size of the attendance on any occasion relates to the age and status of the deceased.

The huge crowds which are a feature of chiefly rites derive from the size of chiefly families and lineages and the ramifications of their kinship extensions, and from the nature of chiefly office. The symbolic demonstrations at the grave are statements about political office and historical truths, and show that while a chiefdom is autonomous in one sense, in another very real way each is linked to like units by obligations which are exemplified in different kinds of prestation.[1] I refer to the reciprocal obligations whereby rival chiefs attend each other's death rites, install each other's successors, marry each other's daughters, and compete in the giving of hospitality, the attracting of retainers and the founding of herds. Chiefs are also honoured by their rivals' followers through 'begging dances' (*mudu*), and compete among themselves in gift-giving.

While exchange and prestation link two chiefdoms (for, as Mausse pointed out, there must be one to give the gift, confer the honour, or express the condolences, and one to receive them) it would be incorrect to assume that chiefdoms are paired in any permanent or specific way. Linking is arbitrary, although it tends to be based on a history of reciprocity and certain factors are helpful in bringing it into being. These may be the sharing of a common boundary, or at least a near neighbourhood, which gives a field of common interest in which the reciprocal relationship is also meaningful. Whether friendly exchanges come into being and persist is dependent on happenings which affect the two clans concerned. I found a number of linkings between neighbouring chiefdoms who shared dry season grazing or watering places and who had intermarried in both their chiefly and collateral lines, as well as linkings between powerful immigrant (non-client) lines and established landowners where land for settlement had been given. Such a linking exists between the Jokari and the Dari

[1] M. Mausse, *The Gift* (1954).

because the Dari gave the Jokari land. These clans intermarry, and the Jokari installed Mar Are, the last installed chief of the Dari, in office. At the Jokari mortuary rite, the Dari were important mourners who brought gifts. The Dari and the Mokido also had such a reciprocal arrangement before their recent affray. Something similar exists between the Dari and the Nyayo and the Nyayo and the Mokido; these linked groups are affines. Again, around the Mount Tindalu area, linkings are found between neighbouring Bora chiefdoms, although here landowning lines who consider themselves related do not intermarry and the affinal relationship is missing.

The death of a baby affects only its parents. A stillborn infant or one which dies at birth is laid in a termite mound and only the mother laments. She must then hide her grief, for 'If too much notice is taken of the death of a new-born baby Creator will be angered and not send the woman another child—Creator can send one, and does not like to hear people making a fuss.' The parents observe mourning for three days and then the mother is washed in hot water, the skin which she was wearing when the infant died is placed in the hut roof, and she dons a new one: when she feels fit she sleeps with her husband.

An infant's social range is so limited that only parents can be adversely affected by its death. When, as occasionally happens, a grossly malformed baby is exposed in the bush, a small rite follows before the couple sleep together. Three days after the infant has been removed, old women shave the heads of husband and wife and anoint their bodies with cooling oils. When they later enter their hut for intercourse the old women shut the door and call through it: 'Where is your little child that was born the other day?' The mother replies: 'A predator has devoured it' (gworoŋ ŋu kor). The women then reply, 'Oh well, get to work.'

A normal child born alive but which dies before it is three days old is buried in the homestead without ceremony. After three days a child is named, and must then receive modified death rites. Its grave is also swept at a simple rite. After the lower front teeth have been removed at the age of eight or nine, a grave pole is raised.

Another category which may be denied the full sequence of rites is that of clients who lack complete social personality because of specific factors in their affiliation. Those recently affiliated as individuals should have rites performed for them by their patrons, but since they cannot become ghosts (having no true blood-kin) it is debatable whether rites are, in fact, always carried out and I have evidence which leads me to believe that they may well not be.[1] Apart from the burial, the further sequence of death rituals which deals with the disposal of different kinds of effective kinship personality must be carried out where there are roles to be handed on. Effective personality increases in importance as the person matures, marries, bears or begets children, assumes a role such as family or lineage head, or a sacerdotal office like that of landowning chief where the ritual welfare of the land is at issue. Some clients never achieve this full personality because of their peripheral positions.

XI

The mourning observances of close kin must be strictly adhered to in order to avoid ritual dangers. Mourning etiquette observed by distant kin is simply a matter of good manners and is not discussed here.

Spouses and close cognatic kin are the people at risk from subsequent ghost activity and also those who, when dead, can initiate such activity. Within the three-generation grouping a distinction is made between the immediate kin and the collateral kin such as parents' collaterals. The mourning enjoined on the latter is less arduous and breaches of it are less harmful.

Four days after a death spouses and parents shave their heads and then leave the hair to grow until the mortuary ceremonies when it is again shaved and, as mourning is terminated, kept normally dressed. These kin all wear strict mourning—uncut hair, no beads or decorations, ashes on the body and thongs of hide of the burial-ox round necks and waists, and round the forehead as well in the case of women. A mother or widow selects an old cloth or goat-skin from which the legs are cut off to tie round her loins. At the mortuary rites when mourning is removed and bodies oiled, heads shaved and women don new clothes, the old coverings, the thongs of hide, and the hair shavings are buried in the waste-land.

An unmarried sibling mourns with shaved head (the unmarried never grow their hair), without ornaments or red-ochre, and wearing bands of hide on neck and wrists, until the grave-sweeping only:

[1] See *Chiefs and Strangers*, p. 115.

paternal cousins and half-siblings act similarly. A uterine sibling may choose to wear mourning up to the mortuary rite. The senior generation—father's and mother's siblings and grandparents—may either terminate mourning at the grave-sweeping rite or mourn until the mortuary rites.

The distinction drawn between growing the hair and shaving it is important. After the initial shaving following burial, certain kin grow a new crop of hair which remains untended until the mortuary rite. Having long hair or a shaved head represent two modes of mourning, denoting in turn different relationship bonds. Those with long hair, the parents and the spouses, are most closely identified with the dead. Allowing the hair to grow, together with the neglect of personal grooming typified by refraining from plucking the facial and body hair—and the only men I have seen where this has been neglected have been mourners—is a more extreme action than shaving, explainable only when the Mandari attitude to hair is understood. Excessive hair on the head and hair on the body or face—including eye-brows—is regarded as unsightly and plucked out. Long or unkempt hair even suggests to Mandari an association with 'animalness', with the untamed. Thus I was bound to notice that my long hair often brought asides to the effect that I had a goat-skin on my head. Undisguised disgust was expressed for the hairy forearms and legs of male Europeans, 'like wild beasts' (se gworoŋ). In this respect Europeans are seen to have 'primitive' characteristics. Central mourners, therefore, with their disordered hair and unkempt bodies, are expressing grief by personal neglect to the point of losing some essential human-ness; this represents the most extreme of the liminal states.[1] The complete shaving of the head also shows a liminal state but a less extreme one. Shaving not only signifies partial social modification, but also the wiping away of an unfavourable state and a starting anew, as when a homicide or the killer of a marked predator is shaved. It may also be a purely pragmatic concern, as when the heads of babies are shaved to keep them clean, or when young people use head-shaving as a decorative art. But the completely shaved head after childhood implies something special, although something less radical than letting the hair grow. Before the questioning of a widow the long hair of close mourners is shaved.

[1] Other persons with long hair are those with long-drawn-out and often fatal illnesses—mayar for instance—and children who are möjut.

At the main mortuary ceremony, therefore, all mourners appear with shaved heads, some having just removed long hair, others having mourned with shaved heads.

Lineage relatives who live sufficiently close to attend the death rituals do not shave, but remove beads and decorations, wear thongs from the burial-ox, and refrain from dancing. Close affinal kin also wear mourning, removing beads and decorations until the grave-sweeping; but only the immediate affinal kin are involved and not members of their whole lineage. Affinal kin bring hoes, a goat, or money. A wife mourns a co-wife and a co-wife's children until the mortuary rites. Siblings mourn the death of each other's spouses until the grave-sweeping only. Modifications in all mourning may be made in special circumstances.

With the exception of child deaths, the hamlet and village is always affected by death. Drumming and dancing are curtailed— in theory until the mortuary rites but in practice the ban is relaxed after a suitable period, depending on the age and status of the dead. A death in the chiefly family silences the drum for the full period, and other grave-sweepings and mortuary rites are held without dancing during the whole of a chief's mourning. If one death follows closely on another, the prohibition on drumming may also hold as it did during the mortuary rites of the young man of Nyayo clan where no ceremonial dance could be held.

Being a mourner also involves abstinence from sexual intercourse. Since the object of intercourse is seen to be to beget a child a woman must not conceive while wearing 'the clothing of death' since violation of this rule offends against the Mandari dialectic of the separation of incompatibles. The action of procreation belongs to life and must not be introduced into situations associated with death. To mix the two is death-dealing.

Sexual abstinence terminates automatically with mourning except for a widow for whom a rite must be performed before she sleeps with her inheritor. The latter provides a sheep which is killed in the doorway of the hut in which the couple have intercourse. The mother or senior wife of the inheritor splashes his body and that of the widow with sesame oil, saying 'May your bodies be cool.' The couple enter the hut over the dead sheep which lies across the door until the morning. The meat is eaten by the elders of the husband's lineage; the couple abstain from it because 'It is the sheep of their bringing together' (*tonara kok*).

(Prohibition on eating sacrificial meat by the central participants features in all rites which either divide off or bring together.) Omission of this rite of separation is believed to lead to the death of offspring and to introduce *mönöjin* among the woman's kin.[1] The sheep, 'for the life of the husband', compensates for the right of access to the widow, rights in her offspring having been acquired with her marriage cattle. This animal cuts the personal bond with the deceased husband, but none the less the tie between a widow and her dead husband is never completely severed. A widow continues under the protection of the dead husband's ghost and if the inheritor ill-treats or neglects her or the deceased's children, he may fall sick. 'A widow may accuse her inheritor, calling on her dead husband. Bullying co-wives may fall ill because her husband's ghost hears her lamentations.'

Certain elements of liminality which adhere to a deceased after the mortuary rites are reflected in forms of reference. A recently deceased is referred to as 'the late' (*lepeŋ ŋilo* if male, or *lepeŋ ŋina* if female). To prevent confusion the name is sometimes added. A dead chief is referred to in this way for a decade or longer, an ordinary person for about a year. It is thought to be characteristic of ill-disposed persons and those with the evil eye who wish to harm, to refer to a dead person simply by name, or to shout or repeat the name.

XII

I suggested at the beginning of this chapter that the ritual time periods which elapse between burial, grave-sweeping, and mortuary rites are an expression of Mandari ideas about time in general and I now say something about these ideas.

The Mandari record the passing of time by the recurring cycles of seasons and generations. Of these, the cyclic kinship time-units have the greatest flexibility. In addition, the Mandari may date an event by its relation to an important incident, such as a famine or a fight; or, alternatively, place it 'in the time of so-and-so', naming a chief. Further back still they say 'before the Administration' (early this century), or 'before the earth was destroyed' (before the slave-raiding). They lack age-sets and the newly acquired 'bead-sets' are not the equivalent and cannot be used for structural time reckoning.[2]

[1] *Mönöjin*—see Chapter 7.
[2] Evans-Pritchard, *The Nuer*, chap. iii.

The ecological time-unit is the year, since this represents the total of economic activities which are tied to seasonal change. During a 'year' (twelve lunar months and one wet and one following dry season, both called '*kiŋa*', are not exactly equivalent) a person performs activities which are repeated with little variation until death since there are no long-term programmes which transcend the annual cycle. The ecological time-unit is the minimum period a dead adult passes through before his mortuary rites are completed. It represents human routine and endeavour and for small children, who have not yet, as it were, entered time and have no part in economic activities, mortuary rites are not held.

The grave-sweeping should be held at the middle point of the mortuary year, but in fact may take place at an off-middle point marked by some urgent activity. Thus grave-sweeping may take place at three months because the dry season is beginning and people must move off to cattle-camps, but when the rite is later referred to, a six-month period may be assumed. Notional time-units and actual time do not therefore necessarily correspond exactly.

Cyclic kinship time covers the three generations of grandfather, father, and son and varies in time length for every group, but it is a scale of measurement much used because it reflects the basic, operative, social unit which is repeated down the generations; it is also the period during which deceased individuals continue to be evoked as ghosts. Three generations after death, a deceased person is merged in the ancestral collectivity and the dropping-out of the long dead reflects the working of actual memory in relation to passing time. Kinship duties, particularly marriage obligations, drop away over that period. Lineage time averaging five to seven generations (less for client lineages) is made up of two repeating units, the one of dead, the other of living as represented in Fig. 6. In the figure, the person at the bottom of each brace will have known the person named at the top. Thus Korondo was living at the time of my first visit and also his grandson, Shuti; Mar Desa was only remembered as the head of the lineage linking it to other collaterals. He is the last ancestor in the 'real' time scale, since above him clan ancestors represent a telescoped group of forebears who embody the idea of clan heritage for that particular clan.

The gradual separation, marked by the death rites and based on the Mandari conception regarding death and continuing personality, also reflects an understanding of the psychological importance of the passage of time in relation to death and bereavement. The periods between the ceremonies are seen as necessary for gradual personal adjustment to the assumption of new roles in the same way that the time sequence after the rites is necessary for wider social adjustments. The widow, especially, is seen to need a period of

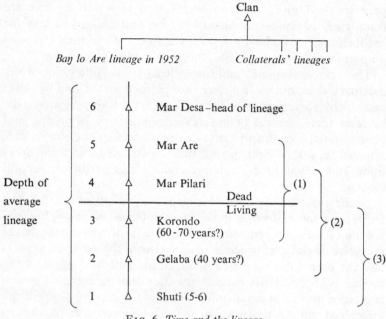

FIG. 6. *Time and the lineage*

recovery before she abandons mourning and makes the radical decision as to her inheritor.

Recognition by the Mandari of the value of time in effecting a degree of personal adjustment to death shows an awareness of important psychological realities.[1] The fact that many societies do not hold mortuary rites does not necessarily contradict the assumption that these rites accommodate a universal psychological need.[2] There may well be needs which the marginal period helps to meet. The fact that they are not taken note of in all societies

---

[1] These were considered by Hertz.
[2] Evans-Pritchard seems to disagree. See his Introduction to Hertz's *Death and the Right Hand*.

does not deny their existence. Some societies inhibit expressions of psychological realities; others allow limited recognition or leave it to people's choice as in our own modern mourning customs. Others, like Mandari, make a point of enforcing a period of waiting which must be followed regardless of personal inclinations, and during which personal adjustments must be seen to be made. A mother losing her baby may well feel this death much more than she feels that of an old relative, but only the shortest mourning is permitted. It may be psychologically correct that it is bad to give way to too much grief over the newly born and healthier for the mother soon to become pregnant again.

Periods of enforced waiting may be therapeutic; so may rules against waiting. Other roles requiring rearrangement are also often involved, as when a father dies, and an elder brother may have to take over the father's role in relation to younger siblings, or when other kin assume parental roles if children are orphaned. The mortuary sequence marks the slow stages in relinquishment of duties and ties.

Thus the sequence of death rites cannot be understood in terms of single explanation. There are personal emotional adjustments to be made, and many societies give recognition to these. There are further, social adjustments. Roles, cut arbitrarily by death, are ongoing and have to be played out. The handing over of important duties often involves replacing one person by another in relation to a third. The phenomenon of personality always implies complicated interrelations with others. After the mortuary rites, uncompleted elements in relationships which linger on are cared for in the ghost rites to which I now turn.

5

DEAD KIN RITUALS

THE Mandari consider that organic life in man, animals, and plants consists of two main elements, the flesh (*lokore*) or body structure (*mugun*), and the life (*ködörö*). Life, the vital force, 'leaves the body at death' and without it man, like all organic matter, is dead.

The word for this *élan vital*, *ködörö*, is also the word for the *shadow* thrown by an animated form and different from *shade*, the simple blocking-out of light. The use of the same word does not, however, imply that the life is the same as the shadow—that a person, for example, can be harmed by attack on his shadow. *Ködörö* is also the word for 'cloud', regarded by the Mandari as a concentration of rain. A common quality of life, cloud, and shadow is the capacity to change, grow, or disappear.

The Mandari see a direct association between life and movement (although movement itself does not necessarily imply organic life; thus fire and water, though in constant motion, are considered lifeless). In men and animals, impaired motive power is a sign that life is weakening, 'his life is getting distant' (*ködörö ny'it ge pajo*), and at death, 'his life has gone' (*ködörö ny'it ge ayin*). In plants and vegetation, drying, withering, and browning are analogous to loss of movement and indicate lifelessness.

When an organism dies, the life released from the flesh returns to Creator who gave it. The Mandari say that 'at death all life goes upward to Creator' (*ködörö wörö ki ko ŋun*), or 'Creator takes the life' (*ŋun jojoŋ ködörö*). The notion of life as a universal animating principle means that it cannot be satisfactorily equated with the concept of the individual soul.

The Mandari distinguish between man and the rest of organic life in that they believe something of him which is neither flesh nor life remains after death. This can best be described as the reflection of kinship personality. I do not speak of it as social personality because this would imply the whole range of social roles and obligations, whereas the continuing personality is only represented in a kinship context. It is the mental image of kinship and kinship obligation in the mind of the living which gives substance to the idea of continuing identity.

The category word for this image is *nulon*, a word also used to describe minor religious signs, psychic phenomena associated with streams and pools, and omens. *Nulon* of human personality may be compared by the Mandari with the dream image. It is on the evanescent quality of the dream experience that the analogy is based because dreams slide into the mind uncalled, slip away, and are gone.

The Mandari have no accepted beliefs about an after-life: 'How can we know, seeing no one has come back from the dead?' Individuals may attempt imaginative comment, for example: 'Up above it is like their homeland (*se baŋ kase*). All life goes up there; that of animals and cows and grass; up there is sacrifice as well as here on earth, when the thunder rolls a bull has been sacrificed and rain will fall. They [the dead] have sacrificed their bull.' A conflict between dead and living is also sometimes envisaged, reflecting the creation myth of Mandari country with the theme of the original joining of earth and sky by a rope. It may be suggested that, at the separation of the two parts, 'Creator and some of the people remained in the upper hemisphere. When life separates at death, it therefore shows the wish of the "people-of-the-Above" to claim their separated kin; they [human beings] cannot go to the sky as flesh, so the life is taken, and the flesh is buried in the ground.'

Nulon as a word to describe the dead personality, implies that the deceased referred to is still potentially able to be externalized in a specific illness. It is rare for this to be the case after more than three generations have followed on from the death. Thus *nulon*, implying ghost visitation, is not used in reference to long-dead ancestors.

II

In some contexts the Mandari refer to the long-dead ancestors as *ŋun*, with the meaning 'of Creator', since ancestors are regarded as 'closer to Creator than the living for their life has been taken by him'. But separateness from Creator is also implied: 'They are not *ŋun* [Creator] but only men *ŋutu* [created]. We have seen them and known them; Creator has not been seen.'

In the context of division in the Universe, the dead are aligned with Spirit-of-the-Below—'they are the Below' (*kok a Kak*). Their former earthbound body, their human and immediate associations, place them in the terrestrial division.[1] In contrast, therefore, to celestial things which are 'cool', the dead are 'hot'. The most usual term of reference for the dead, 'people of the Below' (*nutu ko Kak*), does not imply a continuing physical location on earth. It is particularly stressed that 'The name does not mean they are in the ground. They are "Creator" and come from the above', but the physical body is in the ground—'The flesh is buried in the dirt where it rots and is eaten by maggots: the life goes to Creator.'

As 'hot' phenomena the ghosts of the dead receive 'hot' or 'neutral' sacrifices. Their ideal animal, the hot goat, particularly the large neutered male known as *queto*, is equivalent to the sheep of Spirit-of-the-Above. A bull calf may be exchanged for such an animal for a dead kin sacrifice. Cattle (oxen, and barren cows) are also killed for dead kin (having neutral qualities), and cattle are essential for burial and mortuary rites and also for the killing of the ox-of-the-ancestors on the marriage of a woman. Beer is the standard offering in minor sickness or poverty, having a parallel in the chicken of Spirit-of-the-Above.

The Mandari do not raise shrines to dead kin and ancestors. Graves, with their impressive wood memorials, are not cult shrines, although they may figure in ritual. Thus, if the relatives continue to occupy the same homestead after a death, beer libations are poured on the grave by a wife or senior woman. There are also instances of sacrifices at graves, most often at the graves of persons who have died and been buried away from their homesteads, since this is a disturbing occurrence and can be given in diagnosis as a cause of sickness.

The impermanence of the physical homestead may be one reason for the fact that graves do not become shrines. The length of time a family occupies a particular site is determined by economic and ritual factors, and by inclination; but eventually every site is changed and the grave is left behind in the encroaching secondary bush; the grave poles fall and lie rotting. At the season of grass firing, the family may return to clear away the undergrowth to

---

[1] The attributes of 'rain-power' in certain founder ancestors and chiefs, however, in addition links these dead with Spirit-of-the-Above.

prevent fire actually sweeping over the grave, but it will have long ceased to be a site for ritual.

The Mandari specifically say that the dead 'are not planted' (with shrines). Another reason why shrines are unnecessary is close identification of the dead with the cooking hearth. This is a congenial, mundane place where women cook and people gather for warmth and conversation, the comfortable centre of family life. The Mandari point out that formerly the dead sat there daily and their food was cooked there; thus after death it is the place to boil their sacrificial meat. This does not mean that the actual hearth-place, which may have been abandoned long since, is used but that the hearth is the symbol of close kin living intimately, and is where two living kin are gathered. The meat of other spiritual agents must never be cooked there, but on specially constructed fires *outside* in the open yard; to fail to make these cooking distinctions brings sickness. 'Only the dead belong to the hearth; the Above and Powers are outside. The Above falls down from Up: Powers are far away, and have to be called by their songs.' These external forces require shrines as focal points for communication, whereas, for the dead, such a point always exists while their close kin gather round a hearth.

Lacking shrines, there is often nothing in a homestead to show that a ghost rite has taken place. The sacrificial animal is simply pegged near the hut door; the peg may already be there because other animals have been tethered, or it may be knocked in specially. During the sacrifice, and for a short time afterwards, it is known as 'the peg of the Below' (*köluti na Kak*). Beer will be poured over it when brewed, because it is a point of contact with the dead, but if there is no peg, libations are simply poured down on the ground. When the peg rots it is thrown away, and not replaced as a shrine would be. Sometimes a sacrificial animal is not even secured.

The dead are not only associated with the hearth, but with places with which they were strongly identified, such as the hamlet or the meeting-tree. The identification of this tree with the elders who form the council is so strong that the single word *toket* is used for both the tree and the assembly. At the spiritual divisions of the day—the cool dawn and evening—a concentration of psychic force is seen to pervade the tree, which can cause indisposition. Court sittings always terminate before sundown and, in the morning, people only begin to gravitate to the congenial shade as the heat of the day intensifies.

All ancestors, particularly the long dead, are viewed as founders and guardians of tradition, and the Mandari will explain differences in customs between themselves and other tribes by saying, 'people's ancestors are different' (*merenyegin kade*). Ancestors sanction what is distinctive and unique. But although ancestors are represented as having a connection with custom and tradition, they are not viewed as moral guardians who punish misdemeanours or moral failures, showing an important difference between Mandari dead kin rituals and the ancestor cults of many African peoples where the dead are moral guardians.[1]

Mandari ancestors are only seen to be concerned with morality in a very general sense, in that if there is a lot of unexplained minor sickness, infertility, or crop failures it may be said that 'the ancestors are angry about departure from custom and wrongdoing', but these are not statements about a particular person's sickness, barrenness, or crop failure, nor is guilt attributed to any one individual. This is not to imply that ancestors are considered to be indifferent to the well-being of their descendants; on the contrary, the Mandari see a continuity of interest following down the generations which is not broken off at death, and which reflects the continuity of the descent group. Ancestors are described as 'watching over their kin', or 'helping a man', but in a general and unspecified way.

Kin who have died within living memory, on the contrary, directly affect the living. Where a person is known to have died a creditor to his living kin, as often happens, ghost intervention may be recognized as the cause of sickness. The name of the dead kinsman to whom the debt is owed will be turned up in divination and some sort of restitution will be prescribed. The deceased is represented as visiting his living kin in a very personal way. He is said to 'come to' the one who falls sick—'His father has come to him' (*Monye ly'it yupo ky'it*), or simply, '[It's] his father.' The deceased is envisaged as confronting his kinsman, in the same way as living kin come to state claims or demand debt settlement. Death

---

[1] Middleton shows how the Lugbara ancestors are closely linked with the older living generations who are able to invoke shared ancestors against kin who refuse to conform to norms of kinship behaviour. J. Middleton, *Lugbara Religion* (Oxford, 1960), *passim*.

does not diminish the capacity to enforce payment, and the power to cause ghost sickness is a logical extension of the power of the living by their dispositions to cause the illness of a kinsman, against whom they have a grievance.

Obligations are not relinquished at death, but gradually disengaged. Where the dead is a creditor in any one of his roles, he has power to demand payment, where obligations are due to him he can exact their fulfilment. The grievances of the living therefore tend to merge with those of the dead and to be dealt with simultaneously at the ghost rite. The resolution of the two kinds of debt (those to the living and those to the dead) in ritual, will be considered together in this chapter, with examples of illness caused by living persons brought to light during dead kin rites.

III

The ways in which the Mandari believe that they are affected in daily life by their dead reflect the realities of the kinship structure. I shall, therefore, briefly consider two important kinds of kinship grouping.

The first is the close cognatic group composed of any individual's more or less contemporary kin related to him through his mother and his father. These include kin of the same generation: brothers and sisters; kin of the parents' generation (father and mother, father's and mother's brothers and sisters); and finally two sets of grandparents. Some of the older kinsfolk of this group will already be dead.

Fig. 7 shows the core of kinsfolk, those who are likely to affect an individual as ghosts. Other kin such as the siblings of the grandparents, or paternal or maternal first cousins, are not included because in the normal course of events they are outside the kind of relationship which gives rise to ghost activity.

Kin are also aligned into two sets of lineage kins—and in the case of landowning clans, two sets of clan kin—those of the paternal and maternal descent lines. On both sides dead males are 'grandfathers' (*merenyegin*), dead females 'grandmothers' (*yakanyegin*), no unilineal distinction being made. Since, however, the Mandari trace descent patrilineally and the male line embodies jural authority and is the status-giving, property-owning, office-holding line, it also represents a known, genealogically linked, set of ancestors.

On the maternal side—the non-jural side—forebears are generally not known by name for more than two or three generations; further back they become undifferentiated 'ancestors'. There is less reason to remember by name the maternal forebears, in that after three or four generations from the marriage that linked the two lineages collaterals (the descendants of father's brothers) can again marry into the mother's lineage. It is only for

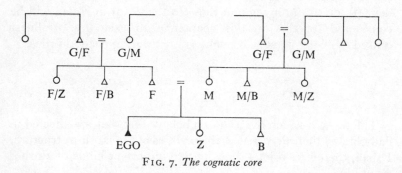

FIG. 7. *The cognatic core*

the three generations while men of the mother's line are addressed as 'mother's brother' and *treated* as such, that intermarriage is considered incestuous. Mother's ancestors are also, of course, different for every set of siblings and become too numerous to be remembered individually by the patrilineage. Mother's lines are less well-defined collectivities, representing the idea of maternal ancestors, rather than groups of named dead.

We must therefore regard the dead from two standpoints, as the Mandari themselves view them: as sets of deceased kinsfolk having relevance for any particular ego, and as lines of ancestors stretching back in time, well-defined in the male line and less so in the female. The cognatic relatives (Fig. 7), are those who as individual ghosts make personal demands on the living. I describe such assumed intervention as 'ghost externalization' and the rite that resolves it a 'ghost rite'. The less specific demands of the lineage ancestors are resolved by an ancestor commemoration rite.

The principal failures and omissions seen to cause ghost intervention and resolved in one of these rites are as follows:

A. *Resolved by Ghost Rite*

I. Failure to complete outstanding cattle debts relating to marriage:

(i) Failure on the part of a woman's father or brother to ensure that members of his patrilineage receive the animals to which they are entitled on her marriage. It is the duty of the woman's father to see that these animals are earmarked at the bride-wealth discussions.

(ii) Failure on the part of a woman's father to earmark the animals which are the entitlement of the woman's maternal kin, (father's affines), particularly the animal of the mother's brother.

(iii) Failure on the part of a husband to complete payment to his affines in reasonable time.

II. Neglect of burial or mortuary rites. Incorrect performance of the rites, the intrusion of quarrels, radical modifications, and failure to kill the required number of animals.

B. *Resolved by Ancestor Commemoration Rite*

(i) Failure to commemorate by pouring routine beer libations.

(ii) Failure to kill the ox-of-the-ancestors, when a woman of the line marries.

(iii) The ancestors have a legitimate entitlement to cattle as the herds which they founded increase, and, although the Mandari do not make unsolicited offerings, they expect this entitlement to be raised from time to time.

IV

A dead person can feature as a ghost in any of the kinship roles held during life. For example, a dead man may be externalized as a father's ghost, a mother's brother's ghost, or a grandfather's ghost, where he has filled all these roles in life, provided that he leaves kin for whom they are still meaningful. He could also in theory be the ghost of a paternal first cousin, but this would be unusual because there are few property obligations due to a father's brother's son in the normal course of events. Ghostly activity would be possible in this category, if the father's brother died and his son inherited his entitlements, or if the father's brother's son was living under the care of his own father when he died, and his mortuary rites were neglected.

An important point arises here in connection with debt. The Mandari see property as due back to older generations, for wives, and for the lives of younger generations. Older generations do not owe a debt to younger generations, though they have legal and moral obligations to provide marriage cattle. This means that ghost visitation is mainly from older to younger generations; a grandson does not make a grandfather ill, a nephew an uncle, or a child a parent.[1] Father's brother's son is of the same generation and is not, therefore, a creditor in this kinship role, though he might inherit a debt.

A woman is a potential ghost in any of her kinship roles but an unlikely role here is that of mother's sister, who is not entitled to marriage cattle on the marriage of her sister's daughter, and who, herself, marries off into another group. But the mother's sister is a part of the 'grandmother' collectivity of the mother's natal line and so indirectly is one of the recipients of beer libations and of broth made when sacrificial meat is boiled.

Kin entitled in connection with bride-wealth payments are the ones most likely to be turned up in divination. When a daughter of the patrilineage marries, cattle should be given to her father and uterine and half-brothers, to her father's brothers, father's sisters, father's other wives for their sons (half-brothers), to her married sisters—particularly those with male heirs—to her own mother (another animal for the uterine brother with whom she is linked), to her mother's brother or his representative. Paternal and maternal grandparents are also entitled kin, although they may be dead at the time of the marriage. If alive, they will claim, but they do not automatically receive on each marriage when there are a number of sisters, but rather take on alternate sisters' marriages. Claims also have to be met alternately where there are several father's brothers and mother's brothers. The eldest brother receives on the first daughter's marriage, the younger ones as other daughters marry. Kin may wait a long time to receive their marriage animal, but an entitled person who dies in theory hands on his entitlement to his heir, though these inherited entitlements are often not taken up. Whether they will be or not may depend on whether a doctor's diagnosis points to them as a cause for sickness on the defaulter's side, which turns either on the doctor's knowledge of the default

[1] A child can become *nyök*, and haunt a parent, something rather different.

or the degree to which the defaulters themselves feel guilty and admit it.

Equally, or even more frequently, ghost sickness follows failures by a man to give enough animals, or animals of adequate quality, to his affines when he marries. Most marriages take place with only a proportion of bride-wealth paid, but outstanding animals must come forward in reasonable time. Tardiness, or complete failure to pay, can affect the fertility and health of the wife but more particularly the health of any children. The defaulting husband and his kin are not harmed, because they are not blood relatives to the wife's living or dead kin. The crucial factor in ghost visitation is that it only operates where blood ties exist. A man's children are the most directly vulnerable target of his default over marriage payments to affines, and child sickness is *par excellence* thought to be due to angry dead or living maternal kin. The sickness stems from the failure at the *affinal* level (the level of the default in the bride-wealth payment) although it manifests itself at the sister's son or daughter level—the level of blood relationship.

It is important to remember that bride-wealth cattle are given for the wife's fertility and children, and if cattle are deficient it is logical that fertility and offspring may suffer. Poor general health, or a weedy, thin body, are often thought to be the result of default. The notion that cattle represent offspring is prominent in people's minds and child sickness, which is very common, is therefore immediately associated with failure in cattle payments.

Few people, however, can keep pace with all their cattle debts because obligations spread out from each marriage and must be dealt with in turn. Marriage entitlements begin to overlap as new marriages take place before old entitlements are cleared. Creditors are satisfied as animals become available, in order of their importance as entitled kin or affines. Cattle debts are a chronic source of grievance, omissions becoming common knowledge, particularly to those doctors who live in the same village and are often related to the debtors.

The following is a typical case of ghost sickness attributed to the dead kin of the mother's line enforcing their entitlement, and also showing the implication of the woman's husband's kin who failed to satisfy his affines in the bride-wealth transaction.

CASE 1. *Infertility of a Wife and Ailing Children*

The young wife of a Nyayo man failed to conceive after the birth of a daughter who, at the time of the ghost rite, was aged about four. An elder boy of about seven was thin and small for his age, while the four-year-old daughter suffered from recurrent attacks of fever. Senior women of the wife's natal line (Nyarkiteŋ clan) had complained to the husband about the barrenness and the poor health and persuaded him to call a diviner. Divination showed that the wife's natal ancestors, in particular the female collectivity—'the grandmothers'—were responsible. A subsidiary factor was the husband's alleged fault—the fact that the animal earmarked for the wife's maternal kin had been undersized.

The wife's father was responsible for producing the neutered goat (*queto*) for sacrifice to his female ancestors, and one had been selected from among the animals forming part of the original bride-wealth. The ceremony, performed by elders of the woman's lineage, was held in the homestead of the mother, the father's senior wife. The husband's kin were not present since their dead kin were not in question, but the husband attended as a spectator.

When I arrived at sunrise the kin had assembled. Those immediately involved were waiting under the veranda and included the young wife, her father and mother and mother's co-wives with their children, the father's sister who lived close by, and the wife's unmarried sisters. The doctor who had carried out the divination and a sprinkling of older men (father's brother and agnates) completed the group.

The woman's father brought up the sacrificial goat which had been grazing on a tether and pegged it. It urinated and then dropped some dung—a good sign, indicating ready acceptance. The doctor opened the rite by scraping up the urine and dung and throwing them on to the roof of the hut. The young wife and her children, the father's co-wives and their children, and the unmarried sisters, who also wished to benefit, then sat down on a mat facing the doorway of the hut and the tethered goat, and the doctor marked each woman and child on the forehead, chest, and back of the neck, with the urine-soaked earth, and then passed flour from a gourd round the head of the goat and threw some on to the hut roof. Next he passed flour round the heads of each woman and child, again throwing some on to the hut. He spat on a third handful and marked the forehead, back of neck, and chest of all the supplicants and, finally, passed the flour round the heads of the parents, throwing the rest on the goat's back. These ritual passes with excreta from the sacrificial animal and flour or unground grain are protective and identificatory acts. They single out the central supplicants and finally the complete homestead, and identify the animal victim with the patients and their home.

The wife's mother then stood up, scraped together more dung and earth, spat on them, and addressed her female ancestors.

You grandmothers, why do you trouble us? Are we not always killing goats for you? Yet you never help us. Now here is the last of those large goats which are neutered billy-goats and which came to us through the marriage of our daughters here. You must allow us all to have good health, and our women and children. You must also open the body of our daughter, so that she can bear a child and the heart of her husband can rejoice.

She then marked the wife with earth and dung.

During the mother's address the father was sharpening a spear-head and, when she had finished, he and the doctor threw the goat on its side. The infertile wife and the ailing children were made to sit on the goat while the father addressed it and explained the purpose of the sacrifice. The women and children then withdrew and the goat's throat was cut. The blood, used in the cooking of the meat, was carefully caught in a calabash, the carcass was immediately cut up and the ritual parts placed on one side to be eaten in the evening. The feet were cut off for tying to the hut roof 'so that the ghosts would see and be reminded that a goat had been killed for them'. Strips of hide were also cut, for placing round the wrists and necks of the women and children, who wear them as protective amulets.

This rite shows women taking a leading part in ritual and illustrates the significance belonging to female roles. In rites affecting women and children and implicating female ghosts, the mother or grandmother often makes the address, particularly if the ghosts involved are those of the maternal line. When ghost sickness is diagnosed as from a 'grandmother', it can simply mean that the female ancestor collectivity 'want an animal', a legitimate claim because the females are the life-givers. In this case there was said to be additional failure in a bride-wealth transaction. The wife's father mentioned it at the rite, suggesting that as the bull for the maternal kin had been small the husband should find a bull calf for sacrifice to the maternal ghosts. The husband later told me that in his opinion there had been nothing wrong with the animal they were complaining about. At a ghost rite, failure to meet legitimate claims will emerge as cause of the intervention, but kin may also see it as an opportunity to extract something extra and more doubtful claims may be brought up. When short-paid, or poor-quality, bride-wealth is made good, the animal is given to the bride's kin who then kill it for the woman and her children in a ghost rite.

In the next rite I show a female ancestor addressed by two interested descent lines, as a ghostly sister and a ghostly maternal grandmother. I saw this rite among the riverain Köbora, but its inclusion here is justified, I think, because the ghost rites performed in the two areas are very similar.

CASE 2. *Death of a Wife and Child Sickness*

This case concerned a young widower whose wife had died nine months previously, since when he and his children had been unwell. He was a member of the powerful Bukana clan. At this rite, heads of collateral lineages were present because, theoretically, a member of the same clan has a right to attend, although in practice distant kinsmen may not do so.[1]

A beer drinking for the ancestors had been held a few days previously and libations had been poured down. The second part of the divination named a paternal great-grandmother, Azande, for whom an ox was to be slaughtered. For the sacrifice, the male and female elders of the man's clan reassembled, together with elders of a lineage of classificatory mother's brothers, who were involved through Azande, their lineage 'sister', a woman born of their line.

When the rite was about to begin, the sacrificial ox slipped its cord as they were bringing it from the cattle camp. After several hours with no sign of the ox, a small whirlwind spiralled round the homestead scattering dust and forcing people to cover their eyes; heavy clouds, which had been blowing up, gathered over the

[1] Lineages of riverain clans live very close together owing to land shortage along the Nile frontage, in contrast to the open spacing of Mandari clans which allows for the development of autonomy and a tendency with it for lineages not to attend collaterals' sickness rituals.

homestead and rain poured down. The elders decided to postpone the sacrifice as ritual is not performed during storms and several signs—the lost ox, the whirlwind, and the storm—had shown the day to be inauspicious.

The next day we reassembled in the homestead of the paternal uncle with another ox, as it was evident that the patients' own homestead and the first victim had been unacceptable. The first ox had escaped a second time after being recaptured, and had made its way back to the cattle-camp some miles away; the elders therefore substituted a fine 'display-ox'. Now only the extended family, a few clan and lineage elders, and the head of the lineage of classificatory mother's brothers, were present. When the rite was about to begin, it appeared that the widower himself was missing and it eventually began without him. His presence was not essential because the father's brother was officiating (the father being dead). This elder stood up and explained the reason for the rite requesting help from the ancestors:

You, my brothers, today we have come together. This is the second time, because the first time the ox ran off, so we changed it, and brought a display-ox. Our grandfathers and grandmothers have been troubling us. The wife of our son died. The diviner says that the grandfathers and grandmothers are troubling us; that they want beer and a bull. Our grandmother Azande [the ancestress] had twins; she lay and took a child to each breast; she was the wife of our grandfather, and bore many children, so why do our children die today? You, grandmother, why do you trouble us? Are we not always killing goats for you and you never help us?

He then sat down and another elder repeated his words ending up:

Before the coming of the foreign administration people knew how to make sacrifices and address the ancestors, but now all the clans have become mixed up [in the nineteenth-century disturbances] and no one knows who their ancestors really are. In spite of this we have brought an ox for the grandmothers and grandfathers and hope that they will let us rest in peace!

Any closely related elder who so wishes may speak, and on this occasion there were several more addresses.

Then the head of the line standing as mother's brother to the sacrificer's lineage stood up and invoked the woman Azande, born of his line and married into that of the sacrificer.

Our father's sister [Azande] married your people and bore children. All have become ill [referring to the suffering of her descendants]. Our people suffer today. Our sister [again Azande] and her husband must take this bull and beer and they must be quiet and help. The foreigners have spoilt the customs, and no one remembers about the evil eye and people cannot tell which illnesses are from the evil eye and which from the ancestors. Today is the last time of coming about this sickness. We have given you, Azande, and you, so and so, an ox which is a favourite ox (*sönö*), you must help us now as you did in the past!

The ox was then speared (the method used here) and the carcass divided up, portions being set aside for the heads of collateral lineages and for the mother's brother's lineage who also eat the sacrifice for their ancestress.

At this rite the dead woman was addressed by members of two different lines, illustrating the continuing interest of a woman's natal line in her descendants (sister's 'children'), together with the importance of maternal kin as ancestors.

v

When sickness is caused by the disposition of the living, the Mandari conceive of the ancestors as identified with the aggrieved kinsman, and the animal handed over by the defaulter is often killed for the claimant's ancestors instead of being retained. The power to harm, however, is innate in the living claimant and is not simply the power of the ghosts exerted on his behalf. A most important relative whose disposition causes sickness is the mother's uterine brother. In the following case the claims of the living intermesh with those of the dead.

CASE 3. *Sickness of the Son of Magok*

The little son of Magok, an elder of Mandiye lineage was seriously ill (I would guess with pneumonia). His mother, Magok's only wife, had died the previous year and her children were being cared for by Magok's brother's wife. Magok called in two doctors, a woman, whose name I do not know, and the well-known doctor, Nyjok.

Magok is an elder of one of the two extended families into which the powerful Mandiye lineage has divided. Only members of Magok's hamlet, about thirty men and women, were present. Members of the other, and senior, of the two hamlets, under its head Butis Agworoŋ, did not come, the division between the segments being now of long standing.

The woman practitioner had just completed rattle divination and had tentatively diagnosed two causal phenomena, Spirit-of-the-Above, which was hereditary in the family and had a shrine in the brother's homestead, and the lineage ancestors (unspecified).

A ewe and its lamb, already dedicated to Spirit-of-the-Above, were pegged since the dedication from a previous illness was to be reaffirmed so that if the present sickness was from the Spirit, it would see the animals and leave the child: 'Above sees and its heart is favourable' (*Ki ge memet, ko to'ly ge a'nabus*). A large black neutered billy-goat for the dead kin was also pegged. Each animal was appropriate to the symptoms of a causal agent—Ki revealed in coughing and chest pains, and ghost visitation in the feverish condition, the 'hot' body.

Ako, the hamlet head, loosed the black goat and paraded it. It was slow to urinate, and Ako declaimed 'Let the goat urinate, so that we can see the grandfathers have accepted it.' Acceptance is to some extent a formality; it is perfectly legitimate to precipitate the 'sign', as was then done by giving the goat water to drink. Ako scraped up the earth and urine and marked the sick child and its siblings. The goat was then tied up and an elder poured beer over the ewe's peg, addressing Spirit-of-the-Above.

Ako again loosed the goat and led it round addressing the ancestors. After each circuit he stopped in front of the hut and invoked: 'A goat has been given to you, and a sheep also tied down for the Above. You must leave this homestead in peace; the people have been suffering from guinea-worm swellings and sores, then our wife died . . . now our children are ill . . . etc.'

Another elder then held the goat while Ako addressed the dedicated sheep: 'You sheep, you have already been dedicated for Ki, to bear young for Ki. Ki must look upon this fertile sheep and let the homestead prosper, and guard the health of its owners.' Other elders invoked. Ako finally took flour and explained the role assigned to the goat, emphasizing each phrase by throwing a little flour on to the animal's back. It was led round again by Magok, when it urinated a second time, and the child and his siblings were again marked. Eventually Magok ordered it to be killed; it was thrown on its side and before the throat was cut the child was lifted on to its back for a few moments.

Nyjok then arrived from attending the son of Butis Agworoŋ (head of the collateral hamlet), and explained that he had killed a goat for the ghosts and a large sheep for Spirit-of-the-Above. (This child died a few days later.) He examined Magok's son and administered medicine, the woody pulp from the core of a medicine root. Nyjok then intimated that as the sun was high he would

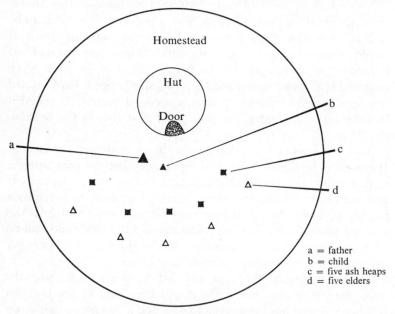

FIG. 8. *Ghost divination*

return and divine in the evening to determine contributory causes. The goat's meat, for eating in the afternoon, was put on to boil and the assembly dispersed.

Before sunset, Nyjok divined. The child was lifted off its mat and seated against one of the hut supports. The ground in front of it was swept and smoothed and five ash heaps placed in a semicircle. The child was lifted into the centre of this, the father seating himself on its right. Branches of *tirioti* (a rain creeper) were split and the forked ends latched on to the backs of the necks of child and father with leaves hanging downwards and the stems pointing up in the air. An elder sat behind each ash heap (Fig. 8). Another poured libations for the ghosts at the hut posts, circled the child's head with the beer, held it against its chest, and finally poured the dregs on the ground. Nyjok, holding a small black chick, squatted facing towards the ash heaps. Each heap stood for a potentially responsible agent:

1. Mother's brother.
2. Spirit-of-the-Above.
3. Kuluŋ—a free Celestial Spirit.
4. A Power.
5. Ancestors.

Pointing the chicken's head at the left-hand ash heap, Nyjok threw a handful of dust on to the bird's head as he addressed the agent. He progressed from heap to heap, smiting the chicken with dust to emphasize his words. At the heap for the ancestors, for instance, he intoned: 'You ancestors, if this illness is from the ancestors let the chicken die here, let it scatter this heap. If the illness is not from this path let it leave the heap.' Each agency was addressed, then the chicken was passed three times round the boy's head while Nyjok recapitulated:

You, Ki; and you, Joksho; and you, ŋutu ko Kak, and Kuluŋ. You, our mother's brother. We have cut a goat for the ancestors, and have dedicated a sheep and its lamb for the Above, you must come out and leave us in peace and return to the place of evil [westwards] and not trouble us any more.

The beak was held open and the child was told to spit in it; beer and flour were added to the spittle. In the centre of the ash heaps a claw was severed with an arrow-head and thrown on to the hut roof; it would later be tied round the boy's neck as an amulet. The head with the beak full of spittle was cut off; later it would be thrown to the west, signifying the consigning of the contaminated spittle to the point of evil. The decapitated body jerked round until it fell on to the heap representing the mother's brother. Everyone laughed and commented on the rightness of the divination. The mother's brother lived in another chiefdom, but it was well known that an animal was owed him from the marriage of Magok's sister (mother's brother/sister's daughter) and therefore it was natural that he should feel irritation. This could make his nephew's son ill, even though he had not voiced his grievance.

The close linking between mother's brother and sister's son is exemplified in the belief that his justifiable anger where his dues have been neglected can cause a nephew's illness or even death.

This capacity carries on to the next generation (great-nephew) as in this case; the mother's brother/sister's son relationship remaining operative for three generations.

I was told that a visit would be made to him because of his 'bad heart' (anger). 'When he hears about the illness and the divination he will come and spit on the child's head', emphasizing his good will; 'My nephew, I have not grumbled against you but if I have had bad and angry thoughts because of my cow, let them be forgotten, and let Creator be with you. May you recover.' When the mother's brother admits his grievance he must be given the outstanding animal to 'cool' his heart.

Because of their power to harm, living kin are put forward at divinations together with spiritual agents, particularly the mother's brother, the grandfather, or father's sister, who are entitled, but are sometimes left out of, bride-wealth distributions because of poverty. Grievance may be suspected even if no complaint is made, or a doctor who follows cattle distributions may expose it. The family may be relieved to face up to the obligation which has become pressing. Many such diagnoses imply tacit recognition of the fact that unless given a time limit, obligations drag on and on, unfulfilled.

When the debt is discharged the animal is dedicated to the receiver's lineage ancestors, killed, and eaten by him and his close kin. In serious illness which shows no improvement, two animals may be recommended, one which joins the receiver's herd, and a barren or neutered goat for sacrifice.

The sacrifice should, if possible, be held in the homestead associated with the ghost or the entitled relative. Exceptions are made when a living person causes sickness and agrees to travel to the patient. When a mother's brother collects his animal from the nephew's home he prays there to his own ancestors, and the animal must urinate to show their acceptance. He then blows a mouthful of water on the nephew's head: blowing water, like spitting, is a conciliatory and protective act. The animal is killed on his return home and there are further addresses: 'Here is your ox brought from our nephew, let them all remain well.' The same procedure is followed when a maternal grandmother is involved.

Sometimes, however, it is considered essential for the patient to reach the homestead associated with the ghost in question. The final decision is made by the doctor, at the divination. On one

occasion when I was travelling to Mount Tindalu in the east of
Mandari, I met a couple with a sick boy whom for three days
they had been carrying for a few hours while it was cool. They
were taking him to his mother's brother as a last resort. The
father admitted 'It is up to Creator now. Perhaps we can reach our
mother's brother and he will kill a goat and our son will get well.'

VI

I now propose to discuss in more detail the kinship roles
carrying entitlements which are most commonly turned up in
ghost ritual, examining those obligations which, if neglected, are
seen to be the cause of sickness.

BROTHER/SISTER

A dead brother may affect his sister through her *children*. Ghost
intervention is likely to follow the failure of his own kin to claim
his entitlement from his sister's marriage. An animal of each
sister's bride-wealth is earmarked for her uterine-linked brother.
A brother does not, of course, receive more than two or three
animals on his linked sister's marriage, and others to secure his
wife come from different sources, but this sister, together with
other sisters and half-sisters, provides the essential nucleus. The
Mandari say that a brother cannot marry and have children without his sister's cattle, and regard a man without sisters as gravely
handicapped.

MOTHER'S BROTHER/SISTER'S SON OR DAUGHTER

When people complete their bride-wealth payments to affines
they are ensuring the health of following generations, because
affines are the people who become maternal ghosts for their
children. The importance of maternal ghosts reflects the importance of the mother and her kin, represented by her brother. The
mother's brother not only receives bride-wealth payments from
the marriages of his sister's daughters, but he in his turn may
help the maternal nephew with marriage cattle. If the father and
father's brothers are dead or cannot provide it, the mother's
brother may give his nephew a display-calf or help to buy his
costly set-beads. Visiting the maternal uncle is a favourite pastime,

and if a father is oppressive a nephew may take up residence with him.

There is a difference, however, between the help available from the maternal uncle and that received from the father. A son has legal rights to property, cattle, and office through the father, but the assistance given by the mother's brother is given from affection; it is a favour, or perhaps more exactly, a moral right. The relationship with the mother's brother is informal and could be likened to that with a natural father. The relationship between nephew and maternal uncle is marked by some permissiveness on the uncle's side.[1] But a nephew must also respect his maternal uncle, whose curse is much feared, while his blessing is particularly beneficial.

A nephew owes some of the same obligations owed to his father to his maternal uncle; for example, if the mother's brother has no male kin, the nephew should inherit his wife.[2] But as the father or father's brother cannot inherit the son's wife, so the mother's brother cannot take the nephew's widow. A dead mother's brother can make a nephew ill, but this power is not reciprocal—the nephew cannot be a ghost for the maternal uncle. Moreover the maternal uncle is not obliged to give the nephew a marriage ox, although he may if he wishes, but he is legally entitled to receive, on the marriage of his maternal niece.

FATHER'S SISTER

A father's sister (*waso*) can be a powerful ghost for her brother's children. In her own lineage she is said to be 'like a man', in that she could have been a male sharing with other brothers in lineage property. A father's sister is respectfully treated and, if she lives near at hand, is a woman elder giving advice in family affairs and rituals. If she lives far away her influence is less strong, because she cannot be constantly consulted; nevertheless, like a man's own sister she remains important, and when she is called in to give her views these carry weight. Her entitlement when a daughter of the lineage marries is a large goat or an ox (as women do not hold animals in their own right, this is for her son), and she may also,

---

[1] This permissiveness relates to the maternal uncle's property which a nephew may beg, borrow, or take. Cattle are not included in this.

[2] I have given examples elsewhere of lines carried on through this kind of link. *Chiefs and Strangers*, pp. 61-2.

because she is 'born of' the lineage, demand meat from her brother's descendants.

PARENTS

Parental ghost intervention occurs where death or mortuary rites have been incorrectly carried out, or where a parent dies during some intense unresolved family quarrel. Parents are unlikely to be brought forward as ghosts in connection with cattle debts, because they, together with a girl's brothers, have the first entitlement, and if they forgo this in favour of another relative, they do this of their own volition, having agreed to it, if reluctantly, at the bride-wealth discussions.

VII

Some categories are excluded from ghost rituals because their roles preclude intervention of this kind.

One such category is the small child. As an informant put it: 'A small child cannot become a ghost and call for meat, because small children are not known; when they get older and are known then they call for meat.' This revealing remark implies that the young lack reciprocal economic and social obligations to and from other members of society. But parents, who are obliged to perform a child's burial correctly, can suffer.

Babies are also not uncommonly thought to become the vengeful agent known as *nyök*, which is particularly feared if a deformed baby has to be exposed. Parents are forbidden to raise a malformed human being, but the course they adopt remains an act against life and carries inbuilt peril. Even the death of a normal infant during delivery can result in *nyök*; implying, perhaps, failure on the part of the parents to preserve the life.

A baby's *nyök* is divided off by an exorcism known as 'settling the *nyök*' (*ŋutu kondi nyök*), which like all exorcisms takes place in the bush. A chicken is held over the heads of the parents while an elder declaims, 'You chicken, take away the "life" of the dead and leave us and our children.' The chicken is killed by 'splitting in half' (*gwalaka*), its body thrown away to the west, and all those present throw up their hands towards sunset, charging evil to depart. This form of exorcism, rather than the more radical destruction of the *nyök* (see p. 255), is used when a blood-relative is involved. A problem may sometimes, therefore, arise as in the case of the sick child (p. 104) where *nyök* symptoms refused to respond to treatment and the doctor told me he feared it might be necessary to destroy the *nyök* (that of a baby sister). He pointed out, 'One is loath to *gorko* the *nyök* of the homestead.'

The possibility of becoming a ghost only exists in relation to blood kin. Lacking these, a dead person has no continuing personality. A client, therefore, is in an anomalous position. He receives 'kinship' in his host's line but he is not the *blood* relative of his host. His own blood kin may be dead, unknown, or left behind in other chiefdoms or countries. Until he marries and leaves descendants, therefore, there is no one whom he can affect as ghost. It is usual for the sickness of a lone client to be attributed to witchcraft or a cult spirit. It is the doctor who reveals the cause, and he is unlikely to name one about which no action can be taken. Over the generations clients build up a network of kinsfolk of their own blood and leave descendants for whom they can become ghosts.

The sickness of a lone traveller cut off from his background also presents a problem, since a person's history is almost essential to diagnosis. The Mandari recognize that a diagnosis made away from home and its spiritual influence is unsatisfactory. If a doctor is consulted he can only diagnose by the procedures familiar to him in his own society.

An instance of a Mandari doctor attempting to treat a non-Mandari visitor involved a man of the Kakwa tribe who was working for me. He admitted that he had called a Mandari doctor who was 'helping' him 'until he could return home'. He had seated him under a shady tree and was swishing leafy branches over him 'to drive away bad influences'; he was also told to sacrifice to the ghost on his return home.

The childless also have a limited range of ghost activity. They may be turned up for a short time after death, in relation to failures in obligation, but they drop out sooner than those leaving descendants. Neither the youth who dies unmarried, nor the dead man whose widow is childless and who refuses an inheritor, are likely to feature much in ghost rites. The Mandari do not readily make 'ghost marriages' but only do so if a lineage is likely to die out, or the family is very rich and the marriage cattle are already accumulated at the time of the death. The Mandari have too few stock for the interests of the dead to be allowed to interfere with those of the living, particularly when there are other sons or brothers waiting to marry. They say that 'The situation is explained to the dead man at the mortuary ceremony to prevent him feeling aggrieved.'

The childless have no one following after them to keep their memory alive, and their names in time drop out of clan genealogies. It is said of a man who has no children or sisters, and whose close collaterals have all died—a man who can never be a grandfather or mother's brother—that he cannot become a ghost because 'There is no one to provide him with meat.' After repeated deaths, the ancestors are rebuked at sacrifices: 'How will you find meat if you kill us all, who will bring you oxen; will you call for meat from people of the bush [the unrelated]?'

VIII

Though the Mandari differentiate between ghosts and lineage ancestors, lineage ancestors include those dead who are externalized as individual ghosts. When a person speaks of 'the ancestors' (*ɲutu ko kak*), or the 'grandfathers and grandmothers', he generally has in mind ancestors of the patrilineage, for it is down the male line that cattle—the status-giving economic possession—chiefly office, and legal rights pass.

Female ancestors cannot reflect a structural group comparable to the male lineage, a fact arising from the realities of a woman's social position. Women gain prominence and influence as *individuals*, as diviners or seers, as mothers of numerous children, or simply as personalities in their own right—they do not hold roles of structural importance, whether these be kinship or political ones. A woman's influence after death, while very important in that female ghosts are more frequently evoked than those of men, tends to symbolize the idea of motherhood and fertility, and it is when these central principles seem to be threatened that the female ghost image emerges. The male ancestor, on the other hand, who is remembered *beyond* the relevant event for living memory, importantly symbolizes the actual continuity of the lineage.

The ghost intervention belongs within the context of the important three-generation grouping, which, as I pointed out when discussing Mandari notions of time, reflects the normal range of memory. The Mandari say, 'One forgets; we have

forgotten the early ancestors, the people of old—they are finished.
They cannot call for meat because they had their meat from our
grandfathers. It is to them [the more recently dead] that we now
give meat.'

The Mandari are very conscious of the three-generation grouping
and of the way in which it is stepped backwards in time, so that an
older generation's obligations extend one generation further back
than do those of a younger generation. They see their earlier
ancestors as bound up with their parents' and grandparents'
generations, who, in turn, are the dead with whom they themselves
are linked and whose names they bring forward in divination.
At different levels in the patrilineage groups of living and dead are
bound together in obligation groupings. After the dead person
moves out of the currently significant grouping, the obligations to
him are either completed, forgotten, or irrelevant.

Because of this, at most ghost rituals the only people directly
concerned are the extended family composed of three generations.
If a grandfather is sick, however, the group enlarges, because to
address the patient's father or grandfather lineage elders, who may
be heads of lineages soon to be divided, or newly divided-off
collaterals, may have to be brought in. It is usual for the person
invoking to be senior to the patient, and in big rites affecting older
people a whole lineage or even a small clan can come together in
order that all important elders may invoke. Even if they are not
actually taking part, senior lineage elders are entitled to attend.

While, therefore, ghost rites are essentially rites of the extended
family, representatives of the total lineage may attend them,
particularly when the lineage is occupying a single village site.
When lineages have divided into large segments occupying
different hamlets (as in the Mandiye case described on pp. 168 ff.),
other segments may not attend. This is particularly true of large
landowning clans, whose lineages link together more than six
generations back, and where the founder ancestors of each lineage
are too remote to feature as ghosts. The composition of the group
attending ghost rituals is a reflection of the size and pattern of
segmentation of a particular lineage and clan.

Certain rites are addressed to the lineage collectivity as a whole.
The killing of the 'ox-of-the-ancestors' (*tey na ŋutu ko kak*) when
a woman of the natal line marries is the most important, and
should be performed shortly after the tying-on of the goat-skins of

married status. After this ceremony, known as *laka*, the bride lives under the care of her husband's mother or senior wife. The couple should not sleep together until after the ox of her lineage ghosts has been sacrificed. In anticipation of this ceremony and of the arrival of the husband's female relatives and age-mates the girl's natal kin brew beer, collect baskets of grain, and assemble basic household utensils.

The young couple return together to the bride's home accompanied by the husband's age-mates leading the ox. Senior women of his lineage including his own mother, mother's co-wives, married sisters, grandmothers, and paternal aunts, 'come to listen and to receive meat'. On arrival the party drink beer. The husband sits apart and does not drink. He takes no part because the ceremony known as 'the son-in-law's *laka*' (*laka na komyit*), which allows him to eat and drink in the mother-in-law's homestead, will not be performed for many years. The husband's mother is presented with a goat, or an equivalent in money. The visitors stay the night and, in the early morning, the husband's age-mates hand over the ox-of-the-ancestors. This is then killed for the bride's lineage ancestors.

Before the slaying, the bride's senior kinsman stands among the assembled women affines and his own relatives, and addresses his ancestors:

You, O grandfathers, and you, O grandmothers, and you also our father [named] here is your cow [ox], and now that this daughter of ours has been launched in marriage with cattle let her continue healthy and in peace. Let her bowels prosper and may she be fruitful.

The young wife is brought forward and splashed with water and anointed on the back of the neck and the chest with sesame oil for 'coolness'. The elder parades the ox until it urinates, while he addresses the ancestors. A portion of the unclassified meat is given to the husband's female kin and age-mates who roast it in the bush. The back ribs (*polyot*) are boiled and hidden in the back of the hut. This ritual 'meat of the Below' (*lokore na Kak*) is reheated next day and eaten by the wife's lineage elders.

When the husband and his entourage return home, the wife stays behind to collect together the pots of food and the utensils for her marital homestead. When she returns there the couple sleep together; sexual intercourse before the ceremony is seen to lay the wife's male relatives open to *mönöjin*. A husband and wife nowadays may cohabit after the bride's *laka*, a departure often given as a cause of the illness of the bride's male kin or her own barrenness.

The ancestors' entitlement to lineage cattle is expressed in terms of receiving meat: 'They must have meat up there as well, so they hover around and send omens or people become sick.' This statement is an acceptance of the fact that herds were founded by earlier generations while being maintained and increased by succeeding ones. A doctor who does not know the details of a family's background, will often diagnose sickness in terms of this right, saying simply, 'The dead [all ancestors] want meat.'

The dead are also said to communicate through dreams, although dreams are not acted upon without expert interpretation. One in which a dead relative makes a request, or a group of important dead kin assemble suggesting a discussion, may be an omen. The following is an example of a young man (the son of the chief of Dari's brother) acting on his own judgement after such a dream. He mentioned to me on one occasion that he had just arrived back in the village after spearing an ox for his grandmother in the cattle-camp. The killing was to do with a dream, in which he had seen his dead grandmother standing by his cattle fire. She had asked, 'How is it I see all these cows, and you have not killed one for me?' Next morning he had speared an ox and tied the horns to a pole. 'My grandmother slept in my head,' he explained, 'saying "Where is my cow?" How else could I act as I was far away on the grassland?' As the son of a rich landowner, he reasoned that it was better to act immediately than to wait and risk sickness breaking out among the herders or the cattle.

His action was, perhaps, untypical. A poorer man would have been less hasty and would have consulted a doctor in the hope that beer libations would be prescribed and the expense of a sacrifice avoided. Spearing the animal was also unusual, perhaps even incorrect (killing in the ritual is by cutting the throat); but it conformed to the practice in cattle-camps, where cattle are killed in connection with young people's activities.

The pouring of beer libations on the hearth is another way of sharing with the dead. The wife addresses the ancestors as she pours, 'Here is your beer, let us rest in peace.' Soup (*sigwor*)—the water in which the meat offered to individual ghosts is cooked—is also poured inside the hut against the back wall (a place of ritual significance, associated with Creator as Spirit-of-the-Below and with the husband as the living representative of the ancestral line), at the hut supports, and at the corners of paths leading into the homestead. A short address accompanies the libation: 'Here is your meat, let us remain in peace.'

Nowadays, when a Mandari may volunteer for the police force or the army, a man returning home on retirement will kill an ox or brew beer for the ancestors, the officiating elder explaining that the serviceman is now returning to live among his kin and to renew his relationship with his lineage ancestors, from whom he has been separated and to whom he has been unable to make offerings during his absence.[1]

IX

The importance of ancestor cults in relation to systems of social control has been demonstrated for a number of African societies. They may provide the greater part of the machinery of authority, particularly in societies with non-centralized political systems, or they may reinforce this machinery.[2] Mandari beliefs about dead kin cannot be said to have a social or political function of this kind. Commemoration of the lineage ancestors certainly embraces the idea of lineage strength and continuity, but this does not play so large a part in Mandari life as do ghost rites, which primarily stress concepts of obligation and indebtedness.

The emphasis on obligation rather than authority in ghost rituals arises partly from the structure of Mandari society. The Mandari have a relatively developed political system, at least at the level of the chiefdom where diverse and, to some degree, authoritarian forms of control are found. Institutions like the meeting-tree, the politico-religious office of *Mar*, and the band of loyal clients embody real elements of potential coercion. Other pressures

---

[1] I attended the reintegration feast given by Anok Pilari when he came home to assume the office of chief of Dari. He had been a sergeant-major in the police; he retired when his brother Korondo's ill-health forced him to relinquish office. Anok killed an ox during the beer-drinking.

[2] On this aspect of the ancestor cult, three books are perhaps of particular importance: M. Fortes, *The Web of Kinship among the Tallensi* (London, 1949); J. Middleton, *Lugbara Religion* (London, 1960); J. Goody, *Death, Property and the Ancestors* (London, 1962); and M. Fortes, 'Pietas in Ancestor Worship', in his collection of essays, *Time and Social Structure and Other Essays*, L.S.E. Monographs on Social Anthropology (London, 1970).

for conformity derive from vital economic self-interest and from the fact that, although the Mandari are a basically egalitarian people, clients and non-landowners occupy dependent positions which imply a certain degree of subordination.

Within the family, authority is not autocratic. A father cannot be said to wield absolute authority even over his own children. The responsibility for bringing up children belongs to the family as a whole and father, mother, and elder siblings each have important parts to play. Authority on the paternal side is spread over a group of males (grandfather, father's brothers, father, and elder brothers) whose power is based on exercising control over cattle. Any of these males can use coercion, but other kin have influence which can temper or check their power. The chief weapon of authority in the family is control over cattle, which gives control over marriage, and authority is seen to be exercised mainly in directing young people's choice of spouse. Girls are subject to greater coercion than men in this respect, but a young man also depends on the goodwill of his kin to make his marriage possible by assisting with cattle.

Outside the crucial marriage context family relationships are seldom authoritarian. The father–son relationship is affectionate; a Mandari father is not a repressive, cold, remote figure, commanding excessive respect—although there is respect. Certain fathers may, indeed, be repressive, but this is their individual character and others have power to modify its effect. The point of conflict is often in the brother–brother relationship, because although in theory brothers are friendly equals a struggle for position and property may show itself here and in mythology it is conflicts between older and younger brothers that are represented.

Within the agnatic group which exercises rights over the cattle-herd, the grandfather may override a father's wishes in relation to his son's or daughter's marriage, or he may buttress the father's authority. I have seen both happen in conflicts over marriage. The influence of senior women also cannot be discounted. The father's sister and the mother, for instance, are often a girl's powerful champions.

For a girl's marriage, the elder adult brothers are virtually equal in importance with the father. By the time a daughter marries, her father has usually made his second and last marriage (except in the case of chiefs and rich men) and it is the girl's brothers who become the interested parties. Pressures often come from brothers, because girls' marriages affect brothers' marriages rather than fathers', particularly the marriage of the linked elder brother. This brother also looks after his younger sister and is responsible in relation to her suitors and lovers, the parents being less likely to interfere.

The manner in which property is allocated among members of a family also helps to inhibit oppressive authority. Sons often begin to acquire their own cattle from the moment of birth. These will be: (i) mother's animals—cattle given to his mother on the marriage of an older uterine sister, or to his mother as 'father's wife' on the marriage of his older half-sisters, and held in trust for him; (ii) cattle given to his mother as 'married sister', when a sister of hers marries, and held in trust for him; (iii) cattle given to him as mother's brother on the marriage of his older sister's daughter. The progeny of these animals increases and a boy should have a nucleus of marriage cattle and a display-ox when he reaches maturity. None the less he will need extra help, and here he depends upon his father, grandfather, and father's sister. There is usually, however, no overwhelming sense of frustration, of having to step into father's shoes in order to reach full and relatively economically free maturity, in spite of the fact that in the last resort senior agnates can block his ambition if they make a common stand.

An individual also has rights in his mother's natal line, and maternal kin provide escape in intolerable conflict with agnates. The tie with the mother's kin is woven into daily life and strengthened by constant visiting. The paternal line is, of course, the one of first preference because it alone gives full legal status. Position in the mother's lineage derives from the original brother–sister relationship, and from the fact that, even after marriage, a woman remains a member of her own descent line. Her fertility, her female labour, and certain legal rights over her person are indeed acquired by the husband, but her own rights in her lineage remain. She may be reclaimed by her brothers if her husband ill-treats her, and in certain circumstances a woman's mother's brother can receive her adultery payment. If a marriage breaks up, a woman takes up her full rights in her lineage again, 'A sister is never refused back.'

The affection and permissiveness associated with the mother's brother's role in Mandari is not counterbalanced by sternness in the father's sister's role.[1] The father's sister (*waso*) is one of the most important females of the agnatic line, but her authority is part of a wider authority exercised jointly by her mother and by senior women married into the descent line. A man's own older married sisters are also influential in his affairs as I showed in my account of the mortuary rite on pp. 141–2. The father's sister is one of the group referred to as *ŋutu nago*, 'female elders', which includes grandmothers, married sisters, and the wives of senior agnates. The father's sister, backed up by these latter, can help to cross her nephew's interests in a way a mother's brother cannot do and has no interest in doing because he is not a member of the nephew's legal descent line. Which illustrates the universal truth that coercion is more effective if backed by legal powers. Residence with a father's sister does not offer the same advantages to a man in conflict with his kin, since she is a member of the same group and may side with her brothers, the complainants' paternal uncles.

Affines may also provide a man with economic security. Support from an affinal line cannot be entirely relied on, because a marriage can break up, but deep affection often exists between a son-in-law and the wife's people. If refused help by all these groups, a man irreconcilably alienated from his agnates may be forced to accept client affiliation.

Because authority is not exclusively vested in any single agency, dead kin rituals do not reflect the authority of the father role as they have been shown to do for some societies. The absence of cult shrines, which can become points of dominance, further militates against the growth of an authoritarian ancestor cult. In societies where shrines are held and administered by a senior lineage male, a person's actions are circumscribed by the necessity of retaining good relations with those whose prayers are essential to religious and physical health.

Indebtedness and obligation are the predominant themes revealed in Mandari dead kin beliefs and rituals; above all, the concept of debt arising from marriage between unrelated parties. The affinal network becomes a maternal network for the children of a marriage, and it is through their health and sickness that payment is stimulated. It would not be an exaggeration to say that many marriage payments are settled because ghost sickness is diagnosed.

[1] As claimed by Radcliffe-Brown. See 'The Mother's Brother in South Africa', in *Structure and Function in Primitive Society* (London, 1952).

Those who are kin, either by blood or by affinity, try to avoid litigating about property with the ill-feeling it causes, but a creditor's patience is not inexhaustible while the vicissitudes of life and the precariousness of a livestock economy make frequent default or procrastination inevitable. The idea of the ghost intervention helps to ensure that debts will be paid eventually and that the consciousness of unfulfilled obligation will not prey on the minds of either creditor or debtor to the impairment of social harmony.

6

DEDICATION, BLESSING, AND RITUAL MEDIA

THE Mandari perform simple dedications and acts of blessing to secure the maximum protection for an individual by placing him under the direct care of Creator. The aim is the physical and spiritual adjustment of the personality and freedom from danger and sickness.

An initial act of dedication takes place at the naming ceremony of an infant. This is the moment when the child is presented to the community. I do not describe the naming here, but would simply mention the final act of 'clapping the child upward', when the married women taking part in the ceremony dance up to the baby where it is lying in its mother's lap, intoning as they do so, 'Your name is so and so', followed by the words 'May you reach to the sky' (*kokokobo yas ki*). This phrase carries the much wider implications of being strong, vigorous, aspiring, striving towards the good. As they sing, the women clap with an upward movement.

I have described the complementary acts of dedication and consignment as the dead person is finally laid in the grave. In between, the passage from birth to death may be marked by changes which require religious emphasis. Thus when a family moves to a new homestead, or when a husband and wife build for the first time, the new homestead is dedicated at a small rite for which beer is brewed. This is drunk in the homestead and libations poured on the hearth for the dead kin; prayers are also offered to Creator for peace and health.

Before a long journey which is not simply a routine move, especially one involving absence from Mandari-land, the traveller is protectively marked by members of his family with the standard flour or unground grain mixed with sesame oil, the substance being passed round the traveller's head while prayers are offered to Creator for a safe journey and eventual return. Forehead, chest, and back of the neck are then marked with the substance. Prayers offered take the form of short impromptu petitions: 'Let all evil be far from you: let it go to the west; let all good things come to you from the east; may Creator go with you and may you sleep peacefully and return safely to us.' Other senior persons in the household may also petition.

Other impromptu blessings require no assembly nor the use of ritual media. They are the spontaneous acts of friends or kinsmen which arise out of some casual and unexpected encounter; for example, protective marking by a friend or kinsman at a chance meeting, the marking of a departing visitor, the marking of a nephew whom the mother's brother meets in the path, or the mutual marking of two friends who meet briefly and part. The one in the senior role marks the junior—the mother's brother the nephew—the two friends reciprocally mark each other. A short prayer under the breath accompanies the gesture. But these gestures, which can be made at any time and only affect the persons concerned, are an important part of personal religion. The only media used are spittle or dust or sand from the path; efficacy does not depend on place, position, medium, or the presence of ritual functionaries. People bless each other because they are linked by bonds of affection and friendship and, in many cases, by kinship as well. The direct appeal to Creator is in line with the belief that 'Anyone may call on Creator at any time.'

The word for ritual marking is *buk*, a special rendering of the ordinary word *buk*, 'to pour': hence also *bukusi*, 'to pour down'—as in a libation—and the common phrase, *ŋutu bubuk bok*, 'they mark each other'.[1] Marking, as I have shown, is also a part of more formal ritual. It accompanies, or follows, rites offered to Spirits and Powers or Ancestors and sacrifices made for sin cleansing. When it follows the rite it implies protection at dispersal. A sick person may also be marked at the rite itself with a variety of different media—flour, homestead-dust, beer, oil, or the urine and droppings of the sacrificial animal. Close relatives of the patient and those taking part may also be marked.

Markings then are integral to the rite and each may represent something different: they may be for protection and for affirming harmony between the person and the particular spiritual power involved, or to show the reintegration of the individual alienated by sickness or sin from spiritual health. There is also the stated objective of bringing

---

[1] The word *buk* is used by Nuer for acts of a similar kind (Evans-Pritchard, *Nuer Religion*, p. 262). In Mandari *buk* does not have the additional meaning 'to sacrifice', nor can it be said to be an act of consecration (ibid., p. 261).

the patient and the sacrificial animal together, an identification achieved by using a single ritual medium which is passed round the patient's head and then sprinkled on the sacrificial animal, or by the use of the animal's urine for the marking of the supplicant.

Ritual media can be roughly graded according to efficacy. Ritual oils and beer aside, those with a food basis like flour (*'bot*) and unground mixed grain (also *'bot*, or more precisely *cima*), stand highest. Their substitute is homestead-dust or dust from a path (*kurun*). Charcoal (*kuksho*) from the homestead hearth has protective qualities (for marking children, sufferers from nightmares, etc.). The standard equivalent for all these in cattle-camps is dung-ash (*phulö*) from the cattle-hearth.

Mention must finally be made of the ritual spitting to which I have referred in connection with departures, meetings, and the termination of rites. Spitting is an act of blessing and affords protection because spittle represents the offering of the living moisture of the one who spits; an association based on the division of the human body into 'moisture' ('water', with its rain equivalence) and 'flesh' or matter. Fluids from the body have inherent virtue (see the urine of sacrificial animals). But even the splashing of water alone has 'cooling', beneficial effects, consequently the sap of creepers with a high water content has therapeutic properties.

A real distinction must be drawn between ritual spitting and spitting which simply clears the mouth of tobacco juice or an unpleasant taste. Ordinary spitting is not a conventional act of hostility; none the less no Mandari would intentionally spit in this way at another person or on possessions.[1] In ritual spitting, the blesser does not in fact spit in the ordinary sense. He narrows his lips and with the tongue between the teeth emits a fine spray with a blowing action which falls on to the recipient's head. A similar action is used to blow cooling water by the individual whose 'hot' disposition has caused sickness.

Although water is described as 'dead' (inert), it is the pre-eminently 'cool' medium. Apart from its wide use for directly 'cooling heat', it is essential for the cooking of ritual meat which must be boiled to prevent it from coming into direct contact with fire. The water cools the heat of the cooking and maintains the essential qualities of the meat, destroyed by roasting.

[1] The Mandari assume spittle to be 'refuse'; it is one of the things which fowls pecking around the homestead are said to clear up.

PART II
PERSONAL IDENTITY

7

CREATORS AND DESTROYERS

I

THE Mandari phrase 'to commit an offence' or 'to commit a wrong' (*konda tönaron*), can be translated in one of its meanings as 'to commit a sin'.[1]

Ultimately, however, sin in the sense in which it will be defined here cannot be distinguished from other kinds of wrong or fault simply on the basis of the Mandari terminology alone, since all the acts I class as 'sin' are not necessarily referred to as *tönaron*, and further, the word is used in its more general sense to describe behaviour which falls outside the specific sin classification, but which is regarded as serious or involves a sense of moral outrage.

Sin as a particular kind of action can more exactly be defined in the Mandari context by reference to its *results*, that is, by the fact that a sin brings into action a specific ritual sanction, a point clearly made by Evans-Pritchard for the Nuer, and a distinction I find convenient to follow here.[2] The minor sins which carry this inbuilt sanction will be considered here under the one heading with the more serious sins (*tönaron*), since all belong to a single body of ideas which form a theoretical category of central importance and deep emotional significance for the Mandari. To the extent that the serious sins are seen as direct transgressions against Creator, they have a correspondence to more universal notions of sin.

---

[1] *Tönaron*, having the sense of 'wrongness', 'badness', 'violation', derives from the adjective *laron* 'bad', and the adverb *anaron* 'badly' or 'wrongly'.

[2] Evans-Pritchard, *Nuer Religion*, p. 177.

It is necessary also to distinguish a further and related, but ultimately distinct, condition, namely the state of pollution, which likewise leads to adverse ritual effects. Since the Mandari, together with Nilotics in general, would seem to have fairly few pollutions, but complex sin concepts, I will first deal briefly with pollution.[1] Using 'pollution' in the restricted sense of conceptual or physical defilement, the Mandari consider certain acts polluting.[2] None of these is a sin. Pollution, in terms of the physically and ritually defiling, adheres to certain unavoidable human states, and does not necessarily result from a breach of religious ideology, from moral wrong, or from faulty action. Cleansing from pollution is also not the same as sin cleansing. Most pollutions centre around death, particularly tasks like grave-digging. Close relatives, homestead possessions, and food, are automatically polluted by a death, as I have shown. A degree of pollution also attaches to the situation of being born and to giving birth, particularly to twinning.[3]

While cleansings, washings, or disposal of polluted materials have a ceremonial and symbolic character, being concerned with the removal of spiritual dirt from the psyche as well as the physical dirt of an exterior condition, these acts lack the distinguishing features of sin cleansings, like confession. Pollution and sin both involve elements of separation and ordering but they are not identical.

While the Mandari have few pollutions, sin and the ritual peril consequent on it relate to a wide category of behaviour. The results of sin are typically revealed in the sickness or accident which often manifests itself in persons other than the one committing the offence. The idea involved here is not that of contagion in the sense of a spreading from a single impure source, but of the by-passing of the source (the sinner) and the manifestation of the ill-effects in another person, usually one connected by some kind of social or biological link.

It is true, of course, that sin also pollutes the sinner, leading to

---

[1] Evans-Pritchard explicitly states this (ibid., p. 317), and Lienhardt implicitly supports it in *Divinity and Experience*.

[2] Mary Douglas has recently introduced a much broader definition of pollution, extending the term to cover all aspects of behaviour governed by principles of avoidance, or separation, the violation of which ('crossing the boundary') is seen to lead to automatic peril or harm. Mary Douglas, *Purity and Danger* (London, 1966), *passim*.

[3] Cf. pp. 244 ff.

the need for cleansing, and many Mandari sins require public confession and the 'marking' of the sinner with ritual oil: serious sin, or sin involving certain categories of person, may require animal sacrifice in addition. An accumulation of unspecified sin inhering in the human situation may also need special elimination. This is clearly demonstrated when, in the transitional period prior to the taking up of a new role or status (chieftainship, wifehood, and so forth), it is symbolically washed away with water. The pollution of the former condition is one of the themes dealt with in all preparations for new states, but it would be an oversimplification to see these ceremonies concerned with the assumption of new roles simply as pollution rituals.

While those actions which constitute sin do not correspond in all societies, and while the mechanisms for dealing with the effects of sin also differ, a common element may often be present in the idea of sin as the ideological violation. The act of sinning varies with the particular ideology, thus actions which appear quite trivial when looked at from another cultural standpoint may be seen to be crucial transgressions of central doctrines in their context. I shall be considering a number of such apparently trivial misdemeanours and show how they are actions violating important theories of being and so become direct contradictions of the principles or 'laws' seen by the Mandari to operate widely in the universe, nature, and in man. Such apparently minor transgressions dangerously offend against the structure of the Mandari world order, and it is only in relation to this background of theory and belief that their significance becomes clear.

In the Mandari context, sin involves the awareness of committing an offence; it is almost impossible for a Mandari to sin unknowingly.[1] A sin is therefore by definition a deliberate act, although one the sinner may regret and from the effects of which he may hope to escape. The element of awareness is one of the criteria by which sin can be differentiated from failures in the human–spirit relationships already dealt with. In those relationships there may be no fault or intention; it is only when the cult relationship has already

---

[1] Even incest, which among some peoples can be committed unintentionally because a couple do not know they are related, is unlikely to be unwitting among the Mandari because of the nature of clan structure. If peripheral kinship was involved and was not known, it would be unlikely that it would be known by others; the diviner for instance, would be unlikely to put it forward as a causal explanation in sickness.

been established that failure and neglect may arise. Sins on the contrary are acts of commission which lead to automatic results because of the nature of the religious law; in the cult relationships the action of a spirit leads to human response. Sin also requires purification, whereas cleansing, confession, and reinstatement have no place in cult relationships and the sicknesses that belong with them.

Serious sins are described as 'angering Creator' (Ŋun *wawaran*), as 'things Creator abhors' (Ŋun *maman*). Of those committing incest or killing within the elementary family, for instance, it is said, 'Creator cannot allow such people to remain.'

II

At the heart of the Mandari notion of sin is the destructive act seen to destroy creativity in man and nature. Sins therefore revolve around offences by creative categories, or offences against them, and around those acts which are seen to kill in one sense or another. Sins are not primarily faults of character, nor acts which are socially wrong.

Since a central Mandari preoccupation is the promotion and perpetuation of all forms of life, it is not surprising that actions assumed to affect adversely procreation and fertility are prominent sins. An important class of sin involves women, the supreme life-bearers and creators. Landowning chiefs are another creative category which may be sinned against, and included here is the rain, the main preoccupation of the chief's creative powers.

I shall begin by considering those sins relating to women, but would first emphasize that women are one of those categories which may be referred to as '*pötö*'. This word, which has a wide meaning, can in one of its senses be most closely rendered by the word 'potent' (in its noun form, '*töpötö*', 'potency').[1] But when in relation to certain persons the potency is seen to be something more than a purely material strength, I shall then describe it as 'psychic force'. The potency of women and landowning chiefs is of this order, and perhaps also the potency of certain animals (pp. 251 ff.). When '*pötö*' is used to describe the effectiveness of doctors and

---

[1] Etymologically, *pötö* is an adjective meaning 'bitter', 'sour' (to the taste): 'sarcastic', 'cutting', 'forceful' (of speech). As a word to describe affective states, it means 'harsh', 'malignant', or 'dangerously aggressive'.

their stronger medicines, something similar is also involved, as is also the case with the opposing human ritual power, the destructive force of witches and sorcerers. Psychic force generally implies a combination of the power to create and the power to kill.

The minutely elaborated rules which protect female fertility are recognized by Mandari as hard to observe and frequently violated. Since many of these rules aim to control and regulate the powerful instincts of sex, they can also be approached from the point of view of male–female relationships. Without a man, a woman cannot use her latent creativity, and for this reason men are the chief participants in many classes of female sin.

Harmful male–female relationships, whether dealt with under the definition of sins or pollutions, have generally been approached in anthropological analysis from the standpoint of the marital relationship. In Mandari, the marital relationship is only one of a number which must be brought under scrutiny. They are:

(1) Father/Daughter   (4) Mother/Daughter
(2) Brother/Sister   (5) Man/Woman (Unrelated)
(3) Husband/Wife   (6) Woman to close male agnates, other than father or brothers

In relationships 1, 2, 3, and 6, the woman is the affecting party in the sense that her sinful action harms her linked male or males. In 5, the woman is the affected party, the male action harming the woman or her child. In 4, mother affects daughter, stressing the mother, who transmits life and fertility.

Regarding the first three (the ones most commonly involved), it is difficult to say categorically which one turns up most frequently in the sin context in real life situations. From personal observation, however, the brother–sister link seems the one most commonly evoked in actual sicknesses and accidents, with the husband–wife relationship following closely. This can be explained by the fact that most female sexual misdemeanours tend to coincide with the period of years between puberty and marriage.[1] After marriage, a woman's sexual behaviour chiefly affects her husband and will be interpreted within the marital situation.

The incidence of 6 (the woman affects lineage agnates) is less

---

[1] The Mandari view immature marriage with great distaste. Girls marry some years after physiological maturity, and while the most attractive marry young—around fifteen or sixteen—unmarried girls of at least eighteen to nineteen can be found. There is, therefore, a long period of free circulation and courtship.

common, and will tend to occur where the girl is under the guardianship of one of these relatives because other kin are dead.

The ritual peril known as *mönöjin* links a woman and one of her male relatives. The word itself denotes both the offence committed and the accident or proneness to sickness which follows it. One of the main sources of *mönöjin* is illicit sexual intercourse, and technically this offence can only be committed by a woman. This does not mean that male promiscuity passes without moral censure, far from it; but a man cannot *sin* by a sexual misdemeanour because a man is non-creative.

The perils follow from fornication, adultery, and incest, and from the incorrect performance of marriage rituals, and affect men linked to the woman in the relationships charted above.[1] A woman in *mönöjin* is doubly dangerous if the male relative is already sick or infirm. The guilty man and woman themselves do not suffer the effects, neither are the kin of the man harmed. Because women and not men are the source of *mönöjin*, the effects devolve on the woman's kin only. Before marriage a girl's fertility belongs to her brothers and father and these are the people most harmed. After her marriage, at which the husband acquires right over her fertility, potential dangers pass over to him, and a married woman's adultery is very dangerous to her husband, who is seen to be particularly vulnerable.

Apart from the fact that *mönöjin* is incurred, fornication and adultery are considered wrong because they are disruptive, they arouse hatred and grievance, and attract public censure.

The Mandari represent young girls as the most frequent offenders, and this may indeed be true. During their teens they are freely meeting young men and the temptation to have a romantic affair is often strong, particularly if the man's social position or his lack of cattle preclude marriage for a long time, or altogether. Girls' secret liaisons are believed to be at the root of much male indisposition, since the sickness and accident-proneness can become chronic with the girl continuing her harmful relationship. If an offence is suspected, various pressures are used to extract confession. The confession is also vital to the girl herself who must also be purified.

---

[1] Incest falls into a special class of heinous sin, with fratricide, parricide, and the killing of a son by a father. As well as spreading *mönöjin*, like all unregulated sex, incest kills in a very special way.

While it is primarily the men of her elementary family who are exposed to danger by a girl's behaviour, remoter lineage relatives may suffer. It is logical that the brother should become the first aim of a sister's actions because there is seen to be a profound brother/sister interdependency, particularly between linked siblings 'born of one mother'. In a special way, this sister ensures her brother's posterity; he also looks after her and is largely responsible for her until she marries; after this he has special duties to her children. Brothers cannot marry without their sisters' cattle, and other agnates like father's brothers (and the father, for his later marriages) receive animals on her marriage. Thus the results of *mönöjin* seldom spread beyond those males who are potentially entitled under the girl's marriage.

The following example shows the typical reactions and the results which are believed to follow. While *mönöjin* generally shows in minor sicknesses and accidents, a case of fornication which occurred near the village in which I was living was put forward as a cause of death. The youth's death occurred while a dispute was in progress over the seduction of his father's brother's daughter by a youth of a lineage attached to his clan. The dead man's older brother attempted to claim homicide compensation. The court hearing the charge of seduction ruled his claim far-fetched and refused it.

Accidents following *mönöjin* include attacks and woundings by wild animals, snake and scorpion bites, falls, and sprained limbs. The Mandari say in explanation, 'Lions, elephant, and buffalo do not usually attack; when they do there may be a reason for it.' Accidents may coincide with disclosures of offences and the next two examples show such coincidental accidents interpreted in this way where an illicit affair was common knowledge.

The first case involved the son of the chief whom I had treated for a scorpion bite. Later he returned saying his foot was worse, and explained that the whole course of events had been provoked by *mönöjin*. He pointed out that a bite is only painful for a while and then the pain wears off. He reminded me that his sister had shortly before been discovered with a lover, who to make things worse was distantly related on the maternal side, thus a form of incest was involved. He added bitterly that had there been a wild beast about no doubt he would have been mauled.

Another case involved a townsman of the Kakwa tribe who

wished to marry a Mandari girl but encountered strong opposition. During the recriminations he admitted having slept with her. The girl was an orphan and lived with her father's brother's son, a professional elephant hunter. There was delay in hearing the case and her guardian went hunting. While stalking he climbed a tree and when the branch on which he was standing broke, he fell, was badly bruised, and narrowly missed cutting himself with his elephant spear. He complained to me that as an experienced hunter and climber he never fell and it was obvious that the branch did not break by chance, particularly as he was nearly impaled, and demanded a black goat for the girl's purification.

Cleansing has two objectives; the elimination of the *mönöjin* and safeguarding of the woman's male kin or husband, and the purification of the sinner herself. While the woman cannot suffer from *mönöjin*, her act is dangerously self-destructive in other ways. Her body is 'hot' (*mugan tomaka*), and heat is contrary to health, fertility, and correct personality orientation. The heat of anger and grievance and the heat created by the discussion of her sin also harm the woman and must be eliminated by public confession. Uncleansed she may later be barren or the children she bears may die.

At the purification the elders splash sesame oil on the woman's chest, forehead, and the back of the neck, while exhorting the wrongdoing, grievances, and angry words to 'come out' so that the girl and her kin may be reorientated and 'continue in health and peace'. When the results of the sin are serious or have affected another sensitive category like a landowning chief, a black sheep provided by the male offender is also divided longitudinally. The meat is eaten by the elders and anyone who has been a victim of the sin. The girl herself abstains, because a sinner never eats the meat of his or her own purification.[1] Harm can also result from legitimate marital sexual intercourse if a series of ceremonies marked by the exchange of gifts between the two affinal groups has been neglected. The first of these ceremonies is the husband's visit to honour his mother-in-law.

This ceremony, 'the bringing of the goat to the mothers-in-law'

---

[1] Mandari may refer to this sheep as '*the goat of mönöjin*'. A doctor insisted, however, that this animal must be a sheep 'because goat's blood is "hot" and unsuitable for purification when "coolness" is the objective'. When the Mandari say 'a goat', they are indicating an animal of the small stock class. There may, however, be occasions when a goat is mistakenly sacrificed; a *female* goat can legitimately be dedicated.

(*mokenya jona kini*), protects the wife's male kin from danger which will follow the exercise of her sexual role as wife unless it is regularized.[1]

After the wife has been *laka* (ceremonially dressed in the goat-skin skirt of the married status), and before she sleeps with the husband, he brings her mother and co-mothers a goat known as 'the goat of the oil' (*kini na welet*). This animal allows the couple to have intercourse without her kinsmen suffering, although, in fact, the woman should not sleep with the husband until after a reciprocal visit has been made by her own kin. The goat is given to her female kin, in accordance with the principle that fertility comes from, and passes through, women—from mother to daughter. If the 'mothers' (true mother and women called 'mother', i.e. father's wives) are not compensated for their son-in-law's acquisition of their daughter's fertility, not only will she herself be barren, but the girl's father and brothers are open to hurt.

The handing-over of the goat underlines the important mother–daughter link, a link which is also stressed in a custom which forbids mother and daughter to be pregnant at the same time. To avoid this it is customary for a father to withdraw from the mother's hut when her daughter is pregnant. A girl rationalized this prohibition by suggesting that it was felt in some way to be unseemly for mother and daughter to be carrying and suckling small infants simultaneously. A married woman told me that a husband might become incensed by a wife's refusal to sleep with him on this excuse. A case could ensue, and the court would suggest the husband seek a second wife.

To return to the rite; the husband's mother and the wives of his close kinsmen prepare butter-fat oil known as *welet na teŋ*, or, if none is available because the cattle are in distant camps, sesame oil (*welet na könyum*), for the anointing of the wife's kin.[2] Money is also collected and 'the goat of the husband' is selected. The husband and wife do not accompany the deputation. On arrival at the wife's

---

[1] I have already described on pp. 178–9 the 'killing of the ox-for-the-ancestors' which compensates her dead kin; this ox is in addition to the animals discussed here and has a different objective. I should add that the meat of the animal under discussion is proscribed to the husband who provides it and to the wife. It is another of the marriage *dunye* (cf. p. 203).

[2] Shea-butter oil (*welet na kumuri*) is never substituted since it is a 'hot oil' and the idea is to make the girl's kin 'cool'. *Welet na teŋ*, made from the milk of life-giving cattle, is the ideal when available.

natal homestead all members of her extended family, including
children and lineage elders, are assembled and splashed with the
oil brought by the visiting women. The latter are then given food
and beer. Arrangements are made for the return visit of the
husband's mothers-in-law, the girl's senior kinswomen. The
husband's goat is also handed over. (This may be a nanny-goat or
billy-goat, a ram or a ewe; all are spoken of as 'the goat'.) A
neutered billy-goat is slaughtered and eaten by the wife's kinsmen,
a female is kept by them for breeding, one of its male offspring later
being killed for the ancestors. A dedicated nanny-goat becomes
'goat-of-the-ancestors' and like other dedicated animals cannot
be exchanged. The money is divided between the wife's young
unmarried kin. Before money was in circulation ten to thirty
arrow-heads were paid.

The visitors overnight in the homestead drink beer the following
morning, and then return home in the afternoon. Before they leave
they are '*laka*', which in this context consists of a promise of
money or a goat which follows later.

In one to three months the reciprocal visit takes place. The
wife's kinswomen ('mothers-in-law' of the husband) bring a
substantial gift of food to the husband's female relatives, including
baskets of grain, pots of flour, jars of sauce, honey, and oil. Essential
furnishings for the bride's new homestead are also presented,
including the small mat (*inyat*) on which the couple sleep and
which remains in the back of the hut and is never brought outside;
the *yika*—ordinary large sleeping mat (on which the *inyat* is laid
for greater comfort), a mat in general use; shell-spoons and pots
including the 'pot-of-the-back-of-the-hut' (*isa na kadi bot*), in
which delicacies exclusively for the husband are stored, a pot not
in general use and with a ritual significance.

These articles represent the wife's contribution to the marriage;
and, in fact, she provides all the hut furnishings. In divorce she is
entitled to the return of certain of these. Some of the food is for
her own use, the rest is for distribution to women of her husband's
lineage.

Until this visit the couple do not sleep together and the wife
lives with her husband's mother or senior wife. The arrival of the
wife's kin gives the husband the right of sexual access, an occasion
marked by a small rite. In the evening the wife is instructed in her
marital duties by her female kin who then ceremonially bathe the

couple, anointing them with sesame oil and placing them in the hut on the new sleeping mat. They have intercourse and in the morning the husband's mother-in-law formally asks whether the husband is pleased with his wife. Nowadays many couples do not observe the sexual abstinence after the bride's *laka*; even so, if the husband has complaints to make—for instance, that his wife was not a virgin—he makes them now. If he intimates satisfaction, a further animal of the bride-wealth is handed over 'so that the mothers-in-law may have meat and blood to make their bodies cool because of the copulation'. Beer which is 'simply a food' can never be substituted for animals at these ceremonies.

The occasion of the ceremonial intercourse is primarily secular, but its neglect is a cause of *mönöjin*. If these exchange visits are omitted or if the appropriate ceremonies are neglected the wife's male kin may be ill, she herself may be barren, or her children may die.

When a man inherits a widow, a goat or sheep must be divided lengthways and the carcase left stretched across the entrance throughout the night; the couple step over it to enter the hut and have intercourse. Next morning the wife is marked with sesame oil and her kin eat the goat's meat. If a widower remarries, a sheep is sacrificed before intercourse, 'otherwise the new wife's life is in danger'. The Mandari say that 'She may become ill because of the dead wife.' This is not strictly a *mönöjin* situation, and the meat of this animal is eaten by both husband and wife. The killing relates to the idea that without ritual severance the surviving partner remains bound to the deceased spouse. In both instances, however, it is the women—the sensitive partner—who becomes ill. A further animal is necessary to legitimize sexual intercourse; this animal, 'the cow of the mat', must be included with the bride-wealth paid for the children the woman may bear. On divorce, it is always retained by the woman's kin.

The situation of *mönöjin* can occur in wedlock as well as in promiscuous unions, since legitimate sexual intercourse is endangering without regulative rites. In fornication and adultery no rite can, of course, be performed. These misdemeanours also lead to quarrelling and even to killing and division of the community. The angry thoughts and words they arouse are, in themselves, a source of sin and danger.

It was suggested to me that because fornication may harm

a father or brother, a responsible girl refuses a lover; a girl herself put forward this argument. But it is difficult to assess the degree to which the belief is really a deterrent. The kind of situation involved and the personalities of those concerned are obviously relevant. The Mandari claim that their girls have a reputation for chastity in comparison with the 'looser' image of the neighbouring Dinka girls.

Safety measures may be taken when illicit intercourse is contemplated, to try to protect kinsmen. Sesame oil may be rubbed on the chests, backs, and foreheads of small brothers and sisters, under the pretence of oiling their skin, so that the boys will be 'cooled' from the 'heat', or a married woman may sprinkle flour in the doorway of her hut so that the flour will cling to her husband's feet.

While it is only the woman's male kin who suffer *mönöjin*, the female sinner and her offspring face other dangers. In later years (or concurrently) infertility, death in childbirth, and weak, sickly, or even dying infants and children may result. A woman enduring an exceptionally long labour will be questioned about youthful misdemeanours, and if she admits to these a former lover will be asked to provide a sheep for purification. The animal is eaten by female elders of the woman's *natal* lineage; at the same time, the woman is anointed with oil. Difficult delivery or death in childbirth does not, however, automatically prove promiscuity, because many agents can be involved—witches, dead kin, Powers, or Spirit-of-the-Above.

INCEST

Also causing *mönöjin* and viewed as particularly destructive are sexual relations within the prohibited kinship degrees. In large clans hundreds of people fall under the sexual prohibition although, in fact, the Mandari clearly distinguish incest within the closer kinship group from incestuous relations with remoter kin.

The question of incest can only arise in a case of illicit sexual intercourse, because the antecedents of both parties to a marriage are so scrupulously scrutinized that incestuous marriage is virtually impossible. It can happen, however, that where there was a former kinship link a couple may wish to marry and may challenge the assumption that the kinship involved is still prohibitive to marriage. Agnatic kinship is not usually involved because then marriage would force the splitting of the descent group, but rather kinship through a recent maternal or affinal link. A new marriage may eventually be allowed here, after 'blood-relationship' has been severed by the dividing of a black goat.

The Mandari have no specific word for incest, which is simply described as 'sleeping with a relative', or by the word for 'evil' (*tönaron*), or by analogy with sorcery, 'to commit sorcery-ness' (*konda turubian*).

The range for prohibited sexual intercourse is:

(*a*) Within the elementary or extended family.
(*b*) Within own clan—in the case of landowners.
(*c*) Within own lineage—in the case of small client groups and immigrants.
(*d*) With members of mother's clan for three generations.
(*e*) With own clients—proto-'brothers' and 'sisters' (less serious).
(*f*) With wife of clansman, particularly wife of close agnate.[1]

I will deal with some of these prohibitions in more detail. Sexual relations within an extended family or small lineage whose members are living together and giving and receiving marriage cattle (or between maternal kin) is seen to be an unspeakable act. It is impossible for it to happen inadvertently. Of this sexual sin the Mandari say, 'How can you sleep with your sister, particularly as she will bring you a cow?' In these crucial relationships where bride-wealth cattle are regularly shared the offence is most serious.[2]

Various safeguards protect against unwitting incest. Lineage members usually reside together and are in close daily contact. Courtship is organized through courting-huts and when visiting one a youth states the name of his clan or lineage. In cattle-camps where youths and girls work together, girls have their own

[1] This is not the *same* as incest with a related category, although it is a serious offence. A man can inherit a clansman's wife, and is obliged to inherit the wife of a father or brother, the mother's brother's widow in default of a male of the maternal lineage. The sin here is the anticipation of the inheritance and the fact that two closely related males are having sexual intercourse with the same woman.
[2] Even long-split-off sections of clans or lineages living apart can, on a rich marriage, lay claim to cattle. While this kind of 'historical' kinship is still given recognition it is 'kinship' in the cattle and incest situation as well. All these people are *yuŋi*, but both the sin and the social repercussions from it become less as the relationship gets more remote.

rest and recreation areas outside the camp. Distinguishing terms are used for 'related' and 'unrelated' girls.[1]

The Mandari persistently denied that incest within the family or closely knit localized lineage ever occurred. In the face of denials I eventually discovered that a case had occurred in a neighbouring chiefdom, had been brought before the chief's court, and had been dismissed because no action could be taken since there was no customary procedure or precedent for dealing with the offence. The only remedial action is the ordinary *mönöjin* rite to protect the woman's kin. The woman herself cannot be protected or cleansed.

The Mandari have conventional images to portray the evils of sexual relations between close kin or within the elementary family. They liken it to bestiality, homosexuality, witchcraft, patricide, or the killing of a son by a father. All these are destructive acts, and, in the same way, people 'die' because of close incest. If conception follows, 'The child swells in the womb killing both mother and infant'; should a child of incest live, it would be blind, dumb, mentally deficient, or a monstrosity. Incest cannot, by its very nature, result in the birth of a normal human being.

In relation to the mother's kin, the incest range is limited to the mother's own lineage. If the mother comes from a large land-owning clan, marriage may take place with members of its collateral lineages. The incest and marriage prohibition only relates to the affinal lineage actually linked in marriage (Fig. 9). The exception to this is the very small, highly localized clan, where the lineages may be acting as if they were virtually a single lineage. The prohibition on new marriages for the two lineages directly concerned in the first marriage lasts for three generations, then the relationship lapses and marriages may be allowed again. By this time the mother's brother/sister's son link, with the behaviour appropriate to it, has become nominal. Sexual relations which constitute borderline incest usually tend to occur at this point, and there could sometimes be genuine ignorance of the original marriage if the territorial separation was considerable. This is the point where doubt still remains in the minds of the elders as to the desirability of again allowing marriage, although this is the theo-

---

[1] The word '*ködite*' means 'courtable', unrelated girl. '*Saser*', 'sister', related girls. A woman's children are all *nyrinye* (nephews and nieces) to her natal lineage and the male kin of her own generation are *mananye* (maternal uncles) for her children.

retical turning-point at which *yuŋi* ends. Before this kind of marriage the rite of kinship severance with the black goat is performed. The anxiety which surrounds such a marriage arises from fear for the offspring, or fear that the girl may be barren; our own idea that first cousin marriage, or too-frequent cousin marriage, leads to feeble-mindedness might be a comparable apprehension.

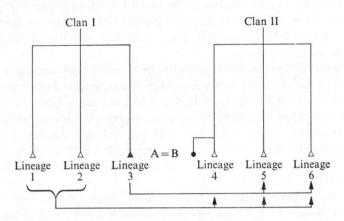

FIG. 9. *Marriage Prohibitions: classificatory affines and mother's brothers*
After marriage A = B, lineages 2 and 4 cannot intermarry again for three generations (mother's/brother's/sister's sons). Lineages 1 and 2 can marry lineages 4, 5, and 6. Lineage 3 can marry 5 and 6. These are 'affines' of collaterals, a relationship no bar to marriage.

III

Some female sins do not involve sex relations with men and are not classed as *mönöjin* but none the less they upset the sensitive balance of fertility and health. These sins are not moral wrongs, although they cause annoyance and anxiety. No purification rite follows their commission and little can be done to remove their injurious effects.

The first of these is the breaking of one of a class of ritual interdictions, described as '*dunye*'. (Two other *dunye* are common to men and women; all relate to transition states.) The specifically feminine prohibition is the '*dunye na yema*', the marriage interdiction explained as 'given by the ancestors' or as 'given by Agoya' implying an exclusively female rule. This is the prohibition which states that an affianced girl or a wife must refrain from drinking milk from the cows or goats received as her bride-wealth. If she breaks this rule her child will be born deaf or with pus in the ears. Further, before marriage and while she is still at her father's home, a girl must not eat meat, fish, or food or drink milk brought to her parents as gifts from her future husband; all these are 'her *dunye*' (*dunye ny it*).[1] After she has been *laka* she may eat the game-meat of wild animals killed by her husband, and drink milk from his cows provided that none of these will later be handed over as part of her outstanding bride-wealth. These, together with their offspring, are permanently *dunye*.

Should a woman inadvertently drink such milk attempts are made to nullify the effects. An elder dips a blade of grass into a gourd containing milk from the cow in question, places the milk on the girl's tongue and then passes the milky grass round her head. This gesture, which is said 'to make the milk safe for her', is not thought to be really effective, and I was told that 'Because women are so careless about their *dunye*, there are many people about with bad ears.'

A female prohibition which is not *dunye* relates to menstruation. When menstruating ('with blood') a girl or woman avoids drinking cow's milk or the cow providing the milk sickens and its newly born calf dies. She is also forbidden the fresh meat of cattle and freshly killed game-meat or fish; the latter part of this rule is explained on the basis that 'The hunter's spear will be spoilt, and he will fail to make kills.' The Mandari point out that this is because 'both have blood'.

There is further a different, but associated, rule which prohibits girls and women drinking milk for certain specified days in every month throughout the years of their fertility as marked by the continuance of the periods. The number of days milk is forbidden is calculated in relation to the number of sisters within an elementary family and is not based on the physiological period. These days of abstinence are additional to the days of the actual period, and a minimum of ten in each month must be observed by the daughters of any one family. The way in which the ten-day period is divided up between the girls of a family presented me with a problem and I was never able to fully grasp the method of

[1] Tobacco is also included under this head. After the consummation the husband gives the wife a small fragment of a pipe or a piece of a bracelet; then they can smoke together.

calculation. However, I give the information for what it is worth. Talking with a group of girls, I gathered that the days were divided out roughly as the girls decide among themselves. Thus in a family with say:

One daughter—she cannot drink milk for ten days.
Two daughters—neither can drink milk for five days.
More than two—they share out the days; the eldest may take
    four, the others between them take the rest of the ten.

If a sister dies, the remaining sisters add her days to their own. In a large family of girls, the eldest may take ten days, the next eight, the third six, and the youngest only two. The information given by the doctor Kok, however, suggested that division was in accord with a more specific ratio. It may be, however, that he was simply giving me an example of another way of dividing up, thus:

First sister—ten
Second sister—nine
Third sister—eight
Fourth sister—seven.

By this method one day from a total of ten is taken off for each daughter after the first. Kok also said that sisters might reverse the order if they wished.

Another alternative in a family of three sisters is after the first has taken ten, for the next two to make an equal division of seven each. The equation here being, three sisters, three from ten equals seven—taken by the younger two. A single sister always takes a full ten. The restriction is said to be observed until the menopause like the prohibition on drinking milk during the actual period. I was not able to find out how this affected girls after marriage, but was assured that the sharing of the total of ten is always between girls of one mother and not between half-sisters. Kok told me that goat's milk may be drunk because, as he put it, 'the goat is only an animal' (jaka), implying that, in this context, it is not on a par with the cow which is perhaps seen here as the equivalent of the woman herself. Sheep's milk is not involved because sheep are never milked. Again goat's meat may be eaten but freshly killed cows' meat is forbidden.

If the ten-day prohibition is broken, the cow which gave the milk dies, and the girl also becomes thin and wastes away. This is said to be because menstrual blood has 'potency' (*pötö*): 'It forms the child.' This association also holds good in the menstrual prohibition. If the latter is broken the woman may later be 'dry' and unable to nurse her babies; the cow also develops distressing symptoms affecting its milk-yield and udders: 'Its skin becomes hard and its hairs rise, its milk dries up and its body and udders become a mass of sores. When a man sees his cow in this state he guesses that a menstruating girl has drunk its milk.' There is no way of counteracting the effects. In cattle-camps where girls are living on milk, abstinence is difficult. Dried meat or fish is sometimes available, and a few animals will be bled daily and the blood cooked with the butter-fat from churned milk. This is given to toddlers and girls avoiding milk. A girl who has to abstain for more than a few days goes home.

Regarding both these prohibitions, the Mandari simply state that the behaviour is customary. Doctors and male elders told me that 'it's a woman's matter and one of the rules of behaviour given for them by Agoya'. The old women confirmed this saying, the rule was 'given by the ancestors' or 'by Creator'.

IV

Certain male actions can destroy a woman's fertility and her child's health. If a man, particularly a stranger, handles a woman's breast it may swell painfully, and if she is suckling, the infant may die. Committing this sin is said to be like the act of a witch. If a man inadvertently strikes a woman's breast in an argument he must provide a goat for purification. A neutered billy-goat is killed and its fat, mixed with sesame oil, is smeared on the violated breast; the meat is eaten by the woman's male and female elders. A nanny-goat is addressed at the rite when the woman is anointed; it then enters the protected class.

When I was staying in Köbora on the Nile such a violation occurred.[1] A group of fishermen were exploring the fishing potentialities of a local lagoon for a government fishery scheme. A man flirting with local women put his arm round the waist of a young mother and, she alleged, handled her breast. In court the woman, who appeared very distressed, claimed that shortly after her

---

[1] As described, Köbora are a closely related people.

marriage eleven years previously, a similar misdemeanour had been committed by an Aliab Dinka. After the incident she had been infertile for ten years, then she gave birth to the baby she was now suckling.

The official in charge of the fishery urged the local court to award a £S15 fine; eventually it settled for £S5 to provide a large goat for purification and something extra for the woman.

Even the breasts of young girls should not be touched indiscriminately, although the offence is less serious than if the woman is married and bearing children. In love-making in the courting-hut, suitors should be careful not to knock or excessively handle a girl's breasts. 'Courting (*lemö*) is by talking, holding hands, necks, waists, and thighs; or playing with a girl's loin-cloth.'[1] If a youth accidentally grabs a girl's breast in amorous horseplay she may hit at his testicles with some such comment as, 'Don't you know one's breast hurts?' Here breasts and testicles are equated, although the hitting of the male testes is simply a breach of good manners and painful, because the male body cannot be sinned against.

A woman's legs are also sensitive to male aggression. Should any man—including her husband—violate a woman's leg by grabbing it during a quarrel, or dragging her by it, he must produce a goat for purification; the woman's mother anoints her and the violated limb with sesame oil. Uncleansed, she may be barren, or her body may break out in sores. Two women or two men can assault each other's legs and a woman may grab a man's leg with impunity.

It is not difficult to understand the logic behind the violation of the breast—the source from which the infant is nurtured—but the leg association is more obscure. The Mandari perhaps regard a woman's legs as a prominent part of her sexual personality (an association which appears widespread).

V

Certain prohibitions, breaches of which do not constitute sin nor lead to hurtful results but which form an aspect of the ideology of creative roles, are the prohibitions on eating together in a potential,

---

[1] A euphemism for modified sex-play.

or newly formed, affinal relationship. Blood relationship (*yuŋi*) alone gives freedom to share food. The Mandari do not eat with non-relatives; thus in the very basic context of eating kinship is constantly evoked. Two separate factors are involved in the prohibition. First, non-kin do not eat together; secondly a person should not even see an unrelated member of the opposite sex eating if there is any possibility of marriage between them. Even within marriage itself, the husband cannot eat with his wife's kin until after the ceremony *laka na komiyit* (*laka* of the son-in-law).

Prohibitions on eating with unrelated persons of the opposite sex are explained by the Mandari in terms of 'shame' (*yu na kwe*). The Mandari explain that such persons cannot eat together because 'they respect each other' (*rujeju bok*). The social notion of shame is so strongly entrenched that real shame seems to be felt in violation, as for instance, if a youth sees a girl or her mother eating. Should a young man see unrelated girls eating he hands over a forfeit—a string of beads, a coin, or tobacco .A man is careful to avoid seeing the girl he is courting eating, but he observes the restriction more rigorously in relation to her mother—his future mother-in-law. If he sees his mother-in-law eating, he withdraws a short distance and waits until a child is sent to ask him his business. He then explains his misdemeanour and promises a he-goat to 'recompense' (*depaju*). Only a token payment is made for seeing the father-in-law eating. Husbands observe respect of the mother-in-law because persistent breach may endanger a wife's health. All kinds of manœuvres may be necessary in order to preserve it. At one mortuary ceremony which I attended, a sub-chief from a distant chiefdom had brought over his young wife, the dead man's sister, He told me that during the two days of the rituals he was more or less ostracized in an empty hut, without food or drink, because he had not been *laka* and 'feared' (*wuwuton*) his mother-in-law's food.

When the Mandari say that the mother-in-law is 'dangerous', they are not thinking primarily of danger to the son-in-law—although it is thought that the latter can die because of his mother-in-law's curse—but to his wife. The anger is seen to turn back on to her daughter, making her barren and her children ill. The Mandari here again emphasize the profound mother/daughter link. Discussing this bond with a Mandari husband, I was told that

'It is because the mother-in-law bore your wife that she has the power to affect her health and fertility.'

A woman is seen to have the power to influence her own fertility and her children's health, and also to exert power over the fertility of her adult daughters and, in turn, over the health and fertility of the daughter's daughters over a span of at least three generations. I have shown how this interlinking is also exemplified in beliefs about dead female relatives and female ancestors.

VI

To understand the ideas and actions which cluster round the female biological role we must examine the coherent and explicit ideology which dominates the Mandari approach to acts of creativity.

Of the two sexes it is the male who, in the Mandari view, is the least creative, though the Mandari are, of course, aware of a man's role in conception. They state quite specifically that 'Men are not creators and bearers like women.' A man's actual disadvantage because of this emphasis is shown in the fact that, in default of objective proof, a woman's word is taken in a case involving fornication or adultery often, as I have seen for myself and as the Mandari also recognize, to the detriment of justice. In the marital situation men are as much restricted as women since divorce is difficult for either party where there are children. Men also have to fulfil arduous inheritance obligations and their freedom of manœuvre here is more limited than the woman's in that a widow can choose an inheritor, but a man chosen by a widow cannot refuse her.

A basically female-centred ideology could be accepted only by a society which accords women a high status and values them deeply; there is, that is to say, a direct connection between the high status of women and the explicit ideology. However the ideal of female value is often contradicted in daily life by the ambivalence inherent in actual male/female relationships. Further, Mandari women, though displaying dignity of person, independent-mindedness, and influence, are, from the point of view of property-ownership and the exercise of political power, much less advantageously placed than men. Greater creative importance is balanced by subordination in executive affairs and femininity involves paradoxes alien to the simpler maleness. The extra sensitivity and greater vulnerability of a creative role is not, however, absolutely confined to women but is found in almost identical form in the office of landowning chiefs, whose creative powers are essential for the continuity of the life of the community.

The Mandari strikingly reveal their attitudes to woman and woman's role in statements like 'Women are paramount, they bear man' (*ŋutu wate a duŋ, yuŋu ju ŋutu*): 'Women have psychic force' (*ŋutu wate pötö*). Psychic force is said to derive from female physiology: 'Women have psychic force because they have the vagina' (*ŋutu wate pötö gwa ko liapiath*). The vagina is *par excellence* the female bodily part which symbolizes fertility. It must be covered after childhood; from the age of around five a girl wears a small cloth or apron of metal links around the loins. (Although at the time of my visit some girls went naked in courting-huts if Dinka suitors were expected—a new departure disapproved of by the older generation.) The male organ is not covered.[1] If the vagina is accidentally exposed, as when a loincloth catches to one side, it is said, 'She has spoilt her vagina.'

Consistent with the Mandari assumption that creative categories also have the power to kill, women are said 'to have death' (*ŋutu wate gwa ko twan*). If they themselves sin or if they are violated and cleansing does not follow, 'People may die.' To contain lethal feminine attributes prohibitions regulate the conduct of others towards them, above all, that of males, the complementary partners. Rules also centre around the female rhythms and those times when these are particularly active; they also protect the parts of the female body singled out as particularly significant.

Female sensitivity begins at first menstruation, the moment, according to Mandari theory, when conception becomes possible. At the first period, women elders anoint a girl with cooling sesame oil. Milk prohibitions are observed. She enters the courtship phase, and is physiologically able to commit dangerous sins against herself and others.[2]

---

[1] Chiefs and prominent persons wear clothes, but at the time of field-work the male population living in Mandari was unclothed.

[2] Girls go to courting-huts much earlier but do not conduct courtships. See Buxton, 'Girls' Courting Huts among the Mandari', *Man*, no. 56 (1963), p. 49.

The assumption that cows and women are linked by their common fertility, and that women as the more dominant of the two can affect the former is based on complex ideas which arise from the Mandari situation. Cattle are literally life-supporting through their milk and meat. They represent women in important structural exchanges at marriage, and human life in homicide and injury compensation. Compensation is the same for a woman and a man, or in the words of one informant, 'even higher for a woman because woman bears man, because of the children'. Milk, a common property of women and cows, is the supreme Mandari fertility symbol. Cow's milk is used in the central act of chiefly installation. It may also be poured on a chief's grave or a cow and its calf be killed there, as his creative powers are committed to the earth. The clear identification between parts of the woman's body and the cow's anatomy shows in the menstruation/ten-day milk abstinence rule: if this is broken the woman's breasts become 'dry', and similarly the udders of the cow are damaged. That the udders 'break out in sores'—raw, red patches—is a form of imprinting through analogy, the sores are like drops of menstrual blood which, through the act of drinking, have been brought into contact with the animal's milk in a dangerous antipathy. Flecking with sores or spots also follows violations of animal personality, although then the pattern is reversed, the human violator, not the animal, becoming impressed.

It is apparent that the observation of relational biological factors lies behind these assumed antipathies. A woman is not pregnant and does not suckle while she menstruates. When menstruation ceases it is a sign that a foetus, nourished by the menstrual blood, has been formed. Menstrual blood and breast-milk are therefore inadmissible in a single context, and through an identification of the creative attributes of women and cows, woman's menstrual blood—stronger than milk because of its primary human qualities and also its colour/mood associations—annihilates the yield of the lactating cow and kills the calf.

Another important association in this complex of ideas is the spoiling of the hunter's kill which belongs to another series of antipathies relating to different kinds of blood, and is a further elaboration of life/death symbolism. The blood flowing from the hunt-kill and the bloody quality of freshly killed meat is neutralized and arrested by the potent flow of menstrual blood. Freshly killed

meat or fish is therefore forbidden, but dried meat or fish is allowed.[1]
Blood antipathy of a most destructive kind lies in human blood
shed by a homicide, the most dangerous blood of all, which 'kills'
the culprit's fertile wife. In the hunt example, the properties of
life-giving menstrual blood are seen to be stronger than, and to
neutralize, the power of the hunter's spear to shed animal blood,
whereas in the case of the homicide, the human blood which
is actually spilt is more potent than the woman's fertility and
destroys it.

Mandari biological theory states that a woman is at the height of
her creative phase around the time of the period. This, therefore,
is considered the most advantageous time for intercourse if conception is desired. At the basis of the theory is the idea that the
menstrual blood is essential for the formation of the foetus.
Husband and wife may avoid having intercourse on the first and
second days of the period when the flow is at its height, the third
and fourth days, or just before it begins, being preferred. Outside
these times, the Mandari consider the woman less likely to conceive, 'because it is the blood coming down and joining with the
semen which makes the child', although the fact that there may be
a variation in individual cases is recognized. When I suggested that
this theory was incorrect the Mandari maintained that it applied in
their case. An assumption regarding 'blood' compatibility follows
from this. The Mandari consider that some marriages are childless
because the blood of the marriage partners fail to 'mix'; the bloods
are, as it were, sterile in relation to each other. If such partners
separate, the Mandari say they have observed that the parties may
later be fertile with other partners with whom their blood 'mixes'.

I attended a court case which emphasized the supposed link
between the menstruation period and conception. A girl who had
been impregnated by a lover admitted having slept with him on the
fourth day of her period instead of waiting until she was completely
clear, a safe time; the Mandari use these safe or 'safer' periods
to avoid unwanted pregnancy, while admitting that they are not
reliable. A married woman told me that, because fertility increases

[1] A further extension of this 'blood antipathy' is shown by the fact that if
a wife of one member of a hunt-group is delivered of a child, the hunt is called
off, since the blood flowing at the birth neutralizes the chances of a kill. This
situation is known as *puru*. Further, a man whose wife has given birth to a stillborn baby will not hunt until she again conceives. If she does not conceive again
he can release the prohibition by the rite of 'licking the spear'.

around the time of the period and a husband with several wives must give each the maximum chance to conceive, the senior wife privately advises him when he should visit a particular wife, saying, 'Go to so and so, her "Creator" is close' (Ŋun *nyit ge pelenya*), the circumlocution 'Ŋun' (Creator) being used here since all life-giving processes derive from Creator. (The word for the period is *bönok*.) Since the period is associated with the greatest fertility it is then that a woman is most endangering and her span of nominal danger lasts until the menopause.

We have also to consider the permanent prohibition on drinking the milk of bride-wealth cattle, and the subsidiary one on eating food and meat given by the husband's kin while a wife is affianced and her reproductive powers are still poised between natal lineage and husband's lineage. Cattle here are the means by which the woman's fertility is acquired; if this fertility is lost to the husband's lineage—for example if the wife refuses to cohabit or is barren, or if the couple divorce—the animals go back. They are not completely owned by her natal kin until their value has been matched by children. Then there can be no divorce. In the rare instance of a mature woman being divorced, no animals go back if she has several children or has passed the menopause. The food prohibition is removed when the woman's marriage is established by her *laka*. Food lacks the importance of cattle; it is simply a courtesy payment within the courtship context. It is included in the prohibition because it forms part of those gifts given when the transfer of the girl's fertility is in the balance.

Mönöjin perils relate to a woman's natal kin, because a woman is never completely separated from them even after marriage. They can suffer if the rites which transfer her reproductive powers to the husband's lineage are omitted, and they are affected by her divorce or her failure to produce offspring. She and her child are vulnerable to her husband's failure to complete her bride-wealth and by the failure of her own kin to satisfy entitlements among their relations (particularly the important obligation to her mother's brother), and later her husband's relatives' obligations to her own brother at her daughter's marriage. The most dangerous situations, however, are those relating to the specifically female physiology and the practice of sexuality within and outside marriage.

The sensitivity of femininity is distinct from the risks to which a woman may be exposed in her role as a toiler in the fields and homestead. Vulnerability centres entirely round the creative role, and being a sensitive category never frees a person from toil and objective danger. Landowning chiefs, the other protected category, were war-leaders and many died in fights.

The ritual dangers which are believed to threaten the process of conception and birth are, to some extent, a reflection of pragmatic anxieties about real dangers which surround delivery, infant weaning, and rearing, where the infant mortality rate is very high and where pregnancy and childbirth not infrequently lead to the death of both mother and child. Some of the rules relate directly to women's anxiety about the dangers of their precarious role as life-bearers. This also explains the extra care taken during the first pregnancy, when a doctor is consulted, a protective talisman may be worn, the woman behaves circumspectly, and she observes traditional pre-natal and post-natal rules to assist delivery and benefit the child. Rules restricting and modifying behaviour guide a woman through the physiological changes of menstruation, marriage, and childbirth and on to the routine of controlled conception.[1] Each stage is marked by a lesser or greater change of state. A woman's seclusion after delivery compares with the seclusion following chiefly installation. Her re-emergence is also marked by ritual. The comparison must not be taken too far, however, and women and chiefs are not identified.

The most dangerous crisis is the birth of the first child, and all earlier prohibitions are focused on this. Provided it is successful, later pregnancies should not require excessive protective measures. A doctor is only called then if the woman is ill or there is threatened miscarriage. But the continuum of fertility–pregnancy–delivery is threatened until the menopause. After this, ritual perils associated with the fertile period end automatically, and a correspondingly greater social mobility is enjoyed, together with an ending of some female restrictions. While a married woman is actively bearing children she circumscribes her activities. Thus while unmarried girls have freedom of circulation, married women do not, without a special reason, hang about bush shops—gossip and flirtation

---

[1] A woman must not conceive again until the first child is weaned. Babies suckle for two, or even three, years. During this period intercourse is forbidden, but sometimes takes place after the first year—'Before this a man is ashamed even to be seen entering his wife's hut.' Should conception result during the feeding period it is a great disgrace. The Mandari stress the desirability of a man having a second wife, or sexual abstinence must be practised for long periods.

centres—go alone to dances, or seek out, or talk to, unrelated men unless they meet them through the demands of hospitality. Greater public reticence or restraint relates partly to the married status, but more importantly to the idea that a woman, whose fertility is overt, must be careful of dangerous contacts, including the 'eyes' of those jealous of her person and her children. Mobility attracts gossip which can make her ill, or lead to the temptation of an affair culminating, perhaps, in a harmful appearance in a court.

A married woman loses her girlhood freedom, and does not have the freedom of middle age when, as a female elder, she again has a greater part in communal affairs. Older women are active in ritual; they walk around freely at ceremonial beer drinking, talking and exchanging courtesies, younger women remaining modestly under the dwelling hut. Informants, commenting on the free circulation of older women at rites, explained to me that it was 'all right because those are women who are past child-bearing; a young woman does not walk about like that.' Old women can litigate on their own behalf and give evidence in court, and while girls now attend meeting-tree courts as defendants or witnesses, I am told that this is a relatively new departure and that formerly cases affecting them were heard in an elder's homestead to prevent undesirable public appearances. If a young woman had to be represented at the chief's meeting-tree, a male relative acted for her. An older woman is not endangered by grave-digging, but this could destroy the fertility of a younger one. But while the menopause enlarges a woman's mobility she still follows the conventions of feminine behaviour.

While the Mandari view women in certain respects as destructive, they do not consider them inherently evil, impure, or polluting. This is true even for attributes of female physiology like menstrual blood.[1] The Mandari only view menstrual blood as dangerous in relation to lactating cows, hunting, and fishing. Apart from these instances it is not the focus of prohibitions and cleansings, and women are not secluded during their periods. There is no restriction on visiting the sick, seeing a new-born baby or youths recently

---

[1] The statement made for the Southern Bantu, for instance, that menstrual blood is regarded as 'dangerous to all things virile', would not hold for the Mandari. Max Gluckman, *Politics, Law and Ritual in Tribal Society* (Oxford, 1965), chap. vi, p. 224.

initiated. (The only woman dangerous to initiates is the one who has conceived in a state of *mönöjin*.) A menstruating girl may continue to sleep in the girls' courting-hut; it is up to her whether she receives a suitor, although I gained the impression that it was more usual to refuse one, because a girl is often not feeling her best, or may have a headache. To have 'a headache' is the conventional excuse both for turning away unwanted suitors, and for excusing oneself when menstruating. During their periods girls bind themselves tightly with rags and avoid wearing their best cloth if they have one. They cannot strip and simply wear beads; therefore they are not dressed for flirtation. One girl told me that suitors are not received because menstruation is 'dirty' (*wasak*); here she was referring to actual soiling and *not* to ritual pollution, which is not involved. In marriage the menstrual period is not avoided in intercourse.

Any reticence in connection with the period is related to the kind of reserve about female biological functions which is generally widespread. In discussing these matters I found men and women quite open and less embarrassed than men and women in our own society might be.

It cannot be said either 'that women have evil in their very nature'[1] because the Mandari do not differentiate between the sexes along these lines. The evil eye and night-witchcraft constitute the two evil human powers that are inborn. Women are seldom thought to be night-witches because they are not nocturnally mobile; in general women are less often suspected of having the evil eye, and all the notorious suspects I heard of, who were believed to kill or seriously injure, were men. That this is so is related to Mandari ideas about these powers, and the socio-political factors which define peripheral status and provide community scapegoats.[2] The common and, in many societies, the correct assumption that witchcraft accusations follow tensions and conflicts arising in relation to women and marriage is not applicable. Such tensions are not resolved by the Mandari, as they may be elsewhere, in this particular ritual idiom. The only witchcraft accusation within marriage which came to my notice was one where a wife accused her husband of killing their three children.

---

[1] Gluckman, *Politics, Law and Ritual in Tribal Society*, p. 224.
[2] See my 'Mandari witchcraft' in *Witchcraft and Sorcery in East Africa* ed. Middleton and Winter, pp. 107–20.

The accusation was considered far-fetched and was dismissed by the court.

The maternal ancestors are not thought to be especially capricious or dangerous. It might rather be suggested that they are more sinned against than paternal ancestors. The fact that female ancestors are very often shown to be implicated in child and wife sickness reflects ideas about debt and the righting of debt imbalance between intermarrying descent units. The overt recognition given to the bilateral blood tie, and all this implies, means that conflicts arising through rights over women and offspring are more openly faced and resolved than they are in some societies.

The link between ideas and behaviour is further illustrated by Mandari avoidance relationships. Thus avoidance is much more severe when it regulates a man's behaviour to his mother-in-law than to his father-in-law, while the behaviour of a woman to her in-laws is unrestricted. The Mandari state quite clearly why they give the extra respect to the mother-in-law:

She [the mother-in-law] bore one's wife. She must be respected because she suffered in bearing the wife; when one's wife was a child she tended her, rebuked her, went short of food for her; when a baby, one's wife urinated over her, abused her body, sucked her breasts; the mother-in-law toiled searching for food for one's wife.

In marriage, a link is established between husband and mother-in-law through her daughter; the husband acquires a right to that fertility nurtured by the wife's mother and passed on in her daughter.

Male sexuality does not involve danger to men, nor are men creative categories, and therefore the rules of avoidance between men are negligible. A man's contacts with his father-in-law are hardly restricted and breaches of respect have slight consequences: there is no avoidance between brothers-in-law, who are 'equals'. In contrast it is dangerous to touch the mother-in-law: 'The mother-in-law must not be touched or a man will fall ill.' He must never bury her: 'She cannot be buried by the son-in-law or he will die'; but he can, if necessary, bury other affinal kin.

It is clear that respect of the mother-in-law is not simply an extension of general avoidance behaviour in general.[1] Nor in the

---

[1] Cf. Radcliffe-Brown, *Structure and Function in Primitive Society*, chap. iv, who suggests that avoidance helps to preserve harmony between groups linked through marriage when the marriage is in an early stage and may be insecure.

Mandari case, can the perils which follow its breach be explained in terms of bolstering the position of affines who are unfavourably placed because they lack the objective means to enforce their superior status.[1] If this were the basis of respect avoidance, it might be expected that the son-in-law/father-in-law relationship would be the one most stressed since males exert authority, but this relationship is free. A mother-in-law has no reason to exert control over a son-in-law, who anyhow often lives at a distance. This explanation would be more plausible if respect were required of the daughter-in-law who may live with her mother-in-law at the beginning of her marriage; in this relationship there may later be a struggle for the control of the upbringing of the children. Yet this relationship also is free. But perhaps a different kind of potential conflict is relevant. As I shall show, the Mandari consider personal disposition and, more especially, verbal conflict to be lethal, particularly in connection with sensitive categories and it is a commonplace that words need to be guarded against in relationships which can be stressful. The son-in-law/mother-in-law relation-ship contains such stresses, both because the wife's mother may take the wife's side in quarrels with the husband and his kin, and also because she may try to exert pressure on her married daughter. In child rearing, which includes rites for child health, it is the wife's mother backed up also by the husband's female relatives, who is most concerned with the children's upbringing and especially likely to demand sacrifices for ailing health and to complain about a son-in-law's tardiness in carrying them out. What may be worked out here is conflict over the children, between husband and mother-in-law, and even between married daughter and her own mother. Thus it is significant that the re-strictions on eating and moving around the mother-in-law's home-stead are removed for the son-in-law after children have been born and are beginning to grow. The crucial avoidance ends once the daughter's fertility is proved and the children are over the dan-gerous early years.

We come back again here to the mother/daughter link, a link as important as the father/son link, but one which has received far less attention in anthropological analysis. Its importance has been shown here in a number of situations. When a woman commits a sin or is sinned against, it is her mother or female representing

---

[1] Douglas, *Purity and Danger*, p. 132.

the mother who assists at the cleansing. The mother's mother is implicated again and again in dead kin rituals. Fertility comes from women and passes through them. The lines of fertility stretching through women—the life-giving mothers—cross the socially well-defined property and office-holding lines traced through men. Avoidance and respect are one means by which this inheritance is safeguarded and by which a woman can continue to exercise control over her adult daughter and her daughter's children. The respect avoidance associated with this tie is charted in Fig. 10.

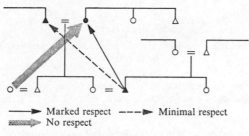

Marked respect ----► Minimal respect
No respect

FIG. 10. *Respect based on mother–daughter tie*

Burial prohibitions emphasize another link in the 'fertility' line, the brother/sister link. A woman's brother may not bury her children; if he does 'her whole line will die out'—she will leave no descendants. The mother's brother does not even attend their burial, and after his symbolic demonstration of hostility, is promised compensation for their death. As a male he takes this on behalf of the maternal line (on behalf of his sister), the line which gave the life in the first place. The assumption that it is lethal for a husband to bury his wife's mother has a similar explanation. A sister's son, however, can safely bury his mother's brother because by the time the sister's son is adult the creative inheritance has already been passed on. Some of these relationships and the burial patterns associated with them are set out in Fig. 11.

VII

Most female prohibitions are not ultimately to do with the sex act itself, except in so far as this is basic to procreation. The strongly expressed Mandari view that sex has true purpose and right function only when directed to procreation is supported by jural norms. Female barrenness and male impotence are grounds for divorce, although a husband may prefer to marry a second wife rather than divorce a barren one. A wife has the right to litigate against an impotent husband who refuses to appoint a kinsman to impregnate her, and traditional tests for male impotence can be

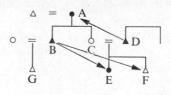

————▶ Cannot bury

FIG. 11. *Prohibited burial in the affinal and mother's brother–sister's son relationships*

B cannot bury E or F, or all C line 'dies out'
D cannot bury A—leads to 'death'—and cannot bury wife's brother B
B can bury C before C's marriage
D ,,   ,,   C
F ,,   ,,   B
C ,,   ,,   G (Her brother's child, in default of males, provided she is not un-married or a young wife (burial a danger to her fertility). C is important female elder to G, but G gets his 'life' from his own mother, and not from C—link is broken here by B who is a male.)

carried out by the council of elders and, if conclusive, the wife may be granted a divorce.

The Mandari regard sexual perversion as non-creative and actively destructive. When trying to discuss homosexuality I had difficulty in making them see the point of my inquiry, and they kept repeating 'What is the point of a man fornicating with another man, when by doing this he cannot bear a child?' If sexual perversion occurs in adolescence, it is severely punished; it is incomprehensible that adults should regularly practise it unless they are witches reversing the normal sex act expressly to harm. Sexual perverts risk being harmed as witches. Somewhat analogous in seriousness is penetrating an immature girl. Formerly a man guilty of this offence had his throat cut, now a major court-case follows. Conception through sex is the sought-after good, and female fertility acquired with cattle alone give this. Men aim to marry in order to engender numerous offspring, but homosexual practice directly denies these values.

Expressed attitudes to sex, of course, reflect the accepted social stereotypes, and there are also minority views held by some individuals or by many individuals at some period during their lives; and there is, further, the way people act in spite of, or contrary to, the standards which they themselves accept. Thus there is a more 'romantic' ideal, prevalent among the young. The romantic attachment represents what people may feel during their courtship days, and it is not always incompatible with a socially approved marriage, although it is frequently modified, as in most societies, by economic, social, and authoritarian factors. The sometimes rather hectic romances of sought-after youth are indulgently regarded as part of the activities of young people, and as correct when confined to this age-group, but they sometimes come into conflict with the conventional model of marriage, and elopements, illicit liaisons, and, in a few extreme cases, suicide, may result. In order to conform to important Mandari theories about procreation, social conventions regarding sex and marriage must be upheld.

The Mandari ideology does not hold that sex is intrinsically impure or destructive. There are no prescriptions on properly regulated marital sexual intercourse, or required abstinence before performing religious rites, before hunting or raiding. (At least, in the latter case, any abstention is for expedience. As informants pointed out, if a hunter or fighter has to rise early and be 'on form', he does not spend the night in copulation.) Promiscuous sex is always dangerous, so also is sex when people are too lazy or too poor to organize their married sex life correctly by regulating rites.

VIII

It is clear that a complete explanation of the Mandari theory regarding the life-process must be sought at various levels, and that the complex notions relating to woman's biological role cannot adequately be explained in terms only of the structure of particular social groups, or in terms of tensions and conflicts inhering in the marital situation alone. It is, however, self-evident that these ideas are consistent with social realities and the alignment of social groups. In the case of *mönöjin*, the fact that a girl's brother and natal kin bear the brunt of her sin before her marriage, and after it the husband, demonstrates the two kinds of legal rights in fertility; while the mother/daughter tie, emphasized in avoidance relationships, shows consistency with the importance given to maternal kin and to linking between women.

Correspondence can be demonstrated between structure and ideas, and ideas can be shown to support specific areas of behaviour. None the less, it would be wrong to seem to explain the ideology and the linked behaviour-patterns simply in terms of supporting social order or authority.[1] Take, for instance, the suggestion that the question as to which party—the man or the woman—is seen to suffer from adultery and female sin, may be related to the distribution of authority exercised in marriage, so that the danger falls on the wife where she cannot easily be chastened, but that where the reverse is the case and the husband is hurt, the wife is under control and the marriage tends to be stable.[2] It does not seem possible to correlate such a proposition with Mandari sin perils. In the first place, both men and women are affected: the man (the less creative category) in his health and safety; the woman (the creative bearer) in her fundamental nature. But it could be said that the position between the sexes in Mandari is fairly equal in these respects.

When we look at marriage and the proximity of a wife's kin, we find the situation varies with the class of individual concerned and with a particular chiefdom. Members of large clans are always more circumscribed in their choice of partners than small client groups because many more people come under incest prohibitions, so marriage partners must be sought from further afield. Whether a man or a woman is involved is also pertinent. Members of chiefly families also must make marriages based on political considerations or to resolve political tensions, marriage being a means of bringing peace. Some affines are therefore next-door neighbours, others may live far away. Marriage is subject to such a range of variables that it is difficult to speak of a typical marriage, still more so to correlate sin perils with marital residence, male dominance, and the presence or absence of wife's relatives.

The conclusion to be drawn would seem to be that there are no set patterns of residence or of male dominance, and that both parties are open to hurt of different kinds—that there is a general consistency between the way ideas are applied and forms of social structuring.

---

[1] Something rather like this is implied by Douglas in her proposition that such rules (prohibitions of the kind just discussed) sanction social order where the latter is weak. *Purity and Danger*, particularly pp. 133–4.

[2] Ibid., p. 135.

That sin perils are instruments for arousing and channelling moral indignation and that such ritual sanctions can replace active human punishment are further propositions.[1] The first is hard to prove, since it is difficult to separate the personal indignation of kin who are angry about spoilt economic values, loss of face, and feelings of shame, from moral indignation which is usually exhibited by the wider community.

The whole problem of how far ritual sanctions are any real deterrent to behaviour is raised here, and comparative evidence tends to be conflicting.[2] My own evidence from the Mandari leads me to wonder whether, in fact, moral indignation is involved and, if it is, how far it is the result of a belief in sin peril.[3] It is certainly true that indignation surrounds offences against Mandari women but, significantly, this indignation is generally confined to those interested and injured parties who are closest to the offended person; there seems little evidence that it carries over into the community at large—*unless*, as in the case on pp. 229–30, there is open obstinacy and defiant continuation of the offence so that behaviour becomes a public affront. In the case on p. 195 the brother's claim for homicide compensation after the girl's action was discovered was considered far-fetched and dismissed by the court—the disinterested party. While there is general agreement that adultery and fornication are wrong, I would question the suggestion that it is the ritual perils following after the offence which arouse the indignation, or that the indignation aroused is necessarily of a moral kind.

The degree to which belief in sin peril is a behaviour determinant is inevitably qualified by the individual character of those concerned. If it is believed that female sin endangers relatives, it is likely that the more conscientious and conforming will refrain. But the belief is unlikely to have much effect on the strongly nonconforming or selfish person, or on one facing conflicting pressures —for instance the girl divided between love for her suitor and her loyalty to her family, who may well elope in spite of possible

---

[1] Ibid., pp. 131–2, 133.

[2] The reference to the Nuer husband dying of pollution and the presumed moral indignation this arouses and the deterrent it provides, is in contrast to Richard's material on the Bembe: 'no fear of adultery pollution deters anyone from adultery.' Douglas, *Purity and Danger*, pp. 130–2, 137.

[3] Evans-Pritchard is also of the opinion that sins do not arouse moral indignation. *Nuer Religion*, p. 189.

consequences. A stated norm always has *some* effect: 'Our (Mandari) girls are better behaved than those of the Dinka' is held to be self-evident. The supposedly more permissive, or weaker, norm among the Dinka may imply that ideal behaviour is less commonly expected or maintained.

Finally, it is difficult to demonstrate that sin perils are less likely to be found where established machinery of coercion exists or where the political system is centralized, although it is true that ritual sanctions will *appear* more important where legal sanctions are lacking.[1] In centralized states elsewhere in Africa sin ideologies are found.

It would seem that we must look at the nature of the offences which attract the ritual sanctions and how they dovetail in to the wider ideological background. In the Mandari case, other acts which are sins must be borne in mind as well, particularly the sins of killing and wrong speech. Although these latter sins are considered in the next chapter, it is convenient to take the theoretical propositions regarding all sin together. When we look at these three kinds of act, it is clear that ritual danger is associated with strongly sanctioned offences as well as with unsanctioned ones. Killing, adultery, and seduction are the important legal wrongs which inevitably require restitution. At the ritual level, these socially sanctioned acts are classed together with other sins by their results. The three kinds of act—'killing, sins against the female role', and talk—have more in common than may at first appear. And all are linked together in Mandari reasoning as divisive, as having a spontaneous quality, and as often leading to one another—the wrong against the woman to killing, the woman's sin to talk.

All sin (whether or not it comes under a moral or legal sanction as well) is contrary to the central Mandari philosophy regarding life and creativity. It negates life or destroys it, whether by killing as in homicide; by preventing fertility or annihilating it, as in the female sin; or by destroying the community by divisive talk.

[1] Douglas, *Purity and Danger*, p. 133.

8

HOMICIDE AND VERBAL KILLING

I

THE Mandari regard killing as a sin against Creator—'Only Creator gives life.' It is not therefore legitimate to take it and a killer must be purified whether his victim is related to him under one of the kinship categories or is a stranger of another tribe or clan.

Within the immediate family taking life is the ultimate sin, polluting and dangerous and seen to lead to the homicide's own death. The immediate expectation of death after such a killing is exemplified by a case which occurred in a village in which I was living, where a father killed a son who had become the centre of a whispering campaign arising from witchcraft suspicions. After the killing the father surrendered to the police but died three days later. His sudden death was accepted by the villagers as the inevitable result of his action, which, although commendable in that it removed a ritual killer, was self-destructive—'He died because of his son's shed blood.'

Killing within the related degrees (lineage, clan, maternal kin, close affines) is not only a serious sin but also a social wrong. But except in the case of affines no compensation can in theory be paid, although if the killing occurs between members of widely separated collateral lineages of a large clan a token payment is sometimes made. The killing of an unrelated person belonging to the same village or chiefdom is a sin and also socially wrong because sharing a territory gives a form of brotherhood. Such a killing has serious political implications and is a threat to unity, and for this reason the victim's kin forgo their right of retaliation but receive compensation.

The killing of non-related persons of other chiefdoms or tribes is a venial sin and traditionally could be morally correct as, for instance, in retaliatory killing; but purification is always required. Serious wounding, and accidental killing and wounding, also require it, as did the formerly legitimate execution carried out with the agreement of the meeting-tree council, and put into effect by three or more persons in order to divide the responsibility and reduce the danger of *nyök* (see below). Executioners were purified in the bush by the killing of a chicken, the feathers of which were singed above an open fire and rubbed over the head, face, and back of the neck of each supplicant while the officiant prayed that the dead man's blood be taken away and health protected. The heads were then shaved and anointed with *meje* (sesame oil and red ochre).

In addition to the pollution which results from the shedding of human blood, killing may also release the agent of *nyök*, which derives specifically from the victim's shed blood and which cannot be exorcized before the onset of the sickness which manifests its presence, although purification aims to reduce this danger. *Nyök* follows homicide, the legitimate—indeed socially enforced— exposing of a monstrous foetus, and the inadmissible killing of domestic animals; it may lead to the killer's own death or, more usually, to that of his children. I refer to *nyök* as 'avenging psyche' to distinguish it from ghost visitation.[1]

The pollution of bloodshed is particularly endangering to the homicide's wife and offspring or, if the killer is unmarried and remains uncleansed, to the woman who later bears his children. Something akin to direct physical pollution seems to be envisaged in that the killer's actual presence becomes endangering, and for this reason he scrupulously avoids his homestead. The Mandari stress that 'women are vulnerable' (*ŋutu wate bak riŋet*). To have sexual intercourse uncleansed is absolutely out of the question, the life-giving sexual act becoming an act of death under the shadow of blood pollution.

An uncleansed killer sleeps and eats in a goat-kraal or disused hut while seeking a neutered goat for sacrifice. The lineage elders gather for the rite, which takes place in the bush outside the hamlet, the homicide being too dangerous to enter a homestead.

[1] Comparison may be made here with one aspect of the Nuer concept of *cien*, 'haunting'. The Nuer *cien*, however, results from all wrongs towards the dead, including what in the Mandari context would come under the 'ghost' visitation (Evans-Pritchard, *Nuer Religion*, see Index under *cien*). Mandari *nyök* on the other hand is only involved in the specific context of actual killing or shedding blood. The avenging agent exists in the spilt blood and not in the ghost personality of the deceased. The ceremony which eliminates it is exorcism not sacrifice.

The goat is passed round the killer's head and charged to take away the blood of the dead man and to allow the killer's head to be 'cool'. The throat is cut and the meat cooked and eaten by the elders in the bush: the killer abstains. His head is shaved and anointed with sesame oil for coolness by an elderly kinswoman.

In former times, after cattle raiding, each side carried out its own homicide purifications. Captured oxen were slaughtered at the meeting-tree and eaten by the elders and those who had shed blood. (The skins belonged to each lineage head who had purified his own men.) A bow was ceremonially broken at the meeting-tree.[1] Whether or not additional rites of reconciliation were performed to allow those involved to eat together depended on whether they were linked by meaningful social ties.

Accidental wounding requires a neutered billy-goat or barren nanny-goat for the cleansing of the man who wounds. The slaughtered animal is eaten by elders representing both parties, and by the two persons involved; water and sesame oil are splashed on the wounds. Both parties eat together for the rite combines cleansing and reconciliation; as the victim is only wounded no time need elapse before it. If the victim dies, the kin also eat a horizontally divided animal either at the purification or at a separate rite known as 'eating the intestines together' (*ɲutu wasut moynettes*).[2]

If a killer is simply purified and his kin and those of his victim do not attend a reconciliation rite they are under the 'blood interdiction' (*dunye na twan*), and mutually endangering; the interdiction also prevents intermarriage. There is no way of counteracting breach of it which is said to result in leprosy, the word for which is '*rima*', 'blood'. The interdiction remains in force for three generations or until the dividing and eating of a goat. After three generations a symbolic gesture of reconciliation takes place. The killer, or his descendants, visit the victim's relatives who provide a pot of water in which the petitioners place their feet, splashing the water over

---

[1] The Mandari complain that nowadays those who have been involved in inter-tribal skirmishes are liable to be taken away by the chief's police before purification, leaving wives and children endangered. Killers try to sacrifice a chicken before this happens. Professor Evans-Pritchard makes the same point for the Nuer.

[2] A horizontally divided animal is used to symbolically divide off a relationship or to bring persons together. Those separated by shed blood are reunited by the eating together of the two halves. For those who are already together and must be separated (distant relatives dividing in order to marry), the two halves eaten mutually by the kin of the suppliants effect separation.

themselves; then they trample the pot to fragments. Coolness in the renewed relationship is introduced through the water and the old hostility is 'broken with the pot'.

The bloodshed prohibition is the third prohibition described as *dunye*. The *dunye na yema* is operative for the life of the wife concerned, the *dunye na twan* for the period from burial to mortuary rite, *dunye na rima* covers the three-generation period, an important general time unit, and the one which marks the ending of debt and obligation, in this instance the debt for the dead man's life.

II

Important notions regarding sickness on the one hand, and of positive benefit on the other, are associated with thought, disposition, and speech. It is not by coincidence that the word *pötö* is used to describe the spoken word, and while it would be an exaggeration to suggest that this is seen to have a psychic force equivalent to that attaching to human categories, something not altogether dissimilar is implied.

Thought and speech, while being important creative activities, can also be harmful. Talk is difficult to control. Gossip, for instance, snowballs and distorts simply in the process of passing between persons and round a community. While recognizing this, the Mandari are also great conversationalists. 'Sensible speech' (*kulya na'bus*) and conversation (*wuya*) are valued, and the ability to entertain with conversation, to write songs and compose cattle poetry, are valued creative outlets in a society offering few diversions.

While the good and the bad side of talk are recognized, the harmful side features the more positively and includes angry argument, particularly that severing a relationship; constant grumbling and complaint by members of a community against the object of their dissatisfaction; the public wrangling which surrounds some disputes; and malicious gossip even if it is true. I have shown how disposition is seen to cause illness when discussing ghost activity; the more general hostile thought which issues in talk is dangerous in non-kin situations.

Chronic verbal discord is known to disintegrate a community but spiteful talk (*kulya naron*) and quarrelling (*kulya jore*) are also an accepted characteristic of community life. When they are shown to have caused sickness, purification of the guilty talkers and of their sick victim is required. Uncleansed parties are 'hot', but after purification the 'words fall to the ground' together with their harmful effects. Purification involves at least two parties because talk takes place in a dyadic relationship or is directed at a target.

Another source of sickness is meeting-tree litigation. All disputes involve argument, but some are recognized as being particularly pernicious. These often involve wrongs against women or wrongs committed by women. Strong emotions, feelings of outrage, hatred, and grievance are aroused; those adjudicating may be divided in judgement. The woman involved is in danger because of the public discussion on her misdemeanour—'She has brought much talk and there have been many eyes upon her.' This comment is both a reference to the evil eye—people who have it are believed to attend public hearings in order to harm—and the fact that she is the centre of comment or abuse. Her particular vulnerability derives from her femininity, and after a major case involving a woman a sheep is killed and she and all those concerned are purified. The animal may be slaughtered at the meeting-tree itself. then members of the court are among those who eat it. The woman abstains (the meat of purification is forbidden to the central party) but her kin eat, and she herself is marked with the fat mixed with sesame oil.

The installed chief was another vulnerable target who 'must not draw hostile talk', who must avoid argument and be protected from shouting and wrangling.[1] After a dispute involving a chief, a sheep, described as 'the medium of the marking and cleansing of the chief' (böböyarikin Mar), is killed. The rain of the chiefdom can also be harmed by hostile comment directed at the chief. Purification of all sensitive categories is carried out at once and never delayed until sickness occurs.

Public confession is a feature of purification. This must be accompanied by sincere repentance and freedom from thoughts of revenge since the cleansing is only effective where genuine intention is present on both sides. The following is a typical case involving a sensitive category and illustrates confession and cleansing.

The couple involved were a Mandari girl and a man of another

[1] Chiefs are now no longer installed; however, the former associations given by installation tend to persist, and present day chiefs may be purified in the traditional manner, particularly when they are rain officiants.

tribe employed by myself. As the proceedings developed, a senior elder harangued me, angrily pointing out that I had brought the man to the village and was responsible for his behaviour. Because of the ill-treatment the girl received from her angry guardian (her father was dead and she lived with a paternal first cousin), individuals were antagonized against him as well. There was also acrimonious disagreement between those who felt that, in the circumstances, the couple should be allowed to marry, and those who opposed this. When the case first broke, I was due to leave with the man for a visit to the Nile Köbora and the girl threatened to follow her lover there. To prevent this her guardian tied her up, binding her hands and feet with cattle ropes, tying a rope round her forehead and anchoring it to a cattle peg. Her screams echoed through surrounding homesteads and neighbours were shocked. She eventually freed herself, and ran off into the bush where she spent the night.

At a preliminary court hearing, hastily arranged, it was decided that there could be no marriage but the seducer should pay £S5 compensation. When the girl heard the verdict she protested violently that she would rather kill herself than give up her lover, tearing off her loin-cloth and beads in front of the assembled elders and throwing dust over her head. Most spectators looked shocked, some laughed unpleasantly, and one old woman shouted abuse. The court broke up, and the next day we left the village. On our return two months later the girl and the man reaffirmed their determination to marry. The man had saved £S5 and I promised an advance of pay. Eventually the marriage was agreed.

That evening the girl was purified at a ceremony attended by the Dari chief and elders, the guardian and male and female elders of his lineage. The defendant and myself and others who had given evidence or pleaded were also ordered to attend. The chief summarized the events, instructing us to have 'cool hearts and forgo ill-feeling, heated words, anger and malice, and only to have favourable dispositions towards each other'. He pointed out that the marriage was agreed and there must be no new recriminations. He was followed by Are, an important elder attached to Dari clan, who emphasized his words: 'Everything is now settled and the people can disperse without resentment, the man can take his wife with him to Juba town where he lives, from where she will return in due course to visit us.'

The girl's guardian came forward and made a long confession, stating how he had beaten the girl and tied her up, how he had spoken angrily to Awuk (myself), to so-and-so, and so-and-so. He repeated word for word, as far as he could, all he had said and done. By midnight, when the talk had been 'talked out', the girl was anointed with sesame oil and flour and blessed by the elders and her guardian, 'so that she may go safely to Juba town, and not fall ill, and may bear children and return soon to visit her people'. Other relatives directly implicated, like her guardian, were also anointed.

III

Some kinds of family quarrelling are said to be 'punished' by Spirit-of-the-Above through death by lightning. As Mandari put it, 'Above is angered by the talk' (*Ki wawaran*) and 'shoots people' (*norju ŋutu*).[1] A lightning victim is described as 'someone who has died from wounding by Above' (*ŋutu lugu ŋu bönöju ko Ki*). The lightning flash is referred to as 'fire of Above' (*cima na Ki*), the series of thunder, flash, and strike, as 'the bow of the Above has shot' (*day na Ki ŋu norju*). Mandari do not inevitably associate lightning and divine punishment. Harmless lightning is a feature of rain weather—'When black clouds gather there will be thunder and lightning; without thunder and lightning there would be no rain.' But when lightning appears to be selective, striking a person or property, it is assumed to be a religious instrument.

A place where lightning has killed or seriously injured is purified by a doctor of Spirit-of-the-Above, the bereaved family producing a sacrificial sheep and the doctor making an address on the following lines: 'You Above. You have killed; now a sheep has been killed for you. Take back your arrows. Be cool.' Failing a sheep, sesame oil is poured on the spot.

Following death by direct strike, the chiefdom's drum is beaten morning and evening until the grave-sweeping, while women wail. Burial is the same as for ordinary death but here the rain creeper, tied to the little finger and laid across the grave, is absolutely vital or the rain is taken into the ground. Grave-earth is also mixed with water and splashed into the air with a rain

---

[1] Among the Nuer, lightning death is attributed to God and is not punishment of sin. Evans-Pritchard, *Nuer Religion*, pp. 52–3.

creeper. Because of the 'fire of the Above' a lightning victim is dangerously 'hot'; should ghost sickness follow a sheep must be killed to cool this heat.

Mandari-land, lying on an ironstone plateau, may actually be more than usually vulnerable to lightning strikes.[1] Whatever the case, the Mandari respond by endeavouring to control lightning at the rain rites so that if sin is present, 'Above will not destroy when the rains break.' Particularly relevant is quarrelling which severs ties between close kin or friends, the most dangerous kind being the emphatic repudiation of ties which is openly declared with such words as 'I will never re-enter your homestead!' If two persons quarrel and part with these words, ritual is essential before the relationship is resumed. If it is omitted, and the offender visits the man with whom he has quarrelled, or accepts food or drink from him, 'the Above may be angered and kill him.' Here we have the idea of a verbal 'killing'— a relationship literally annihilated—and a rite of reconciliation, somewhat similar to that which ends the bloodshed prohibition, is required to resuscitate it. In the case of a quarrel, the parties are only separated by words, so while a rite is necessary they do not, as in homicide, wait before performing it.

If a man who has verbally 'killed', wishes to make up the quarrel, his lineage elder together with senior men accompany him to the homestead of the other party. The reason for their visit is explained, and if the other party agrees to a reconciliation, a gourd of water is produced and the man seeking forgiveness repeats word for word the whole circumstances and content of the quarrel. The officiating elder circles the gourd of water round his head, then throws water up into the air, saying 'Let all the harsh words leave so-and-so', naming the culprit, addressing the man who has received the insult, 'Let all the evil talk come out and let your heart be cool.' Then again addressing the offender: 'May you remain safe, and if Above should approach when the rain falls, may you suffer no harm.' Spirit-of-the-Above may also be addressed: 'You Above, fall coolly: leave us in peace.' As he speaks the elder may flail his arms in a whirling movement, signifying dispersal of the words.

[1] Stigand, writing on the Lado Enclave, remarks on the violence and frequency of thunderstorms: 'cases of people being killed by lightning are of fairly frequent occurrence.' C. H. Stigand, *Equatoria, the Lado Enclave*, new impression (London, 1968), p. 12.

Tobacco is distributed to symbolize the healed relationship. As everyone smokes an elder reaffirms: 'Let the talk be forgotten and let us be protected and at peace.' This ceremony is *rata*.

If offenders fail to '*rata*' they may be killed when the rains break:

Even if the offenders are sitting in a hut together with other people, the Above will seek them out and they will be struck while others remain unharmed. If people in one family are always bickering and never *rata*, the Above becomes tired of their behaviour and wipes them out; the hut or byre is struck and the occupants are hurled outside together with goats, sheep, dogs, and other possessions; the Above spares nothing and destroys all.

Two cases of death by lightning in Dari village came to my notice. In one case there had previously been dissension over the marriage of the youth who died, the girl involved being a distant relative of the affinal class. The other death was that of the Dari chief's senior wife whose hut was destroyed by fire after being struck. Quarrelling also preceded the death.

IV

Cursing comes in a different category from harmful talk of a more general kind, because it represents a stylized pronouncement directed at an individual which is intended to harm because of its form and because of the relationship which links the two parties. The curse of a landowning chief can make land unproductive and destroy crops, the land's fertility being linked to the disposition of the chief who curses. Not surprisingly, the Mandari say 'The cursing of the son-in-law by the mother-in-law brings death. If your mother-in-law insults or abuses you, remain silent and never answer back; her curse can make your wife barren and kill your children.' The angry father's curse makes the stubborn son ill, and the curses of senior kin, like grandparents, mother's brothers, or father's sisters are regarded as very dangerous. Cursing between close kin is an irrevocable repudiation of the bonds of blood relationship, and after a curse close relatives may separate for good. A blood relative only curses after prolonged provocation, and there is often a feeling of moral outrage in the individual who curses.[1]

---

[1] The idea that cursing between brothers leads to repudiation of kinship features in the Bora myth; see *Chiefs and Strangers*, p. 23.

The logical opposite of the dangerous talk situation is the benevolent word and disposition, most commonly, perhaps, the diffuse
praises giving good report of popular and generous persons. Diffuse
good is assumed to be cumulative, like its opposite, the ill arising
from grumbling. Counterbalancing the formal curse is the prayer
or blessing generally expressed within the kinship relationship,
but also playing a part in neighbourly relations.

Not unnaturally the benefit which has accrued from favourable
report is seldom pin-pointed, since, in general, good fortune tends
to be accepted uncritically. People are more aware of having to
cope with problems than of receiving benefits; and, moreover,
adverse events must be scrutinized so that their source can be
dealt with. It is consistent that the Mandari explain good fortune
rather vaguely as coming from Creator, an all-embracing principle,
whereas misfortune—including illness—is attributed to a wide
range of causal agents. Significantly also, those who lead upright
lives are said to have a certain immunity from dangerous talk—
an assumption related, of course, to the realities of the diagnostic
situation.

V

Because the Mandari ascribe dynamic qualities to the mental
activities of thought and emotion, and to speech, the overt manifestation of intellectual and affective processes, when thought or
speech is directed at human targets it is seen to assume something
of the concreteness of action.

The building of this concrete image is partly the result of the
Mandari habit of introspection and self-examination. In divination,
introspection and preoccupation with the psyche and with the
attitudes and emotions of others are encouraged. Preoccupation
with the interior condition and the awareness of the power of the
emotions lead the Mandari to regard much of their suffering
as coming from within the self, or from the relation of the self
towards others. Making a link between one's own or other people's
thoughts and words and external illness does not, however, exclude
an awareness of internality, but rather the reverse: the projective
images are formed *because* internal thought and disposition are seen
to have a vital reality.[1]

[1] Jung, who assumes that for the primitive a much greater range of real

The fact that a man may not even know he has harmful thoughts until it is revealed by a doctor simply demonstrates that he does not always know what is going on within his mind until this is revealed by a trained expert.[1]

Since it is always in the context of grievance that thought/speech images build up and since it is almost impossible for a man to prove, even to himself, that he has not, at some point, given thought to his grievance and that this thought has not led to illness, he makes the kind of statement I report on p. 172. The power of the mind is seen to have an inner and an outer aspect, the latter projected image has the power to harm and must be dealt with. In somewhat the same way, the power of witchcraft is seen to come from inside the witch and to be projected at the victim—with the difference that only a small proportion of the population has, by Mandari theory, the power to make the witchcraft projection, whereas everyone has the power to project through talk.

VI

It has frequently been demonstrated by anthropologists that while sin includes the action which bears the moral condemnation of society, many important character faults escape definition as sin. In Mandari also the moral wrong which is a fault of character and reprehensible but which does not violate essential doctrines in general escapes the ritual sanction.

The Mandari regard some morally wrong behaviour and disliked personality traits as self-punishing—the disliked habit of gluttony, for instance, in that greedy people are unpopular and may become targets in 'attacking' songs. Greed is inhibited by the fear of being shunned. Young people, particularly, dread the laughter of age-mates; folk-stories about the fate of youthful gluttons figure extremes like suicide. Character faults like cruelty, meanness, and bad temper make people unpopular: the behaviour may attract injurious talk, and if the offenders come from non-landowning

and natural occurrences are interpreted within the psychic category of 'projections', considers that this tendency for the experiences of the psyche to be carried outwards reflects a much greater failure to recognize interior content. C. G. Jung, *Collected Works*, vol. 11 (London, 1958).

[1] A fact which seems to suggest that the Mandari may recognize that thought can exist at a deeper level than that of conscious awareness, an assessment perhaps borne out by their attitude to dreams. See p. 293.

families they may, in extreme cases, be suspected of having the evil eye. The wealthy with similar personality traits are thought to attract the attacks of witches whom they have slighted, and the angry complaint of those they have neglected. Although theft is not a sin, it has moral, social, and ritual implications and is also subject to legal sanctions. It can have a witchcraft association because it takes place secretly and involves someone else's personal property. Thefts of cutting objects—spears, knives, and axes—release dangerous forces; the thief is thought to fall ill with symptoms of bowel or throat disorders, 'because the stolen implement cuts these parts of the body'; he may also be savaged by a predator.[1]

In a more positive sense the Mandari say that the good man is 'loved by Creator', and may escape the dangers which threaten bad men. Continual moral violations are seen to attract a concentrate of harmful power, so that if the whole man is 'bad', 'Creator may cut him off'.

Sin (the act linked with the automatic peril) by contrast is the ideological violation—the threat to central doctrine—which may have little to do with the fact of being a bad person. It is partly for this reason that the sinful act carries integral mechanisms of reinstatement in the rite of purification. The sins of incest and killing within the immediate family, however, allow no reinstatement.

A comparison can perhaps be drawn between the Mandari sin as ideological (doctrinal) violation, and the 'crime' against the state or party in certain totalitarian societies which carries a more extreme sentence than behavioural deviations like murder. Ideological crimes always require 'confession', followed by some form of rehabilitation. If the crime is serious, it cannot always be expurgated.

---

[1] A statement in symbolic terms may be made to exact confession from an unknown thief. The owner of the stolen object makes a formal statement of the loss: then the chief's drum is beaten with the 'dipp dipp note of death'.

9

THE MONTHLY RITE OF ELIMINATION

I

THE Mandari know that most sins and omissions never come to light, and a monthly rite of elimination is performed by every household, as the Mandari say, to ensure 'peaceful sleep' (*toto nabus*). 'Peaceful sleep' implies lack of worry and a feeling of positive well-being which a burden of guilt or worry disturbs. The Mandari, simply as they live, are not free from stress. On the contrary their precarious livelihood and the lack of scientific medicine mean that hunger, sickness, and death must continually be faced, as well as the mundane worries of daily life and sorting out complicated personal relationships.

The monthly rite known as *duŋgu na koljok* ('cutting the cucumber') is said to be 'for Creator', the emphasis being on unification as well as on elimination. (A free-spirit-of-the-Above or a Power of the homestead is included in the offering, together with dead kin.)

The ceremony takes place at the waxing of the new moon described as 'the waking of the moon' (*yapa ŋupuri*). When a homestead head sees the new moon rise, he takes down a wild cucumber (*Cucumis prophetarum*), now referred to in many parts of Mandari by the Dinka word *koljok*. Bunches of the round, prickly fruit are kept hanging under the hut eaves or on the branches of a shrine ready for use, for cucumber seeds are a basic ritual medium which can be used protectively or therapeutically by anyone in a wide range of emergencies. In doctor's homesteads or those of persons with shrines, cucumbers are cultivated, often at the shrine.

Each elementary family cuts its own cucumber each month, a man with several wives cuts one for each homestead, or his adult son does so on his behalf. Women and children, together with clients or visitors who may be staying temporarily, gather in the yard outside or by a homestead shrine and the senior man passes the whole cucumber round the head of each supplicant making a short prayer: 'You Creator (*Ŋun*) this is my *koljok*, if it finds favour with you accept it, because I have no cow or goat to offer. If there is any trouble let it fall to the ground.' He also prays: 'You Creator and you the Above and the Below, and you our Ancestors, let us and our young children remain healthy. Keep death from us. Take this "cow", and let Creator come and stay in the back of the hut so that we can be at peace and make sacrifices.' If there is any special worry this is mentioned; then he halves the cucumber and throws both pieces on the ground. The way in which the pieces fall indicates whether the prayer is acceptable and is also an omen for the future. In a good fall at least one half falls with the seeds facing 'the sky', representing health and well-being; the half facing the earth is the bad one, representing sin, evil, and sickness, and if both halves fall face downwards the pieces are thrown away and another cucumber is cut. If bad falls continue, or follow a month of illness or family bickering, the family head may consult a doctor who may advise him to kill a chicken or pour beer libations, or to make good some neglected obligation.

If the cucumber has fallen with one half up and one down, the officiant passes the bad half round each head, saying as he does so 'Let all evil and bad talk come out'; he then throws it away towards the west (*kotiaŋ*) in order that it may 'take sin and sickness to the place of evil'. With some of the seeds of the good half he marks those present on the forehead, chest, and back of the neck, while he prays: 'You must sleep peacefully; let all evil keep away, let everything bad disperse. May all good things come from the east (*yure*), from Logobong.'

If a homestead has a shrine to a Celestial Spirit or a Power, and if the month has been plagued by indispositions, the family head may make an offering. I attended such a rite in the homestead of a neighbour, the head of a family of retainers attached to the local chief. At the rite the doctor Deŋdit (as it happens a brother of the chief to whom the family were attached) acted for them. The rite followed the standard pattern of supplication for the patients, protective passes with the sacrificial chicken, and the stressing of the oppositions of good and evil as the doctor walked first to the west side of the homestead and raised his arms towards the west crying 'Let all evil remain in the west', and then crossed to the opposite side and beckoned to the east crying 'Let all good come from Logobong in the east.' During his address,

Deŋdit trembled and shook, showing typical signs of celestial possession.

The chicken was decapitated and used to seek an additional omen, in this case reassuring, as the chicken fell dead by one of the patients. (In such falls, it is important that the bird does *not* fall facing the west, a bad omen.) It was then cooked, eaten by the whole family, and the head thrown towards the west.

The monthly rite is the only ritual directly addressed to Creator as the unifying principle; it automatically incorporates all other religious agents. The principles of good and evil, embodied in east and west, and united in Logobong, are also stressed in word and action. Further, the rite also embraces all individuals who are present. All receive its benefits, if not the actual removal of anxiety and guilt, at least the breaking down of the formless load of time into smaller units which can be dealt with one by one. It prevents disorientating and disheartening accumulation without materially altering the situation of the participant, who will, after all, sin again and be purged again, month after month.

II

Since there has been a good deal of discussion regarding the role of the wild cucumber as one of a number of symbolic substitutes in Nilotic areas, I will now consider its role and meaning among the Mandari.[1]

In the first place, the prognosticatory aspect of cucumber-cutting at the rite of elimination is very important. The Mandari wish to determine the proportion of good and bad in a particular time-sequence.

Cutting the cucumber also gives additional emphasis by concretization, to the intention and the spoken word. This is integral to the formal blessing, although it can be dispensed with in emergency. Spontaneous prayer has its place in the unpredictable, individual crisis but, in formal ritual, media which can be endowed with some properties of the situation will support the verbal statement.

The most important ritual media are 'things of the homestead'

---

[1] Evans-Pritchard, *Nuer Religion*, pp. 128, 141–2. Audrey Hayley, 'Symbolic Equations: the Ox and the Cucumber', *Man*, vol. 3 (1968), no. 2.

and are food based, like flour or beer.[1] But for use in the routine elimination ritual and in the often-occurring mishap, anxiety, or threat, the medium of concretization and prediction must be easily available, expendable, and cheap. It must also be something which is whole and can be severed in order to represent the division of experience into good and bad, and it must be easily cut into more or less equal parts so that it can be thrown down equitably. Cucumbers meet all these requirements; they can be cut and thrown down, they can be hung-up by their clinging tendrils, they can be stored. More important, they are easily halved since unlike many other common fruits with hard kernels, cucumbers contain small oblong seeds set in a pulpy substance; the latter can also be used for marking and the supplicant can be seen to have been marked because the seeds adhere.

But apart from its expressly prognosticatory role and its use as a ritual marker, another role is suggested for the cucumber by the reference to 'ox'. I must stress, however, that while the cucumber is sometimes spoken of as 'ox', it can never be used in a situation in which an ox would feature, therefore it is not, in fact, a substitute for a sacrificial animal. Here we appear to have a contradiction, a descrepancy between description and use. How does this arise? I believe the explanation is not so obscure as at first appears, and that the solution lies in the not uncommon procedure whereby common denominators shared by two things are transferred from one situation to another, resulting in a form of metaphorical statement. This conclusion seems justified if we look again at what is involved.

Some references made by the Mandari give the impression that cucumbers are regarded as actual substitutes for cattle. Thus, if one asks a homestead owner what they are, hanging in a bunch under the eaves, he may give the 'botanical' term *koljok* (Dinka name), or *kitöli* (Mandari name), or he may answer '*suk ko Ki*', 'Spirit-of-the-Above's cattle'. Further, the Mandari say that the prayer addressed to Creator might contain the statement, 'take my cucumber, I have no cow.' (I have not heard the reference to cow actually made.) But here it is necessary to bear in mind other principles of Mandari sacrifice, in particular the fact that sacrifice

---

[1] Wild creepers or plants—the rain creeper used in various ceremonies—are not ritual media but things which have qualities that link them by analogy with life-giving rain, hence their use is therapeutic.

is not offered to Creator, and that the Mandari in fact say this: 'We do not offer back to Creator what is already His' (namely cattle). Moreover, Creator is not an agent of sickness, and it is in the situation of sickness that cattle or their substitutes are sacrificed to his agents. The rite of elimination is regularly performed whether or not sickness is present. When there is sickness, a cucumber is not used because it does not replace an animal victim and sickness cannot be removed with it.

It is not, therefore, as among the Nuer, the poor man's animal substitute, and when sickness occurs a real animal substitute must be sought. If it is not found the rite cannot be performed; in most cases, however, a minor offering can be secured when urgently required because it is an obligation of kinship and patronage to guarantee the health of dependants. While cutting a cucumber is protective, it is not sacrifice. Family elders do not assemble to 'sacrifice' cucumbers, but to kill animals or offer substitutes or to anoint with ritual oils. Sacrifice may follow the elimination rite in special circumstances, as in the case recounted on pp. 238–9, when the humble family produced their small chicken.

The scale of sacrificial substitutions[1] does not include media which are simply ameliorative or concretize prayer. These latter are another kind of media in their own right; they are flour, cucumbers, spittle, ashes of the homestead wood fire, and ashes of the cattle-camp dung fire. They will be selected partly on the criterion of availability within their own class, although some, like flour, are seen to have greater efficacy than others and may be sought when considered essential. Unless an omen must be taken, words alone or together with spittle may be equally effective. The special value of the cucumber is that it can give visible reassurance or foretell the future, as other media cannot because they cannot be severed.

If we turn to the Nuer the distinction becomes clear. For the Nuer the offering of a cucumber is indeed a sacrifice in that they themselves class it with other kinds of sacrificial offering. The difference between the Nuer killing of a real ox and the severing of a symbolic one—a cucumber—lies at the level of economic stringency and not at the conceptual level where an ox and a cucumber are seen to be interchangeable. Evans-Pritchard makes this quite clear by showing that the Nuer do not only *refer* to

[1] See p. 399

cucumbers as oxen, but *use* them as oxen. He gives examples of cucumbers actually being used as cattle substitutes in death rites, in cleansing for minor incest, and as stop-gap offerings in default of a ready animal.[1] The latter use only is reported by Lienhardt for the Dinka. The Nuer also use the fruit of the sausage tree in the same way.

What we are dealing with in Mandari, on the other hand, is not a stated substitution, but metaphor based on a number of common denominators shared by two things—oxen and cucumbers. Both have organic structure, both have 'flesh' which can be cut, and interior parts which can be manipulated. Further, in the same way that 'ox' is a general descriptive word for cattle substitute in many situations, it may perhaps be used also in a different context, where the link is the significant act of 'cutting'. Thus a severed cucumber represents an ox in a rite which has little to do with sacrifice, but a lot to do with the stating and resolution of the crucial human predicament presented by the fact of good and evil.

Another factor which may be significant for the verbal image-building is the fact that there is only one word, *duŋgu*, for 'to cut' and 'to sacrifice'; therefore different meanings of the word 'cut' can only be clear in the situation in which the cutting takes place. 'To sacrifice' is an appropriate translation of *duŋgu* in the case of killing an animal in a rite. But at an elimination ritual where the contractual element implicit in the Mandari relationship with spirits which lies at the heart of sacrifice does not exist, it would be more correct to speak of 'severing' in the general sense. Yet, while the background of ideas in sacrificial cutting and in cucumber severing are very different, the *act* of cutting is the same whether an animal's throat or a cucumber is involved, and this may also contribute to the merging of images. (It is relevant that 'spearing' (*rembu*), while it may have ritual implications, is not sacrifice.)

I would suggest that a complicated metaphor is involved here, based on the perception of similar qualities which have little to do with 'cucumber equals ox' at the level of symbolic substitution but much to do with the fact that oxen and cucumbers have common properties and in some respects can be manipulated in similar ways.

There is also a further possible explanation: that the word 'ox'

---

[1] Evans-Pritchard, *Nuer Religion*, pp. 146, 184.

and the phrase implying substitution have been borrowed from the Dinka in the same way that the Dinka word for 'cucumber' is now used in many parts of Mandari. This would not imply that the rite itself is simply a Dinka borrowing (too many important elements, typically Mandari, are present for this to be the case), but that having heard these statements made by Dinka in similar contexts, and finding that they fit some features of their own situation, the Mandari have taken them over.

10

BIRTH VARIANTS AND
BIRTH ABNORMALITIES

THE Mandari consider that some persons are endowed for life with special associations through the circumstances of their birth. Three kinds of birth variants are seen to be a sign of Spirit-of-the-Above: multiple births, breech-births, and babies born with teeth. The first, for the Mandari, means twins. (Those with whom I discussed it had never heard of more than two babies being born at one time, and when I pointed out this could happen, exclaimed that this was 'like animals' and asked whether the mother could survive.) Mandari make their primary distinction between twins and other birth variants on the one hand, and deformed infants on the other, by viewing the former as a spiritual sign and the latter as falling in the malign category of *rube*.

I

TWINS[1]

Mandari welcome twins but recognize that their delivery presents a greater danger for the mother and for the infants than the single birth and that the life expectation of twins is less good than that of the singly born. Because they are seen to be a sign of Spirit-of-the-Above, and in a precarious position, ritual is performed following the twin birth. The fact of being a twin also sets the pattern for all sickness rituals performed throughout the twin's life; in a sacrifice for a twin an animal of the 'cool' category must always be used.

The word for twinning is *kurudu*; but twins also have the bird association reported from the Nuer, and when a woman is delivered of twins, therefore, the idiomatic phrase 'She has been

[1] The main sources of material on twins among the Nilotics are Evans-Pritchard, 'Customs and Beliefs relating to Twins among the Nilotic Nuer', *Uganda Journal*, vol. 3 (1936), pp. 230–8; *Nuer Religion*, pp. 128, 130–2. Seligman, *Pagan Tribes of the Nilotic Sudan* (London, 1932), *passim*.

delivered of birds' (*kurudu kwen*) announces the event. The association is particularly strong around the time of birth, but becomes
less emphasized after the naming ceremony. It is when they are
newly born and, like all babies, still unnamed and confined to the
delivery hut with the mother and when even their sex is kept secret,
that the verbal identification of twins with birds is clearest. An
inquirer will ask, 'Are the birds still there?' If one has died, the
reply is 'No. One has flown away.'

Since they are classed as 'Celestial', the 'hot' goat cannot be
used in a twin sacrifice for illness, but a goat, together with a sheep,
features in the initial rite immediately following the birth. The
sheep is killed 'because they are Above', the goat is 'for the cleansing, because their birth is *nulon*'. After this rite, the celestial link,
not the *nulon* aspect of the birth, is the one stressed. (As pointed
out, *nulon* is a miraculous sign that is not an unequivocal celestial
intervention. It often presupposes a terrestrial association, although
this distinction is not absolute.) It is understandable that twins—
human beings, physically located on earth—should require recognition of the terrestrial in the sacrifice. The sheep–goat offering
also represents the separate realities of earth and sky, with their
attributes of hot and cold, which are united in the dyadic element
of the birth.

The father produces the goat, and the mother's brother the
sheep. One animal should be male, the other a barren female;
it is immaterial which relative provides which sex of animal.
The father and the mother's brother exchange sacrificial meat,
the father and his kin eating the mother's brother's sheep, the
mother's brother and his kin eating the father's goat. In this
way both families are identified with each sacrifice, both give
recognition to the celestial association and both are cleansed
from the birth which affects the parents and both sets of kin
equally.[1]

The link between twins and birds is derived from the primary
association with Spirit-of-the-Above. The recognition of the
celestial nature of twins is crucial and its violation—for instance
by killing a goat in a twin sickness rite—has lethal consequences.

---

[1] Seligman reports for the Nuer that the father and the maternal uncle must
each kill a bullock in order to relieve the father and mother from the twins'
dangerous influences which are seen to present a threat on a cross-sexual basis
Pagan Tribes of the Nilotic Sudan, p. 227.

But why is the stereotype of 'twin' a bird and not an animal? In the first place, in the Mandari context, an animal association would be ideologically inadmissible. This is made clear if we consider the place of birds and animals in Mandari thought.

Birds come in that category which embraces the upper part—the sky and its phenomena—but we must be careful not to assume that birds are therefore *manifestations* of Spirit-of-the-Above, because this is not so. Only two birds are *spiritual* representations; one of these is Kulaŋ, 'black-bird-of-the-Above', the other, Mardit —'white-bird-of-the-Above'.

Evans-Pritchard has already pointed out a reason for the link which is seen to connect birds with the 'upper'. They fly high and are therefore imaginatively seen to be nearer Creator ('God', in Evans-Pritchard's terminology) than terrestrial things: the fact that some birds may not fly at all is irrelevant to the *idea* of bird as a flying category. Levi-Strauss's diagram based on the Nuer material emphasizes the point Evans-Pritchard makes regarding the physical and the ideal place of birds and twins.[1]

Although the Mandari do not use the bird as the symbol of the life or soul, an association made in some cultures, they believe life moves upward to Creator at death. Rising from the earth (like a bird) suggests spirituality. The phrase 'to walk high' means to be well directed; the doctor 'walking high, high' (*wörö ki, ki*), epitomizes the committed, dynamic person, active in curing and saving life; the person immobilized by illness, the 'grounded one' (*gwa kak*), is the useless and frustrated.

While the association of birds with the celestial is largely a perceptual connection based on the spatial habitat of birds and their soaring flight (a reason why chickens by 'latent birdness'—they seldom fly—are reserved sacrifices for Celestial Spirits) the twin/Spirit-of-the-Above identification is largely a conceptual one, deriving from signs of Celestial Spirit seen to be present in twins. But the fact that for different reasons twins and birds come within a single ideal division does not necessarily explain why twins should be *called* birds, since other persons also in this division (like the breech-birth) are not so called. Something further is needed to connect twins with birds, and this is found again at the perceptual level, the level of assumed observation or the

[1] C. Levi-Strauss, *Totemism*, transl. R. Needham (Boston, Mass., 1963), pp. 79–80.

common characteristic of multiple birth. An association with an animal on the multiple birth element is inadmissible since animals belong to the terrestrial, and also because animal–human analogies are considered malign, or, at least, ludicrous. They would be wholly out of place in the twin context.[1] The good side of both twins and birds makes their linking ideologically correct; the bird association actually helps to distinguish twins, essentially good, from abnormal infants which are bad.

Another element in the bird association is drawn from the analogy of flight and what this represents in terms of soaring away. Twins, especially when newly born, are considered to have a tenuous hold of life, and as a bird soars away, so the precarious twin life may 'at any moment return to Creator'. This ephemeral quality is constantly stressed and the twin death expressed in terms of flight.

A breech-birth, however, which might be considered at least as dangerous, lacks the bird association, although it is also 'Spirit-of-the-Above'. It would therefore seem that it is the multiple birth, linked to other 'bird-like' features, which lies at the basis of the stereotype. A somewhat similar building up of particular images out of the material of shared qualities and common resemblances will later be considered in the context of animal stereotypes.

Twins do not eat birds or their eggs, a prohibition not extended to twins' relatives, and the prohibition on eating birds and eggs by other categories derives from other notions. The bird association, however, means that chickens can never be killed in twin sacrifice, beer is therefore substituted. The Mandari also share with the Nuer the idea that birds respond to twins, so if a village is ravaged by weaver-birds, twins enter the fields to disperse them, waving their arms in the air (like wings?) and crying, 'You birds, leave our grain and go into the bush to eat your own.'

A most important feature of the twin situation is the notion of single identity shared by a pair of twins. The special relationship between one twin and another is stressed at all major changes of state, where twins are treated as a single personality. If recognition is not given to this the excluded twin may fall ill or die.

---

[1] Contrast the Nuer, who link twins with crocodiles, an extension of the link with birds through the fact that crocodiles lay eggs. Evans-Pritchard, *Nuer Religion*, p. 130.

At the age of around seven, when the lower teeth are extracted, those of twins must be removed simultaneously. Twins should marry at the same time. If they are boys, and cattle to allow this cannot be accumulated, the first-born marries first. When one twin is of each sex, the male should betroth his wife at the moment his twin sister puts on the goat-skin of married status. If twin sisters cannot achieve simultaneous marriage the elder marries first and the younger enters the nuptial hut and lies for a short while at the side of her sister and her husband. As one would expect in view of female vulnerability, it is considered more injurious for twin girls to be separated at marriage than for twin boys, or twins of different sex.

At death, great care must be taken that the body of a twin is not buried entire, an irrevocable splitting of the single personality which may lead to the death of the survivor. To prevent this, the little finger of the dead twin is amputated and left outside on the grave. There is some analogy here with the burial during the early rains when, as I showed (p. 116), the corpse must be linked to the open with a rain creeper so that the moisture of the human body is not separated from the falling rain.

Certain names are given to twins although these can also be given to ordinary infants. If one twin is of each sex the girl is Agoya, the archetypal female, the boy Kulaŋ, the archetypal male (together representing perhaps the archetypal pair?). When both are female the first-born is Agoya, the second Körimit, 'child of Creator'. The names of the two celestial birds are used for two boys, the first is Kulaŋ, 'black-bird-of-the-sky', the second Mardit, 'white-bird-of-the-sky'.[1]

Twins are one of those categories which are said to have 'blood relationship' with the scorpion (*yuŋi ko kito*): others with this association are *Möjut* (p. 249) and those possessed by Spirit-of-the-Above. The link between all these categories and the scorpion is, I assume, the fact that the scorpion, with the tail carrying the poisonous sting erect and pointing towards the sky, makes a characteristic sign by 'pointing up'. (Such a sign should also be made by the sacrificial chicken for Spirit-of-the-Above, which dies on its back—'facing the sky'.[2])

[1] It will be remembered that the two Kulaŋs are different.
[2] The association may be reinforced by the suddenness and the sharp agony of the sting (cf. Chapter 2 on the characteristics of celestial illness).

The logic of blood relationship proscribes those 'born with scorpion' from killing scorpions, and assumes that the latter will not sting them or if the person is stung he will suffer no lingering reaction. The assumption is that things in the same category cannot be inherently mutually destructive. If a scorpion stings its human relative and swelling or death follows, the scorpion has 'violated its kinship'. The blood-relationship between humans and creatures never leads to verbal identification and a person is never referred to as a scorpion.[1]

II

OTHER BIRTH VARIATIONS

Like twins, a breech-birth is a sign of Spirit-of-the-Above; 'It shows the Above wishes for meat.' A sheep must be severed lengthways—analogously with the baby's divided legs which show first. A child born with teeth is also in this category, and necessitates the killing of a sheep.[2]

MÖJUT

This is a birth situation which requires protective dedication and has the scorpion link, although not specifically described as Spirit-of-the-Above.

Möjut is a male child born after several previous babies have died in succession. He is dedicated to Creator and protectively singled out at childhood changes of state, although after maturity further attention is not required.[3]

At his naming ceremony special pleadings are made to Creator to spare his life. The baby is raised upwards at each corner of the homestead by a female elder who prays as she holds it up, 'You Creator, spare this child; this is our last child, spare us one, all the rest have been taken by You.' The baby is marked with ashes (of mourning and protection) and a chicken is decapitated.

At the end of the month following the birth a second chicken is sacrificed when the monthly cucumber is severed. Ordinary

---

[1] This is not a contradiction of the Mandari assumption that some lions are 'men'—for Mandari an actuality and *not* an identification.

[2] The daughter of the seer, Deŋdit, was born with teeth—another example of the association with Spirit-of-the-Above in this family.

[3] The word *möjut* not only describes the child's state, but is a personal name as well.

babies' heads are shaved and kept shaved for hygienic reasons, but the hair of *möjut* must be allowed to grow freely. Growing the hair is a sign of mourning and it is said 'This child is born after great sorrows.' Children with long hair are *joro*. Should the hair become excessively tangled it may be trimmed, but never shaved off because long hair is the sign of the child's special position—'Creator sees and spares it.'

At the removal of the four lower front teeth, a purely social occasion marking a maturation stage, the child's head is shaved. A chicken is first passed round it by a female elder and prayers are offered for health and in thanksgiving. The chicken is decapitated and beer-drinking and homestead dancing follows. The teeth are then extracted in the normal way.

Sacrifice is never offered at tooth extraction unless a child in need of special protection is included.

ABNORMAL BIRTHS

When a radical physical abnormality shows in the newly-born it is inauspicious (*rube*), in two forms considered to be associated with sorcery. (Formerly the baby was secretly taken to the bush by an old woman and buried in a disused termite mound, for hyena.) Abnormal infants are

1. Monstrosities.
2. Babies with extensively marked bodies, 'mottled like leopard'.
3. Males born without testicles (*liss*).
4. Males born with only one testicle (*loweri*).

The two latter are now reared, but are regarded as potentially unlucky and never included in hunting or raiding expeditions for fear they should 'spoil the spear' or 'cause the deaths of their brothers'. Women giving birth to monsters and mottled babies keep this secret for fear others would suspect them of being witches.

11

PSYCHIC FORCE IN THE MAN–ANIMAL INVOLVEMENT

I

ENCOUNTERS with animals of many kinds provide an immediate and intense part of Mandari daily experience. In this chapter I shall consider the aesthetic and emotional responses that animals evoke, and the images or stereotypes which are built up around certain of them, attempting to show how these are evolved and how the idea of animal personality leads to the ascription of something similar to the psychic force of important human categories, to some animals.[1]

The Mandari classify animals, in the first place, by their spatial distance from men, humans, in the same way that we distinguish domestic animals, pets, wild animals, and so on. The smallest residential unit, the homestead (baŋ), contains the intimately connected animals described as 'homestead animals' (jaka ko baŋ). The most ubiquitous is the dog, which is important both in idea and sentiment as well as in mundane affairs. Dogs play the usual canine role of watch-dogs in homestead and cattle-camps, and of faithful companions. Good hunting dogs are particularly prized, the saying being that 'One hunter with four good dogs can kill a buffalo single-handed.' Dogs are liked as pets, and the Mandari appreciate good colour markings and general good points in dogs as they do in cattle. Clan histories and, more generally, folk-lore refer extensively to the closeness and reciprocity of human–canine relationships. Primal dogs in legend had the power of speech and warned humans of impending danger; they also taught the use of fire. 'Dog-horns' (see pp. 344 ff.) featured in the early Bora rain rituals.

The chicken is also classed as homestead bird, but like birds in general it also belongs to the category of 'celestial things'. As

[1] The material in the first part of this chapter was published as an article under the title 'Animal Identity and Human Peril'. See *Man*, vol. 3 (1968), no. 1. In rewriting it I have altered some of the terms originally used.

'bird-of-the-Above' it is a standard sacrifice in minor rituals, but it lacks the dignity of animal personality and 'it may be seized at any time and sacrificed.' Also inhabiting homesteads, although of the category 'wild nature' (*ko mudiŋ*) are small hut- and grain-store-dwelling mice, rats, snakes, and lizards. Some of these un-domesticated creatures receive immunity from harm because of their physical location in homesteads.

Baŋ also means hamlet, village, or social space, and here cattle and small stock are felt to belong. Sheep and goats may be actually kraaled in the village, but cattle are always camped outside it. Cattle, and to a lesser extent, small stock, are central to social, economic, and religious activities, but it is cattle alone which offer important emotional and aesthetic outlets, and feature in history and myth.[1]

The wild (*mudiŋ*), the reverse of *baŋ* in both the physical and conceptual sense, lies beyond the immediate domestic sphere. *Mudiŋ* is both the neighbourhood 'bush' and the true wild; both are complementary to the social unit. At the fringes of the cul-tivations lies the neighbourhood wasteland, used for defecation and the disposal of refuse from ritual and mundane cleansings. This belt is constantly crossed when fetching water, searching for firewood, and visiting. Small animals frequent it, but while game and predators sometimes penetrate it, it is not a hunting area and seldom dangerous to cross. The hyena, because of its scavenging nature, is closely associated with it, and performs an important function by disposing of the carcasses of stock killed in exorcisms, polluted food, and the monstrous human foetus.

Beyond the neighbourhood wasteland is the untamed bush, primary woodland and long-abandoned secondary scrub, the en-vironment of two important animal categories; 'game' (*jaka*)—animals hunted for meat—and the 'predator' (*gworoŋ*)—the large carnivore which attacks and eats men.

In addition to the classification which places animals in relation to man as domestic, game, and predator, the Mandari divide creatures into zoological classes by biological similarity. The main ones are animals (*jaka*), birds (*kwen*), fish (*somot*), snakes (*munu*); all subdivide into named varieties. When there are many animals to a variety, there may be a further designate—the 'small wild cat' variety (*gwagwe*), for instance, embracing the polecat, serval,

[1] We have seen the involvement of humans in the display-ox.

wild cat, and lynx. Many larger animals lack generic names, although a number are recognized as 'of a kind'; for example there is no designate 'ape' or 'monkey' and each is referred to by its specific name.

Game includes antelope, buck, gazelle, and wild pig, and from the hunting and meat viewpoint buffalo and elephant, although these two important animals are more often distinguished respectively as *mekor* and *tome*. Both can be placed in the predator category, particularly the buffalo, which relentlessly hunts down and tramples a man, and while neither has the central predator characteristics of being man-eating, both can be 'game' or 'predator' according to context. Their correct class, however, is 'game', because in general men hunt and eat *them*.

True predators are the large man-attacking, man-eating carnivores—lion, leopard, and the lesser, but more common, hyena. The predator category is loosely framed, as the occasional inclusion of buffalo and elephant shows, and the Mandari are aware that it crosses the 'zoological' classification. (Hyena go with jackal and wild dog, and lion and leopard with the smaller wild cats.) The Mandari, however, seldom refer to predators except in the *gworoŋ* context since they are primarily thought of in their common position in relation to man.

Wild animals have their own spatial location and men theirs, but wild animals also enter the domestic range, sometimes specifically to prey—and men spread out over the bush visiting, herding, and travelling. Dry-season camps, extensions of the social unit, are situated in the far wild, where encounters with predators are likely. Although man is primarily homestead-centred and wild animals are bush-centred, animals and men meet in frequent encounters, and the Mandari have a keenly developed knowledge of animal nature and likely animal responses, and it is important to keep in mind the extent of the man–animal involvement.

The Mandari are quite clear about the basic separation between man and animal, but also show a preoccupation with eliminating what they consider to be animal characteristics which may be impressed on humans. Babies mottled 'like leopard' as described earlier, must be exposed. Some human action also destroys the correct distinction between men and animals leading to other kinds of marking or impressing with animal features or, as in the case of the *mönöjin* sin, to animal attacks.

II

Animal personality is associated with dogs, cattle, and, to a much lesser degree, small stock. It is the dog, particularly, which is regarded as having that extra quality which gives psychic force (*töpötö*) and makes the killing or the shedding of its blood dangerous. There is even an analogy with the situation of killing a person, the difference being that whereas human homicide involves both the ritual uncleanness of the killer and the avenging psyche (*nyök*) of the slain, only vengeance is feared from domestic animals wantonly killed in anger. The killer's wrong emotional condition— his anger and aggression—is an important element here, since the accidental animal killing, the sacrificial killing, and the killing for socially recognized entertainment, do not lead to vengeance, although even in sacrifice the officiant addresses the animal and states the reason for its death.

The Mandari explain the ability to release animal *nyök* as deriving from the close man–animal involvement. Killing a dog is particularly dangerous—'The dog has psychic force (*diuŋ pötö*) because it grows with man.' On one occasion I offered a shotgun to end the misery of a fine hunting dog injured by a leopard, but was told that it was unthinkable 'to kill a dog just like that, for no reason'. On another occasion a man came to my homestead in some agitation asking if I had seen his dog which he had clubbed in a fit of temper after it had stolen food. He feared that, if it crept away to die, his children would fall ill. Dogs most commonly release avenging psyche because they hang around the hearth and irritate people by knocking things over or snatching food and, while reasonable beating is legitimate, the inflicting of serious injury is not. The ensuing peril searches out the innocent target. The dog's killer is unharmed, the danger devolving on to his or her offspring either alive at the time or born later. The wounds of the mutilated and bludgeoned dog appear in multiple form on the child when 'sores break out all over it, or it is born with its body smothered in sores'. These dog-wounds are seen to lie dormant, in wait for a victim, almost indefinitely.

When the diviner diagnoses this condition, the victim's close kin gather in the bush, a hole is dug into which sesame oil is poured, and a chicken is placed beside it. The doctor instructs the avenging psyche to 'take the meat and leave the child'; the chicken is decapitated and head and body laid in the hole and covered over. The bird is not eaten because the avenging psyche is said to directly enter it.

More specialist treatment which involves the destruction of the avenging psyche is *gorko na nyöksho*. The hole in the bush is baited with grain, beer, groundnuts, and the heart and intestines of a goat killed for the exorcism, then the patient is laid beside it. The avenging agent is 'called' with the divining rattle:

> It may come quickly, or be slow and have to be tempted with further delicacies. When the doctor sees it go into the hole to feed, or hears it squealing from inside, he impales it. The *nyök* screams 'Ahrrrrrrr!' The doctor wrestles with it swaying to and fro and pressing on the spear while spectators assist him. He foams at the mouth or blood pours from his nostrils. Eventually it weakens and ceases its struggles. Sometimes it refuses to come, or escapes slipping to one side, then the doctor only wounds, and treatment must recommence.

The earth is filled in and the spear left standing for four days, then a fire is lighted over the spot. In exorcism, the doctor induces possession by rhythmic rattling, a mechanism adapted to many uses.

Cattle or small stock can theoretically become *nyök* but it is unlikely that a valuable animal would be wantonly killed, nor are cattle described, like dogs, as *pötö*. But cattle *nyök* can follow killing simply for meat,[1] or killing under false pretences, which can happen when people place cattle with friends for herding. They may sacrifice a loaned animal and fear, or feelings of guilt, may lead to the pretence that the animal died naturally or was taken by a predator. A suspicious owner can invoke the animal's blood: 'All right, let the blood of my ox seek out the killer'; the culprit's children may then sicken. The correct action is to inform the owner and promise a calf in compensation.

III

Most wild animals are not seen to have special personality although even these are not killed gratuitously. Game animals, together with smaller edible creatures and birds, may be killed for food without ritual imperilment, and this licence is supported by

---

[1] As also in Nuer; such a killing falls under one aspect of the concept of *cien*. Evans-Pritchard, *Nuer Religion*, p. 265.

statements relating to initial creation, such as 'These animals were put there by Creator to provide men with meat', or 'These animals are only meat for each other [predators] or men.' Even the elephant is 'meat' for ordinary people, although for the professional elephant hunter it has a special significance, and ritual follows his first kill.

Of predators in general, the Mandari say that their characteristic is to withdraw in face-to-face encounters; but they may have to be killed because they attack people or stock, and then ritual is carried out. This is not to expel *nyök* (which is exclusive to domestication) but relates to the inherent qualities of some predators.

For the 'type' predator, the leopard, a mortuary leopard dance known as *damaya na koka* is held. For this ceremony the killer's head is shaved by an old woman who also paints his body with spots to imitate leopard markings, using the traditional mixture of powdered red ochre and sesame oil known as *meje*.[1] Beer-drinking and ceremonial dancing follow during which the killer and other hunters charge around shouting ox-names, throwing spears, and shooting arrows into trees. The leopard skin, which is displayed on the meeting-tree during the rite, is afterwards worn by the owner at dances.[2]

Failure to hold the mortuary dance is said to result in the killer's body becoming 'spotted (*akwackwac*) like leopard'. It is also said that 'leopard is like person' (*koka se ŋutu*), and 'We dance for it as we dance for a dead relative.' Here, the danger surrounding the killing is represented by the impressing of leopard marks on the killer himself, in contrast to the marking of an offspring with wounds.

The ceremony which lays the psychic force of the leopard contains components similar to those of human death and homicide rites. The leopard killer's head is shaved like a human homicide. As the human corpse is anointed with shea-oil, a dark oil, with the association of 'black', the colour of death and of veiling, so the leopard killer is marked with spots of red ochre,

---

[1] Red ochre is not a ritual substance as such, although it may have a ritual use—it is primarily a 'decorative dress' *jupusi*.

[2] It is prestigious to kill a leopard and wear its skin, both because the animal is dangerous and also because of the qualities of leopard itself. A historical myth describes how one landowning chief rewards a client by giving him a leopard skin, at the same time handing over to him duties in connection with the woodland and game. There is no rule, however, that only chiefs and their relatives can wear leopard skins.

red having the association of danger and 'heat', and perhaps here being the mark of achievement, the triumph of human over animal.

By imitating the essential leopard attributes, spots, and holding a leopard death rite, the leopard presence is symbolically eliminated. Also stressing elimination is the beer-drinking, which at a human death demonstrates progression. Initially it represents 'wiping-away', a release from the earthbound; later it shows establishment of new identity. Leopard rites have wiping-away qualities but lack additional transitional features, because although both animals and humans have life which returns to Creator, and although vengeful animalness can hang about harmfully, animals lack a continuing personality. In leopard death rites, as in those for humans, past conflicts are played out. As at chiefs' mortuary rites war is mimed, so at rites for leopards the hunt is mimed.

Hyena killing, by contrast, requires no ceremonial, although the killer's body must be patterned with red ochre splodges to ward off hyena marks. The lack of ritual may be related to the Mandari view of the hyena as a low creature, typically mean and cowardly. Hyena are primarily scavengers; leopard are real predators— bold and cunning. They are also considered aesthetically beautiful, particularly for their perfect markings. Hyena are considered ugly, their image of 'predatorness' is faint, their markings less distinct.

The Mandari readily describe the characteristics of those pre-dators to which the distinction *pötö* is applied.

1. *Inedible and preying*

They must not be eaten because they eat human flesh. Apart from their gratuitous preying, the Mandari use them to dispose of corpses and filth which cannot be dealt with by the community. In pre-Administration times the bodies of outcasts—witches, sor-cerers, chronic thieves—executed after meeting-tree consensus, were thrown into the bush, and predators are still utilized for the unobtrusive dispatch of grossly deformed babies. The Mandari view defiling things as belonging to the bush, the sphere of predators.

2. *'Eyes'* (*kwen*)

A most important source of the psychic force of predators is being 'night animals with eyes', and a number of notions converge here. 'Things of the night' form a category, which includes night-witchcraft, owls, and predators.[1] Day-hunting predators are rare; if seen by day they simply walk away. At night they become aggressively active and the dark hours associated with human (ritual) predatorness are also their working hours. The dangerous power of night animals contrasts with the ritual harmlessness of day animals, even those objectively dangerous ones like elephant and buffalo.

The image of 'eyes'—'which gleam in the dark', or 'glow red in the dark'—carries other malevolent associations. Eye redness is a stereotype of the evil eye; 'watching and looking'—too steadily or too meaningfully, with intent—are involved here. When speaking of danger inherent in the eye associations, the Mandari often simply say 'eyes'; this conjures up the standard associations. Some ritually harmless night creatures, of course, also have glowing 'eyes', like small wild cats. But no day animal has them; these sleep at night, and even if awake do not stare and watch and their eyes do not glow. In view of the Mandari preoccupation with eyes as a feature of both human and animal physiology and in relation to looking and watching and the psychic relevance of these acts, it may not be irrelevant to comment that the eyes of leopards, when seen close to, do have a strikingly impelling quality. Peaceful daytime encounters with leopards are by no means rare and for me the memory of them is marked by the outstanding magnificence, steadiness, and depth of immense tawny eyes. They move slowly off, turn and look again; move further, turn and look again; until with seeming boredom they glide into the undergrowth. Hyena are more nervous and their eyes lack this brilliance, but they are seen much more frequently glowing in the scrub around village outskirts at night.

3. *Markings (wurusi)*

An essential property is having markings. Leopard conspicuously, and hyena to a lesser extent, are marked—dark on light. But lion are unmarked and though they are among the

---

[1] Ill omens also include night animal behaviour or reversed animal behaviour; for example the persistent hooting of an owl perching on a tree overlooking the homestead, a hyena howling on the edge of the homestead (portending death—'It comes to mourn'), and flying ants swarming by day rather than by night, the correct swarming time. A diviner may be called when events confirm an omen.

predators, this lack excludes them from the *pötö* category. I cannot stress too strongly the general perceptual and emotional importance of patterning and marking for the Mandari, a characteristic already remarked in other Nilotics.[1]

In Table 2 I set out certain animal characteristics. Animals in columns 1–5 are *pötö*; the lion misses the absolutely crucial column 5. Those animal characteristics which have a special relevance for the Mandari are picked out—'eyes', night activity, tameness, and so forth. Other characteristics are ignored, and therefore some animals are ignored, in the image building. Analogous elements seen to exist in the chosen attributes and in the emotionally charged situations—such as those associated with witchcraft—are used to build up the stereotypes. The formation of any image always involves an interplay between the properties of the object and the selectivity of the observing subject[2] and the Mandari animal images can be seen as selections from a special range of perceptions.

The two categories implying the greatest polarity—domestic and dangerous wild—can of course be arranged in a sequence close–domestic–helpful–subservient, and far–wild–hostile–aggressive. The principle of benign domestication is expressed in statements like, 'The psychic force of the dog is good; the dog is a black person, and is very important, having taught many things to men'; the danger of the wild and of predators in statements like 'The psychic force of predators is bad; they have no kinship with men.' Distinction between 'us' and 'them' is quite clear here—the dog is one of 'us', the predator is not one of 'us'. Their personality enables domestic animals to harm through their avenging psyche in much the same way as humans, the animal manifesting itself through 'wounds', persons through 'sickness'. Predators (which cannot become *nyök*—'they are wild') manifest their personality differently.

While the logical element inherent in the idea of complementary duality is undoubtedly of importance in the polarizing of these two kinds of identity,[3] it would seem that it is subsidiary to the more significant emotional and perceptual components, which are the

---

[1] Evans-Pritchard, *The Nuer*, pp. 41–4, and Lienhardt, *Divinity and Experience*, pp. 13–15.

[2] Rudolf Arnheim, *Art and Visual Perception* (English edition, London, 1957).

[3] Cf. C. Levi-Strauss, *The Savage Mind* (trans., London, 1966), *passim*.

S

TABLE 2. *Sources of psychic force in animals*

Elements often indicating *pǒtǒ*					Elements never indicating *pǒtǒ*		
1	2	3	4	5	6	7	8
'Night'	*Prey on men*	*Non-edible*	*'Eyes'*	*Markings*	*'Day'*	*Dangerous (non-preying)*	*Edible*
Leopard	Leopard	Leopard	Leopard	Leopard	—	—	—
Hyena	Hyena	Hyena	Hyena	Hyena	—	—	—
Lion	Lion	Lion	Lion	—	—	—	—
Wild cats	—	Wild cats (most)	Wild cats	Wild cats (some)	—	—	Wild cats (a few)
—	—	—	—	Snakes (some)	Snakes	Snakes (some)	—
—	—	—	—	—	Elephant	Elephant	Elephant
—	—	—	—	—	Buffalo	Buffalo	Buffalo

ones that give the animal images their particular form and their compelling force.

IV

In another man–animal relationship, metamorphosis, persons are believed to assume the physical form and nature of dangerous animals. This capacity is distinct from the notion of *töpötö*, and any dangerous animal may be involved.

The Mandari statement that some men 'have wild beasts in their bodies', is not a statement of certainty, like, for instance, 'some people have the evil eye or are night-witches.' As might be expected, actual experience of man-into-beast transformations is rarely claimed, so the Mandari have little occasion to clarify ideas about them, whereas almost everyone believes that they, or their family, have experienced witchcraft phenomena; the suspected witch and man with the evil eye are often known persons. Beast-men are outside the range of everyday experience and accounts of them are vague. The usual assumption is that these are persons with the power temporarily to assume the form of animals, rather than animals which assume human form, although uncertainty is clear from the evidence.

The Mandari seldom apply metamorphosis accusations to other Mandari,[1] but rather to non-Mandari neighbours who live to the east of their country, at Khor Bya where the Nyangware–Bari–Tsera boundaries converge on the Nile frontage. (The inlet is about a hundred miles from Mandari.) The location has a good deal of relevance. Thus it is around Mount Tindalu, on the eastern boundary (permanent lion country with rocky outcrops and perennial springs), that most metamorphosis incidents are claimed to occur. Those Mandari who live at Tindalu also have contact with Nile-dwellers sharing dry-season camps at Tombek and sometimes intermarrying. Nile-dwellers have a witchcraft association for the Mandari, and metamorphosis also falls within the category *rube* which includes ritually evil human powers. A number of important associations therefore converge to make metamorphosis credible for the Mandari of this region.

---

[1] I was told of a form of metamorphosis which could occur inside Mandari which resulted from the ill-treatment of an inherited widow (*körubi*). In such cases the *ŋulon* of the dead husband might enter a leopard and savage the culprit.

The appearance of beast-men is not random; they are deliberately summoned by those who feel themselves denied justice
through customary channels, and are a recognized, if rarely used,
ritual sanction. An informant first raised the subject of them with
me in this context, comparing them with acts like deliberate 'rain-
spoiling'. All are legitimate but dangerous ways of drawing attention to wrongs, because the user, who confesses in the hope of
gaining redress, runs a calculated risk if widespread harm is
thought to have resulted.

The phenomena materialize in the form of preying or dangerous
animals including snakes and buffalo, but most reported cases
involve lions. The following description was given by an informant
who claimed knowledge of an actual encounter.

When a man has been injured but cannot get satisfaction, he may
go down to Bari, south of Terekeka to Khor Bya. The people who live
there are called Jabour, and their clan owns wild beasts; these are
loaned out by their chief. The wild beasts are, to all appearance,
ordinary people, usually handsome young men, but they have the power
of changing into dangerous animals during the night, for instance
lions, leopards, and snakes. A buyer brings a bull, a calf, and 50 piastres
to their chief, and tells him the victim's name and the country
which is to be ravaged. The beast-men are instructed to go to so
and so's country and maul people. They do not touch anyone on the
way. When the buyer goes home the beasts may accompany him at
once if they have no other work. He will find them roaming around him
in the bush or springing by him on the road, and becomes alarmed,
but they do not touch him. These people are *rube* and lions and other
beasts are in their bodies. They only attack the people of the man who
has injured their buyer.

When they reach the victim's homestead they begin killing. The buyer
goes and confesses to his own chief that he has bought wild beasts to spoil
so and so's homestead because of his grievance. This is then rectified.

During the day the beasts look like young men, and spend this time
in a place other than where they are to work. If they are to kill in Mijiki
they will go to Borenye during the daytime and eat there as visitors,
changing at night and descending on Mijiki. This is for fear people
should realize who they are and spear them. They start biting early in the
evening about sundown and continue during the night: then again in the
early morning before first light. During the day they are only people.

Around 1947, a man named Lado confessed to bringing lions to
Chief Gali Lado's country on the Mandari–Nyangwara boundary,

complaining his wife had been lured away; at the same time people were killed by man-eating lions. Lado claimed to have planted a rain creeper (used for 'anchoring' rain) round a cattle peg and to have instructed the beasts to maul up to that mark. The Province Court awarded Lado a token imprisonment. Lions had also visited my informant's own village in Mijiki while passing to another destination. He told me that one of his father's wives was approached for food by a party of good-looking strangers to whom she gave roasted ground-nuts. Instead of splitting the husks and extracting the kernels, they seized handfuls and crammed them into their mouths with the shells on, using both hands, and disappeared into the bush. Later, people heard lions grunting. The woman alerted the village and small stock were kraaled and people barricaded their huts. By their dress and appearance the visitors had been Nyangwara; later news reached Mijiki of fatalities from lion in Gali Lado's country.

Here suspicion is aroused by a train of coincidences. Hungry people arrive and eat like animals, then disappear into the bush and animal noises are heard: later people of a neighbouring group are mauled. There is clear proof that the 'lions' had spent the day in Mijiki before going to work in Nyangwara.

It is, however, important to bear in mind the weight given by the people themselves to a claim or statement, and in the case of metamorphosis it is clear that this is a peripheral belief. Information is either vague hearsay, or a record of individual experience. These notions lie around the fringe of more important and widespread assumptions about man–animal relationships and also, perhaps, about man–man relationships of the witchcraft–sorcery kind. All the same what is involved is the idea of actual identity and not simply metaphor regarding the polarity of human behaviour, although at a different level (the psychological one) this might be said to apply.[1]

Another example where the distance between persons and animals is seen to be narrowed so that the animal advances menacingly is, of course, the *mönöjin* offence, one result of which is the animal accident—trampling, mauling, snake and scorpion bites—which befalls the woman's close male relatives. Metaphor

---

[1] This seems also to be the case among the Dinka where Lienhardt reports that it is said that 'some men are really lions and can change into lions'. *Divinity and Experience*, p. 117.

and analogy here play a part in the selection of the association links between several kinds of behaviour. Unregulated sex (sleeping around, adultery, incest) is animal-like, and leads to animal-derived dangers. Illicit sex often takes place in cultivations—'like dogs'—humans should copulate in homesteads. Much Mandari behaviour metaphor is animal-based (as indeed is much of ours); 'You sleep around bitch-like', for instance, is a Mandari woman-to-woman insult.

Metamorphosis, of course, involves a much more extreme boundary crossing, because here persons are not simply behaving like animals but are animals. Problems of personal integrity are involved, and concern about 'humanness' which may be destroyed by a too radical departure into deviant behaviour.[1] The merging of images is also connected with the idea of predatory characteristics in both humans and animals. Witches prey on neighbours, for instance, and may be compared with animal predators—'Witches are like wild beasts who pass their time preying', and 'witches devour a victim's life.'

Finally, the metamorphosis stereotype is one among a number of other anxiety images which operate in the situation of the dangerous neighbour threat, and which represent fears displaced on to an appropriate model. The 'Dinka Power' is the one which follows out the manifold links the Mandari have with their Dinka neighbours, and minor variants of this are found around other tribal boundaries. The dangerous neighbour within, the prolific and ambitious client, is dealt with in the witchcraft–evil eye idiom. The witchcraft stereotype draws its roots from the multi-ethnic constitution of Mandari society and the apprehension of patrons in regard to the threat of the reversal of the *status quo*—something which has actually taken place in some areas. The Mandari have difficulty in accounting for this reversal when no obvious explanation can account for it; the rationalization is that it is linked in some way with the rise of clients.

Metamorphosis is a particularly appropriate model for those Mandari living on the eastern boundary where contact with neighbours is irregular (an uninhabited arid plain lies between) but sufficient to introduce uncertainties. Two kinds of anxiety are fused, that about real predators which are encountered because of

---

[1] Cf. Douglas, *Purity and Danger, passim*, particularly chap. 3.

environmental factors of terrain and associated fauna, and those about potentially 'predatory' neighbours.

I would again emphasize the extent of the territories and the numerous populations which surround the Mandari, and the fact that the sparse Mandari population is itself made up of levels of immigrants dispersed around separated cores of indigenes—a situation in which fears of survival as a people, and even doubts of identity, can readily be understood.

The creation of anxiety stereotypes where a group is threatened or feel themselves threatened by internal minorities or by external majorities has been widely discussed, but the exact way in which a society generates its stereotypes and the reason for the selection of a particular image has not yet been satisfactorily demonstrated. Our own society, at any given point in time, provides examples of new forms of stereotyping created to meet anxiety or threat situations. An important point to remember, however, is that the existence of such stereotypes does not mean that all who use them are anxious as *individuals* (although some may be); the stereotype is simply a conventional model used automatically. The original stereotype, however, arises in the first place under particular conditions and in response to particular stress.

The specific metamorphosis image is no doubt also in part a reaction to a more direct kind of danger which is always present in Mandari country, the danger from wild animals. It would be reasonable to assume that this contributes to animal imagery and explains some claimed man–animal confrontations. Death and wounding are not uncommon, and indeed it is perhaps surprising that there is not more anxiety. The impression created is that of sensible awareness. The wild is respected and utilized with care and discretion. Assurance breeds the optimism of statements like one already quoted—'A man crosses the bush, a wild beast watches him from the cover, it lashes its tail, but the man walks safely by.' In our own society, a similar paradox can be seen where anxiety about the traffic jungle does not prevent most people from mingling in it with sophisticated assurance.

v

A number of other animal stereotypes have also been evolved around a variety of animal species. The first impression of these is of a completely random selection. Why one particular animal and not another? This question is, of course, a part of a much more general problem as to why some experiences and events are sufficiently impressive or significant to give rise to a conventional stereotype. Why do certain ones catch on and become the centre of attitudes and behaviour patterns while others do not? I shall try to show in my discussion of particular examples of animal selection how the Mandari perception of certain animal characteristics and animal responses becomes relevant and leads to a particular kind of stylized relationship being established between the persons and the animal. Some general guides to the selection are what the Mandari consider to be characteristics shared between a person and an animal and what are considered human-like responses in animals.[1]

The first example involves a convention which is common to all Mandari that the house mouse (*miji*) must not be harmed, which is justified by a story of the assistance given by a mouse to primal man. Humans are portrayed as originally unaware of the birth process so that when a woman neared her time, men gathered round to cut her open to remove the child, leaving the woman to die. A mouse arrived at such a scene, called the men into a hut and effected a delivery. As its reward it chose the freedom to roam around dwellings feeding here and there.[2] Nothing equivalent to the psychic force of domestic animals exists here, nor is the killing of a mouse endangering; none the less the mouse is considered to have a legitimate place in the homestead; it is a domestic animal although not a domesticated one. Its ubiquitousness requires some kind of response and the Mandari prefer to give it a conventional immunity rather than to try to eliminate it—perhaps because of its very harmlessness and its use in clearing up cooking residue, a role somewhat similar to that of the predator in the bush which disposes of more dangerously polluted matter. That the justifying story sees the mouse as central to a successful delivery scene

---

[1] These relationships are quite different from what is generally described as 'totemism'—either of the kind involving a complex system of classification, sometimes based on logical opposition (cf. Levi-Strauss, *Totemism*), or that built up in a more random way around a central organizing principle. Cf. Peter Worsley, 'Groote Eylandt Totemism and *Le Totemisme Aujourd'hui*', in *The Structural Study of Myth and Totemism*, A.S.A. Monograph (London, 1967).

[2] The mouse story has a wide distribution, including among others the Anuak and Murle.

may be connected with the fact that mice are exceedingly prolific.

Similar immunity is given to the harmless green house snake, *logwirinun*.[1] Its appearance is a favourable omen (*nulon*). A bowl of brewing residue is placed for it to eat.

Both these examples reflect close and intimate living with a harmless and, in the case of the mouse, a very common homestead creature. Both are fed, the mouse indirectly by helping itself. Creatures that can in this way live unmolested near a regular source of food may well become semi-tame, appear responsive, and show little fear of people.

The Mandari also have a number of more individual animal linkings based again on the idea of a favour done by the animal or a reciprocal favour. The human descendants thenceforth declare that they share 'blood relationship' (*yuɲi*) with the animal. This prohibits killing or shedding the animal's blood and binds both the human group descended from the particular ancestor and the animal species involved. If the animal violates its kinship by harming the human relative it may in turn be killed. These associations are inherited and thus they become an appendage to lineages, but the link with the descent system is purely secondary, and few descent lines have these associations. A number of clans do not kill monitor lizards, which may otherwise be eaten, because a lizard is reputed to have done a favour to an ancestress. The woman involved left her baby in a sling while she went to the river; it cried and a monitor came up and rocked it until the mother returned. The Bari Kujutat clan are 'kindred' with lions. During a famine a lion entered their village, causing terror, which it allayed by gently growling and mimicking the act of eating. The ancestor followed it and it showed him game that it had killed. The starving people ate the meat and survived. Another version portrays the lion's jaw as wedged open with a bone; it rolled playfully on its back, the ancestor extracted the bone, and it led him to meat.

I am suggesting that in these animal stereotypes we see a reflection of some kind of real experience—not of course as actually portrayed in the story—but one having about it enough of the

---

[1] I do not know which species of snake is involved. The Bari also give immunity to a snake which they refer to as 'grandmother' (*yakanye*). It seems likely this is the same snake. Cf. Fr. Spagnolo, *Bari Grammar*, p. 413.

eventual model to provide its substance, and arising from an instance of anomalous behaviour in an animal. If we consider for a moment the claimed animal experiences which feature in Call dreams (Chapter 12) where animal behaviour is not merely regarded as odd or unusual, but also as significant, it seems likely that something similar is involved at the source of these other relationships.

Another kind of animal stereotype reflects a quite different kind of experience, that is a marriage link with a foreign woman from a tribe with a system of so-called 'totemic' classifications, the superficial details of which have been carried over into the marriage relationship. This is known to be the case in regard to a newly acquired form of man–animal blood-relationship taken on from a Dinka wife. Thus a man and his offspring 'respect' (*rujeju*) the clan animal of a Dinka wife or mother. The Mandari know little about the ideational background of such respect and simply observe it out of politeness. It is inherited, and extended families and small lineages now exist with such Dinka- and Atwot-based associations, all of whose members refrain from killing and eating the respected animal. The doctor Kok respects python (*kitun*) in deference to his Atwot mother, for example.

Probing the reasons for this respect, I was told by a Mandari, 'In Dinka an animal and a human foetus can be delivered of a woman at the same time.' Pursuing this dual birth notion further with him, I got him to admit that this seemed strange, but that 'perhaps it could happen in Dinka'. After further thought he suggested that perhaps, when a baby was delivered, something else was expelled which 'looked like an animal'. The reaction to my question, probably of a kind he had never been asked before, is of some interest. Explanation was first sought in different ranges of experience of Mandari and Dinka, then an explanation in terms of the logic of similarity was put forward.

Another way in which the Mandari say blood-relationship arises is when an animal is seen to produce anomalies in human appearance. This is known as *kekelaju*, a word also used to describe hereditary likeness between parents and offspring in humans and animals—an ordinary genetic similarity. Animal-like features are believed to occur when a woman is frightened or deeply impressed by an animal while carrying the baby, later seen to be stamped with some feature of the animal, in the womb. Fear of undesirable animal marks on a foetus leads pregnant women to avoid baboons, hippos, or crocodiles. (Avoiding the latter two is hardly difficult as they are not found in Mandari and few Mandari women visit the Nile regions.) She will also shun wild cats 'because of their staring eyes' (association with the night/evil eye) and, as the likeness can show in motor activity, the small red monkey *teleme* with its jerky, scrabbling movements. Informants assured me that one could meet individuals who had these animal resemblances and who avoided eating their imprinter, if it should be edible. Fairly common are certain skin markings said to be 'like python'; a harelip (elephant)—'the lip divides and the teeth show like elephant tusks'; and baboon-shaped or hippo-shaped physiognomy.

Such impressions are regarded with some amusement, but they are not so remote from a much more radical and serious kind which is not amusing, namely the new-born baby with the extensively mottled skin—'like leopard' (*se koka*). The mottled baby not only looks like a predator, but worse still, like the worst type of predator, the leopard. The Mandari are concerned to avoid any resemblance to a predator and it is for this reason that they dislike persons who do not extract their bottom front teeth. 'People with mouths full of teeth look like predators' (*se gworoŋ*), particularly, 'like hyena'—an observation made rather pointedly to me on several occasions. The Mandari are uneasy about persons from tribes whose members not only keep all their teeth but file them to points, like the Azande. This custom confirms for them the rumour that Azande are cannibals—'human predators'.

Bodily movement is seen to be the link associating an animal with a form of convulsions; the sufferer from the convulsions does not eat the animal, to which he is 'related'. The relationship link can be broken by symbolic action, after recovery. A small striped rodent called *nurumsho* (a bush rat or squirrel?) infects an infant with convulsions if the child clutches the leg of a dead one or the parent treads on the tail of a live one. The spasms (*boko*) are treated by mixing the animal's droppings with herbal medicine and marking the chest, back of the neck, and forehead. The rodents are edible, and to break kinship and allow the child to eat them after outgrowing the convulsions, the child must mimic the act of killing one by shooting three miniature arrows of wood slivers into a stunned rodent, saying with each shot, 'Our relationship is ended.'

Markings, movements, facial similarity, receiving a favour from an animal as from a kinsman, all in some degree transfer the human being over to the side of the particular animal. The sequence of reasoning behind this kind of animal stereotype appears to proceed something like this:

Ordinary people can kill and eat the animal freely because there is no association of likeness, and therefore no 'kinship'. Marked people, on the other hand, cannot do either because it is axiomatic that animals do not kill and eat their own kind (nor do persons). But on what *basis* is the assumption made that marked people are 'of a kind' with their imprinter? The Mandari know that genetic likeness derives from blood-relationship—from the birth situation. People who look like an animal, therefore, have something in common with it in terms of the *idea* of the 'birth' situation which gives basic likeness. Even the terms used, *yuṇi* and *kekelaju*, are those used of genetic inheritance. 'Kinship behaviour' follows as a corroboration of the 'birth' linking.

VI

The information given by Evans-Pritchard on the ways in which the Nuer consider that their totemic symbols are acquired seems to suggest that they choose them in somewhat the same way as the Mandari select their animal stereotypes.[1] The ownership of a particular Nuer totemic animal may be justified by a story of a man–animal encounter, or by an experience or happening in which an animal is claimed to have made a particular impression. Other totems are seen to come through something very similar to the Mandari animal imprinting.

In the *selection* of the totem, therefore, there appears to be some similarity with what we find in the Mandari. The Nuer also add new totems as new experiences occur, and these new additions can be accommodated because of the segmentary nature of Nuer descent lines; as new segments form and spread, gaining autonomy at the religious and social levels, they provide scope for the incorporation of the new totems. It is at the level of *selection*, however, that all similarity with the Mandari animal stereotype begins and ends.

The structural framework of the Nuer totemic system itself is far from fortuitous. Every lineage has a totem and the symbolic

[1] Evans-Pritchard, *Nuer Religion*, chap. ii, sections i–iii.

representation of the animal—its 'spirit'—is integrated into the wider ideational pattern of over-all religious belief and practice. The spiritual representation of the totem is an important part of Nuer 'theology', and specific spirits may receive sacrifice. The nature of the Nuer totemic relationship can only be understood, as Evans-Pritchard makes clear, in terms of the symbolic relationship between the totem, the group who owns it, and 'God'.

Much the same is true in the Dinka case. Again a certain element of chance—embodying many features basic to stereotype selection that we find in Mandari—is portrayed. But Lienhardt points out that the way in which an individual may acquire his 'clan-divinity' (totem) is only secondary to the idea of a divinity as something given and laid down by Divinity in the ultimate sense.[1] Thus everyone has a 'clan divinity'—although sometimes the way in which it was acquired may not be known. Clans accumulate divinities, and sub-clans may come to have secondary ones.[2]

The element of chance, again, as in the Nuer, operates at a low level, while the structural pattern is clearly defined. The ideational background is again integrated into the religious order. Clan divinities are included in invocations at sacrifices, and play an important role in the notion of religious protection accorded to the clan members. According to Lienhardt they represent the ideal and permanent values of agnation for the Dinka.

The contrast between these Nuer and Dinka relationships and the man–animal linkings of the Mandari need hardly be stressed. Mandari animal stereotypes have no comparable supporting structure, either at the level of social group identification, or at the level of symbolic idea or religious action. Mandari animal stereotypes not only lack any organic link with descent groups, but are absolutely unrelated to religious belief and practice. The only common principle which links the various man–animal relationships is a minimal kind of behaviour and a recognition of certain standard 'clues', which indicate where and when a relationship may be built up.

The Mandari animal stereotypes embody few irrational elements (mystical notions) although they show a special kind of perceptual selection and a formal pattern of behaviour. The integration of the stereotype in an over-all conceptual religious framework never

---

[1] Lienhardt, *Divinity and Experience*, p. 116.
[2] Ibid., p. 119.

occurs in Mandari; the step from the perceptual to the conceptual level is never taken as it is by the Nuer and the Dinka.

Few Mandari lineages and clans have animal 'relationships' and these are the exception rather than the rule. The Mandari would appear to be more selective about the animal experiences they use as the basis of their stereotypes than either the Nuer or the Dinka. Many claimed animal encounters could offer excellent occasions for acquiring a totem, but this does not in fact happen because 'totem' is not a significant Mandari idiom. If a culture provides a strong totemic idiom, then while people may not be consciously on the lookout for new totems, it could at least be suggested that they will tend to interpret many kinds of experience in these terms. Dinka totems, which are not only animals, may be quite trivial in themselves, as though almost anything may be chosen as a totem. Where everyone must have one, and where there are so many forms of totemic duplication, this is likely to be the case. In Nuer, also, the ways in which totems are acquired often have the appearance of triviality as, for instance, in the case Evans-Pritchard describes, where a bird becomes a totem after perching on a man's head.

VII

Mandari of both sexes observe a prohibition on eating birds, homestead chickens, or eggs during their years of peak fertility. In theory a woman should not eat them between the time of her first menstruation and the menopause, but in practice it seems that mature married women with growing children may do so. Elders of both sexes are free from the prohibition, but as to be an 'elder' is a matter of status rather than age, a family head who is still relatively young may decide to eat a chicken sacrifice. All those who are old in years eat as they like, and small children do likewise.

There is clearly a connection between prestigious young people's activities, courtship, marriage, and perhaps also the critical early years of child-bearing and rearing, and the bird–egg prohibition, although I have never heard that contravening it causes infertility. (It might be suggested perhaps that eating an egg is analogous to eating an embryo?) The Mandari simply explain the prohibition in terms of the shame a young person incurs, particularly a man, if discovered eating a bird. 'Chicken eater' (*könyöit na sukuri*) is shaming abuse, reducing the target to a laughing-stock among contemporaries.[1] In serious famine prohibitions may be set aside since everyone is under the same duress. Satirical songs, however, are composed around situations of wrong eating even here, as demonstrated, for example, in a song which mocks poor clients who during a famine ate baboons (proscribed because of their human appearance) and after eating them fell sick.[2] Chicken- and bird-eating tend to imply destitution and low status. Single clients and needy people eat such things because they have nothing to lose; in the same way the very sick may eat chicken meat.

VIII

A special association is seen to exist between a professional elephant hunter and elephants. This dangerous and skilled craft is hereditary and confined to clans of non-landowning status. Non-professionals do not hunt elephant although they may assist in tracking and so forth.

While the elephant lacks psychic force and no ceremony follows its killing (although there may be dancing and celebration), each professional hunter completes a series of rituals after killing his first elephant. 'These allow him to go on killing elephants in safety.'

Two days after his first kill the hunter's head is shaved and anointed with red ochre by an old woman—'to protect him from the killing'. This rite, known as *karama na tome*, is held, a hunter told me, 'because you have killed a person'.[3] (It will be remembered that the leopard is also described as 'like a person'.) Apart from this ritual which cleanses and protects from shedding elephant blood, a second rite must be performed to 'make elephant meat safe', and enable the hunter to eat the meat of further kills without illness. The meat of his first kill is always proscribed. To immunize elephant meat a tripod of wood is erected, the hunter crouches

---

[1] A youth suggested that young people abstain from chicken because chickens have scavenging habits, pecking around the yards. He particularly stressed the way they peck at spittle.

[2] Buxton, 'Mandari Witchcraft', p. 114, see verse iv.

[3] *Karama* has the meaning 'ceremonial celebration': the word is Arabic. In Bari, clans of elephant hunters constitute a special class, and it is noteworthy that one lineage of elephant hunters attached to Dari clan is named 'Yari'. *Yari* is the category word for 'elephant caste' in Bari. Seligman, *Pagan Tribes*, pp. 257–8.

inside this with cut-up elephant meat piled on his shoulders; a bundle of grass is ignited and thrust inside the tripod, the hunter runs out scattering the burning grass and the meat. He must further be formally introduced to elephant meat when, on another occasion, a senior hunter will bring him meat of his own kill and place pieces in his mouth; the novice spits these out, then he swallows three pieces. Afterwards he is washed and anointed with oil.[1]

After this ritual sequence is performed at the beginning of the hunter's career no further ritual is required. The shaving of the head and the use of red ochre echo the leopard rite; no markings are made, however, because the elephant is unmarked. Elements common to other situations of changed relationship or role are included; the symbolic introduction to meat, its rejection, and the swallowing of three pieces followed by ritual washing and anointing, bears comparison with the ceremonial introduction of a man to his mother-in-law's food and drink which precedes the relaxation of strict son-in-law respect. The hunter has a continuing and life-long association with elephant; he watches, tracks, and kills them or may himself be killed by them. The elephant is not simply a game animal for him as it is for ordinary persons who eat its meat without ritual preparation. Before he can do this he must pass through a form of abbreviated initiation which allows and legitimizes his permanent relationship and his licence to kill.

Because elephant are also objectively dangerous, and for fear that the hunter may be additionally endangered by sins and undisclosed wrongdoing, most hunters perform a protective rite at the beginning of each hunting season. At one such rite I attended a female doctor performed a rattle divination. The hunter's gear, including his special elephant spear, was piled in the yard and the blood of a beheaded chicken, 'red like meat', was sprinkled over it; prayers were offered for safety and success and beer drinking followed. When sin is present, a goat is killed and flour sprayed on the hunter. Prayers are offered to Creator for a safe return and kills.

---

[1] Interesting comparisons may be made with the relationship between elephants and men among the Nuer. Cf. Paul Howell, 'A Note on Elephants and Elephant Hunting among the Nuer', Pt. I, *Sudan Notes and Records*, vol. 26 (1945), especially pp. 4 and 6 where the comparison with the human homicide is made, and p. 8 where the ritual performed before a man can claim an elephant found dead in the bush, which includes burning a grass hut, is described.

PART III

MEDICO-RELIGIOUS PRACTICE

12

THE RELIGIOUS CALL AND ITS RELEVANCE TO HEALING

PART III assesses the role of the doctor in relation to the Mandari theory of illness and cure. I shall begin by considering the Call which justifies a Mandari in becoming a doctor. I shall then examine possession as a medico-religious technique, looking at the same time at other forms of Mandari possession. Finally, I shall deal with the social status of the doctor and his methods of work.

I

Before describing those individual experiences which the Mandari interpret as signs of a religious calling, I should stress that the medico-religious vocation is always assumed to be good and socially beneficial when the doctor is practising traditional healing; this is confirmed by such statements as 'The power [to heal] is from Creator': 'The power is traditional' ('of old'—*töpötö na beron kodaje*); or, 'When Creator made man he also made the doctor.' While the power to heal is seen to be intrinsically right and good, it is recognized that a doctor may not himself be a virtuous person, and that a few doctors may even have the evil eye or practise night-witchcraft. When both beneficial and dangerous powers are found in the same person, each power is seen to be concentrated towards its particular end, the healing power working for cure and the support of life, the evil power for destruction. The good power is never corrupted by the bad, neither does the evil power enhance the ability to heal. It simply enables the doctor to harm enemies, sometimes under pretence of treating them. Any association, therefore, between good and bad ritual power is purely coincidental. When a patient is thinking about his sickness he will be concerned with the doctor's reputation for healing and not with witchcraft suspicions—although a person who believes himself to have been actually harmed will obviously avoid consulting the doctor concerned again. In Mandari thought it is never legitimate to use witchcraft to further any cause however admirable, and the powers which fall in this category are always antisocial and proscribed.

Witchcraft affects the doctor's profession in so far as practice is open to persons of either sex and of any social status, while some individuals of non-landowning background can become suspect and assume roles of community scapegoats. Well-known healers may come from such suspected backgrounds; a few are even openly accused persons. The extent to which a suspected practitioner can, in spite of these disadvantages, build up a good practice depends partly on luck (in that his patients do, in general, recover or at least do not die in suspicious circumstances) and partly on the doctor's personality and popularity. In my experience a certain ambivalence is displayed towards such persons: 'We do not know one way or the other', 'No one is suspected by everyone.'

Persons who are ineligible for political office (or would have been in the traditional field) because they come from client groups, can excel as doctors, and although I have no evidence to suggest that more doctors are non-landowners than otherwise, many doctors of my acquaintance did come from such a background. Obviously it would be difficult for a chief, because of his position and responsibilities, to practise, but the close kinsmen of chiefs in fact often do so.

II

I use the word 'Call' to describe those experiences which mark the doctor's election to his profession and which are regarded as his inspirational authority to practise. The Mandari isolate the Call experience in idea, but have no single word for it. They describe certain sorts of events as the prelude to the practice of a particular doctor, and many of the accounts include statements that the person was 'called' or 'summoned' (*luluŋa*) by a religious being.

A religious Call is virtually essential to practice; instances of practice where no Call is claimed are very rare, for signs of Calling are the determining factor and make it possible for the would-be doctor to proceed to a recognized training. Call can be manifested in a variety of ways; its signs may be physical or mental illness, significant dreams, or remarkable happenings. All Calls are ultimately seen to 'come from Creator' (*po ko Dun*); but this universal source of inspiration is often interpreted more individually as a directive from Spirit-of-the-Above or, nowadays, from a Power. A dead relative may also appear in a dream and summon a person, informing him that he is chosen, but ancestors are never claimed by practitioners as spiritual guides nor do they directly possess individuals.

The association with Celestial Spirits or Powers in Call experiences, and the form of partnership set up between these 'guides' and the doctor, exemplify the supposed desire of these spirits to establish direct contact with human beings. Where a family has already raised a shrine to a spirit this is often claimed by a novice as his mentor and the source of his inspiration; or, after a Call, a man may raise a shrine to the guide which has been revealed during the Call period. The acceptance of multiple causes in sickness, and the diversification of professional skills to meet such multiple causes, are logically reflected in the notion that Call may originate from equally diverse sources. A Call, however, may come from no named source but be explained in terms of power given 'by Creator', and some doctors work without specific spirit 'guides'.

The extrinsic nature of the Call is of great importance—'Doctors do not choose, but are chosen'; 'The power falls down upon a man (*du'un ky'it*), in spite of himself.' Even if the Call is initially rejected, as it may be, it is believed that the chosen individual must eventually acquiesce, because otherwise he or his family will continue to suffer chronic Call signs (sickness and so forth), which are diagnosed as evidence of the persistence of the spiritual power. It is recognized that suffering is an integral part of Call and that it takes a variety of forms.

The 'hereditary' element, considered to be almost as important as the Call, is demonstrated where any cognate up to about three generations back in kinship time has been in practice. Referring to such heredity, the Mandari claim that at death the doctor's power 'waits to enter' the child or grandchild. The most common heredity is through a parent, a mother's brother, or grandparent. The form of heredity which supports practice cannot, therefore, be seen in terms of agnation, since it descends through cognates of two to three generations. There is often a maternal link or a link through a mother's mother; but ultimately linking is quite arbitrary, and it would be incorrect also to interpret the frequency of claims traced to the maternal line as an example of ritual healing powers being complementary to, or a compensation for, the jural powers of the paternal line.

I have found instances of hereditary healing established on the following relationships:

(a) Father/son.
(b) Mother/son.
(c) Mother/daughter.
(d) Grandparent/grandchild (male or female grandparent, in matri- or patrilineage).
(e) Mother's brother/sister's son or daughter.

The only important relationship of which I failed to find an instance was with father's sister, though while this may be an uncommon form of heredity, there seems to be no reason why it should not be valid, particularly if a woman who practised lived in the same village as her brother's child and contact between them was regular.

While it would be inaccurate to speak of lineages of doctors, short chains of practice are often found averaging a three-generation depth. Or there may be a 'broken' heredity; the breaks allowing for the fact that in any one generation no individual wishes to practise or has the essential qualities. A number of independent factors finally determine which individual in a generation, if any, will come forward. Those who are poorly endowed intellectually, or who have ineffectual personalities, are unlikely to succeed in the profession.

Unless there is some indication of a wish to practise, a person showing symptoms that could be interpreted as a Call would be likely to have them attributed to another source. There may, however, be exceptions, in that if overwhelming evidence for a Call is shown, a person who has never himself considered practice may eventually be persuaded that this is indeed his vocation, and will take it up after initial doubts. In the initial period of genuine confusion and uncertainty about the true significance of symptoms, the decision to embark on a healing career is seldom taken without consultation with relatives. Established doctors also play a part in the selection of new candidates, through their diagnoses and their encouragement or the reverse.[1]

A person strongly drawn to the profession will find an opportunity to show suitable Call evidence. This is borne out by the range of experiences accepted as Call evidence, some of which hardly seem to relate to the claimant at all, but rather to close members of his family—even to dead relatives. A whole family sometimes seems to be showing signs of frustrated Call, which is eventually interpreted and resolved in relation to one particular member. If no one comes forward, these signs are passed off as frequent illness. In other cases—and mainly in those where practice is already strongly represented within the cognatic family—individuals may begin to practise on apparently slender supporting Call evidence.

The claim to involuntary selection, however, separates the doctor's profession from mundane professions like elephant hunter or blacksmith. It also gives authority to the doctor when making diagnoses and prescribing cures. The idea of being in some degree set apart is important where a theory of non-empirical cause is combined with the treatment of real physical symptoms.

The other essential factor is the return to normal health. Those who do not recover cannot enter practice. While some individuals are known to undergo long-lasting Calls, it is only by definite *recovery* that a person can prove that the symptoms were manifestations of religious power and not simply illness.

III

The following case histories illustrate the points just covered. They were given to me during my 1952 visit by doctors whom I knew well, or with whom I had at least some regular contact. Unfortunately at that time I did not fully realize the significance of the histories, and made no attempt systematically to collect a larger number, so that any conclusions drawn must necessarily be tentative.

[1] Here I would mention the case of the young girl (p. 107) whose family were worried about an apparently serious illness, but where there was also an awareness in the community that she was manifesting a behaviour pattern very typical of Call, and that her 'illness' might resolve itself along these lines.

Although these Call histories are accounts of individual experiences, the general pattern revealed in them represents something of a social stereotype, in that any doctor—or any layman for that matter—who is questioned will at once mention the various elements they feature.

When presenting the case histories I paraphrase informants' own accounts in the interests of clarity. Details of the clans or places of origin of the persons concerned are included because these can have some bearing on the kind of techniques later employed in practice, particularly where a 'foreign' background is involved. I have no independent corroboration for any of the case histories, all of which referred to events in the past, but laymen who were present and heard them recounted, confirmed that they are typical.

Since histories are largely a record of experiences claimed by the individuals concerned, it would be difficult to get corroboration or refutation of particular incidents.

1. *Ako Akurukway (also known as Deŋajot, Bariyei lineage)*

The hereditary link here came through Ako's grandfather Desa, and his own father. When Ako was a youth, two of his brothers, followed later by two sisters, died after illness diagnosed as a Dinka Spirit-of-the-Above for which a shrine had previously been raised.

Shortly after these deaths Ako passed through his initiation, and when he was wearing the pinkish-purple bead known as '*eyor*', and worn at that period for the first few years after initiation, he became mentally ill.

Around the onset of symptoms, Ako told me, Spirit-of-the-Above took him out into the bush at night; he slept outside, and had a dream that a 'religious being' (*ŋun*) came and stood over him and looking down on him addressed him: '*Doalo!*' 'You!' Then it vanished.[1] Ako woke up and walked home in the early hours of the morning, while it was still dark. On the way he saw a brilliant white light burning ahead of him in the bush. He went towards it until he came to where it hung suspended, burning a few inches above the ground. He likened its brightness to that of my pressure lamp. He went up to it and placed his feet in it and at once felt

---

[1] This term of address has the strong emphasis of the slang phrase, 'You there!'

a sensation like plunging into cold water pass up his legs and envelop his whole body. Passing on through the light he eventually reached home, where he quietly called up an age-mate whom he managed to persuade to accompany him back to the spot where the light was still burning. He warned the youth to tell no one about the encounter. Ako explained to me that the light was the same as that which belonged to his grandfather (the doctor), who had two lights which burned with a white light and which were used by him when he journeyed at night.

After this encounter Ako stayed at home for about four days keeping his experiences to himself. His brother was in the cattle-camp, and his father in Rumbek (a Dinka township) so he lodged with his elder half-sister. Shortly afterwards he attended an evening dance. While he was dancing he felt a violent blow on the head as though he had been struck with a club; he staggered and fell to the ground dazed. The dancers crowded round and asked him what was wrong. He replied that someone had hit him on the head. They answered, 'What are you talking about, no one hit you.' Eventually, the age-mate who had also seen the light, came forward and explained to the others—'I know what is wrong with him, it is to do with the light of the other night.' They then asked 'What light? What is wrong with him?' An elder escorted him home. A phase of derangement followed during which, as he described it, he talked and behaved 'like a madman' (*se ko kapur*). His half-sister, with whom he was living, was deeply concerned, and went to the cattle camp to fetch a barren sheep, 'because it was obvious to her that the Above had fallen upon him'. The family elders assembled to sacrifice the sheep for Spirit-of-the-Above and to hold a ceremonial dance. Ako told me that during this dancing the Spirit spoke to him again, saying: 'Now I will depart from you, because I have slain your brothers and sisters. I am not alone, a Power of your grandfather is with me.' After this revelation the family sacrificed a goat for the Power and an ox for Spirit-of-the-Above. During the rite the latter spirit spoke once more telling him: 'It is now all right: we will both stay with you [Above and the *Jok*] and guide you. If someone falls ill you will be called and you will place medicine into his mouth to cure the seat of the illness. Do not grieve that I have killed your brothers, you will bear male children to replace them.' Then there was a flash, 'like lightning', and a tremor shook his body.

Not long after this, Ako recovered and began to practise, after having raised a shrine to the Dinka celestial spirit, Jombai, the spirit which had earlier been diagnosed in connection with his brothers' deaths. Ako was evasive when I asked who taught him his techniques, particularly those for treating Powers, and simply replied: 'Jombai taught me.' On a different occasion, however, he told me that when his brothers died a doctor from the Atwot tribe was called in and named the cause of the deaths as Jombai. This doctor may have instructed Ako. There is a strong non-Mandari content in Ako's methods and his family have several foreign connections; his deceased mother was a Cic Dinka, and in his narrative he spoke of his father being in the Dinka town of Rumbek. Ako's elder sister, also married to a Dinka, now lives with her husband in the same hamlet as Ako in Mandari. Ako treats Mandari and Dinka patients, specializing in treatments of both Spirit-of-the-Above and Powers and using possession and spirit mediumship.

The Call sequence in this case is initiated by a dream summons, followed immediately by a miraculous encounter which, in Ako's view, precipitates acute mental illness.[1] Ako would probably have been in his late teens or early twenties at that time. (Age may be of some significance in relation to mental crises of this kind.) Direct revelation—'the Above spoke'—is claimed.

The description of a brilliant light is significant in that light, and the colour white, symbolize spiritual power and transcendental qualities.[2] Two possible explanations are suggested by Ako's claim regarding the light.[3] Either he was subject to hallucination—not inconceivable in view of his subsequent mental illness, or—and perhaps more likely, in view of the confirming statement by the age-mate—a bog will-o'-the-wisp was encountered. Ako's vivid description of his sensation of plunging into cold water as he walked through the light could have indicated that he crossed a seam of cotton-soil marsh. Such marsh is not very common

---

[1] The idea that miraculous encounters may be harmful features in other contexts. See pp. 345–6 where I describe how an elder dies after seeing a lost rainstone.

[2] I take this up in Chapter 21.

[3] M. J. Field (*Search for Security*, London, 1960) gives two instances from rural Ghana of claims made by noviciate priests regarding 'fires' in the bush; but in one case (p. 74) it would seem an ordinary fire was involved, in the other (p. 75 and n.) deliberate deception.

in Mandari, but it is perhaps significant that Ako's father was the ritual 'owner' of a pool on the land of Rokwe where the family may have been living at the time of the encounter. Evans-Pritchard, in his study of Nuer religion, notes that marsh phosphorescence when encountered by the Nuer is regarded as a manifestation of Spirit.[1] I have not heard a Mandari explanation of luminous miasma, and if indeed it is rarely seen this might account for its significance in a Call experience.

Later, and during dancing, Ako seems to have suffered a form of black-out—'the blow on the head'. I shall be considering a possible association between drum-beats and convulsions and it is possible that something similar, but more extreme, was involved here. This is seen to precipitate an acute mental illness showing a typical syndrome—leaving home, wandering, and fasting. After several months of intermittent wandering, Ako was considered by his family to be very ill. Although of modest means they made costly sacrifices, the initial ones to remove what was believed to be serious illness, the final one to establish the spiritual guides which had gradually been revealed. Ako himself sees the final sacrifice as the turning-point towards his recovery.

2. *Kok (also known as Ajaych: Atwot born, but domiciled in Mandari since childhood)*

In this case there is practice on both sides of the family. The mother and her brother worked as rattle-diviners, on the paternal side his grandfather was a specialist of Powers.

Kok was orphaned as a child. His father was already dead when his Dinka mother died during a visit to Mandari country, where her late husband's sister was married to a Mandari of Dari clan. This husband's sister, whose own daughter Iom later married Chief Korondo of Dari as his third wife, eventually took Kok to live with her in Mandari, where he grew up in Chief Korondo's hamlet.

Much of the sequence of Kok's own Call involved the paternal grandfather, long dead by the time Kok was old enough to know about him. The events occurred in Atwot, Kok's father being from the Atwot tribe. In addition to practising as a doctor the grandfather was a professional elephant hunter. A time came when abnormalities began to appear among his hunt victims. First he killed an

---

[1] Evans-Pritchard, *Nuer Religion*, pp. 98, 136–8.

elephant with an excrescence on its back, similar in appearance to the small mushroom-shaped deposits of laterite, which protrude from the ground over much of the region. Then he killed an elephant with metal rings—'like bracelets'—in its ears; then one containing cooking gourds; then one with four tusks. Shortly after making these kills he died; the death of his son, Kok's father, followed and then the deaths of Kok's two elder brothers. As the only surviving son, Kok was told the story by his father's brother. The deaths were ascribed, in divination, to the killing of four elephants which were '*Jok*'.

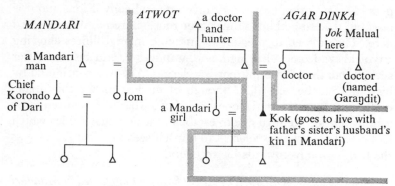

FIG. 12. *Kok's kinship and affinal links*

Kok's own Call symptoms were unexceptional. As a youth in Mandari he suffered from chronic ulcerated sores which failed to respond to treatment, so his mother's brother Agaraŋ (the Dinka practitioner) was called to Mandari to diagnose and declared that Malual, a Power of the mother's natal family, had followed her from Agar and was now troubling Kok. The sacrifice of an ox and the erection of a pole shrine for Malual was prescribed. Kok, who had expressed an inclination to practise, was then trained by Agaraŋ. Kok paid 50 piastres for his tuition—a token payment —because his teacher was his mother's brother.[1] Agaraŋ presented Kok with his string of medicine roots and showed him the kind of terrain in which he could dig further supplies. After his apprenticeship and when beginning practice, Kok expressed a wish to return to his father's people in Atwot, but was persuaded

---

[1] A doctor requires a much higher fee to train a non-relative. but a mother's brother helps a sister's son 'for nothing'. Medicines must always be bought or the Power which 'owns' them will be angry and make the user ill.

by Chief Korondo to remain in Dari, where he eventually married a Mandari girl.

Here, there is a duplication of hereditary elements. Kok sees his Call as linked, on one side of the family, to the histories of his grandfather, father, and own dead brothers, and his ability to treat Powers as stemming from his mother's people whose family Power he inherited.

Kok is a child of mixed stock and there is every reason to assume that his techniques would reflect his cultural background. His family connections are so varied they are worth charting out (see Fig. 12).

Kok showed none of the signs of psychological disturbance shown by Ako during his call, neither did he mention to me any experience which would suggest such a disorder; in his treatment of patients he uses a fairly extreme kind of possession.

3. Asek (of Jarra clan)

This case has already been discussed. After a long history of chronic physical sickness among members of the family two brothers died and then Asek himself was ill. Ako Akurukway was called in after other practitioners had failed, and he diagnosed the Power Mutiaŋagok. Asek recovered, planted a shrine, and became apprenticed to Ako. Asek has no relatives in practice and his is one of the rare cases of potential aptitude being discovered during treatment. Call signs were physical and linked up with other illness and death in the paternal line. Asek uses possession in his treatments.

4. Wale (a Mandari domiciled with Mandari Böri, a Nile-dwelling off-shoot from Mandari country)

Wale, although a Mandari, lives on the Nile with his second wife's family who are Böri, a group of long-established migrants from Mandari Bora. Before leaving Mandari to live with his affines he claimed to have been apprenticed to Ako Akurukway and other practitioners.

Wale admitted to being trained in the use of the diviner's rattle and medicine only, but told me that, by the Nile, he had begun to treat Spirit-of-the-Above and Powers—again only with medicines —'because the Nile-dwellers refuse to raise shrines'—a fact confirmed by my own observations during a four-month visit there. Wale made some scathing comments on the state of Nile practice, which he told me is female-dominated—'Men do not like the profession here.' He considered methods of diagnoses and techniques of treatment were very limited: 'They put everything down to ancestors (*mulökö*) and so no one gets well.' He also remarked that Mandari country is renowned for the potency (*töpötö*) of its doctors.

Wale's father was a Mandari of Pukun lineage of Rume.[1] His maternal kin are Nyangwara, a Bari-speaking tribe living east of Mount Tindalu. On his maternal side his grandfather's mother was in practice and his mother's brother, Lomole, still practises in the country of Nyangwara chief, Lopore Wala.

In his youth the idea of practice never occurred to him until one day as he was playing in the homestead yard a kite swooped down on to one of his chickens. He managed to catch and tether it. The same night he had a dream in which a miraculous being (*ŋun*) stood over him and instructed him not to harm the kite, so in the morning he released it. Instead of flying away it remained in the homestead and fed tamely with his chickens. The next night he had another dream in which a man and a woman appeared and instructed him to follow them. He got up—as he put it, 'during sleep'—and accompanied them to a small rocky hill named Rumkwac, in the back of which there was a cave—'a kind of room, like a hut'. He went inside and found an open box containing books—'like those you write in, Awuk'; a man whom he described as 'white' (the word could also mean 'light' or 'bright') was standing by the box and drew his attention to it.[2] He remained inside the cave for two days without food or water, then returned home. On arrival he began to act 'like a madman' (*kapur*), refusing to speak or eat. His family sacrificed a sheep but with no result. Some months after this he was found sleeping with a poisonous snake wound round his neck, which glided away harmlessly. After this, according to his account, he was 'ill for a long time—at least two years'. (It is not always clear what the Mandari mean by a 'year', but the indication is that a long illness followed.) He recovered and, at this point, his maternal uncle (the doctor) came from Nyangwara bringing with him a diviner's rattle which he presented to Wale. Later Wale raised a shrine to the Power Gurumbek, which became his guide.

---

[1] The Pukun are of Moru extraction and retainers of Chief Fulai Nyegwere.
[2] It cannot be assumed that Wale means a European when he says 'white'.

Practice is hereditary on the maternal side with a great-grand-mother, mother, and maternal uncle in practice. Call experiences are similar to those described by Ako Akurukway and one might suspect collaboration, if it were not that the two men live over 100 miles apart and have not met for years.

Like Ako, Wale claims that miraculous signs preceded mental illness, wild creatures (the kite and the snake) show a reversed behaviour pattern, acting as though domesticated. He walks in his sleep after a summons and foreign symbols are introduced. The Mandari, who are non-literate, regard books and writing as one of the clues to European dominance; the white being thus introduces him to esoteric knowledge. 'White' also symbolizes traditional knowledge in its association with chiefship. Its appearance in a Call experience supports the assertions of doctors that during their withdrawal in the bush they acquire knowledge of a special kind.

Wale does not use possession in treatment, perhaps on account of the general dislike and suspicion which attaches to anything savouring of Dinka behaviour in the area where he works.

5. *Nyjok, landowning head of Nyayo clan*

This distinguished doctor is the head of the long established landowning, but no longer politically independent, Nyayo clan. He is an old man, the typical dedicated, conventional practitioner. His mother and his maternal grandmother both practised, and as a child Nyjok helped his mother to search for medicines and to prepare them, also accompanying her when she visited patients.

While still a youth he had a revelatory dream in which he saw an elephant and other animals; the images faded and he found himself beside a wide river, which turned into a man who summoned him, saying, 'I choose you to be a doctor; if anyone is ill you must go out and heal him.' In the morning Nyjok explained his dream to his parents, and it was decided that as he already had a working knowledge of the diviner's rattle and medicines he should begin apprenticeship. He soon established himself as a sought-after practitioner.

The hereditary element is strong on the maternal side and there is already a good working knowledge of the profession. There is no mental or physical illness and practice automatically follows a dream 'summons'.

The theme of a river which changes to a man is of interest

because Nyjok married a woman of Nyarkiteŋ clan which 'owns' a similar metamorphosed river myth (p. 903). In both myths the river, as a man, gives a command. The river is a Mandari 'life' symbol and since doctors are also concerned with preserving life, . a river is a particularly appropriate Call dream symbol. Although it is unlikely that Nyjok was married at the time of the dream in view of his youth, he may have known the Nyarkiteŋ myth.

Nyjok uses rattle divination. Although he specializes in the cure of celestial sickness and has a shrine for Spirit-of-the-Above raised after a physical illness, he never uses possession. He does not treat Powers and in fact expressed some concern about, and even disapproval of, these and the diagnoses relating to them.

6. Deŋdit lo Mar Pilari (brother of Chief Korondo of Dari)[1]

Deŋdit, a man in late middle age, is primarily a seer claiming precognition. He practises in a minor way, exploiting the hereditary association with Spirit-of-the-Above found in various forms in the chiefly family. Like Nyjok, he comes of chiefly stock, but his clan is much the more powerful politically. In 1958 Deŋdit performed the Dari rain ceremony.

Deŋdit claims that power came to him directly 'from Above by a sign' when he was a mature adult. During a visit to a cattle-camp, a bracelet fell at his feet from the sky. That same year he foretold a famine in which a number of people died; he then declared the death of an important elder of another chiefdom before the news of it could have reached him. He appears to have suffered from a nervous disorder which was marked by shaking and trembling. He told me that when he first became afflicted in this manner his enemies dismissed his claims to religious power, saying that he was 'mad' (kapur). Deŋdit told me that they were all wrong and that his claim to be 'with Above' was proved by his curative work as a doctor.

Deŋdit uses a mild form of non-induced possession confined to shaking and quivering and the giving of directives in a trance-like state. He does not treat Powers.

While no close relative practises, there are several pathological manifestations of Spirit-of-the-Above in this family. (I have discussed the nocturnal convulsions with which his brother Chief

---

[1] Deŋdit is a variant of Deŋ, the name for the Dinka sky spirit, and means 'Great Deŋ'.

Korondo was afflicted, which I would think may be due to a chronic febrile infection, or infection of the filaria order affecting the spino-cerebral area.)

Deŋdit treats his neighbours and members of his family but does not appear to be ambitious to practise on a large scale. He is not one of the busy doctors constantly seen at rituals and in patients' homesteads. He is thin and frail with a retiring, withdrawn manner. Though he was very friendly towards me I always felt that there was something a little odd about him. The unkind comment that he was mad leads me to think that I am not alone in feeling this. Incidentally, I have never heard this comment made about other doctors of my acquaintance, in spite of histories of pronounced disturbance around the time of their Calls.

The 'bracelet', may well have been a piece of meteoric iron. The bracelet association being suggested by the shape, or simply from its clearly being iron of some kind.

7. Apu (a female practitioner of a lineage attached to Bukana clan— Nile-dwelling Köbora)

This married woman is one of the Nile Köbora. I have included her case history here, because of the similarities with Mandari Call experience, and because she is the only woman practitioner about whom I have any details.

Apu's grandmother Kako, her mother's brother, Munda, and her younger sister are all practitioners. This feminine orientation is what we would expect in the Nile area, where, as described, the profession is almost exclusively in female hands in contrast to the more even balance shown between the sexes in Mandari practice, with even perhaps male predominance in that the most renowned Mandari practitioners, with a few notable exceptions, are men.

While still an adolescent, Apu began to hear noises in the head and voices. She began to shun her age-mates and to wander alone in the bush. When her parents tried to restrain her she ran away. Her family assumed that she was ill and her elder brother produced a chicken for sacrifice, 'to persuade the influence to depart from her'; senior relatives attending the rite marked her protectively, and spat on her head. Shortly after this she was found sleeping with a poisonous snake coiled up beside her (cf. also Wale's case).

She regained her health for a time and married a lively deaf-mute, a retainer of Chief Buvu Deri of Bukana clan. Following the birth of her first child she suffered a relapse. After a difficult and painful delivery with her second child some years later, she was again 'ill for a very long time'. Her next infant died at birth, then she miscarried twice. Another child, which survived for a time, subsequently died and, at the time I met her, only one remained. Apu had begun to practise at about the time this last child was born. The owner of the land on which her family have built, an elder named Legwere Lekwac, brought her a divining rattle and suggested to her that she should begin to practise. Beer was then brewed and a goat sacrificed for her future health. Apu worked for about three years as assistant to a woman practitioner named Agor, learning to specialize in the art of *mömöröju* (the extraction of witchcraft substances); she also learnt to exorcize *nyök*. Apu was instructed free of charge, but when she began to earn she gave Agor £S1, and still accompanies her as assistant.

I did not know this woman well, and the information about her is very sketchy. A typical Call syndrome seems to have been present, perhaps with auditory hallucinations—'noises in the head'. I did not inquire closely into the kind of ill-health she complained about after the recovery from her initial illness and her subsequent marriage. I assume from the way in which she spoke that these were relapses, probably precipitated by the strain of difficult pregnancies and the emotional shock of child deaths—and not new illnesses. Judging by her appearance and the details of her history, Apu was in her thirties, which would mean that she might well have been recurrently ill for ten years or more and would have taken up practice at a later age than is usual for the male Mandari practitioner. She told me that her health was now improved.

IV

Although the Mandari themselves do not make a distinction between the various forms of Call, for the purpose of analysis these fall into two main classes. First, the Call that manifests what appears to be psychological disturbance of some kind involving a single individual, and which shows a quite distinct symptom pattern and occurs in a sufficient number of candidates for any Mandari, whether doctor or layman, to describe them. The second kind of Call is more diversified, covering a range of physical illness—even deaths—and affecting a number of related persons. Here the symptoms are often spread over a long time, until a candidate eventually comes forward to justify in his work the multiple illnesses. The Mandari consider both kinds of Call as equally valid, but different ways in which religious power is revealed. One of the reasons why they do not precisely differentiate the two kinds of Call may be that, unlike ourselves, they do not make a theoretical distinction between mental and physical illness, although they recognize the symptoms as different and requiring different treatment.

Mandari accept the type of Call which involves a psychological disturbance as a form of illness; they accept, at least, that a Call manifests itself in a similar way to some mental illness. Only those who *recover*—and this is constantly stressed—can go on to train; therefore, by definition, all doctors who claim this type of Call are admitting—unless the experiences claimed are fraudulent—a period of emotional disorder from which there has been a complete recovery, usually around the late teens or early twenties. I have no information about particular persons who have suffered similar symptoms but not recovered, although they obviously exist and are presumably among those described by the Mandari as 'persons permanently disabled by Above', or as 'mad' because of 'the placing of *kapur* in the head'.

The symptoms of the disturbance syndrome can be summarized:

1. Abrupt withdrawal to the bush and wandering about there alone, which can be a dangerous activity at any time, and is particularly so at night—often the time of wandering.

2. Refusal to eat or speak; a severance, in fact, from all important social communication. The reverse of this pattern is the manic 'talking like a madman'.

3. Visual or auditory experiences, or both. A number of variations again appear, such as lights and bright apparitions; the direct summons from a voice speaking when the recipient is awake and conscious; the voice in the dream; or in a more degenerate form, the noises in the head.

It is clear that a form of visionary experience is not only culturally acceptable to the Mandari, but is even anticipated during periods of heightened emotion or 'spiritual' receptiveness. A sensation of elation is perhaps deliberately promoted by ascetic practices such as fasting, hardship, and isolation, or this sensation may follow from the hardships endured after a compulsion to make the initial act of separation. The importance of cultural suggestion cannot be ruled out. If it is considered that religious power may be manifested in this way, individuals will be found who will claim, or deliberately seek, these experiences.

The comments of a Christian Dinka law student, whom I met when travelling between Khartoum and Juba, on the Call as claimed by Dinka practitioners, are of interest for comparison. For Dinka, he told me, Call is also manifested through illness. With regard to withdrawals to the bush, my informant considered that he had observed an increase in intellect, an implied development of consciousness resulting from the separation, with its isolation and hardship. He attributed this to the fact that 'the individual has time to think'. He considered that real powers were acquired, although these were not of the kind actually claimed by the doctors themselves, particularly stressing the development of the personality. The course of events surrounding a Call could lead to the novice being treated as a special person and therefore in time actually assuming a new personality.

In some cases a perfectly natural occurrence such as marsh phosphorescence may explain experiences. Other experiences may be deliberately simulated. While this may sometimes be the case, it is not essential for a doctor to undergo the extreme kind of Call experience (and only three out of my sample of seven did so), so, while it is a recognized cultural pattern, it is by no means the only one. It is difficult to see why persons should go to the trouble of simulating these experiences, with the attendant worry to their families, the expense of sacrifice, and the medical treatment involved, when this is not essential professionally. The degree to which relatives of sufferers, who are aware of the facts of Call experiences, appear worried and anxious, suggests a recognition that something is actually wrong. We cannot, I think, rule out the possibility of a psychological disturbance of a kind known to modern medicine.

On reading Field's ethno-psychiatric study of rural Ghana, it is impossible not to be struck by the similarity in the experiences claimed by some Mandari medico-religious novices and those undergone by some candidates for shrine priesthoods, particularly 'running to bush', and its associated austerities.[1] The symptoms seem to

---

[1] Field, *Search for Security*, chap. iii, 'Spirit Possession'.

be less acute in Mandari. The words 'running' or 'rushing' to bush are not used; persons are simply said to begin to wander in the bush—that is, they separate themselves off from their previous surroundings and interests, and go off alone.

Even after reading Dr. Field's very full analysis, I am not clear, however, whether medical science would see the illness which gets better, and seems in Mandari, as in rural Ghana, to develop and mature the personality, as different in kind from the illness with similar symptoms which becomes chronic and terminal. Are two quite different conditions involved—as the Mandari themselves would say? Or does the difference lie in the basic personality type involved, the same illness in a weak or poorly endowed individual leading to deterioration, and in a strong and intelligent person (basically 'good personality' according to Field) leading to new insights?

It is difficult to say in any particular Mandari case how far illness is involved, how far imagination, hysteria, and suggestion, or which of the phenomena have a natural explanation. I was not able to see any of the persons concerned during the Call crisis or question them shortly after their recovery. I have only seen one case of a possible disturbance syndrome in operation, that of the adolescent girl already mentioned.

Whatever may be the explanation in terms of scientific medicine, the Mandari themselves believe that a person cannot treat illness in others without having first experienced illness and passed through treatment and cure (with the exception of the few who already have an intimate knowledge of the profession, when a Call dream alone may be sufficient qualification). Specialist roles require some distinguishing mark, and the Call provides the justification and the visible change of state for a doctor.

Dreams are very significant in relation to the Call and this is one of the few situations in which the Mandari give weight to dream experience. They consider that most dreams are 'simply dreams' (*rudesen kanaŋ*), a form of mental process continuing in sleep. People are said usually to dream about daily events, or friends and relatives, and those who are emotionally close are thought to dream about each other—for instance lovers, who may anticipate their hoped-for marriage in a dream. Dreams of future events are generally considered unimportant and the dream does not specifically foretell the future, although 'if a man dreams he will acquire a cow, and if he does so, he may comment to himself, "My cow which slept in my head has materialized." ' Death dreams do not foretell the dreamer's death, but merely represent the human condition of mortality. Frightening and persistent nightmares may lead to a household head 'marking' the dreamer, or members of the family may 'mark each other' (bubuk bok).

A small class of oracular dreams foretells or confirms an event and requires expert interpretation, and Call dreams come in this category because they occur in a situation with other recognized and related symptoms. Dreams in which dead relatives appear and make demands and dreams about cattle sickness have already been considered, together with the protective action, like pouring libations, taking omens by chickens, or the offering of prayers to Creator, which may follow.[1]

Animal symbolism is another feature in Call experiences, and any unusual animal encounter at the time of the crisis may be viewed as a part of the revelation. In the case of Apu and Wale the dangerous or predatory element was eliminated, showing power in the person. The snake which features in two cases also has other religious associations.

V

A Call, of whatever kind, is seen as a once-and-for-all experience, and as with the receiving of other kinds of spiritual power, like rain power, I was unable to find any instance of the psychological symptoms experienced at a Call returning after practice had begun. My probing never produced anything more concrete than the remark by Ako Akurukway that 'his Above' would sometimes visit him during the night and take possession of his body, causing him to wake up shaking. Ako was prone to minor physical indispositions over the year during which I knew him, but as many people suffer from chronic febrile illnesses and infestations, 'feeling under the weather' is not unusual.

I found no evidence to suggest that doctors are emotionally disturbed persons who find an outlet for their neurotic tendencies in practice, while at the same time playing a useful role. It is of course true that, by the time I met them, the persons whose case

---

[1] In general, dreams for the Mandari lack the significance and oracular content described for dreams in Azande culture. Evans-Pritchard, *Witchcraft among the Azande*, pp. 135–47, 378–86.

histories have been recorded had been in practice for some time, so that the symptoms claimed would have occurred anything from ten to fifteen years previously. It is also difficult to know, even on close acquaintance, how far individuals may suffer emotional disabilities which they have learnt to conceal. What is certain for the individuals concerned is that if there was any such disability it had led to no obvious impairment.[1] On the contrary, the observer is struck by the above-average intelligence of doctors who are able persons who show a reflective and inquiring turn of mind, and a sophisticated insight into human affairs. Several of those I knew had reached positions of influence, Ako, for example, and his cousin Nyöki (whose Call history I did not record) both represent their lineages as government headmen. There is no reason to think that a man like Nyjok has at any time ever suffered from mental ill-health. Such a speculation only arises in relation to a small proportion of doctors.

The question whether drugs are sometimes used as aids to dissociation should perhaps be raised, but I feel confident that it can be dismissed in the Mandari case. The common hemp (*Cannabis sativa*) is occasionally and illegally grown and Mandari understand its effects, partly because of government propaganda against it. They appear genuinely to dislike the idea of smoking it, which, they say, is incompatible with a gruelling cattle-camp life. However, the comment made to me on one occasion, that 'some people who smoke hemp and "rave" may claim Spirit-of-the-Above has fallen on them', seems to indicate the possibility of an occasional history of hemp smoking. Mandari assert, perhaps with some truth, that the Moru, their sedentary neighbours to the west, grow and smoke it. The owner of the only homestead in which I saw hemp growing hurriedly explained that it was for sale 'to the Muru', which was doubtless true, as the boundary was just up the road. Hemp has no place in traditional medical practice, although I would not care to state categorically that Mandari doctors never smoke it. It is not in any case a stimulant and it is difficult to see how it would assist in promoting a possession.

[1] There is also no reason why a doctor should not be neurotic, but this does not mean that most are.

13

POSSESSION

I

BY possession I mean the convulsion known as *molja*, already described in the context of mortuary dancing and medico-religious diagnosis. In examining the physiological and psychological factors involved in possession I shall draw on experimental evidence provided by other scientific disciplines and suggest additional factors which may play a part in some kinds of Mandari possession.

Having considered the nature of the Call, it may be useful to inquire whether any link can be found between the kind of Call showing a psychological disturbance, and an ability to dissociate, in order to discover whether those doctors who use convulsion techniques have a history of nervous disorder.

TABLE 3. *Incidence of disturbance syndrome and use of possession*

1 Disturbance syndrome	2 No disturbance syndrome	3 Uses possession in diagnosis	4 Does not use possession
Ako	—	Ako	—
Wale	—	—	Wale
Apu	—	—	Apu
—	Nyjok	—	Nyjok
—	Asek	Asek	—
—	Kok	Kok	—
Deŋdit	—	Deŋdit	—

The evidence is set out in Table 3. On this evidence two doctors, Ako and Deŋdit, have manifested a disturbance syndrome during the Call and also use possession as a diagnostic technique. (In the case of Deŋdit the possession used is mild.) Two others, Wale and Apu, suffered severe disturbance at Call, but do not use possession. Asek and Kok had Calls without any psychological symptoms, but use a violent form of possession.

This leads to the conclusion that the ability to dissociate, in controlled situations, has little to do with a past history of disorder, although individuals with such a history may also have this ability. This form of controlled possession, therefore, may have only a random association with illness.

At some of the ceremonies at which the kind of possession I am discussing occurs, certain sensory stimuli are always present. These are of particular interest in examining the possession state, especially since laboratory testing has shown that some forms of auditory stimulus play an important part in precipitating convulsions.

Most possession states in Mandari are not random. As I have shown, the convulsions of *Jok* doctors are deliberately induced. Those of doctors possessed by celestial spirits are spontaneous but not random. Adolescent female possessions occur at mortuary rites and are incidental to, and not a part of, the ceremony. But a significant factor is that a rhythmical sound accompanies both mortuary rites and seances. I have attended both and witnessed the forms of convulsion which take place at them. The stimuli offered on these occasions are charted in Table 4, together with similar stimuli offered at other events where possession does not occur.

TABLE 4.

Sensory stimulus associated with possession

Sensory stimulus	Place	Event	Category affected
(i) Drumming Singing Dancing Heat	Round a grave at midday	Mortuary rite	Girls in middle and late teens
(ii) Shaking divining rattles Clapping Singing	Hut	Ritual diagnosis	Doctors

Sensory stimulus where no possession occurs

(iii) Drumming Singing Dancing	Dance ground day or night	Recreational Secular	No-one possessed, although sensitive categories present

In considering (i) and (ii) in Table 4, I have found Nehler's article on the effects on the nervous system of rhythmic drumming most useful. It provides some systematic proof for my own assumptions regarding the link between auditory stimulus such as drumming and the shaking of divining rattles and the convulsive reaction.[1] The main proposition of his thesis is that drumming in the range of 8–9 cycles per second has frequently been shown to precipitate an emotional response. Nehler considers that other factors also play a significant part in helping to precipitate convulsions where an underlying susceptibility is present.

With Nehler's article in mind, I shall examine the events with which possession is associated and the forms of sensory stimulus concurrently offered, and consider other events where similar stimulus is offered but where no possession occurs.

1. *Mortuary dance*

At the mortuary dance a number of sensory stimuli are presented simultaneously. At the height of the dance several drums of different sizes are in use and provide a very complicated and rapid beat pattern. There is also strong and well co-ordinated singing. The auditory effect of the drumming and singing on those taking part is, therefore, one form of stimulus. Further, the dancers themselves are singing and the rhythmic dance movements and the singing may go on for several hours at a time.

The actual movements of the ceremonial dance are different from those of secular or recreational dances; they are more monotonous and controlled. Dancers progress slowly round and round the grave or, when lack of space prevents this, round an adjacent dance space. I know from personal experience that a relaxed, semi-hypnotic state is achieved after a time which makes it possible to dance for very long periods without awareness of fatigue. However, the known effects of fatigue as a precipitating element in trance states should not be discounted.

Intense heat is another feature of mortuary dances, which are in full swing by the hottest time of the day—the time at which the sun is directly overhead. It may, of course, be coincidence that this is also the point at which girls begin to dissociate. I do not know how far heat could be shown experimentally to speed up a response to basic auditory stimulus. Nehler mentions hyperventilation as

[1] A. Nehler, 'A Physiological Explanation of Unusual Behaviour in Ceremonies Involving Drums', *Human Biology*, vol. 34 (1962), pp. 151–60. (My attention was drawn to this article by Sturtevant's letter in *Man* in response to an article by Needham. See R. Needham, 'Percussion and Transition', *Man*, N.S., vol. 2 (1967), no. 4, and W. C. Sturtevant, 'Categories, Percussion and Physiology', *Man*, N.S., vol. 3 (1968), no. 1.)

a possible accessory factor in inducing abnormal behaviour, and in the mortuary dance the combination of rhythmic movement with singing must of necessity enforce a particular kind of breath control.

Nehler (quoting Ulett) also makes the point that the emotional response has been shown to be greatest at the point of 'highest driving'. It is certainly true that an increase in the tempo of drumming, in the volume of singing and in the total co-ordination of both dance and dancers, actually takes place, and that this whole build-up tends also to coincide with the rise of sun temperature and with possession. A single dance sequence, in whatever kind of dance, always generates a climax of energy and co-ordination, which is held for a time; then the momentum is gradually lost and the dance period begins to run down, the drumming stops, and a break separates that dance sequence from the one which follows it.

Another, and I believe a very important form of stimulus, but one less easily isolated and proved, is the unique atmosphere of the mortuary dance. A mortuary rite assembles the largest concentration of persons for the purpose of performing ritual. No other rite brings together so many, linked by such random ties. This is particularly true of those for important persons, where massed dancing and, indeed, possession, most often feature. In a real sense it is possible to speak of a common emotion. All those who attend consciously, come to express a common sentiment about an important situation. Of course everyone present does not *feel* exactly the same; the emotional response of bereaved wives and close relatives is generally much more intense than the response of others whose mourning is largely formal. None the less, people are affected by the occasion, which marks an overwhelming human experience. Every adult will have attended mortuary rites, perhaps for someone close and loved. An occasion which centres round an event as fundamental as death creates a special atmosphere, and evokes special emotions.

For a few at least of the participants the rite will mark the end of the mourning year and the moment of radical role-changing. It may bring back memories of the initial trauma and feelings of anxiety and apprehension. Such emotions can be communicated to others. Feelings which have been held in check for a year are released in the dance; the demonstrations of older women and close female kin, their shrill ululations and the violence with which they throw themselves down in demonstrations of grief, are in keeping with the convulsions portrayed by young girls who have been 'seized'. This emotional atmosphere is undoubtedly of outstanding significance.

2. The ritual divination

In the ritual divination we have, in contrast, an example of a very sophisticated control and manipulation of stimuli and possibly of innate physiological and psychological susceptibilities.

Rattles, not drums, are used here. A significant factor in the seances, where the doctor must, for the success of the diagnosis, ensure possession, is that the shaking of divining rattles, the individual singing, and the audience responses in the chorus, are directly controlled by the doctor himself, supported by his trained or at least chosen, assistants. Because the doctor controls the tempo of the rattling and the audience participation, he can ensure the quickest and most sure response.

The sequence of the seance has a standard pattern of lead-in by the doctor with a song passage, followed by the taking up of the chorus by the audience, who also clap in unison in time to the beat; this sequence is then repeated. During the singing and clapping the doctor and his assistants are vigorously shaking divining rattles. I do not know whether the rhythm of the rattles is across the rhythm of song and clapping, or whether it reinforces it. The doctor's movements are relaxed and in time to the rhythmic rattling.

The Mandari themselves always isolate the songs as the important factor in possession—'Sing well so that the Power can come': 'If the singing is bad, so and so Power will not come.' It is hard, therefore, to know exactly where the doctor finds his own stimulus. He may not separate the amalgam of sound into its separate elements; and indeed it may be essential for the conditioned subject that all the stimuli should be provided together. Judging by the evidence of the laboratory tests carried out on the effects of auditory stimulus, however, one would tend to see the rattle-shaking as the precipitating factor. In the random possession, on the other hand, mentioned on pp. 42–3, the novice practitioner became convulsed in consequence of singing and clapping alone, and himself stressed these two elements. This was clearly the

6. Kok: doctor of Powers

response of an undisciplined subject who had received some conditioning, but lacked the finer elements of control.

Direct heat is irrelevant in the case of the doctor's possession, since seances never take place at midday. Whether or not there are some uncalculated elements in the seance atmosphere conducive to convulsions, it is the degree of precise control in divinatory possession that strikes the observer. The possibility of failure to induce convulsion is openly recognized, but I have never seen this happen with Ako, Nyöki, or Kok. The well-established practitioner seems consciously to have worked out an almost infallible combination, as is implied by the remark, 'Such-and-such a doctor is more successful than another because he has been practising longer.' The type of stimulus involved is, I believe, only provided in this precise form at the seance, which may account for the fact that established practitioners, like those just mentioned, never dissociate at random.

Nehler suggests that some persons become conditioned to specific rhythms so that possession will always be induced whenever these are heard. He also suggests that the amount of control subjects can exert over possession is limited. While it is clear that doctors undergo deliberate and systematic conditioning, it also seems that the experienced practitioner can exert at least a degree of control. At the rite described on pp. 88–90, where two doctors worked in conjunction, each was possessed in turn in orderly fashion. After Nyöki's possession had run its course, he was followed very swiftly by Kok, suggesting that Kok was ready in the sense of being stimulated but able to release possession at the appropriate moment. It is difficult to substantiate this, and the reason may simply be that some persons respond more quickly to stimuli than others, and that doctors who work together frequently plan their performances accordingly.

The doctor, who does not use drumming as a part of his repertoire, does not appear to respond to drum stimulus; I have attended dances where doctors who use possession were present but showed no signs of reaction while girls were reacting violently. It is perhaps to be expected that the rattle, the symbol of office used by all doctors, should be the medium adapted to this new use. Where it is not used as an aid in precipitating convulsion, it offers a focus for concentration. The divinatory position, with doctor and patient sitting face to face, cross-legged, eyes fixed on each other, against the background of rhythmic sound, continuing for perhaps an hour or more, with breaks for questions, may lead to a relaxed semi-hypnotic state and help to promote the free expression of worries and problems by the patient, even perhaps in some cases helping to establish telepathic communication. Convulsion never follows this use of a single rattle and the auditory driving is at a very slow rate, the rhythm far less complicated than at a seance. It would be interesting to discover how the shaking of a diviner's rattle, or rather the simultaneous shaking of several diviners' rattles, compares with the drumming frequencies shown to be a norm for the stimulation of convulsions.

Rattles can obviously be adapted to such a use. They are, apparently, so used to induce convulsion in the exorcism sheep by continuous rattling over its head while it is stretched out, and firmly held; here the convulsion is claimed to kill the animal. I am prepared to accept that death may sometimes occur from heart failure, bearing in mind the terror which must accompany the performance for an animal which will probably be old or unhealthy.

There is little doubt that response is conditioned in the doctor who grows into, and deliberately develops, his responses; and indeed it is essential for his work that his conditioning should be absolute. The reverse seems to hold good for girlhood convulsions: the girl grows out of them and this is also to her advantage. Her convulsive attacks are spontaneous in the sense that they are never deliberately sought, and her sensitivity should resolve itself naturally.

Girls are not systematically conditioned, and the fact that those who have the susceptibility convulse only at ritual and not at secular dances, although at both the drumming and dancing are vigorous and the tempo fast, suggests that the mood of the occasion contributes to their possession states.

As I have pointed out, dances differ in form and style, in objective, and above all in atmosphere. Mortuary dances take place in the hot sunlight, while, in general, young people's recreational dances take place at night.[1] Temperature may be a factor in inducing convulsions, but I believe it is the difference in the 'psychology'

---

[1] The exception to the evening timing is the *Mudu*, the dance initiated by a young person to elicit gifts. *Mudu* continue over two or three days and nights. During a *mudu* in Dari, girls were convulsing by the middle of the second day.

and function of the dances that is decisive. The comments made by Deren regarding the fundamental ambience of different kinds of dance, demonstrates the distinctions between them very well.[1] Recreational dancing occurs in the context of entertainment and courtship. It involves personal display and adornment, and attempts to attract the opposite sex and to vie with rivals. The occasion is inappropriate to the revelation of spiritual forces, as in possession. Their appearance would represent a confusion of situation and be aberrant. At mortuary dances, on the other hand, a spiritual sign is fitting. Moreover young people only attend these because they have a link with the bereaved, which presupposes for some a degree of emotional involvement. Each kind of dance has its appropriate emotional mood and the atmosphere of the occasion develops this.

II

An element of adolescent maladjustment or mild neurosis may be an accessory to female convulsion although, in general, Mandari young people give the impression of good emotional health and stability. The possible association of female possession with a culturally determined deprivation syndrome of the kind isolated by Lewis should also be considered. Lewis's proposition[2] is briefly, that women and other deprived categories, those in inferior or peripheral roles, may exploit possession to gain desired ends or make a protest which cannot be expressed overtly because of inhibiting social pressures. The possessions described by Lewis are spontaneous, although they follow some kind of pattern in that certain kinds of recurring situation precipitate them again and again. They appear to be genuine hysterical symptoms in that they are compensatory, representing an escape from a disagreeable situation: an attempt to gain a desired end, or make an implicit protest.

There is little evidence to suggest that the possessions of adolescent Mandari girls come under this head. During the age-span when they commonly occur girls have a greater freedom and can exert a more capricious influence on the opposite sex and on

---

[1] Maya Deren, *Divine Horsemen* (London, 1953), chap. vi.
[2] I. M. Lewis, 'Spirit Possession and Deprivation Cults', *Man*, vol. 1 (1966), no. 3.

their own relatives than at any other time. They pick and choose suitors, have little arduous work and few responsibilities; they also freely accompany the young men to all but the most remote dry season camps. In fact they constitute a favoured category.

Where individual girls face serious emotional problems in unhappy love affairs or forced marriages, they do not experience possession, but tend to react in a positive way by openly rebelling or running away. In situations of extreme frustration, they may even commit suicide. Older married women, perhaps emotionally deprived by the husband's neglect, do not seek compensation in possession either.

Adolescent convulsions may be symptoms of mild *individual* neurosis, but it would be difficult to determine the cause and form of this without medical investigation. The Mandari themselves accept that a few attacks are a growing-up symptom; this recognition is implicit in the pragmatic way in which attacks are dealt with, and in the fact that these are only seen to be radical maladjustments if they continue into what should be a stable maturity.

The Dinka offer some comparative evidence in that Dinka also consider female adolescent possessions of little importance. It would appear, however, that older Dinka women occasionally suffer a return of attacks around the menopause; this is then regarded as more significant, and the woman will be questioned after the convulsion and asked to state what the possessing spirit requires.[1] Thus attacks occurring in maturity have become significant, requiring attention.

Since it appears that some girls have a natural predisposition to convulsion, it is rather surprising that women practitioners do not make use of it as a diagnostic technique. A point to remember here, however, is that the deliberately induced convulsion of the doctor treating Powers is something new even for men, and that women doctors on the whole are more conservative and less experimental in their methods. Anyhow, few women specialize in treating Powers. It would be surprising to find a woman using *induced* possession because this is not the technique of the traditional specialist—the typical female practice. The traditional form of possession is always mild, and a woman may show very mild symptoms of this kind when treating a patient. I have never heard

[1] Verbal communication from a Dinka friend who is practising as a doctor in England.

that women are deliberately discouraged from using possession, but here the emphasis on the elimination of the arbitrary possession in the mature woman may be relevant.

Doctors who use induced possession owe many of their ideas and methods to foreign (Nilotic) influence. I have no doubt that the sophisticated Dinka and Atwot are well aware that responses can be obtained with auditory stimulus and that we are seeing now in Mandari the use of a similar technique to the advantage of some young and middle-aged doctors. While doctors, whether Dinka or Mandari, are not aware of what takes place in the cerebral cortex when the auditory stimulus is produced, they are certainly aware of the effects of the stimulus, and that without it there is no response. This does not preclude a genuine belief that spiritual power is channelled in this way, and that possession is the key to higher levels of consciousness.

III

No systematic singing, clapping, or rattling accompanies the mild possessions associated with treating Spirit-of-the-Above. The rattle may not be used, although divination with a single rattle may precede a convulsion, or the doctor may convulse after singing rain hymns.

I do not attempt to explain the condition involved here; possession may sometimes stem from a nervous disorder, as perhaps the example of Dendit suggests. But even here some control has been established which allows it to occur at one moment and inhibits it at another.

Comments made by the Mandari, such as 'Only those who really have Above can *molja*', 'Ordinary people cannot *molja*', suggest that they view the capacity to dissociate as an inborn personality trait, and that only a certain type of person is involved. The Mandari conviction that faked possession can always be distinguished from genuine possession relates to the notion that the capacity to dissociate is an integral part of the psyche (though in Mandari there would be no point in faking because so many other techniques are available to a doctor. It is only where every doctor is expected to show signs of possession that faking becomes necessary.) Possession is seen to follow the action of spiritual power on a special type of personality.

The Mandari believe that at a certain point in the individual's development the personality pattern is established and that, after this, it is very rare for a radical change to occur. Most Mandari know that they will never be possessed; that possession is simply not in line with their innate capacities, and this will be clear to them while they are still youthful. Normally it will be as a person approaches maturity that the signs of vocation will be seen. Any particular susceptibility will usually have been established by the late teens, and people generally start to pursue their vocation in early life. Youth is the time to undergo training, not middle age. The late developer, who manifests vocational symptoms late in life, does exist, but is the exception in Mandari as elsewhere.

It is clear that auditory stimulus of the kind discussed by Nehler provides some of the answers to Mandari possession, perhaps the main answer in the case of the deliberately induced possession. In the case of the possession affecting girls at mortuary rites, it would seem that other factors are also involved and that these lay the girl open to the stimulus then offered by the rhythm. The real life situation of the mortuary rite—what it represents in emotional terms, what it is seen to achieve, and the psychological responses it exacts—exerts an influence which is, of course, absent in the clinical conditions under which possession may be induced in a laboratory. Social and emotional pressures always add another dimension, which strongly affects the sensitive psyche. One of the reasons why possession is regarded as appropriate, and even a matter of course, at mortuary dances, may be that the Mandari are aware that these occasions, which provide a high degree of both auditory and emotional stimulus, promote this kind of response.

14

MEDICO-RELIGIOUS PRACTICE

I

IT will be clear from descriptions of sickness rituals that it is rare for an afflicted person to diagnose his own condition. Inevitably, when it becomes clear that more than an indisposition is involved, a doctor is called. The patient and members of the family then assist diagnosis by giving, as far as possible, a full history; the doctor elicits further evidence during divination.

It has often been pointed out by anthropologists that a divination brings to light a history of bad personal relationships which has built up a reserve of latent anxiety and stress, and this is also true to a certain extent in the Mandari case. The exposing of 'social' sickness is apparent when the doctor uses the prolonged rattle divination, where he concentrates on a single patient and his problems for perhaps an hour or more; it is less evident in the new divinatory seance, where a number of people all wish for guidance and the seance is inevitably at a shallow level of inquiry. The doctor cannot sustain a persistent inquiry into one case, but must give a mass of superficial judgements and guidance. He is not attempting to do more than this because he is concerned to give the whole audience the opportunity for direct participation. In the Mandari seance there is little of the element of healing the community, so marked in the superficially similar, but in fact very different, shamanistic trance sessions described by Audrey Butt for the Akawaio, a society where the shaman is the central, almost the only, mechanism for adjusting, through his spiritual authority, the disrupted social relations of the community.[1] Seances relating to Powers, because of their alien character, cannot have this fundamental social function, but even traditional Mandari medicine only has it in a limited degree. Sorting out strained social relationships has always been the primary concern of the family, lineage, or clan head and, in the wider sphere, the duty of the chief and his

[1] Audrey Butt, 'Trial by Trance', chap. 21 of *Trances*, by S. Wavell *et al.* (London, 1966).

meeting-tree council. The doctor, of course, has a function in bringing interpersonal conflict to light, but having pinpointed this, and having prescribed the required sacrifice, his responsibility ends. He may give advice but he never admonishes or censures or himself effects reconciliation. This is the duty of the family elders, who carry out the action the doctor recommends. In the purification described on pp. 230-1, for instance, a doctor did not even figure.

Many Mandari sickness situations are seen to arise in breaches of a spiritual relationship, which are non-social breaches and cannot be resolved by social resolutions—the only social element in an association with Spirit-of-the-Above or a Power and the train of sickness it explains, is the link of kinship through which it passes. Sicknesses seen to result from the evil eye or witchcraft, from sin, and, to an even greater extent, from ghost sickness, have a more direct social root.

It is perhaps because the doctor cannot enter the conflict situation directly, beyond the strictly professional point, that he is not a socially influential person merely on account of his profession. Influence depends on his being both a doctor and an important elder as well. Both doctor and lineage elder have roles to play in guiding spiritual and social health, and their functions tend to be complementary; the elder cannot act without the doctor's diagnosis, the doctor, with his specialist powers alone, lacks the social authority. While the rite is the responsibility of the elders, the doctor who diagnoses and prescribes is invariably asked to attend it, and may be one of those who 'marks' the sufferer and invokes. He should be present if only because he is entitled to meat and beer. A doctor is essential for shrine planting.

I have discussed a number of diagnostic techniques and techniques for what the Mandari describe as the 'working' (*kita*) of spiritual and super-sensory agents.[1] But the basic professional tool remains the diviner's rattle. Every doctor makes use of this whatever other method he introduces. No medium, as I have shown, gives such scope for detailed investigation. Doctors not only attach great importance to 'smelling-out' with the rattle for themselves, but they consider it essential for the patient, in order to create confidence and an openness of response without which

[1] I list the various departmental skills and techniques in a note at the end of this chapter (pp. 314–16).

doctor and patient cannot attain the rapport necessary to carry through together the diagnosis and treatment. A celebrated doctor told me that if a rattle were not used the doctor would not be believed when he diagnosed, that diagnosis by symptom and medicine alone would be considered worthless. While he himself considered the medicine of primary importance, the patient tended to lean on the divination, which provided proof of the doctor's correctness.[1]

Doctors see divination as inseparable from treatment—'As the doctor fixes his eyes on the patient and shakes his rattle ideas about the illness come to him'; '. . . are put there by Above or another spirit'. Doctors believe that they link on by the rattle technique to a stream of consciousness which exists beyond the level of ordinary awareness. It is possible that telepathy and hypnosis sometimes play a part, but this is not easy to assess. Medicines are also considered vital; 'they (medicines) have been handed down over the generations and he (the doctor) works with these and with his head.'[2]

The Mandari recognize that nothing can be made of the initial Call without hard work. A young practitioner begins by treating minor illness among relatives and neighbours until he becomes known. Youth is not necessarily a disadvantage, and a young doctor may be 'stronger' than one with years of practice—'some doctors always remain small' (they are unsuccessful or have non-descript personalities), others 'grow and become powerful'. They gain in reputation by what are seen to be cures. Success can be instantaneous with a spectacular cure, particularly when the patient is a prominent figure.[3] A reputation for success draws patients, the doctor becomes known, begins to charge higher fees and grows more selective in the cases he takes on.

The importance of instruction is particularly stressed by doctors treating Powers. The novice must be coached by a sponsor in the techniques of induced possession, and the 'question and answer'

---

[1] Several doctors pointed out the importance of clothing knowledge in palatable form so that even the most unsophisticated would accept it, 'making it easy for "simple" or "stupid" people to understand'. They feel divination could not be abandoned without seriously prejudicing their work—'If a doctor only gave medicines people would think he was useless or an amateur.'

[2] See Evans-Pritchard, *Witchcraft, Oracles, and Magic among the Azande.*

[3] Ako Akurukway made his reputation thus, by his cure of Chief Kulun Shuli.

method. When I asked Kok why a Power questioned by Ako had 'spoken' much more clearly than had his own Power when he questioned it, he replied without hesitation: 'Ako has been trying longer' ('*yu jum beron*'—'is more practised'). As in every profession, success depends on genuine ability, personality, and hard work, with that indefinable addition of luck. It is essential that a practitioner is not involved in serious mistakes. This can be disastrous—and by a bad mistake I do not mean simply the death of a patient, but death with 'proof' of neglect or involvement.

II

The profession has a code of ethics, strict adherence to which depends for the most part on individual conscience, although a doctor who is continually guilty of flagrant violation will get a bad reputation.

Fees come under this head. A doctor should fix fees in accordance with the patient's ability to pay. It is correct to treat the poor free, for nominal sums, or on long-term credit, and to demand a recognized maximum from the socially prominent and wealthy. If the doctor is unsure of a patient's position, he suggests a fee and waits for the reaction; a form of bargaining usually follows and it is often tacitly understood that the whole fee, although agreed, will never be completely paid. In default the doctor can exert various pressures, but some leniency is often in his own interest.

Nyjok gave three principles which, he maintained, were basic. First, that payment should never be demanded unless a cure was effected; a stringent qualification, as a doctor may put in a lot of work with a patient without much result. (The fee referred to here is the main fee and not the small charge for the divination made at the time.) Secondly, that poor people with no prospects should be treated free; and thirdly, that no patient should be refused because of inability to pay. Nyjok told me that abuse of these principles 'angers Creator'. He suggested that doctors might expect a reasonable return, but must never abuse their powers which are given 'by grace' ('of Creator').

Many doctors fall short of this standard and Nyjok is exceptionally respected. Two factors may explain his scrupulousness; one is his genuine sense of dedication and his real affection for, and

understanding of, people, and the other is that he comes from
a secure, landowning background, and is not therefore involved in
the struggle for status and recognition which faces young practitioners from less secure backgrounds. While there are instances of
exploitation, most doctors only make an unobtrusive living. They
are the only class of person that is obliged to work regularly, and
which often cannot herd its own cattle. They also have professional
expenses, in that they usually wear a garment (shirt and shorts or
an Arab style *gallabia*), and these must be bought for cash. Most
payments they receive are negligible—such things as tobacco,
chickens, grain, a few piastres (pence)—and are soon consumed in
daily living. Payment is now often, at any rate in part, in cash.
(To get this a patient sells a bull-calf or grain.) Labour and services
can also be taken in lieu. Wealthy patients, where there is a substantial fee, are the exception. A doctor watches his debtors, and if
they default where there is ability to pay he may refuse further
treatment. In some long-drawn-out illnesses where payments fall
behind and where, on recovery, the patient's hair must be shaved
by the doctor, he may refuse to do this till payment is made.[1]
If the patient shaves independently the illness returns.

Doctors of Powers seek to justify themselves against accusations
of overcharging or disinclination to accept poor patients by
explaining that their training is long and arduous, that Powers are
'greedy', and that treatments involve exhausting possession and
lengthy seances for which high fees are a legitimate return.[2] The
accusation of overcharging and even of fraudulent activities sometimes laid against *Jok* doctors by traditional practitioners, is partly,
at least, related to the antagonism existing between the traditional-
ist and those using new and lucrative methods. But it may not
necessarily be *Jok* doctors alone who come in for criticism and the
charge of financially 'devouring people'. I heard the same charge
made against a doctor who was himself hostile to *Jok* practitioners.
This man had built up his own unique treatments on a basic
traditional practice. He was a sophisticated man who had lived

[1] After illnesses such as Mayar (and in some chronic complaints), during the
course of which the patient does not shave, the doctor shaves the patient and
anoints his body with cooling oil to mark his return to normal living.

[2] Doctors also say that the Power or its medicines will become 'angry' and
turn on the doctor himself if he fails to demand a fee. A doctor may stir medicines
proprietary to a Power over a fire and address them; 'then the Power itself seeks
payment'!

in a township and had been a patient in a government hospital, so he is not typical. Among the paraphernalia which he showed me were the parts of an old telephone, which he used like a rudimentary stethoscope.

A doctor is not expected to take on a hopeless case and if the patient is dying he tells the relatives and leaves after warning them that he has done his best, and 'the rest is up to Creator'; in this way he protects himself. A doctor of Powers suggested to me that a death-bed had an adverse effect on the doctor. 'If he (the doctor) remains in a place of death, the Power in his body falls upon the corpse and devours it, then the Power acquires a taste for flesh and its use is spoiled because it sides with the agent in the patient's body, saying; "Let us kill this man and we shall have meat." ' I only once heard this theory put forward, but there is a convention that the doctor withdraws from the death-bed itself, though, in fact, doctors may happen by chance to be with patients when they die.

III

While there is concealed and even openly admitted jealousy within the profession—'the hatred of those who are small for those who are great'—there is also informal co-operation between individual doctors, particularly when techniques are complementary. A doctor who works with the general skills usually calls in the same specialist when he feels that a case requires it, particularly if the latter is a friend, sponsor, or relative. Ex-patients who practise after successful cures often retain permanent associations with the practitioner who cured them. Persons so linked are spoken of as 'brothers' or as having blood-relationship (*yuŋi*). When a doctor travels he stays with such a 'brother'.

While two or more doctors may decide to work a case together, a patient's family may also consult several opinions. A number of divinations may then support or supplement each other, or new agents may be exposed. Payment is shared or, if the doctors are working together, they agree their proportions beforehand; each has a part of the sacrificial meat, the leading operator and the owner of the sacrifice taking a half of the hide each. The leading operator is not necessarily the most experienced doctor, he simply leads in that particular case.

While rivalries divide the profession on the inside, in public doctors support each other. While malpractice and deception may be admitted in private, names are never given. The importance of maintaining a united front, a characteristic of all professions, is recognized.

If a doctor himself or one of his family is ill, he seeks a second opinion. On one occasion when visiting Ako Akurukway, I found his cousin Nyöki Berok advising on an indisposition and asked Ako why he did not treat himself. He replied that while he could easily do so, it was usual to seek other advice.

IV

Certain activities, some legitimate, others less so, lie around the periphery of correct practice. One is selling a spirit guide or Power to a buyer who has not acquired it in a valid Call or through heredity. If a doctor agrees to sell, he kills an ox in his own homestead to protect himself. When he plants the shrine he kills the ox supplied by the buyer. The transaction is made expensive as a deterrent. A man may buy in order to help a sick relative which is legitimate, or to harm an enemy which is not. Medicines can be bought for a pound or two. At a revenge shrine a chicken is killed at the rise of the moon in the name of the enemy, and the agent is given a directive. Medicines are 'cooked' and directed. I have doubts about the shrine raising, but instances of medicine buying have been reported, sometimes leading to allegations of poisoning, particularly where a medicine is acquired from another tribe.

Areputed malpractice is the destructive divination, something doctors claim they will not be a party to since 'the power over life and death should never be used to harm innocent people who have fallen out with neighbours'. High fees (a cow and calf) are demanded as a deterrent and because the work is 'dangerous' for the doctor. The 'Life' of the victim is drawn into a gourd of water with the divining rattle and impaled. The work takes place *inside* the hut, instead of under the open veranda, destructive medicine, like sorcery, being secret and hidden. I was assured that doctors have been discovered in such work, which is a debasement of the legitimate method of destroying witches and sorcerers. It was suggested that a doctor who undertook such work was powerful rather than evil. As an informant put it: 'He has the power and if he is paid sufficiently he uses it, it is not his business to ask whether the request is right or wrong. He is approached, he is paid, and he uses his powers. He does not know good or bad people, he only knows the reward.' As a moral individual, however, a doctor uses his judgement, and when in doubt tries to dissuade. If he co-operates it is because he is afraid the inquirer is a witch. It is said to be wisest to evade the issue by pretence or with excuses, rather than by outright refusal. The doctors I questioned were emphatic that they would never perform this kind of divination.

Note: DEPARTMENTALISM IN MEDICO-RELIGIOUS PRACTICE

Specialization arises in the profession because of the multiplicity of causal agents. Doctors with a limited qualification do not treat some of these but most can diagnose and make recommendations in minor illness. The following are the main curative skills. In category I are listed skilled persons who are not qualified doctors.

CATEGORY I

(*a*) *Bone-setters*. Practised people who set broken bones, sprains, and dislocations by tying them firmly with creepers, often to wood splints. Hot poultices are placed on the swellings and incision may be made at the point of a break and the bones pushed together. Stitching is not used to sew bone fractures, but split scrota may be sewn.

(*b*) *Medicine owners—Dutu ko Winiko*. Owners of simple remedies. The most common are for snake bites. Curative snake medicines are pounded and bound on the bites; prophylactics are cooked over a fire and inhaled before journeying at night. Small stocks of other medicines may be bought from a doctor who has cured the purchaser of the agent to which the medicine belongs. The doctor may also show the user where to dig new supplies in order to continue his own treatment or help friends and relatives. Medicines are often handed over if a shrine is planted; where, in fact, the Mandari see a chronic element in the sickness.

'Household' remedies such as herbal purgatives, the pungent roots of wild garlic chewed to relieve colds, and herbs used for treating infected wounds, are available to anyone.

(*c*) *Midwives*. Experienced old women; each lineage has its own.

CATEGORY II

(a) *Doctor of the Rattle—Bunit lo Tu'ya.* These are doctors who divine only with the rattle (*tu'ya*), described as 'smelling-out' (*wöwöndu*), or 'following with a rattle' (*dodoa ko tu'ya*). These doctors own general medicines and recommend and assist at sacrifices to traditional agents of disease (particularly Spirit-of-the-Above and ancestral ghosts) and carry out purifications and hunting rituals. They supply protective charms and talismans to pregnant women and people in liminal conditions, and advise on suspected bewitching and nightmares. Women work in this category, although some also exorcize and extract. These general practitioners are an integral part of every community and several will be found in a sizeable village.

(b) *Specialist of Celestial Sickness—Bunit lo Ki.* These specialize in Spirit-of-the-Above, working either traditionally with the rattle and medicines or with a Celestial guide and a shrine. Types of possession employed vary.

(c) *Specialist of Powers—Bunit lo Jokan.* Doctors of the new cult who conduct mediumistic seances and use induced possession. All have shrines and a named guide. There were no women in this category during my field-work.

(d) *Exorcist—Kagorkeit.* The specialist in exorcism.

(e) *Extractor—Kömuryeit.* Specialist who removes witchcraft objects. Maser is a famous *kömuryeit.* Women work in both these mediums.

DOCTORS AS CHIEFS' AGENTS

Before the establishment of the Administration, a practitioner was attached to each chief's household, whose duties were to hold divinations before raiding or vengeance forays. Such a practitioner never took part in the raid himself, because of having 'worked on the life' of important leaders on the opposing side, in order that 'they would be delivered into the hands of the attackers' (it is claimed that 'the blood of those whose death he had divined for would seek him out in the fight'). Divinations were also ordered by chiefs to determine the guilt or innocence of suspected witches, sorcerers, and persons with the evil eye; in this way the doctor kept the chiefdom free of undesirables. Chiefs no longer have personal practitioners with public duties, although most chiefs have their favourite doctor who regularly attends them. Some of these are clients or retainers who have long formed a part of the particular chief's hamlet. They may also divine about rain failure, hunting, and important journeys. A chief consults other doctors and specialists as he wishes; similarly, his own doctor is free to take other cases.

15

THE THEORY OF SYMPTOMS

I

IN discussing theories of causation in relation to illness, something must be said about the diseases of domestic animals.
Most diseases of stock, particularly cattle—the only animals
primarily relevant—are understood to have a natural cause and
Mandari have an elementary body of empirical knowledge about
these. Thus infectious diarrhoea, when diagnosed, involves isolating
the infected herd and means a radical modification of cattle movement. There is also a common-sense appreciation of the harmful
reaction to bites and stings.

But cattle are also thought to be directly affected by the actions
and dispositions of their human owners. Like the human illness
which can often be explained by a man-to-man or man–Spirit
relationship, many cattle diseases are explained in this same idiom.
Ghost activity, breaches of female prohibitions, deliberate 'overlooking', and sorcery, are the non-empirical diagnoses generally
given in cattle sickness. The evil eye, the envy weapon, explains
cattle barrenness, poor milk yield, aborted and dead calves. Many
cattle-less persons come from non-landowning lines and are therefore suspected of 'overlooking'.

Rites for cattle are usually simple acts like killing a chicken or
rubbing ashes on the animal's back while prayers are offered,
although a goat or a young ox may, in exceptional cases, be killed
as well. Ritual is not, however, performed each time an animal
sickens (as it would be for a human being) but rather when there
appears to be a threat to all the cattle a man herds together, or
when a valuable animal is in danger.

Theories of cattle sickness have been modified in recent years
since the Mandari now accept that the epidemic, killer diseases, can
best be controlled by using the services of the Veterinary Department. After initial suspicion, the benefits of cattle inoculation

have been recognized, and few owners hide their herds or openly refuse to bring their animals into field centres periodically set up in the vicinity of Tali by mobile veterinary units. Chiefs and headmen are responsible for seeing that this is done, and there are penalties for default.

It is perhaps ironic that it should be animals rather than humans who benefit most from modern preventive medicine, or indeed from any scientific medical treatment. Herders who have themselves never visited a government dressing station, still less a hospital, bring their cattle for inoculation.

At the time of my visit the only medical assistance provided for the people of Mandari consisted of the simple bush dispensary at Tali Post, under a Nyangwara medical assistant and a medical dresser. The efforts of the staff could not compensate for its limitations; the lack of a refrigerator or microscope and the constant shortage of drugs made anything beyond the most elementary diagnosis and treatment impossible. The Medical Assistant complained to me on several occasions that medicines and supplies failed to arrive from Juba township. As far as it could do so the dispensary served the needs of the mixed population who live in, or around, Tali Post itself; it also acted as a collecting-post from which those who were prepared to go for treatment to Juba—about two hundred miles away—could be ferried on any available merchant's lorry. It is not surprising that most Mandari preferred to use their indigenous medicines and 'to die at home'.

The C.M.S. Hospital at Lui, situated near the Moru District Headquarters at Amadi, had a very good reputation during the years it was in operation and Mandari who bordered the Moru might take lorry lifts or be carried there on litters. For Mandari as a whole, however, the lack of medical facilities was one of the problems resulting from their isolation.

To return to domestic animals. Cattle alone receive medico-religious treatment. Mandari are too poor to call diviners for small stock, but they will do so for cattle which represent essential wealth and are substitutes for persons in many situations. Because of their value, and through identification, cattle are brought within the range of human socio-religious experience. Comments on wild animals, on the other hand, emphasised that 'they are things of the bush and outside, people cannot think about what they may be suffering'.

I attempted to make a classification of sickness symptoms to see whether certain symptoms were generally associated with specific agents; for instance, whether a fever and swelling would be a sign of the presence of the Power Mayom, and treated as such. It was soon apparent that a simple categorization of this kind was totally inadequate to meet the complexities of diagnosis, since, as I have shown, classification by symptom is only one way by which cause is determined. In diagnosis doctors assemble evidence as follows:

1. Symptoms   → determined on physical level   → treated by
                        by external examination   medicine,
                                                                extraction, etc.

2. Socio-medical,
   religious, 'history' → determined on both objective   → treated by
                          and mystical level, by divination,   sacrifice,
                          questioning, etc.   cleansing, etc.

Physical symptoms are not consistently differentiated or aligned; there is overlapping, one symptom showing for many causal agents and dissimilar symptoms for one agent. Western medicine, of course, also recognizes that different diseases may manifest similar symptoms or that dissimilar symptoms may indicate one disease. The layman in either case is unable to diagnose (in one he lacks the mystical, in the other the scientific, experience) although in either case he may make a guess. Scientific medicine has clinical procedures for determining symptoms, and history is less important. In Mandari medicine, on the other hand, it is essential to all diagnosis, symptoms being secondary.

If several agents are diagnosed, different levels of reality and different ranges of experience are seen to combine in a single illness. A patient's own sin or moral failing may lead to self-induced sickness, the interpersonal relationships of members of the wider community—relatives and neighbours—may also be involved, and finally a whole range of external religious phenomena.

The Mandari themselves believe that there are certain basic guides to symptom diagnosis, and any doctor I talked to would give his particular version of this classification, which in general terms was also confirmed by other doctors. Ako, for instance, told me that sensory criteria were one useful starting-point for diagnosis, and gave the following examples relating to two common afflictions, eye complaints and chest disorders, to explain this. He told me that he deduced that eye complaints were caused by Celestial Spirit if the eyes were watering, sore and red, and were caused by the evil eye when there was swelling, pus, the eyes smelt bad, or were closed-up. The two sequences of data involved are (*a*) running < rain < water < Ki, and (*b*) matter in the eye < something put in them by a witch < loss of sight, the intended objective. In complaints involving pains in the chest, he differentiated by whether the rest of the body and head were cold and damp or hot and dry, the sequences then being (*a*) pains < cold < Ki, and (*b*) pains < hot < Power.

On the basis of information given me I arrived at a general classification which showed areas of overlap, but which none the less is seen by Mandari to be of diagnostic value if used in conjunction with case history. I was specifically told that the new causal agents (Powers) were partly responsible for the confusion and overlap in the diagnostic procedure. The symptoms align as follows.

THE EVIL EYE AND SORCERY

Here something has been placed in the victim's body, particularly in the belly or bowels. Thus the patient often says he feels 'a snake'. He may be right in the sense that this kind of diagnosis follows symptoms which suggest radical worm infestation.[1] Bewitching manifests the additional symptoms of infestation, like weakness, debility, and vomiting. Such patients complain, 'my life is being eaten away', or 'my body is weak.' When the patient believes his joints have been tampered with— 'I am aching in all my joints, they are stiff or sore'—he may be suffering from rheumatism, yaws, or a chronic febrile condition. Bowels are another favourite point of sorcery attack, resulting in what is probably dysentery, enteritis, or the reverse, bad constipation or blockage.

The persistently 'bewitched' grow listless, their resistance is low, and they become wasted, and if they contract another infection they often die, a point noted by the Mandari—'He is persecuted by witches until his body is so weak he cannot withstand

[1] A youth who worked for me, told me he was undergoing treatment for stomach pains diagnosed as bewitching with hippo meat placed during our visit to the Nile Köbora. When he was later admitted to hospital the diagnosis was amoebic dysentery and angostoma, a parasitic infection.

the attacks of Above and *Jok*.' Bewitching is also the trigger which starts a descent into madness. Barrenness, death in childbirth, and milk drying up may also be attributed to this cause.

Many of these symptoms, however, if combined with fever, are likely to be attributed to other causes, particularly if death is swift, for the 'witchcraft' death is long-drawn-out.

CELESTIAL ILLNESS[1]

Symptoms cluster around the head and the upper part of the body: severe headaches, infected eyes, madness, nervous disorders, delirium, convulsions, sore throats, coughs, and pains in the back and chest. A cold fever is present; onset is sudden and violent and death may follow. The symptoms can extend down into the body's lower regions, although these are not typical of this agent's disorder areas. Barrenness again features.

POWERS

These cover all the body areas associated with Celestial Spirit and the ghosts of the dead. Distinguishing features are said to be the violent and sudden onset of the illness and its often fatal course. Swelling diseases are particularly typical. Heat in the body distinguishes these agents from Celestial ones, but leads to overlap with illness from ghosts. Barrenness also features.

THE DEAD KIN

Parts affected are similar to those affected by other agents and include chest, throat, and bowels, but illness is often long-drawn-out and not necessarily fatal. The body is hot. Female fertility and the health and physique of children are very common targets, for reasons already explained, as are unhealing wounds. Wasting and debility theoretically differentiate these illnesses from those caused by Powers.

SIN

Here the symptoms relating to male indisposition overlap with the possible results of bewitching. Reproductive problems in females and child sickness and death duplicate other agents.

[1] See also Chapter 2.

HYDROCELE AND HERNIA (*Tulu*)

A swollen scrotum and hernia are both *tulu*, the word for testicles. (Women can only suffer from hernia, although the Mandari informed me that women have internal testicles.) Cause is divided between the mystical breach of death prohibitions, and the common-sense realization that excessive load-carrying can lead to rupture.

MEASLES (*Kujugi*) AND SMALLPOX (*Dando*)

As with all epidemics, both are said to be 'sent from Creator'. Fatalities are numerous, particularly among children. A measles epidemic in a village where I was staying, decimated whole families. No sacrifice is possible, but attempts may be made to contain the spread by felling trees and firing grass around the infected village.[1]

LEPROSY (*Rima*)

This is said to result from a breach of the vengeance prohibition. Is uncommon.

VENEREAL DISEASE

The Mandari know that this is a town disease and for this reason fear urban residence. It is not included in traditional classifications and the empirical explanation is accepted for the genital sores, but the malaise which surrounds advanced cases is explained under one of the traditional headings, after divination.

NATURAL CAUSES

The Mandari are aware of natural indisposition, and symptoms which are neither violent nor prolonged come under this head. As in our own case, it is only when the doctor is consulted that the vague aches and pains, minor upsets and indispositions from which most people suffer from time to time, are confirmed as illness and treated as such. The Mandari know that unwise eating and stale food cause stomach upsets, and assume individual food allergies

---

[1] The purging destructive qualities of fire are seen to be effective beyond the purely physical level, hence also the kindling of the fire on the spot where *ŋyök* is exorcized, and the prohibition on roasting sacrificial meat the quality of which is destroyed by fire.

(warm fresh milk and millet beer make some people sick and they will avoid them).

'Childhood' complaints, whooping-cough, colds, inflamed eyes, cuts, and bruises are not given a mystical explanation. Diarrhoea and constipation are home-treated and only considered illness if persistent. This is also the case with tropical ulcers and guinea-worm infestations which are endemic. Only when these become radically incapacitating are other causes sought. A paste of sesame oil and powdered red ochre is used on both types of sore, and poulticing is employed to speed the exit of the guinea-worm which is then skilfully wound out. Guinea-worm infections which involve complications may be explained in terms of association with grave-dust, and there is a theory that the infection is present in rain-pools, because 'it comes from the sky, in the rain'.

A distinction is also implied between the symptom and its cause. When a patient first falls ill, he is mostly concerned with his symptoms. He will describe what he is feeling, saying for example, 'I am "ill" (suffering)' (*Nan tatana*), or 'I feel bad' (*Nan a naron*). Explicit details may be added like, 'I am suffering with my "head", "stomach" ', etc. (*Nan tatana ko kwe, ko pele, etc.*), or the condition may be expressed as 'having a head, bowels', etc., or that such and such a part is 'painful' (*mimyen*). There is a large vocabulary to describe parts of the body and internal organs based on knowledge of animal physiology. When the condition has been diagnosed, the name of the agent and possibly the details of sacrifice required will be given.[1] As proceedings advance, and cause is revealed and ritual arranged, the emphasis shifts to the agent concerned. By that time the symptoms may have improved or disappeared.

[1] The reaction of the patient in our own case is very similar. The layman is more likely to say that he has a stomach upset or a sore throat, than that he has gastro-enteritis or streptococca, the causal state tending in both cases to reflect the specialist's diagnosis—the doctor's against the layman's.

16

THE SYSTEM: OPEN OR CLOSED?

WHILE the cures practised by the Mandari may be ineffective, I found no evidence that the natural medicines used were damaging to health and, as a whole, the system appears humane so far as it goes. Mandari doctors also practise a form of elementary individual and group therapy for the cure of the whole person or whole family, with the emphasis on relieving anxiety and guilt and bringing tension and stress into the open. In these later aims we may suggest that their medicine has real value (in combination, perhaps, with some of the herbal medicines). But doctors fail completely over a wide area of serious physical and organic disorders, including those which would only be amenable to hospitalization or to modern drugs. But it must be remembered that many of those conditions would also have been fatal in Europe some fifty years ago.

In giving a diagnosis which is correct, that is, which can help the patient, the doctor relies on the honesty and integrity of the patient and his family. Having taken note of the observable symptoms, he can only proceed to his assessment on the basis of what the patient says about his own and his close relatives' personal circumstances, together with particulars of any previous diagnoses or spiritual attachments. Where there can be no clinical testing the openness of the patient to the doctor and his honest statement of his case is the basis of successful treatment. The doctor uses the information he receives, together with any he may already have, and selects from this intuitively— 'led by his spirit'. The smallest detail may be relevant and this is one reason why the Mandari are often so discursive when discussing their illnesses. Even when the doctor cannot achieve much in the way of physical cure, he may be able to help the emotional health of a whole family. The fact that problems are constantly talked out with an interested but independent party may account, in part, for the sound mental health of the Mandari.

Mandari doctors are fully aware that their knowledge and

abilities are limited, that their efforts often fail, and, from my impression, they are concerned about this. But, like their patients, Mandari doctors, conditioned by their culture, are unable to make a completely objective assessment of their own beliefs and actions. They are also aware that some of their practices involve deceptions, but this does not invalidate their own system for them, since even laymen recognize that an element of deception—the placebo—plays a part in some cures.[1] The fact that there are other kinds of treatment available in European hospitals does not necessarily lead to a loss of faith in their own profession. They believe their particular type of medicine is justified by their situation as Mandari—an attitude which is justified by their wider philosophy which places the unique and specific above the general and universal.

They apprehend an over-all human condition but they also assume that there are limited and unique conditions; thus their particular form of medicine, with all its limitations, is peculiarly suited to their way of life and to their relationship with the moral forces which are believed to control this. They do not suggest that it necessarily has a wider validity—although it can have, since Atwot and Dinka attend their doctors. It is for this reason that, while they allow European medicine an over-all superiority, and even in relation to themselves, a superiority in some spheres—particularly those with a pronounced 'empirical' element such as serious physical injury, or 'splitting-open and sewing' (operating) which they do not attempt—they will generally prefer to treat illness by their own methods. They suggest, and logically, that as Europeans neither recognize nor believe in most of their agents of illness they cannot have perfected techniques for dealing with them: 'You do not have a medicine to cure something you do not believe in.' They consider (in some cases, perhaps even rightly) that Europeans do not suffer from many of the illnesses they face but rather have their own afflictions, with associated curative techniques.

They see a common human element, none the less, and they allow that there can be a beneficial overlap between the two healing systems at certain points, where European medicine may be useful to them, while their own treatments may even be helpful

---

[1] It is probable, however, that like all specialists everywhere they are more aware of the limitations and failings of their own profession than ordinary people are. Cf. the 'myth' of the infallibility of 'science' in our own culture.

to other races, particularly perhaps to members living in their country. I myself gave the Mandari proof of a successful treatment of a European in the following circumstances. For no apparent reason my foot became swollen and painful. Ako Akurukway who had called that day, at once left to fetch medicine. On his return in the evening he bound on a poultice of shredded, pounded, and moistened roots. By the morning the pain and swelling were gone.

The Mandari theory of medicine provides a number of standard rationalizations of failure at the level of laymen's opinion. These are expressed in such comments as 'some doctors are useless', 'the spirit refused', 'it is up to Creator', and so forth.[1] Moreover, laymen and doctors alike recognize the mis-diagnosis and the failure to recognize additional causes. Rationalizations of specific failures (so often considered to have a 'safety-valve' function and to inhibit any challenge to the system itself) do not necessarily, in the Mandari case, provide an absolute barrier to modification in theory and practice. I believe, in fact, that many systems of folk medicine have a much greater flexibility and are more open to rational scrutiny than has sometimes been suggested, and that they can and do accommodate both the internal modification and the external pressure which leads to change—although it would seem that some systems are more closed (self-validating) than others. Thus, I find it hard to accept that the Mandari medico-religious philosophy is anything in the nature of a given absolute, something impervious to change and never examined. In the first place, while the over-all philosophy on which it is based rests on certain basic assumptions, this philosophy cannot be said in any sense to be a unified whole. It does, however, embrace a number of symbolic centres, inner cores with a high degree of stability. Change at the centre is a gradual process which cannot be observed, and the emotional involvement here is so strong that change requires radical alteration in the psyche of the individual adherents; it involves, in the Jungian frame of reference, the equivalent to a changing of cultural archetypes. Around the cores, however, there is a peripheral area, where the symbolic and theoretical meet the assaults of direct experience. Here new ideas gradually make their entry and are slowly assimilated, even becoming new dogmas, or alternatively are rejected and thrown out. A continuing attach-

---

[1] Professor Evans-Pritchard, in his Azande study, also lists a number of similar ones.

ment to the symbolic centre can be combined with the acceptance on the periphery of revised extraneous elements, even with a gradual widening of the recognition of empirical cause. Folk medicine and scientific medicine then begin to exist side by side without conflict. A good example is given by Field for rural Ghana; she shows that acceptance of religious cause and treatment in hospital may go together.[1]

The Mandari also accept new evidence but keep some of it outside their central categories; they have not, for instance, assimilated Powers to their religious (*Ɉun*) category, although most Mandari are prepared to deal with them on the symptomatic level. There seems to be no reason why elements from Western medicine should not also be so accepted.

It can be said, therefore, that while the Mandari do not automatically incorporate new evidence to affect theory, they show a considerable flexibility and a willingness to examine it. (Further examples of this will be given later.) In many ways Mandari medicine in its theory and practice shows itself more receptive to new proof and more capable of modifying accepted dogmas than has been the case formerly with some Western theory and practice. We need only look at the struggles of certain nineteenth-century medical innovators to get what would seem indisputable evidence accepted in the face of persistent and blind resistance (the history of the struggle to get antisepsis accepted comes to mind as an example), to see that openness to new ideas and evidence is a very recent phenomenon in our own society.

[1] Field, *Search for Security.*

PART IV

RITUALS OF THE COMMUNITY

17

CHIEFLY OFFICE AND THE RITUALS OF INSTALLATION

I

I HAVE so far discussed rituals which members of extended families or lineages perform for healing, purifying, and comforting their individual members—what all religion answers to in the way of individual need and rehabilitation in fact. In Part IV I consider rituals of the territorial chiefdom performed by hereditary officiants to benefit members of the chiefdom collectively.

In these community rites, the doctors who play such a crucial role in family and lineage rituals are no longer central figures. Their diagnoses, and their position as links between individual patients and spiritual or other agents, are irrelevant here. Instead, the land-owning chief, in consultation with his elders, decides when to hold the ceremonies, officiates at them, and is the expert in their procedures. His power to perform them is hereditary and innate. A doctor is called only if something goes wrong, when he may be paid to divine why the chiefly rites have failed.

In theory the landowning chief himself is the unique link between his whole people and their land, and the religious sources of rain and fertility in nature.[1] In practice, close agnates of a chiefly family and, in the last resort, even persons of its collateral lineages may be empowered to assume religious duties, since all have the status of

---

[1] The internal structure of the chiefdom, the nature of chiefly office, and the rules of succession have already been described in *Chiefs and Strangers*, chaps. v and vi.

'landowners' (*komonyekokak*). The sharing of power ensures its continuity should a chief die without an heir, or (a greater misfortune) the chiefly office devolve on a collateral line. It is not uncommon for a brother or paternal uncle to deputize during the sickness of a chief, and religious duties may be shared within a group of siblings.[1]

The innate religious powers of a landowning chief derive 'from Creator', and for rain and the fertility of the woodland, he addresses Spirit-of-the-Above and Spirit-of-the-Below. Community rites are never offered to the free-Spirits-of-the-Above or Powers nor to the ghosts of the dead. As the scale of the group widens to embrace the chiefdom instead of its individual descent segments, the religious power addressed becomes universalized and a single hereditary leader represents all groups, including in addition to the landowners affines, maternal kin, clients, and settlers. Chiefly office unifies politically and religiously all diverse interests.

The hereditary religious power which gives the right to intercede for rain derives from valid forms of landownership. Landownership (the state of being *komonyekokak*) is based either on being 'born from the land'—an autochthon—or on having ancient ownership which, although not absolutely primary, is validated by religious charter as in the Bora myths.

The Bora myth does not represent a cultural heritage shared by all Mandari, but it comes nearest to a unifying history, in that besides a feeling of common identity to all those of Bora stock its main theme is known also to non-Bora.[2] Bora clans are widely recognized as rain-clans, and it is also accepted that in former times the Bora nucleus had considerable influence beyond its own territory. Particular features of chieftainship like installation and even the present-day mortuary ceremonies are claimed by Bora to be based on an original Bora pattern. The two main myth themes state the original unity between man and Creator through the joining of earth and sky by the rope. In the myth two brothers 'fall to earth from the sky', or 'come down the rope'. (For the implications of the 'fall from the sky', see Chapter 2.) One remains on earth and begets two sons who figure respectively as the prototypes of political power and religious rain power. The elder is instrumen-

---

[1] In Appendix IV I give the serial placing of rain powers in Borenye chiefdom.

[2] For accounts of Bora myths see *Chiefs and Strangers*, pp. 19–26.

tal in killing the younger, the miracle worker. The killing of the younger brother, representing the life-giving side of office, is followed by 'the death of the land', featured in the myth by three days of darkness and a year of sterility and barrenness. The death of every landowning chief, who is spoken of as 'the land', embodies something of this initial disaster and during the interregnum the chiefdom as a living force ceases to exist, although its mundane affairs continue, in modified form, while the people mourn their dead rulers.

The first fratricide initiated the break-up of the Bora people, the Bora 'rain' dividing at the same time following the new political divisions as each leader assumed responsibility for his land 'together with the rain which falls over it'. Immigrants then arrived and settled, some bringing their own rain with them.

II

The death and mortuary rites for a deceased ruler, and the installation of his successor, are linked as a single sequence. As I have shown, new roles of whatever kind cannot be assumed before a lapse of time allows people to adjust to the kinship personality of the dead as dead. Political office-holders must, however, be replaced without too long a delay in the interests of orderly social life, at the end of the standard mourning period of one year. Installation followed as an extension of the mortuary ceremonies, or alternatively a few days elapsed between the ceremonies. Once the living political and religious personality of the dead chief has finally been relinquished, a lengthy waiting period could not be allowed. Yet while the year of interregnum was represented as very dangerous it could not be avoided because of the need for adaptation to the deceased's personality as deceased, because installation could not be held during mourning, and because the central dogma of chieftainship decrees that two persons can never simultaneously occupy the one office. The three reasons were in essence one: a candidate could not assume office before his predecessor's occupancy was seen to be terminated.

I have referred elsewhere to the reciprocal linking whereby installation required the assistance of a rival chiefdom linked by reciprocal duties,[1] and also to the role of the client selected for

[1] See *Chiefs and Strangers*, pp. 83–7.

installation with the chief in order to assume certain obligations of chieftainship and stand between the chief and damaging contacts. The role played by the client not only represented the historical position of chief and client, but saved the chief from hostile speech or action, direct involvement in argument—even indeed from a too close involvement in mundane affairs—potentially harmful to an installed chief, who should maintain a greater physical and emotional detachment than others.[1]

Installation was divided into a public accession, attended like the mortuary rite by representatives from a wide area, and afterwards a private ceremony of blessing. As a prelude to installation chief and client, feigning reluctance, hid in the bush where the visiting deputation sought them out and presented them to the people. Then followed the washing with water, symbolizing the elimination of mundane impurities and the laying aside of the former status, and the pouring of milk over heads and shoulders, symbolizing for the chief, endowment with life-giving qualities, and for the client, his transfer from a menial status to a chiefly one. Finally the anointing with oil brought by the visiting delegation and carried by young brides newly wedded 'who were beautiful and well adorned'.[2] During the five day seclusion which followed, chief and client were renamed.[3]

At the rite at re-emergence, a sheep was killed and prayers were offered for the chief's well-being, his 'coolness', and for spiritual assistance in 'holding' the country and 'feeding' the people.

Mandari chiefs are no longer traditionally installed.[4] The possibility of forced retirement or removal of a chief, and particularly the appointment of a substitute, destroys the Mandari principles that two chiefs 'can never be installed in one place' and that once installed an office-holder can never be removed. Clearly no modern administration can function through an office held on such terms, neither can it wait a year to fill a vacant post. The Mandari,

[1] *Chiefs and Strangers*, pp. 83–90 and 108–10.
[2] The fact that young married women and not virgins feature here is of some interest, and is consistent with the fact, already pointed out, that correctly regulated sex is not polluting.
[3] It is characteristic when referring to chiefs to prefix the installation name with the title 'Mar' 'chief' e.g. Mar Are. Title and name become equivalent to a composite name.
[4] Because of anomalies introduced by the Administration, in particular the grouping of smaller chiefdoms into administrative units and the selection of single office-holders as administrative chiefs.

feeling that they cannot perform the sacred rites of installation under the conditions required by the Administration, have preferred to allow the ceremony to lapse.

The Mandari are well aware who their rightful leaders are, and whether or not they are selected as administrative chiefs, they are accorded the respect and continue to embody much of the virtue of their predecessors, particularly when they come from landowning stock.

Although identified with the fertility of the land, the person of the chief is not absolutely linked with the natural order in the sense that an automatic disruption of this follows the decline of his physical powers.[1] Nevertheless, if angered he might refuse to perform rituals, and usurpation of his political authority is seen to disrupt the rain. It is also assumed that it is unsatisfactory for rain rituals to be performed by a sick office-holder, and while an ageing or infirm chief retains the qualities of office received at installation, a brother or son may perform the ritual in his name. Even favoured clients 'who became great people of rain' are said formerly to have done so. The delegation of ritual performance allows rain to remain vital and an installed chief need never be disestablished. In no circumstances whatsoever could an installed chief be killed. His death was the ultimate disaster; as the Mandari express it, 'the chief *is* the land.'

III

Through his capacity to pray and sacrifice for the community the landowning chief synthesizes the two divisions of the universe in relation to the particular chiefdom, the upper part symbolized in the rain, the lower in the land and woodland shea-trees.

In Mandari ideology two categories especially are concerned, each in its own way, with the regulation and guardianship of fertility and life: the landowning chief who ensures the continuing fertility of all nature, and woman, who ensures the continuity of the individual family and descent line. This is not to suggest that chiefs and women are equated in Mandari thought and action, although there are seen to be shared and analogous qualities, and some symbols and restrictions are common to both. Both are associated with the supreme fertility symbol, milk. For the chief,

[1] Cf. the Shilluk *reth*.

the milk association is deliberately created, for a woman it is inborn. Chiefs and women as wives both enter their roles through rites of passage. But the rite of accession is much more complex than that of marriage, and the chief undergoes much greater change of state which corresponds to his wider area of responsibility. He must actually become a *new* person, whereas a woman simply fulfils her natural powers in her role of wife. She is essentially creative and all that is required is ritual recognition of this fact in order to ensure her maximum fulfilment. The chief elect, on the contrary, although endowed by birth with potential creativity, is male; his maleness must therefore be transformed. In order to sustain his transformation throughout the years of office, a continuing shielding is required. The virtue of chiefs, like the virtue of women, can be damaged, hence the chiefly substitute. Chiefs also have the power to destroy through their curses. Qualities of sensitivity and ambivalence belong to aspects of both roles and, in this sense, women and chiefs have something in common for the life of the community.

18

RAIN RITUAL:
ITS THEORY AND PRACTICE

I

RAIN rites should traditionally be carried out by all clans with landowning status, and where a number of landowning clans have now been combined in a single Administrative division, it is still the identity of the traditional order which is ritually important, not the administrative division. In my account of rain ceremonies, therefore, I speak of landowning 'chiefs' and rain 'chiefs'.

The individual ownership of rain, which is seen to exist in combination with the recognition of the more general laws controlling all rain, has its basis in the Mandari assumption that rain is not only associated with particular chiefdoms but also with particular people. Rain is therefore vulnerable to spoiling and loss, and rites for it can develop special features in some places. The main distinction between types of personal, 'owned' rain is that between Bora rain and the rain of non-Bora groups. Among the non-Bora clans in turn rain procedures differ according to differences in history and origin. Dissimilarities in the performance of rain rites may also arise in a single chiefdom as officiants succeed one another. Some chiefdoms have acquired unique rain paraphernalia (rain drums and spears, or, in the past, rain-stones) while others have not.

Rain rites, therefore, vary far more than those sickness and affliction rituals just described. I include later details of the rain ownership and rain rites of the more important landowning clans, but since this ethnographic detail may be initially confusing I first describe the rain-ownership in Dari chiefdom and its rites which I attended. I know this chiefdom well and have details of its rain rituals over a period of eight years, during which the ritual duties passed between several brothers because of illness and death.

The Dari, though not autochthons, are a clan with ancient

Mandari residence.[1] Long settlement in their land thus validates the Dari claim (sometimes challenged in theoretical discussion with other landowners but never challenged in practice) to belong to the category of landowner (*monyekokak*).

The Dari claim to have hereditary rain brought with them from Lugbara, their country of origin. During my 1952 visit, their rain rite was performed by Chief Korondo. That was a famine year following the failure of the previous rains, and the rite was performed with two chickens. Korondo explained to me 'the earth is hungry', hence there was no rain-ram.

Although rites are performed on behalf of all members of a chiefdom, only members of the performer's own lineage actually attend them, the people at large simply attending the rain-dance held the evening before which announces their performance.[2] In 1952 the dance was omitted because of mourning for Korondo's married daughter whose marital homestead was situated nearby. I did not see this rite but Korondo told me that at sunrise beer was circulated among elders of the chiefly lineage and its retainers. After the beer-drinking Korondo placed a pot of water by his shrine for Spirit-of-the-Above. This water represents the previous year's 'new rain', although it is usually water from a nearby rain-pool or river. Korondo crushed a frond of the rain creeper *dölöŋi* so that the sap ran out and dipped this into the water which he splashed up into the air. As the water was thrown up, he invoked Spirit-of-the-Above and the Rain: 'You, The Above, and You, so and so [naming Dari ancestors who had important rain powers, including his own father and grandfather] and You the Rain. We need you now. You the Rain must fall. Here now is your ox [a chicken].' Korondo sprayed the water in the air with a circular movement at the same time making a whirring sound. If the rain is near at this point, he told me, it may fall; 'if it is far away it delays for a day or two', he said. The chickens were then beheaded. (A ram is divided lengthways and the stomach contents washed.) As the 'ram' (chicken) was killed, the Dari rain-drum, brought out for the occasion and placed behind the shrine, was beaten with a 'dirr, dirr' beat, which calls to ceremonial dancing. The drumming is described as 'the dance of the Above' (*löri lo Ki*), and 'calls the

---

[1] For the history of this clan, see *Chiefs and Strangers*, pp. 27 and 30.
[2] Since Dari lineages are now widely separated, Rokwe and Surukulya lineages may tend their own rain. Officiants are Möjut Awol and Deŋ lo Bugga.

rain'. A rain-drum is considered a sensitive instrument which affects the weather when beaten, so it cannot be used indiscriminately. (When I asked if I could borrow the Dari drum for a dance before leaving Mandari, Korondo apologetically pointed out that it could not be lent since the rainy season was beginning and nothing should be done to interfere with the rainfall.) Violent or excessive rainfall can be moderated by rubbing the drum with ashes. The use of ashes (the hot residue of a fire) to mitigate the violence of rain is based on the idea that fire and water—the extremes of hot and cold—are mutually antagonistic and, if brought together, their effects are neutralized or, as in this case, the stronger controls the effects of the weaker. Similarly at burial rites in the rainy season the ashes from mourners' fires are moistened before being thrown away.

When a rain-ram is sacrificed, its meat is divided up and the sacred parts are boiled and eaten by the attending elders. All then wash their hands and hold them out with the fingers hanging down so that the water from them drips on to the ground 'like falling rain'. In the evening (unless the country is mourning) the rain-drum is beaten for ceremonial dancing in which the elders and rain officiant take part. The skin of the rain-sheep is later made into a loin covering for the officiant's senior wife. At the site, a strip of hide is cut off and stretched, 'like a rope', from the officiant's shrine, across the homestead, to the roof of his wife's hut, or if there is no shrine pole strips are simply placed on the hut roof. This 'rope' represents the tying of the rain to the earth, perhaps (although the Mandari do not say this themselves) the rope joining earth and sky severed at the beginning of time.

At a rain rite of the Nile-dwelling Köbora I saw a more complicated arrangement of creeper ropes employed, one for 'bringing the rain down to earth' and one pegged from the foot of the shrine out along the ground to 'catch the wind and the thunder and disperse them, making the rain safe', in effect a form of storm or lightning conductor.

During my six years' absence from Mandari, Chief Korondo died, and the rain ceremony was taken on first by Jurlay, his youngest brother, who had charge of the rain-drum.[1] The year

---

[1] The eldest son and the youngest son have a special position in ritual, as I have described in connection with shrines. Jurlay himself later fell sick (with a Power originating from the Moru) and ceased to carry out the

before my return Korondo's eldest son, Gelaba, performed it and also provided the sacrificial sheep. In that year, I was told the Dari had plentiful rainfall.

In 1958 the rite was carried out by Deŋdit, one of Korondo's younger brothers, the seer and doctor. The evening before, the rain-drum, now kept in Deŋdit's homestead, was beaten at his shrine for Spirit-of-the-Above to summon the Dari to the rain-dance. This had to be called off, everyone having gone to the much larger public dance held at Tali Post five miles away, to celebrate the combined Aliab Dinka/Mandari/Atwot quarterly court which was in session. The court sitting also accounted for the poor attendance of elders at the rite itself, senior men who were required in connection with disputes being absent.

The rite took place early in the morning at Deŋdit's home in Lomindot, a few miles from Dari village. Those present in addition to Deŋdit's family were the adult sons of Korondo's dead brothers including Mörut lo Nyöyi and senior men of the two client families attached to the chiefly lineage, together with one or two old men and women neighbours. As well as providing the sacrificial animal, Mörut had provided the beer. Mörut's father had been a wealthy man, whereas Deŋdit presides over a modest household. The rite therefore represented a combined effort by the chiefly family to ensure rain when there were signs that it might be seriously delayed.

When I arrived the beer-drinking was finishing. The rain-drum had been placed behind the shrine for Spirit-of-the-Above and Deŋdit was in the process of parading the black sacrificial ram up and down the yard. Mandari symbolism rules that a rain-ram should be dark, for were it 'red' or one of the light browns, the sun would become intense and blazing. A white or a light-coloured animal would also be inadmissible, making the sky light and driving away dark rain clouds. A piebald animal, though, whether white and black or red and white, would be acceptable. A light-coloured ewe should also be dedicated ('tethered for the Above') and its ear clipped to mark this. The white ewe is a neutralizer, used to avert violent or damaging rain and lightning. It is not always available and is not as important as the dark ram without which 'there is no rain'. I have not seen it used.

rite. (One man told me that even when he had performed it, it had not been successful.)

After circling the homestead leading the ram, Deŋdit tethered it near his shrine and stood to sing the rain hymn:

Verse I—Mandari text

Gulumbek yiyiŋa kulya ko kutuk
Monaja na nyiyo
Perere ko yapa
Gwoloŋ a lawa,
Kudu na Mareŋ, Yi kwakwa madaŋ.

Verse II

Yi wöwöju, a juru kadi
Wurusi ko Akwac, wurusi ko duöt lyiyo
Lolowa.
Kudu na Mareŋ, Yi kwakwa madaŋ.

English translation

Gulumbek harkens to our prayers.
That of our daughter is tied up,
Luminous moon-rays waiting
Spread out in the sun
Oh, Rain of Mareŋ, we are beseeching you gently.

We are 'praising': we of different countries.
Patterned Akwac the markings of my ox
Are spread out to dry in the sun.
Rain of Mareŋ, we are beseeching you gently.

Gulumbek is a free-Spirit-of-the-Above associated with Dari clan. The three following lines refer to the sacrificial animal which was acquired through the marriage of a Dari daughter. As it quivers in the sun it calls to mind the vibrations of the luminous ring round the moon (in turn 'cool'). *Lowowa* means in general usage 'to lay something out in the sun to dry'. The last line describes how the people pray softly, so that the rain may fall softly. The second verse describes the Dari singing 'praise' songs (as for a display-ox): they are people 'of different countries' because other small clans, who also require rain, are now joined administratively to Dari. The markings of the ox (which is 'spotted', *akwac*) are 'spread out' in the sun; the refrain of 'praying softly' to the rain of Mareŋ, a Dari ancestor, is then repeated. After singing, Deŋdit became possessed. It is unusual for the rain officiant to be possessed, so this is an example of a personal technique used by a rain officiant who is also a doctor.

Deŋdit was then handed a calabash of water, 'the calabash of the Above'; the sheep was untied and held by its cord while Deŋdit poured water slowly over its back. After washing, it stands a perfect rain offering, soaked and dripping. Deŋdit then lifted it up and holding it upside down by the four legs and facing east ('towards Logobong') he raised it three times above his head praying as he did so:

> Do Ki, teŋ löluk alo.
> Yi ga'yu sipi.

> You, the Above, behold your ox [sheep].
> We want water [rain].

He then scooped up the remaining water in his hands and splashed it into the air. (He told me that, unlike many officiants, he does not use a rain creeper for this splashing.) The sheep was then thrown and divided lengthways down the belly with a spear. Deŋdit used more water for mixing with the chyme (*möyok*), splashing the water into the open stomach from a small spoon-like gourd. The washing and splashing of the stomach contents ensures consistent rain and prevents light, spasmodic falls which are damaging.

The ram was finally skinned and the skin laid behind the shrine. Parts of the carcass with religious significance—particularly *polysho* (small back ribs) and *lamasho* (front ribs)—were placed on one side in the hut, 'for the Above', to be eaten later by the owner of the sacrifice. The remainder was put on to boil for the ritual meal. While the meat was cooking, beer was circulated; before drinking, each elder poured a few drops beside the shrine, 'for Above'. Deŋdit told me that a cucumber may also be divided and thrown up in the air if the officiant so decides. After the ritual meal the elders wash their hands and again splash drops of water up in the air.

The rite just described contains the core of all rain ritual. Every rite begins with beer-drinking and is followed by the sacrifice of an ox or sheep preceded by prayers or hymns. The lengthways division of the animal and the washing-out of its stomach, and the symbolic gestures with water, feature in descriptions given from all over Mandari. The rite is always completed by the ritual meal.

The sensitive link between the owned rain and the person of the rain-officiant is seen to endure beyond the situation of the rain sacrifice itself. Thus, during the rain which follows his sacrifice, he can provoke excessive or violent falls of rain by his use of water. During the rainy season, therefore, particularly if flooding threatens, an officiant is frugal in his bathing and avoids pouring water over his head so that it cascades on to the ground splashing it about carelessly which may precipitate heavy downpours. I was told that in former times during feuding, rain-experts might bathe and throw water in the air to cause violent thunderstorms and hamper attackers and snap their bow-strings.

II

An important source of variation in rain ritual is the diversity of the Mandari population. In the following summary of ethnographic material from the different areas of Mandari country, I shall show the distinction between the 'rain-expert'—a person of non-chiefly status—and the rain-chief. I shall also consider the special features of the rituals of the important Bora clans, which invariably distinguish these rites from rites performed by non-Bora groups, including the use of 'rain-stones' and 'rain-horns'.

(a) Non-Bora rain[1]

Autochthons, now merged with Bora neighbours or non-Mandari incomers, may or may not perform rain rites. The Mayar, for instance, the lineage living at Mount Tindalu who claim to have been in Bora 'before Marnykwac the Bora founder came from the sky', attend the Mandari Bora rites. Wejur clan, on the other hand, the landowners around Tali, although administratively combined with the Jabour, perform rain rites. They told me that they formerly owned a rain-stone (now lost) given to their ancestor by Mar Desa, the son of the Mandari Bora culture hero, during a visit. The Lorogak, landowners under the Mokido Administration, consult the Mokido female rain-expert. The Nyarkiteŋ say they may take a ram to the rain-expert of Jabour clan if, by the middle of April, no rain has fallen.

Four large immigrant clans 'brought' rain from their homelands: the Dari come under this head. The Gworoŋa brought their rain from Fajelu, and an ox is speared at their rites which are

[1] Reference may be made to Map 2.

performed by a descendant of founder Mar Wurubek. In spearing sacrificial animals the Gworoŋa follow their own custom.[1]

The Mokido use a female rain-expert, who succeeded her husband, also a rain-expert, in the following circumstances. A severe drought had followed shortly after the rain-expert's death, and divination revealed this as due to his anger at his burial 'in the bush'. (He died on a visit to Jungwa and was interred there.) An ox was then taken to Jungwa and killed at his grave. Rain then fell. It was finally decided that his wife should continue his work since his rain power had been shown to be still 'active'.

Rain was introduced into the dominant, non-landowning, Jabour clan through a female link and after a miracle. A son of Dimu (the non-Mandari founder) had married a girl of Mandari Bora clan, named Wörda. After visiting her natal rain kin at Mount Tindalu, she returned home with a black pot of ground sesame and flour for beer-making. When she brewed rain fell, although it was January, the height of the dry season. Her son became a rain-expert, 'because his mother had brought the rain back with her from Bora'. The office is now hereditary in Kawöri line, the chief's brother officiating. The Wejur, the indigenous landowners living with the Jabour, also have rain.

The notion of 'miracle' has much the same connotation for the Mandari as it has for us. It is always a sign outside the natural order of things, an event which is contrary to accepted knowledge and experience. Most Mandari miracles I recorded related to rain falling out of season or in extraordinary circumstances. Miracles are never deliberately sought or expected; 'they are from Creator.'

The rain-experts referred to above, like doctors, are chosen by signs. They are not religious leaders, but work under the direction of a chief who supplies the sacrificial animal. They therefore lack the immunity which chiefly office gives, and may be subjected to ordeals if rain fails.

(b) Bora rain

Bora populations enjoy a reputation as 'great people of rain', particularly the Mandari Bora clan itself in the ancient Bora homeland, being a well-known source of rain and justice from whom neighbouring groups 'collected rain' and sought judgements. A

---

[1] Spearing sacrificial animals is a Bari custom, common to most Bari-speaking tribes including the Nile Köbora and Tsera.

number of instances of soliciting Bora help in drought, of Bora rain being carried out into non-Bora lines by marriage, and of the giving of rain-stones by Bora to non-Bora were recounted to me.

All sizeable Bora clans, even those who claim to have long separated from their homeland, follow the same rain procedures on the assumption that, 'As the people divided, their rain divided and went with them.' The Bora clans who live around Tindalu can attend the annual rain rite performed in the homeland, although a process of gradual dropping-off from this assembly is in operation. Until shortly before 1950, Bari Kujutat used to travel the fifteen miles back to Tindalu for the joint Mandari Bora–Somöring rite, but no longer do so, their links now being remote. They do not hold a ceremony of their own.

Where Bora leaders moved far out and established new chief-doms, on the other hand, they tended their own rain.[1] For example, the Jungwa in the west have not returned in known memory, the present officiant, Muŋgu, being a descendant of the Jungwa founder's son. The Borenye perform rites independently; the Mijiki who separated within living memory, severed kinship and ritual ties after hostilities.[2] Having 'lost' their traditional rain, the Mijiki perform a minor rite 'to help the rain' at which Phulö lo Diyö of Kamana lineage kills a chicken. Rume rites are performed by Chief Fulai Nyegwere; the Jokari also perform their own.

The three characteristics which distinguish all Bora rain ritual are first, that the rite takes place at the grave of a clan founder. Thus there is a direct link-up with founder ancestors lacking in non-Bora rituals where, although a father or grandfather may be mentioned by name in prayers, clan founders do not figure centrally and rites are not held at the site of a carefully preserved ancestral grave but in the officiant's homestead. The ancestors addressed in Bora rites are not ghosts, but the embodiment of the hereditary rain power referred to as 'Power-of-the-Above', or, 'Our power-of-Above of old'.

In the original Bora homeland the site of the grave of Mar Desa (son of the celestial founder 'who brought rain to earth') is cleared annually of undergrowth and swept for the rain rites. The grave stands in open bush at the foot of Mount Tindalu—the point of

---

[1] For a chart of the Bora clans see *Chiefs and Strangers*, p. 57, and for their distribution see the map at the end of that book.

[2] The account of the Mijiki–Mandari Bora feud is given ibid., p. 53 n.

Mar Desa's reputed fall. At my visit it had not yet been cleared for the ritual and the site was difficult to distinguish. It is claimed to contain the bones of Mar Desa and his renowned client, Lupöyot.[1] The grave is a meeting-place to which anyone can 'bring a ram, beer, grain, and shea-butter oil to exchange for rain'; now only Mandari Bora and Somöring meet there. The latter are the descendants of Mar Desa's first wife, a girl of Mayar, the ancient owners of the mountain; the descendants of Mar Desa's second wife, the Mandari Bora, have moved out from Tindalu. The Somöring thus combine Bora landownership and ownership of the mountain through maternal links.

In Rume the graves of the founder, Gumbiri, and of Nyegwere, father of Chief Fulai, are cleared and swept and both are addressed. In Jarra, the ceremony takes place at the grave of Mar Leot, the founder's son; Bömu, the present head, kills an ox and supplicates Mar Leot 'for rain, flying ants, grain, shea-butter, and plentiful game animals'. Other dispersed Bora segments hold rites at the grave of their own founders, or simply in the rain officiant's homestead.

A second Bora characteristic is (or rather was, as they have long since been 'lost') the ownership of rain-stones known as *raga*, rain-spears, and the 'dog-horn' (*oŋgwora na d'uŋ*). The dog-horn is said to have been used in rain rites and is still a mystery to me. Perhaps the horned dog represents a mythical animal akin to the unicorn. As Jung points out, the idea of the single horn embodying a force and virtue was not confined to unicorns as such; horned fish, dragons, and scarabs are also reported in mythology. The theme of the single horn is widespread.[2] A 'dog-horn charm' is mentioned by the Acholi poet, Okot p'Bitek.[3] This reference has some comparative interest because of similarities between the Mandari Bora of Mandari and some Acholi groups. Girling also mentions 'trophies' including 'about a dozen horns and trumpets . . . used in the installation of the Rwot', and gives a drawing of one, clearly that of an ungulate.[4]

The Borenye clan told me that they owned the rain-spear named Jaliye and brought by the archetypal ancestor Mar Nykwac 'from

[1] For particulars of this client culture-hero, see *Chiefs and Strangers*, p. 110.
[2] C. J. Jung, 'The Paradigm of the Unicorn', *Collected Works*, vol. 12, p. 415.
[3] Okot p'Bitek, *Song of Lawino* (Nairobi, 1966), p. 156.
[4] F. K. Girling, *The Acholi of Uganda* (London, 1960), pp. 120–1.

the sky', a dog-horn, and a rain-stone. The spear controlled the rain, the woodland, and the game; all these originally featured in rain rites. The spear was lost by Nyarkiteŋ lineage (landowner prior to the Borenye); then the dog-horn and rain-stone 'disappeared'.

The object known as *raga* was described to me by a Wejur elder as being 'like a piece of iron or stone'. He told me that their ancestor had received a stone from Mar Desa of Bora who instructed him to anoint it with sesame oil and to sacrifice a ram over it. When Wejur lost political independence to the incoming Jabour, the rain-stone was handed over to them and eventually 'lost' during the slaving incursions. The Wejur description tallies with that given to me by elders of Bunja, a Bora segment, who had seen their rain-stone before its loss.

The Bunja rain-stone was brought by their founder, Mar Dirushuk, from Borenye together with his 'horned dog' when he left behind his elder brother, Kulaŋ, as chief, and founded his own chiefdom at Uguluma in western Mandari.[1] (These are perhaps the rain-stone and horn said to have 'disappeared' from Borenye?) The rain-stone and the dog-horn eventually passed via Dirushuk's son Dokulu to Mar Möndi, at whose death 'it went away.' Mar Dirushuk's display-ox was also tied up and washed during the rite. Dirushuk's descendants now perform the ceremony. The present officiant described the rain-stone:

The *raga*, together with other rain objects like the dog-horn, fell from the sky. They were kept in a hut and when rain was needed were brought out. Beer was brewed and all the people came together. The body of the *raga* was washed with sesame oil, and then laid at the pole for the Above in the rain officiant's homestead. When rain was about to fall, it was taken inside the hut and the rain fell.

The rain-stone was said to be a piece of iron (*witi*), tortoiselike in shape, with a hole through the middle. A literate Mandari present at this discussion sketched it under the elder's instructions (Fig. 13). The Bunja elder recounted the following incident relating to the lost rain-stone which took place during his lifetime:

Some time ago, a man of Bunja named Jurun went into the bush near the old disused Bunja village site and saw a piece of iron with legs

---

[1] The myth theme of younger sons leaving because an elder brother whose dog is hornless is jealous, emphasizes the idea that life-giving powers lie with the younger and political power with the elder.

walking in the grass. He returned home and said nothing about it. The same day he fell ill, and as he lay on his death-bed, he explained to his relatives that he had gone back to the old Bunja village site and seen a piece of iron walking which then disappeared. The elders realized he had seen the lost rain-*raga*, and that seeing it had caused his death.

Chief Aznaba Lakuli of the linked Mandari Bora–Somöring clan confirmed that they had owned a rain-stone which was anointed with sesame oil at rain rites, but was later mislaid.

From the evidence given by Bora clans now widely dispersed, it is clear that some kind of rain-stone, together with rain-spears,

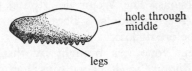

F IG. 13. *Sketch of* Raga—*rain-stone*

and something represented as a 'horn' and said to belong to the primal dog which was unicorned, featured in Bora rites. Rain-stones filtered out from the central homeland with the dispersal of Bora segments and were eventually lost. Their disappearance or their 'walking away' often coincided with the death of a famous ancestor. Loss may be claimed to have been concurrent with the disturbances of the last century and that would certainly have been a time when small objects could be mislaid in hurried dispersals. The notion that rain-stones and rain-spears 'fell from the sky' suggests that they were brought with the Bora (whose ancestor also 'fell') when they entered Mandari.

Some interesting comparative material is provided by accounts of rain-making among the Bari, particularly those living on the east bank of the Nile.[1] Rain implements and rain-spears were of great importance there. To quote Seligman: 'There can be no doubt that certain stones, generally of quartz, are the most important, but certain sacred spears also seem to play a part in the ceremonies.' Seligman saw a number of rain-stones and rain-spears.[2]

---

[1] C. G. Seligman, *Pagan Tribes of the Nilotic Sudan*, pp. 281–9.

[2] Seligman suggests that some of these stones were worked artefacts, perhaps lip-plugs used by neighbouring tribes, or natural or worked stones. (Compare the Bunja *raga* with its 'legs': can this have been an Eolith or a prehistoric tool?)

An informant described to him how the rain-stones were smeared with sesame oil, and a black goat then sacrificed near them. He also states that rain sacrifice 'undoubtedly takes place at the grave of the rain-maker's father', and notes invocations made at rites, addressing ancestors, and associating them with rain; for example 'truly this cloud *from long ago . . . of my father* and soon it shall fall . . .' Using Whitehead's account he notes that ancestral rain-makers are called upon—'the great Janggara, who lived five generations ago', and a collectivity of ancestral rain-makers.

In addition to minor rain-experts in the style of those found in Mandari, there is an important Bari rain-clan, the Bekat, which from Seligman's description may be compared with the Bora, in that it was influential, over a wide area. The Nile-dwelling Köbora told me that they remembered the former visits of the Bekat rain-chiefs to their territory, when substantial tribute was paid for rain.

The third characteristic of Bora rain rites is that the landowning chief or a landowning elder performs the ritual; Bora clans never employ rain-experts. Where a Bora clan—for instance Mijiki—has been amalgamated administratively with a politically more powerful non-Bora group, the Bora clan sacrifices for the rain in its part of the territory, while the other clans in the amalgamation may sacrifice for their own parts.

Apart from these three special characteristics of Bora rain the ritual itself is on the pattern described for the Dari rite.

The combined Mandari Bora–Somöring rite is the largest assembly for sacrifice, partly because the Bora are renowned providers of entertainment (a fact confirmed for me during my stay in Bora) and partly because of the association with the authentic Bora homeland. Unfortunately the rite took place when I was staying with the Nile Köbora.

Chief Aznaba told me that beer is brewed in his own homesteads, in those of Barisho, the Bora head, and in those of Mayar lineage the mountain owners. The beer drinking is 'for the whole country', and representative elders assemble for it, beginning in Barisho's homestead. Then they walk the five miles to Mar Desa's grave at Tindalu, leading the sacrificial ox, supplied alternately by Aznaba and Barisho. More beer is carried from Aznaba's homesteads to the grave-side and drunk there while libations are poured on the grave and prayers offered. Barisho rises first to address liturgically Spirit-of-the-Above and the rain-founding ancestor Mar Desa, the prototype client Lupöyot, other ancestors remembered for their rain powers and finally his own father and grandfather: 'You, the Above, and You, the Rain, and You our Ancestors [by name] here is your beer and your ox, send us rain now and flying ants and shea-butter fruit. Let the rain fall now so that we can have grain, and our people and the cattle may prosper.'

As he invokes he dips a frond of rain-creeper into a pot of water and splashes the water in the air. The sacrificial animal is divided over the grave and the stomach washed. The ritual meat portions are boiled on a fire built at the grave-side, and then eaten there. In the evening ceremonial dancing takes place in the cleared space around it.

Barisho told me that the rain, which at this point is imminent, holds off until he returns to his homestead, when it begins to fall. This statement exemplifies the assumption that rain is embodied in the person, that he is, in fact, 'bringing the rain back with him' to his people as the Bora ancestor in the myth initially 'brought rain from the sky'. This gathering-up of rain for later release occurs in the account of the Bora woman who brought Bora rain back with her to fall over Mokido, her country by marriage.

The Bora rite is claimed to provide rain for all the land round Bora, but Barisho told me that when drought is persistent groups living around the periphery bring a sheep or ox for him to kill on their behalf at Mar Desa's grave. In 1952, when drought followed the first rain rite, Barisho killed a second ox, and then rain fell consistently.

I conclude with the rain rites of Bunja, a small Bari lineage living in Western Mandari, whose head sacrifices in his own homestead, the ancestral grave having been left behind in Bunja migrations. After providing a beer drink at which libations are poured at his shrine to Spirit-of-the-Above, he washes the rain sheep and splashes the rest of the water in the air with rain creepers. He stands 'looking around for clouds' as he prays: 'You the Above and you Creator (Dun). I am praying to you. You must let the rain fall, and help us now. I follow after my father, so and so [stating the ancestral succession] who prayed for rain. I have brought you an ox [sheep], etc.' The sheep is divided and the meat cooked and allocated. The elders who eat the kidneys and liver drop small fragments on the ground, at the same time addressing their ancestors under their breath. The rest of the meat is eaten by attending relatives. 'At this point rain clouds begin to gather and rain falls.' Ceremonial dancing follows in the evening.

At the present time a landowning chief is assisted at rain rites by a brother or adult sons. Rain-experts may be assisted by a senior wife. In the past, however, when hereditary client assistants were installed with chiefs, these are said to have 'held rain power in their hands'. When a chief visited kin at a distance, his rain possessions (rain-stone, dog-horns, or spear) were left with his personal client who also assisted him at the rites. The role of those few remaining clients has radically altered but client retainers attend present-day rain rites. (I noted the presence of a small group of Dari clients at the rite performed by Deŋdit.) Clients help in the background at the rite, assisting in throwing the sheep, cutting it up and dividing out the meat. The officiant seldom kills the sacrificial animal himself. He is often an old man and the animal must be quickly thrown and expertly dispatched.[1] Even where an officiant is young and vigorous, younger men present manœuvre the sacrificial animal for him.

III

An understanding of Mandari ideas about rain cannot be reached by concentrating on the rite alone, in isolation from beliefs and assumptions which give this central act its meaning, nor without taking cognizance of other kinds of action directed to rain but outside the situation of the rite. The theory of rain (including the theory of rain failure) and the kind of action which emerges in response to a drought which follows the performance of a rain rite, are crucial to an understanding of what the Mandari seek to achieve by performing the rite. I begin therefore by considering statements made by the Mandari and then examine actual behaviour in the face of persistent rain failure.

Informed elders were emphatic that, 'No one makes rain. It is Creator who sends it, and it will fall when he decides', and further, that, 'If Creator chooses to hold up the rain, nothing can be done to make it fall.' When describing the action of a chief carrying out a rain rite, the Mandari use the word *tetena*, most accurately

---

[1] The Mandari approve of quick, clean killings and dislike inept and inefficient slaughter.

translated as 'tending', 'caring for', or 'nurturing'. (Thus, 'the chief is tending the rain', '*mar tetena kudu.*') The word *tetena* is also used when speaking of caring for other things like fields, homesteads, or cattle. The Mandari may also use the verb *kona* which in one of its senses means 'to make'. But *kona* used in ritual contexts has little to do with this more general sense of 'make'. Thus, the expressions: 'People are "making" each other' ('*yutu kokon bok*'), when they mark each other with ritual substances or bless; or *mar kokon kudu*, employ 'make' in its sense of 'perfecting', 'making whole'.

Attempts are never made to tend rain out of season. Rain out of season is a miracle, and miracles by their nature are unsought. It is also quite clear that the Mandari do not assume that if rain sacrifices were never made rainfall would cease. As one elder expressed it, 'Suppose something was not "cut" (sacrificed) for the rain, no doubt it would come in the same way.' They are perfectly aware of the universal nature of rain and assume it rains elsewhere, and in the countries of whites, who, they know, do not perform rites. They do not think that concern with the weather is only confined to themselves and, indeed, they will inquire of the visitor how he meets weather problems in his own country.

It may be asked then why the Mandari consider the rites to be so important. In the first place, as with much of their ritual, they consider that they are of value 'because they are things of old and we have always performed them'. Here the Mandari are expressing their feelings about beliefs and practices which are a part of their cultural heritage and which have a deep emotional value because they express important truths about the social, moral, and natural order. Rites as the expression of these truths are valuable in themselves. The Mandari are here expressing what has often been described as the affective (emotional) value of ritual.

But rites can also be approached from another standpoint, and one which becomes clearer if we leave the rite itself on one side and consider the assumptions which form the background to it, together with the ideas regarding rain failure and actions seen to destroy rain.

The Mandari theory of rain rests ultimately on the theory that rain has a universal and a specific side. The Mandari accept this fact as proven on the basis of their traditional knowledge and the evidence of their own actions with their apparent results, but they do not assume that this fact is necessarily universally the case.

Those acts which they see to be harmful and destructive to their *specific* rain relate to their own unique predicament. One objective of rain rites is, therefore, to guard their 'owned' rain from actions which threaten it, from sin in the community, from sorcery, and from breaches of rules regarding rain-water or failures to observe symbolic oppositions in ritual in general. As most rain failure thus stems from human failure, it could be said in a very real sense that for the Mandari the rain is within the person. The regularity and predictability of 'owned rain' (*kudu nikay*) is not infallible, but can be subject to breakdown.

The 'rain of Creator' on the contrary—the unregulated, elemental rain—falls everywhere and is outside the control of man. Tended rain falls over Mandari and over other places where rites are performed, and for it human response is essential, thus placing owned rain in a separate category from universal rain and making it a specific of a more intimate cosmos. The linking of rain to territories and its integration with human action means that its failure may be a sign of discord in the community which requires action when, after a reasonable period of time, it becomes apparent that a radical breakdown in the weather has occurred. But not only do the Mandari never attempt to anticipate rain by performing rites before the time of the wet season, they also allow for the fact that rainy seasons may be late, and rites usually follow a period of light showers which indicate the initial phase of the rains for that year. If the rite which is performed then fails, it becomes clear that something is wrong and then much heart-searching and discussion follows. More than one rain rite may be performed together with other ameliorative ritual. The Mandari know what to do when breakdown occurs, although as in illness they are faced with an almost impossible diagnostic situation because of the numerous individual and communal actions which may have a bearing on any particular drought. They are therefore not particularly surprised if their diagnoses and actions fail, although they also believe that their remedies are often partially successful. If the rain holds off after every correct response has been made and all evidence sifted, the Mandari will accept that nothing more can be done; 'they (the elders) have done their best, the rest is up to Creator.' There is no point in continuing to kill valuable stock, people must hope for the unintended 'rain of Creator'.

In some chiefdoms I found apathy about rain rites, particularly where, for one or other of the reasons given, owned rain had been lost or reduced. In established landowning lines, on the other hand, I found an attitude of confidence together with regular performance, although there was little evidence which might have suggested to the Mandari that any local variation in rainfall resulted from the difference in attitude and action.

Because the Mandari break up rain into parts linked to the territorial divisions of their country there is no rain or rite for the whole of Mandari-land.[1] 'Owned' rain is ultimately tied up with people, because territories only exist meaningfully in relation to a given population. Its identification with a human population gives rain its extreme sensitivity and its supposed openness to spoiling— even to total destruction—through the actions of individuals.

The narrow range of responsibility for rain leads to a correspondingly limited placing of responsibility for its failure. This also accords with the fact that rain failure can actually be local in character, although this is only true of the early rains and does not apply once the rains have set in. It is during the uneven first falls that chiefs may call diviners to find out what is happening and to indicate necessary action. Mandari country is so small that after an initial period of variation there is either rain over the whole country or widespread failure. By then the nature of the disaster is clear and all chiefs will have completed ameliorating sacrifices and resigned themselves to a bad season.

Mandari recognize many kinds of rain loss and rain breaking, some final. This is exemplified by the historic loss of rain through territorial separation, through quarrels, or by the permanent and deliberate damaging of 'owned' rain. Ordinary elemental rain which is un-nurtured and wild, and without which there could be no life, is not lost in this way, and this rain is depended on when 'owned' rain has been lost.

Permanent rain loss is a feature of Bora history and movement— a younger brother goes off and leaves his country and its 'rain', or he takes away the rain implements of the chiefdom. Deliberate sorcery also 'destroys' rain.[2] When rain is permanently lost, a chief

---

[1] The central Bora rain rite belonged to a past historical period, and never, even at the height of Bora influence, is it claimed to have covered *all* Mandari.

[2] For example, the new falling rain caught in a pot and placed at the boundary of Mijiki territory with instructions that the rain should not fall beyond that point, is claimed by the Mijiki to have damaged their rain permanently.

either performs a small rite to 'help the rain' or people hope for the untended rain of Creator.

The typical chiefly rain quarrel is exemplified in the Majore case recounted to me by a member of that clan.

In the past, Jarra clan (of Bora) included the ancestors of Majore clan. One day a stranger came from the bush bringing with him a wild fruit. He divided the fruit, removed the seeds, and caught in one half the new rain from the sky. He fed this half to the Jarra breeding bull. The bull swallowed the little container and the rain. A drought immediately followed. The elders called a doctor to disclose the reason for rain failure. He divined, and showed that the rain had been swallowed by the bull of the herd and to release it the animal must be slaughtered. The elders were filled with consternation and called another doctor; however, he and others called gave similar pronouncements. The bull was reluctantly slaughtered and rain fell.

The Mar of Jarra then quarrelled with his brother (the ancestor of Majore) whom he accused of administering the rain to the bull (not knowing of the action of the stranger). At this time the 'Turks' [slave-traders] came to Mandari and harried the people so that they separated out, and Jarra and the Majore founder went separate ways because of their quarrel over the rain. They parted at Reilli Pool. Jarra stayed at Kösipi, and Majore went to the north-west of Tali to Ginyiki. After a while they moved to Ajop, the place of 'black earth'. At present the Majore have no rain.

The dangerous nature of the stranger's act in the Majore story illustrates the Mandari belief that falling rain or rain which has recently fallen 'from the sky', must be left in the open and never caught, enclosed, or taken inside. (Openness and freedom are the quintessence of the celestial, and hiddenness and fettering a dangerous opposition to these qualities.) Customary prohibitions ensure that new rain is not taken into a hut or confined; the rain in long-standing pools or permanent rivers, however, has become simply water and lacks the sensitivity of pristine rain, its use being therefore largely unrestricted.

Because rain is so vital and sensitive—according to Mandari theory, and actually so, for by nature it is erratic and often either inadequate or excessive—everything possible must be done to avoid harming it. The best rain cannot be enjoyed if there is 'trouble or sin in the homeland' (*kulya kata i bay*). Quarrelling, ritual offence, breaches of prescribed behaviour, disrespect to elders, the angering of the landowning chief, or the ousting of true landowners are all believed to precipitate drought. Conflict and sin must be resolved before rain rites are performed or these may be invalidated. The chief summons a doctor to disclose the sin so that culprits can confess and be purified. Then another rite is performed.

During 1952 the rains were late, then they fell lightly and erratically and by May still held off—a serious disaster as the previous season's rains had been poor. There was discussion among chiefs whose countries were situated round the Tali area as to what was wrong, and many possible causes of failure were followed up. They agreed on a combined effort, deciding to keep each other informed about faults which were discovered, and even eventually to take some concerted action. While each chiefdom is responsible for its own rain, it is recognized that there may be causes behind radical failure which need inter-chiefdom action in the same way as, on the political level, judicial action may extend beyond a single territory. This is particularly so when failure is suspected of being due to rain-experts who are holding up the rain either deliberately, because of a grievance, or unintentionally. Such experts may be living in neighbouring chiefdoms, and their acts may affect the rain of several chiefdoms. Further, a sorcerer may be engaged in harming an enemy in a neighbouring country. Unintentional ill-disposition may also be responsible, and that year it was suspected that the displeasure of a rain-expert living near Tali whose new hut had not been thatched, might be relevant, so helpers were mustered to thatch it immediately.

Rains may also be blocked, or falling rain stopped through accidental misuse of rain-water by some one person who has been stupid, or who wishes to draw attention to a legitimate grievance. Some of the careless mistakes which automatically cause rain stoppage are as follows. Recently fallen rain-water from small rain pools in the scrub around villages can only be used circumspectly, and when fetched for drinking and cooking it must never be brought *into* a hut, hidden away or used in indoor work, or rainfall stops. The water of large rivers and permanent or regular seasonal pools is unrestricted, for these are strictly speaking not rain.

Further rain-water, or water from rain-pools, must never be used for plastering or repairing the clay on walls of huts and grain stores, or in any work which comes under the category of *joda* (the act of slapping on wet clay) or *borowa* (smoothing-over a surface with wet clay). A sequence of incompatibilities is involved here: rain is mixed with soil; liquid becomes solid; dark earth diminishes light rain. The pristine, fluid quality of free rain is thereby destroyed. Being aware of this, I was surprised on one occasion to see a friend smoothing the clay surface of her yard during the early rains. When I asked her about it, she said that she had walked to the main Dari river (about four miles) for the water, instead of taking it from the rainfall pools lying around the hamlet. The degree to which people may be inconvenienced by such prohibitions will be appreciated when it is remembered that permanent water is often far from villages and must be fetched and carried in heavy clay pots. The amount of water needed in the operation of re-surfacing a yard or hut is considerable, and the obvious way to acquire it would be to use water from nearby, or to leave containers outside to fill during showers. Both are forbidden acts. The ban on the use of water from seasonal rain pools is, however, relaxed during the later rains when the whole country is covered with pools and streams.

While it is akin to sorcery to catch new rain in a pot and take it into a hut, this is a valid technique of some rain-experts who catch the first falling rain and bury it; this rain is used in the next season's rain-rite. The logic of this action is based on keeping the rain stored in a pot (tied-up and controlled) and then bringing it out (releasing and freeing it) when rain is next due. Mandari rain officiants to whom I spoke said that they themselves never kept rain but used ordinary water, but they agreed that rain was stored elsewhere in Mandari. The rain-expert of the Nile Köbora uses stored rain, but on the occasion when I witnessed a rain rite ordinary river water was substituted because, he explained, his pot of rain had dried out. Bari rain-makers are also reported to use this technique.

A locality may have certain unique natural features which are believed to be fundamentally linked to the rain of that particular chiefdom. A part of the river which runs through Dari chiefdom, for instance, and which is known as *agoratit*, has this association. Here the river bed and its banks are composed of a white flint: the pebbles are white on the outside but when chipped show an opaque dark blue, giving a very striking contrast. It may be this contrast of dark and light, symbolically important in rain rituals, the suggestion of a light sky with dark clouds in the stone, which brings to mind a rain association and gives this part of the river its particular character. This is the only river with this flint bed, others having clay beds and banks of cotton-soil or dark loam.

Dari people claim that the rain may be checked if nodules of soil, flints, or leaves—in particular the leaves of a spotted orchis which are long and shiny and yellowish-green spotted with whitish grey—are removed from the river banks or bed, especially if they are hidden or taken into a homestead either just before or during the early rains. If such things (all referred to as *agoratit*) are removed, a whirlwind is said to sweep down and 'carry the rain away'. Something from this river reach may occasionally be purposely hidden to draw public attention to a desperate grievance, after which the aggrieved individual confesses to the chief and asks for immediate consideration of his case. This is an extreme action seen to have very dangerous consequences and, while legitimate, it is condemned as selfish and anti-social. It may be difficult to induce rain to fall again, since 'rain-breaking' mechanisms are never thought easy to reverse. After a confessed act of this sort an emergency court hears the grievance and compensation is awarded. The complainant then replaces the object (spoken of as 'poison', *sum*). The act of taking it is 'poisoning the land' (*sumba kak*). The offender is accompanied by an elder or the chief, who anoints the offending object with sesame oil (for coolness) and throws it back into the water.

During the search made for the cause of the 1952 rain failure, a man named Kurun, of Jungwa clan (a formerly independent chiefdom now recently merged with Dari) came to the Dari chief and admitted taking and hiding leaves from the *agoratit* river.[1] The man's defence was that a complicated case about his wife's adultery with his brother had not been satisfactorily dealt with by the chief's court. Kurun had a fiery temper; his wife was unyielding and outspoken. Everyone became bored, as the case dragged on inconclusively. The final reckless act on Kurun's part was generally felt to be typical of the whole proceedings which were immoderate and extreme. Feelings in Dari ran very high against him. An elder of Wöŋösek lineage (the owners of the *agoratit*) told me that people should ask the chief's permission or inform him of their intention to *sumba*, and never take irresponsible, independent, action. Following Kurun's confession the elders reassembled,

---

[1] I withhold the offender's true name, and refer to him as Kurun.

Kurun agreed to return the *agoratit* if his case was reopened, and that same day, after he had returned it, some light showers fell, but later petered out. It is a matter for speculation as to whether Kurun did in fact remove something from the river, or whether he simply said that he had done so, to exploit a situation for his own ends. Certainly he took something *back* to it.

(I myself inadvertently became involved with the potentially guilty when I took some moist earth from the Dari river bank for my seedling tomato plants. The Dari chief who visited my homestead and whose attention I drew to my plants, made no comment, but later I was informed that the chief was sure that I meant no harm, but as things were, it would be better if the earth were put back. It was immediately returned, and fortunately that evening there was a shower.)

The situation, however, continued to deteriorate and wider action was planned. It was suggested that a number of rain-experts who lived around the Tali area should be interrogated. A plan was mooted by the more hot-headed, that these people—some of whom might be deliberately withholding the rain—should be grilled by being shut inside a thorn enclosure in the centre of which a large fire would be kept burning. They would be left there during the heat of the day, not with the intention of causing them physical injury, but so that they should endure discomfort in some measure similar to the suffering they were inflicting. This rough justice was vetoed by the chiefs who feared administrative disapproval and were moreover not convinced that proof of intent was present.[1]

When drought becomes serious and people are short of food because of previous bad rains, and are reduced to searching the bush for edible roots and herbs when they are debilitated by the heat, the search for water, and the worry of keeping their families alive, extreme action may be precipitated or threatened. Many possible solutions are turned up because concealed wrongs exist within the community. As each disclosure is dealt with, isolated

---

[1] Seligman writing on the Bari gives an account of the Bari coming to their rain-maker Leju Lugar to complain about the behaviour of his client (*dupiet*), named Lako, in a similar situation: 'They said: "Leju, the sun is shining strongly." They said "Why?" He, Leju, said: "A person is not shining, God is shining." The people of Lika said: "It is nothing to do with God; it is Lako who is shining. Give us Lako to kill." ' Seligman adds in a footnote, 'Lako is taken to a stream, killed, and the rain soon falls.' Seligman, op. cit., p. 289.

showers arouse the hope that the true cause has been found and remedied. Eventually, at some point the rains set in, because the later rains seldom fail totally. Then people cease to speculate about the cause behind the initial failure.

The Mandari will sometimes, however, go further and attempt a more radical explanation of failure which implies a concern with the established rain techniques themselves. A new departure may then be attempted after explorations which suggest *experimental* inquiry and the possibility of a new appraisal of traditional theory. I shall shortly give an example of such an inquiry into the whole theory of rain and human action.

IV

It is in the anti-rain action and the situation of rain failure that we can most clearly see the Mandari concern with explanation and understanding, with effecting ends through ritual and not simply with making symbolic statements. Because the *affective* element stands out so strongly when we concentrate on the rain rite itself in isolation, it draws the attention away from the equally important side of the rite which is concerned with working assumptions about natural processes. The rite cannot, therefore, be analysed meaningfully as a set of symbolic statements in abstraction from its supporting theoretical background.

If the symbolic statement alone entirely justified the performance of the rite, a single rite would be sufficient. It would be emotionally satisfying and final since it would state important truths and represent man's place in relation to essential sources of fertility and regeneration. But it is not the psychological value alone which makes performance important, although the therapeutic value of the constantly evoked symbol which embodies life-sustaining truths is one element (and one that the Mandari themselves recognize) and from this point of view the rite is a traditional form of individuation. This spiritual healing achieved through regeneration is the primary objective of rituals concerned with effecting moral changes like, for instance, the purification rite, but is a secondary objective in the rain rite. The Mandari evidence shows quite conclusively that it is *not* enough to make the single symbolic statement. On the contrary, the rain rite must be seen to effect change at the physical level. Unless it does this, not only is the rite repeated, but other kinds of action follow.[1]

The fact that the rite is the mechanism for bringing about change at the physical level is not to imply that the kind of religious instrumentality involved is seen by Mandari to be of the same order as empirical action. A rite involves a special kind of action held to be valid by a different set of rules. Two levels of symbolic statement are in fact merged through the linking together of religious symbols with symbols representing concrete reality. It is as if it were possible, for example, in our own society, for symbols of the Mass to be meaningfully combined in a single situation with symbols used in the natural sciences—symbols generally seen to belong to two separate orders of reality. Both kinds of symbol would be different from each other and both would be different from the symbols of everyday life. This is also the case in the Mandari combination represented in the law of connection. From our point of view the Mandari combination is incorrect and the symbols are selected for the wrong reasons, but the process of selection has a rational validity.[2]

The difficulties involved in attempting to categorize action based on this kind of connective reasoning derived from a law based on complex analogies, as the Mandari evidence shows, are that often two kinds of operation are taking place at the same time and two objectives are combined in a single instance. There is also no separate language to distinguish the two types of procedure, since all questions of whatever kind relating to theoretical explanation are inevitably posed in the language of religion. It is not easy,

---

[1] Beattie's concern with the importance of the symbolic statement made through ritual and the affective value of the rite, has led him to underestimate the importance of the rite as a part of a statement concerned with inquiry and explanation, and therefore, ultimately, with a theory of matter and forces in the physical world. Since this intellectual element, so important in primitive religion, has been eliminated from contemporary Western religion (becoming the concern of science) a direct comparison between primitive ritual and the ritual of the Catholic Mass, for example, can be misleading, unless the fact of this separation is borne in mind. Primitive ritual is not only instrumental at the level of changing the religious condition but is seen to effect change at the level of the concrete—the material level—something which Christian ritual is no longer claimed to do. Cf. John Beattie, 'Ritual and Social Change', *Man*, vol. 1 (1966), no. 1, *passim*.

[2] As Lévi-Strauss points out, 'men have made mistakes of identification: the meaningful element was not always the one they supposed.' *The Savage Mind*, p. 268.

therefore, to match the single Mandari category with its implicit differentiations, with our numerous explicit categories—'religious', 'scientific', 'common-sense', and so forth. A rain rite, therefore, uses a variety of symbols of different kinds and combines different levels of reality into a meaningful whole.

The anti-rain sequence is relevant for our understanding since it is when rain goes *wrong* that it becomes clear that the rite is not simply an ideal statement of things going right—a wish-fulfilment or wish-expressing statement—but a carefully articulated working procedure which can be nullified by pragmatic actions which have their roots in symbols of the concrete which appear in the rite. Thus the act of plastering a hut assumes symbolic effectuality through the contingency of particular natural events—the falling of rain at a specific phase of the natural cycle—which bring into operation the law of connection in a potentially dangerous way. The longer-lasting or more radical a particular rain failure situation, the more thorough the exploration and the wider the search for the flaw. The methodical investigation of potential causes, the scrutiny of implicated individuals, is intensely practical and directed by reason and inquiry. If human action stands up to the test, the symbolic determinants are correct, and no other fault can be shown, then a final cause—in effect the law of the universe—is invoked. After a certain point a line is drawn—'Creator has refused.'

There is further no doubt that the Mandari subject their beliefs to testing and reassessment and that within the limits of their particular set of assumptions new theories resulting in fairly radical changes can be formulated. It seems that some systems of thought are relatively more closed and self-perpetuating than others.[1] But in the Mandari example intellectual scrutiny and challenge is possible, and may sometimes lead to the modification of theory and action and not simply to low-level failure explanations of the kind that the rite was improperly performed, or some other intervention was responsible. Radical change may, however, be resisted by individuals who consider the new departure bad or dangerous. The following example illustrates the readiness to radically alter ritual practice in response to evidence.

Burial among the west bank Nile-dwelling Köbora was traditionally in the homestead. A decade or so before my visit there was

[1] The Azande theory of witchcraft, perhaps. Evans-Pritchard, *Witchcraft among the Azande.*

serious drought. Diviners were instructed to determine the cause but had no success. It was eventually disclosed that immediately before the drought a man who had been suspected of having hidden the rain had died. The idea was then put forward that the drought had occurred because, at his death, he had finally 'taken the rain into the grave'. As he was by then dead, nothing could be done to prevail upon him to release the rain, and so it was decided that, as a precaution, his body should be exhumed and carried to the swift-flowing Nile and thrown in.

After the immersing of the remains, rain fell. It then became the rule that when rain failed (as it often did) the corpse of anyone who had died just before the rain failure should be dug up and thrown in the river. Eventually, I was told, people became tired of this unpleasant task (described with some relish for gruesome detail by informants) and it was agreed that those dying during or around *kiser* (the rainy season) should automatically be buried in the Nile. Initially the bodies were simply carried in a mat to the river bank and thrown from it into the current, care being taken that they were not thrown in bound up in the mat for fear of 'restricting' the rain. In time, complaints that bodies were washed up on to the banks began to come in from downstream. The authorities investigated and the practice was forbidden. The present compromise is to dig a deep grave in one of the river inlets (*kiget na tör*), and bury the body in this, so that the water, lapping over it, keeps it moist. Informants told me that, in spite of administrative disapproval, those with the evil eye and rain-experts and members of their families would still be actually thrown into the Nile, regardless of the season in which they die. The one category involves people who may tamper with rain, the other those who pray for it. Mortuary rites for those thrown in the river or buried in inlets are held in their homesteads. Köbora chiefs and members of their families alone are always buried in homesteads.

I asked the rain-expert, a member of a small lineage, about water burial and particularly about the claim that he himself and members of his family would be thrown in the Nile. At first he denied any knowledge of the practice; then he agreed that it had become customary, and began to criticize it vehemently, giving an impression of strong personal disapproval. He suggested that far from helping the rain, this kind of action was one of the *causes* of current misfortunes including bad rain. He considered it a 'bad custom' (*konesi narok*), and one 'abhorrent to Creator' (*Ɖun maman*). Water burial is confined to the west bank Köbora, and at least one large group of people on the west bank who originated from Mandari Bora said that they knew nothing of the custom. These latter people live at some distance from the Nile itself and always bury in the homestead.

This controversy over rain and burial provides an example of inquiry and experiment: the search for an alternative theory and new action taken in response to apparent new proof. It is also a comment on attitudes to the laws of nature and of human action. It shows that knowledge of the universe is seen to be incomplete and open to enlargement, that the relation between human action and the processes of the natural order is scrutinized and reassessed. Certain clues to the right workings of the universe are received through cultural traditions, but new ones can be added. Not everyone, however, is convinced by new evidence; in this case, the rain-expert—the traditional holder of knowledge—rejected and decried it in much the same way as Mandari traditionalists reject the evidence regarding Powers.

A particular feature of new modifications is the fact that new theoretical knowledge is always presented in the traditional idiom (one which we should describe as 'religious' or 'mystical'), because no other idiom exists in which to conceive or express it. Knowledge can only be extended in this way, and while we may consider the knowledge and the experimentation erroneous, the aim of the inquiry itself is not markedly different from that of science. The Mandari work from a different premiss and use a different order of exploratory technique but, as in our own case, new theories will accord with the theoretical premisses already acceptable. In our culture progress can only be made through *scientific* explanation; proof presented in other terms—in a mystical or supersensory idiom—is inadmissible. Both systems of inquiry are equally closed in their own ways: both arise from certain assumptions, accepted as proven, about the nature of the laws of the universe and matter.

19

RITES FOR POOLS AND RIVERS

I

THE difference between the principles embodied in woodland rites described later and those for rivers, pools, and swamps is a basic one, implicit in the nature of the phenomena and of the spiritual powers seen to be involved in each case. Although water is positioned on earth, rites for rivers and pools, in contrast to those for woodland plantations of shea-trees, are never addressed to Spirit-of-the-Below; and, in its primary spiritual association, the physical location of the water is largely ignored, the association with Spirit-of-the-Above, deriving from the common nature shared by water, rain, and sky phenomena being the one stressed. Not only are water rites offered to this spirit, but the direct link made between the spirit and the rain is carried through in relation to the rivers; this is never made the case with the shea-trees and Spirit-of-the-Below, woodland rites simply being thanksgivings and intercessions for future harvests.

The direct link made in regard to water is consistent with the belief that rain was first given by Spirit-of-the-Above, and that water was once rain. The Mandari speak of 'the Above of the river', but never of 'the Below of the shea-trees'. Further, the idea of direct pervasion is consonant with the nature of water, but not of woodlands. Trees are passive—they cannot directly affect people —whereas water is strongly active; it can be *physically* felt and entered into; the very nature of water lends it the power to cause injury, sickness, and death.

As I have shown, Spirit-of-the-Above is regarded as more than a transcendent reality in that it can be immanent in people on earth. It 'comes down' in rain and lightning; it is innate as hereditary power in landowning chiefs, present in doctors whom it possesses. Its attributes exist in the very structure of the human body—both moist and dry—and in things like the sappy creeper, of which it is said, 'Its body is filled with water which flows out when it is cut.'

In addition to a primary celestial link, an important pool or river also presents an image of 'earthiness' because of its location and its permanence as a terrestrial feature, an association which is missing in the impermanent rain pool. The feeling that permanent water has both terrestrial and celestial qualities is stressed when the Mandari speak of the *'nulon'* of a watering place. (*Nulon* is the word for 'spiritual sign' or 'miracle', but not specifically a sign of Spirit-of-the-Above.) The double reference to *'ki'* and *nulon* made in the twin birth situation is another example of a celestial/terrestrial combination with the stronger emphasis on the celestial.

While the primary association of a water-point is the celestial, the very nature of its ownership and regular exploitation gives rise to those other images described as *nulon*; this word, particularly, is used to describe sub-images which arise around the ownership of a particular watering-place and are unique to it.[1]

Spiritual associations of whatever kind are only seen to exist in relation to regularly used and owned water. If asked about unexploited water out in the bush, the Mandari reply that 'If there is *nulon* there, we do not know it.' The quality of being known, used, or named, is a prerequisite of these spiritual associations. Unexploited water in the bush lacks these qualities and is conceptually neutral—although in relation to the nearer wasteland, it will be remembered that images appear reflecting the bush as the place where dirt and anti-social things find their place and are eliminated in its over-all neutrality.

Water rites serve a dual purpose, arising from the fact that life-giving water is dangerous. While the main objective is to ensure abundance of water and fish, and for this prayers are addressed to Spirit-of-the-Above, the source of water, the secondary objective is protection, and here prayers may be addressed either to this spirit, or to the water-spirit (*nulon*), or to both, depending on the circumstances. A rite in a specific sickness, addressed to either or both types of agent, comes under family ritual, the responsibility of the doctor and homestead elders. The rites for abundant water and the protection of the community at large are the responsibility of the owner of the water. This

---

[1] Mandari may now refer to the *jok* of a river where illness has a water connection, showing the traditional verbal stereotype being replaced by a newer one.

officiant may be the landowning chief, his delegate, the owner of the woodland, or a member of a humble group given the ownership.[1]

Water is known to cause colds, fevers, and coughs, particularly in the season when it is abundant and people are working in it. While many Mandari assumptions about the part water actually plays in illness are mystical, those regarding the effects of getting wet and chilled and the very real hazards of deep, swift-flowing water have no less common sense than our own, although the common-sense explanation may give way to the religious explanation in serious illness. Protection is also required against injury and drowning. Rivers are also rather vaguely associated with smallpox (*dando*). The basis of this link would appear to be the characteristic of an epidemic to sweep indiscriminately over a community carrying off victims, and the analogous random flow of the river in spate. Rivers also come from distant and even unknown sources, and appropriately therefore, smallpox is said 'to come with the river'.[2] When current coughs and colds or smallpox outbreaks are diagnosed as 'spirit (*nulon*) of the river', the owner drowns a bound sheep under the water or throws in a pot of beer.

Möjut Awol, the head of Wöŋösek lineage of Dari, the owner of the Agoratit section of the Tapari River, told me that if after bathing in or fetching water from his stretch of river people were ill, he decapitated a chicken and threw it into the river charging 'Spirit-of-the-Above, through the water, to take the chicken and allow the people to work in the water unharmed'. Alternatively, he threw in a pot of beer or flour.[3]

A separate routine rite should also be performed at the beginning of each fishing season, although because of sparse rains, rites were not performed during my visit. One neighbour who hopefully brewed beer on his own account and built a fish dam, eventually abandoned it. If the initial rainfall is sparse, water levels will be low and ritual is wasteful and pointless. After good rain a diviner is called to explore fishing prospects and if the diagnosis is favourable a bound sheep is drowned; alternatively, a sheep or

---

[1] The officiant is known as 'chief' (*Mar*) or 'owner' (*monye*), of the river (*kare*), pool (*waka*), or sedge swamp (*tör*).

[2] Lienhardt reports the Dinka associate the river and smallpox on the basis of analogy between the weeping pustules and water; *Divinity and Experience*, p. 112 n. 2.

[3] In my first book, this elder was referred to erroneously as the 'head of Dakotian lineage'; see *Chiefs and Strangers*, frontispiece.

chicken is killed in the owner's homestead. The offering is described as 'for the people of the river' or 'for the spirit of the river', because 'if the fish are removed and it is never compensated, the river is angered'. As another elder put it, 'the carcass of the animal can be eaten by the fish and water animals, then the water is made safe.'

A communal fishing party follows the ritual, at which men fish with spears, and women and girls with baskets and nets. The owner patrols the bank, selecting from the catches in recognition of the sacrifice. He places large specimens at any shrine he may have, and divides the rest between members of his family. While it is usual for the owner to initiate ritual, neighbours may press him to perform it, or those who are not owners may, with his permission, make offerings and build their own dams.

All the main Mandari watering places have ritual owners, usually the heads of local landowning lineages (but in at least one case a member of a client lineage).[1] The owner drowns bound sheep or pours in beer. These areas refer mainly to the various sections of the Tapari River and its tributaries which flow across Mandari country in a north–south orientation. Each section of the river appears under its individual local name—Tali River, Dari River, Agoratit, Mina, Mijiki, and so forth. In the north, Roro River and the Roro sedge swamp and outlying pools, and Kösipi in the west, provide other significant networks. Smaller and largely seasonal pools and streams are not the object of communal ritual, although ritual following accident or sickness may be performed. Sometimes operative water ownership may lapse leading to the neglect of rites, as in the case of the part of Tali River owned by Wejur clan whose land has been over-settled by the dominant Jabour. Wejur still, however, regularly present a gift of fish from the first catch to the Tali Police Post, 'because the policemen are our guests'.

II

Water ownership may be supported by myth which shows how the water took form in relation to the activities of an ancestor,

---

[1] A pool south of Roro 'belongs' to Bariiye, a retainer lineage formerly attached to Rokwe. Since Bariiye moved to Dari village, the rites have been neglected. The present incumbent of the office, the doctor Ako Akurukway, told me he would perform a rite as his father formerly did, if approached by Rokwe.

and so thereafter could only be exploited by the ancestor's descendants. The mystical organic relationship between a group and its water may become diversified as the group concerned grows and expands, each lineage taking over a part of the water (as in the case of Dari). A typical example of mythically validated ownership is that of Mina River owned by Nyarkiteŋ clan, and said to have been acquired in the following way:

One day the ancestor was sitting in a tree cutting wood for a bow when he heard a loud roaring sound so alarming that he began to tremble. He looked into the sky and could see nothing: then he looked down and saw a man approaching. Below the waist he was shaped like a snake, but he had the chest and arms of a human being and two heads like the heads of men.

This apparition spoke and said: 'Don't be afraid or you will fall, but come down and I will explain what I want.' So the ancestor came down, and the strange man said: 'Go home and bring me three bulls, and two sheep because I have come a long way from Yei and am very hungry. The first night I slept at Reilli pool and the second night at Paki swamp till I came to Mina.'

So the man assembled oxen and sheep as requested. When all the people arrived with the animals, they found that the trees and grass had disappeared and in their place was a river and a drum was beating under the water. So they slaughtered the animals and threw them into the water.

Then the river spoke and said 'These are my last words; as you have brought oxen and sheep the river is yours. In it are a great number of fish, but if your people come and take them a sheep or bull must be slaughtered first, so that no one shall die. If war breaks out I will beat a drum in the water and you must fight near my banks so that I can help you. Finally, if anyone comes here and sees the river, let him never ask, "Is this the river of Mina?" because if he does so he will die.'

Nyarkiteŋ are still owners of that part of Mina River, and the present Mar sacrifices when water reaches the thighs. A sheep is cut down and beer in a pot thrown into the water. In war, offerings are made, and the people call on the *nulon* of Mina to help them.

Here the river is symbolized by an apparition which comes from Yei, a township in a neighbouring tribal area and, for the Mandari, the direction of the source of Mina. Common characteristics assumed for both snakes and rivers lie at the basis of the images— the winding, looping, restless qualities of each, and the life-giving/ death-dealing potentials—rivers bring fertility and death, killing snakes may be symbols of religious power. The journey through watering places maps out the water-courses of Mandari country, including Reilli pool—the place where the Bora ancestors parted after their quarrel—Paki sedge swamp and its tributaries. Ownership of the river is acquired with the blood of Nyayo sheep, and at subsequent rites this ownership is reaffirmed. The river also defends (rivers divide territory and form natural boundaries). Its life-giving qualities make the river vulnerable, hence the refusal to disclose its name to strangers.

In a Dari myth the ownership of Roro sedge swamp and river is sealed with human blood.

In the old days the Mandari did not eat fish. There were fish in abundance but they were believed to be inedible.

One day, the breeding bull which led the Dari herd was loosed for grazing and separating from the herd it followed the way which leads to Roro. In the evening when it returned the people saw that its body was covered with grass and mud as if it had splashed and wallowed.

And Lubukak, the ancestral Dari chief, and Wöju his 'friend', began to question 'from whence is the bull coming that it is blown up with grass and splashed in this way?' (the bull had gorged itself on the rich grass of Roro). And the people answered, 'How do we know whence it has come?'[1]

Next morning the bull again took the same path, and Lubukak said, 'My friends I am going to follow the bull.' Lubukak eventually found it grazing on Roro, and he found there teeming multitudes of fish— belinyi, rienöki, and kungorun—swimming on the surface, because it was the dry season and the water had almost evaporated.

So Lubukak said to his followers: 'Try and spear some of these fish.' And after doing so they made a fire and placed some fish on it which smelt very savoury as they cooked. Then the people said 'Give some to the dogs and let them eat first, in case these things are poisonous and we die.' So the dogs consumed the fish and then lay down to sleep being satiated. When they awoke they began to run about and play and drink. When Lubukak saw this he said 'these things are safe, come and try some yourselves.'

Chief Lubukak took a fish and removed the head and swallowed it whole, followed by another. After they had eaten and suffered no ill-effects, Lubukak said 'I shall now call my "friend" to come here and

[1] This story pinpoints the ambivalent element in the Dari/Lorogak relationship, Wöju being the ancestor of the Lorogak, autochthons who owned much of what is now Dari, and who gave settlement land to the Dari on arrival. The Dari now suggest that Wöju was 'like a client' in relation to Lubukak. The position tends to vary according to which party is making the comment.

bring the people.' And his followers replied 'Well and good.' Lubukak then rubbed his nose to make a calling sound 'NUUHHHHHHHHH', and called: 'Wörju loooooooooooh, adi yoooooooooooh, tit ana, tit ana tit',[1] meaning, 'Wörju, you there. Come here to this splendid place.' And Wörju came with the cattle and people; the huts and grain stores followed of their own accord. When they reached their destination the Dari pegged down the cattle, and, being tired, lay down among them and slept.

And a young girl came in the night with her mother named Aŋyuŋun, and sat down in the camp. The girl's name was Roro.[2] When Dari awoke in the morning and saw the strange pair they said, 'Since you have heard us break wind in our sleep, you (Roro) must marry our chief.' But she refused. So they replied: 'Then you must die, because you have watched us sleeping.' Her mother begged them to take her in marriage and not to harm her. But as she remained adamant, they cut her throat. Her blood spurted up, up, up—towards the sky. Her body was thrown into the swamp.

Then the mother danced in anguish on the banks, invoking the waters and crying: 'Oh, you river and watering place, bear witness to the blood of my child. If anyone comes to steal this water, the blood will revenge itself on them.' The lagoon was named Roro, because the name of the girl was Roro.[3] These are the events which led to the Dari building at Roro. As they became many they divided and came to their present villages.

A concentration of life symbols appears in this myth. The life-giving water is acquired through the blood of a woman, the central creative category.[4] The association between fertility, women, and water is also shown in the euphemism for pregnancy, 'water in the belly' *sipi i pele*; the word for semen is *kula yuŋusi*—literally 'the urine ("making water") which promotes conception'.[5]

[1] The country round here is still named Atit.
[2] In one account the girl was said to be a Dinka, divorced from her husband, who came to Mandari from Jan Pan near Rumbek.
[3] The linking of the river with woman is also a Dinka theme. See Lienhardt, *Divinity and Experience*, chap. v: 'The Myths of the Spear-Master'.
[4] The death of an unrelated girl endows people with the ownership of land in a Bora myth. See *Chiefs and Strangers*, pp. 24–5.
[5] The theme of the giving or discovering of fish in both myths is of some interest. The Nyayo myth particularly, has much in common with the Toba and Pilaga Indian myth recounted by Alfred Métraux and referred to by Lévi-Strauss. This Indian legend describes how a serpent called Lik strays from the river; it asks men's help in carrying it back, a difficult task because its belly is heavy with fish. Men are afraid, but are reassured by the serpent. Those who help Lik receive the right to take fish provided they never disclose how the fish are obtained. Claude Lévi-Strauss, *Structural Anthropology*, trns. Jacobson and Grundfest Schoepf (London, 1965), chap. xiv.

20

WOODLAND RITUAL

I

As with the rain, the fertility of the land and its harmonious exploitation are obligations of chiefship. Land is abundant and ownership of it is seldom in dispute, but should two claims conflict, the landowning chief concerned adjudicates when a settlement cannot be reached by local elders. He does this as the living descendant of the ancestor who, as the Mandari put it, 'gave birth to the land' (*yuŋi kak*) by forming it out of undifferentiated bush.[1] If disputing parties reject his ruling, the chief may curse the land and destroy its fertility. The sale of land never arises in Mandari but land may sometimes be lent to over-populated neighbours. Then the borrowers take on certain obligations as a part of the population of the owning chiefdom, although they remain under the political jurisdiction of their own chief. Some instances of land lending have turned into land usurpation and have been bitterly resented by the original donors. Usurpation is a standard reason given for bad weather and harvests.[2] The loan of land to a petitioning group may be refused if owners feel that the loan may be contrary to their interests. During my stay in Dari the Mokido, who lack permanent water, asked to settle an occupied area near Dari River but the request was refused for fear it might prejudice future Dari expansion.

II

The Mandari do not perform crop rituals at the beginning of the cultivation season, the beginning of the Mandari New Year. I made careful inquiries on this point, in view of writings on the

---

[1] I have described the different kinds of 'landownership' in *Chiefs and Strangers* (see index under this head).

[2] See *Chiefs and Strangers*, chap. v, ii and iii, for accounts of indigenous groups elbowed out of land.

7. Homestead with forked shrines

Bari which state that crop rites are performed among Bari tribes by persons called *monyekak*.[1] The view was expressed by some elders that a rite was formerly performed at sowing time by a landowner (*monyekak*) or a man possessed by Spirit-of-the-Above before 'the country was spoilt by foreigners'; but no one could say what it was. The rain ceremonies are claimed to cover crops, rain being the primary essential.

People begin to cultivate after the first showers when there is evidence that the rain will continue steadily. Individual families with poles for Spirit-of-the-Above or a Power may kill a chicken or pour beer libations; a small pot of shea-oil, ground from last year's pickings, may also be placed at shrines. These offerings express unity in endeavour between the spiritual forces and human owners of a homestead. When addressing the spirit or Power the homestead head also 'prays to Creator' (*mo'yu Dun*), for a good harvest and freedom from sickness and trouble. Anyone who is worried about his crops may call a diviner—'a man with-the-eye sees his neighbour's fields with a good yield and comes and "stares" [ritually], or a night-witch defecates among the seedlings, then the crop fails.'

Charms, although not widely used, are available to promote growth or give protection. When millet, sesame, and bean seeds are mixed for broadcast sowing, a sprig of a sharp thorn (*yome*) may be placed among the seeds which are addressed: 'You seeds must grow well, and let evil persons stay away' (as people automatically avoid thorns). If a man finds a dead squirrel, civet-cat, or marten, he may place a piece of skin or bone in his seed gourd to encourage large full heads (the analogy here is based on these animals' prolific breeding). Rain creeper leaves (*dölöŋi* and *tirioti*) are beneficial because of the association between rain and luxuriant growth. A tortoise's or hedgehog's foot, representing protection (these animals hide in shells or curl up), keeps grain safe.

When homesteads have surplus grain from a previous harvest, a family may brew 'for vigour' before cultivation. During the poor years of my visits this was not done. A notable or chief with a large acreage will also call on traditional labour by giving a beer feast. Formerly, rich chiefs killed an ox when the first showers gave the signal for mixing the seed; the meat was eaten by hamlet

[1] L. F. Nalder, *Tribal Survey of Mongalla Province* (Oxford, 1937), p. 125, and Fr. L. M. Spagnola, *Bari Grammar*, in a Bari text, p. 353.

elders, and prayers were offered to Creator for a fruitful year. *Gwele*, the traditional cultivation-season dance, followed. (*Gwele* is danced during the later months of cultivation by a whole village, including its old people.) Men who had attended a chief's cultivation feast sent their wives and children to clear his fields and plant.

After harvest, rituals are not performed; although after a good harvest of the main millet crop there may be celebrations expressing 'gladness in harvest'. These are social occasions, although they are marked, like all major social events, by prayer to Creator. Harvest celebrations—'the homestead feast' (*tukeba* or *köri, lo baŋ*)—are dependent on abundance and were not held during my visit, but informants described them to me.

When the grain has been harvested at the end of November (*Kut*) and the women are spreading out the grain heads in the yard to dry, the elder of the hamlet or village calls homestead owners and says, 'Well, my brothers, the harvest is in, let us now pray to Creator and give thanks.' Then people may say, 'Not yet, so and so is not ready.' They wait until all have finished, then a day is chosen so that everyone is at home. Beer is brewed from the new grain in every wife's hut. Then it is taken and drunk in the homestead of the family head.

The day is spent in a round of beer parties, people circulating in each other's homesteads. Lineages which live close to each other or are intermarried (like Are and Mandiye lineage of Dari clan) hold their *tukeba* simultaneously and visit each other. During the drinking the homestead head pours libations on the homestead paths and prays:

You, Creator (Ŋun), and You, the Above, and You our Ancestors . . . now the crops have been reaped, may the people prosper, and come to no harm. Keep all evil away. When the time comes to go to the grasslands may we go to our new activities in cattle-camps in safety.

At *tukeba* all spiritual phenomena attached to homesteads receive beer; families without specific attachments simply place 'the pot for the ancestors' (*agase na Ŋutu ko kak*). A homestead may have several pots set out in their appropriate places, and elders drink from each. The pot for ancestors, also called 'pot of the back of the hut' (*ise na kade bot*, the husband's pot), is drunk at the back of the hut; the pot for a Power is drunk at its own side by its owner, while that for Spirit-of-the-Above is drunk outside, by its shrine, when libations are poured. Libations for ancestors are poured on the permanent cooking hearth. *Tukeba* marks the end of the cultivation year.[1]

While contemporary harvest celebrations are simply convivial occasions with typical religious overtones, the late Chief Korondo told me that at one time a rite marked the end of cultivation. According to him, after the main harvest, each kind of grain could be eaten except for the small millet known as *siaka*. Before eating this, each housewife ground a few heads of *siaka*, mixed this with water, and the old women, accompanied by hamlet elders and a landowning representative or a doctor, carried the pots into the bush. A tree was selected around which the assembly stood, while each elder in turn cut out a chip of wood with an axe. When the tree was about to fall it was pushed over towards the west, the old women ululated and the *siaka* and cooked grain was thrown after it, followed by handfuls of dust and earth. Everyone then returned home without looking back. The fall of the tree to the west, Korondo told me, marked the taking of the sins, illnesses, and deaths of the old year towards the west—the evil pole: looking back was avoided for fear of looking back on evil. This rite is not generally known about, but I am prepared to accept Korondo's word that it was once performed. It seems logical that an annual rite for the elimination of evil was performed in addition to the monthly one and its discontinuance is rather difficult to account for. It could be that the contemporary preoccupation with cattle and a declining interest in cultivation—showing a shift from a balanced mixed farming economy to a more strongly pastoral one—may, in part, be the reason.

III

The Mandari continue to value their natural woodland which provides a rich harvest. Woodland rites which are carried out annually are centred on the shea-butter trees,[2] natural groves of which are a characteristic of much of Mandari woodland. The

---

[1] The word *kiŋa*, a twelve-month lunar period (a year), also defines periods of seasonal activity; 'the cultivation year', or 'the herding year'. The Mandari refer to the end or beginning of a 'year' (*kiŋa*), when they speak of the beginning and end of cultivation or herding. The 'cultivation year' stretches roughly from the end of March or April till the end of October or into November. The 'herding year' begins the end of November or early December and lasts till the end of March or April.

[2] *Butyrospermum niloticum* Kotschy.

fruit is eaten raw, the oil extracted from the kernels then being used as a basis for relishes and as a lubricant with a rather restricted function. It is unsuitable for ritual since its colour and texture make it conceptually 'hot'; its messiness makes it unpopular as a cosmetic.

Shea-trees in the bush can be picked by members of a chiefdom, trees on or near cultivated land are owned. Fallen fruit may be gathered, but it is an offence to rob trees. When a village moves, its people return to collect their shea; a favourite pastime is also visiting the mother's brother to gather shea from woodland in which he has rights. Shea fruit is picked and eaten during May and June; the kernels are then ground and the oil prepared.

Where trees are plentiful, rituals are performed by the land-owning chief or his representative—known as 'the chief' or 'owner' of shea (*mar*, or *monye*, *lo kumuri*)—who performs a rite after the fruit has been collected and the kernels have been ground. Most of my information on shea rituals, which I did not see myself, was obtained from the Mount Tindalu area where groves are extensive.

Allowing for local variation, the core of the ritual is the as-sembly for the splashing of the community with the new oil which is mixed with sesame oil to neutralize its 'heat', the sacrifice of a red goat to Spirit-of-the-Below, and addresses by the owner to this Spirit and to the shea itself and sometimes to founder ances-tors. Feasting and ceremonial dancing follow. The dance featured here is *gwele* (often referred to in this context as '*gwele* of the shea'), the dance of the cultivation season. A proportion of the produce is presented to the owner and to the landowning chief in recogni-tion of the sacrificial animal and the prayers.

The following ethnographic material was collected from chief-doms living in the main areas of shea woodland. It shows that while in theory the rites are performed by landowning chiefs, in practice it is often a member of a small indigenous group who carries them out with the assistance of the chief. Also shown is the way in which the presentation of fruit marks out links of agnatic affiliation and political allegiance.

In Borenye, Ajara lineage, who own the trees, perform a ceremony in *rit* (autumn) when the grain harvest has been reaped and the people are in villages. Kurun, the shea owner, earmarks an ox (goat). The women of his homesteads and those of his male kinsmen prepare beer which is drunk by male and female elders. Kurun prays, calling on his ancestors (particularly Mar Agoya, third son of Borenye founder and founder of Ajara lineage), together with Spirit-of-the-Below (Kak), asking for abundant following harvests. The goat's meat is divided out and boiled and eaten at the grave of the owner's father or other distinguished ancestor. Male elders eat the ritual offal, the chest and forelegs, men and youths the hind legs, senior women the bowels and stomach lining and sometimes one leg. The beer is finished up in the evening when the clan drum is beaten for ceremonial dancing. The shea owner takes the goat's skin for a drum cover. All those attending bring Kurun a basket of shea. Defaulting may result in illness because of his aggrieved disposition.

The Mandari Bora and Somöring clans perform a joint rite for shea as for rain. The presentation of the fruit to the owner, an elder of Bora lineage, takes place in September. He receives fruit from surrounding hamlets and in turn presents some to Barisho. The owner's wives prepared the new oil and food and beer. Hamlet elders assemble to drink, and to eat the food mixed with the oil. The owner prays for a good following crop and splashes the assembly with oil. Ceremonial dancing follows. The presentation fruit is divided between Chief Aznaba of Somöring, Chief Barisho of Mandari Bora, and the owner.

The Bari Kujutat shea belongs to the Mulö, indigenes and original owners. Their elder, Kunyune, receives fruit from his people and from Bari Kujutat. He selects baskets for presentation to Magok, head of Bari Tapir lineage. Fruit is also carried the twelve miles to Mandari Bora and presented to Barisho who entertains the bearers and confirms that their country will have shea, termites, and game the following year. This presentation acknowledges the former attendance of Kujutat at the Bora rain rite. At the Bari Kujutat rite a goat is presented to Kunyune, who mixes 'cool' sesame oil with the new 'hot' shea oil to neutralize it and then splashes the sacrificial 'ox' with it, addressing the shea trees: 'You shea (*do kumuru*), may you bring forth fruit. Here is your ox.' The assembly is splashed, then the oil pot is broken. When housewives later prepare the new oil, some of it is splashed on those eating it.

Mijiki shea belongs to retainers.[1] Gworoŋa (an immigrant group)

---

[1] See appendix IV.

bought their shea trees from Tija and Wörigöri, autochthons and woodland dwellers and cultivators, in exchange for cattle. Around Tali, shea grows sparsely; here powerful immigrant clans like the Jabour and the Mokido and remaining depopulated landowners never performed rites. To the south-west, the Jarra pray for their trees at the rain rite.

Shea grows on Rokwe land in Dari; an elder of a client line attached to Rokwe kills a sacrificial goat. The clients, whose founder came from Terekeka, received the trees from Dari. Their handing-over is said to have followed the neglect of the meeting-tree and the cattle by a Dari chief whose main preoccupation was hunting in the forest. After the loss of the herd leader, the personal client persuaded the chief to leave the woodlands in the client's care and attend to his chiefly duties. Each season, the client owner collects a little fruit from each homestead and presents the bulk of this to Mabour lo Ako, head of Rokwe, who provides the little red goat for sacrifice. The owner prays at the rite: 'You Shea, may you ripen. Let all forest products prosper. You, the Above and You, the Below, let evil be far.' The goat is killed and the assembly splashed with oil using bunches of shea leaves. In the evening and throughout the following day and evening *gwele* is danced and those attending are splashed with the oil. Rokwe employ a larva called *kiryitite*—said to have 'a mouth at each end of its body'—which is broken in half and placed in the mixture of oil and leaves with which the assembly is splashed.[1] This is said 'to make the fruit plentiful'.

In the far west shea is abundant. Small Bora segments—Bunja, Majore, Lomore, Jurkoli, part of Jokari, and Jungwa—live here and rites are performed annually. Jokari shea is owned by Lekelyu, woodland dwellers prior to Jokari's arrival from Borenye.

IV

All nature featured in ritual is to some degree socialized, in that it is singled out, used, and exploited, but the social aspect of wild nature is quite different from that of domesticated nature,

---

[1] I could not identify this worm or larva. Father Spagnolo, writing on the Bari, describes the 'chrysalid of a kind of butterfly . . . endowed with good ghost-like influence upon such seeds as are sown by scattering', and says one of these will be placed in the sowing basket. *Bari Grammar*, p. 416. The Bari word for 'worm', or 'larva of wood-worm', is *kurutöt* and *kuturutöt*.

which exemplifies long-standing human endeavour, planning, and selection. The Mandari point out that they are not directly concerned with, and responsible for, free nature, and that if it fails nothing can be done, whereas they are constantly concerned with domesticated nature. They imply that where there is a direct and persistent interference by man in vegetable or animal life—where this has been stamped with the mark of human personality—it will be drawn into the orbit of personal human ritual and rites for it will be based on a simplified version of rites for persons.

There is, however, one form of nature standing somewhere in between these two extremes, which, although free in character, is subject to personal ritual, namely those trees which are selected as meeting-trees (*toket*).

In a country where much of the woodland is secondary bush, the presence of single, large, spreading trees of great age helps to determine the siting of a chief's homestead, and therefore the placing of a particular community. Meeting-trees show a constellation of images arising from intimate use and close association and from the events with which the trees are connected—congregation, disputes, community cleansings, and, in the past, rituals for war. A meeting-tree can have a dangerous presence because of the accumulation of forces connected with it, and it can also be endangered and polluted. If this happens the community itself is harmed.

Acts which threaten the community through the tree are bloodshed, desecrations, ill-omened happenings, and contentious disputes occurring in its shade. While the community can be cleansed at the tree, the tree itself may also need to be cleansed in order that the community can remain whole. To cleanse the meeting-tree a sheep is presented—often by an elder who 'wishes to be known to the chief'—and given 'for the meeting-tree'. A short statement of intention is made by an elder or the chief's personal client, who splashes sesame oil on the assembly and on the tree itself. The sheep is killed, skinned, and the whole body, including the feet, cooked and eaten by all elders at the tree. Apart from specific cleansings, libations may be poured at the tree by a wife of the chief when she brews beer if her homestead is close by. Thus Awuk, wife of Korondo, used to care for the Dari meeting-tree, Gomiyo, during her lifetime.[1]

[1] When discussing the images of meeting-tree identity, I inquired whether

The influences which are seen adversely to affect domesticated nature (animals and crops) are individual human failings, sins, and acts of sorcery, whereas wild nature is damaged by more general events—failure of political control and effectiveness leading to the incapacity of landowners to sustain the dominant relationship over their rain and land, a situation seen to precipitate all manner of natural disasters, the most fatal being drought.

Rain, however, as we have seen, has a more personal side as well, based on its active properties—its wetting, chilling, disease-bringing qualities and its immanence in human beings. Rain-derived pools and rivers may therefore be drawn into ameliorative ritual and rain itself may have to be protected from human action. Then ritual has a subsidiary, personal side which is missing in relation to passive nature.

v

It would be surprising if the Mandari did not value and exploit their rich natural harvests in view of their poor and limited grass-lands and relatively small numbers of cattle. The Mandari are forced to be mixed farmers and to augment what they can produce by their labours, from the wild. The wild is therefore brought into ritual. Pastoral peoples like the Atwot and Dinka, who have better grazing capable of supporting larger herds, but poor woodland, place less emphasis on edible natural products and neither people performs woodland rites, although they value Mandari shea and honey and regularly obtain these, together with sesame and groundnuts, from Mandari in-laws or by barter.

The exploitation of the woodland by the Mandari and the care-ful singling-out of typical woodland products in ritual cannot, however, be explained simply in terms of economics. Other factors are certainly involved. I have already suggested that part of Mandari-land may at one time have been populated by small scattered groups living by hunting, exploiting the forests, and keeping sheep and goats.[1]

While rain rites are always performed by the chief, in a number something similar existed in relation to Mount Tindalu, the rocky hill in East Mandari where the Bora ancestor 'fell'. Inquiry brought the reply, 'We only know spirits of the homestead. If there are spirits of the outside (mudiŋ), we do not know them.'

    [1] See *Chiefs and Strangers*, pp. 28–9.

of places rites for the woodlands have been delegated to dependent, or virtually client, lines. There is, I think, some evidence to suggest that woodland rites may have been the traditional ritual of the small groups of early landowners, the scattered remnants of a population who were overrun by powerful incomers of diverse origin, the more recent being the Dari, Mokido, Jabour, and Gworoŋa whose migrations can, in a few instances, be directly substantiated.

Delegation may in some cases therefore have represented giving back to original owners the duties recognized as having been theirs initially. There is also evidence that some powerful cattle-owning lines lacked interest in the woodlands and were glad to delegate these to clients who were not necessarily original owners but were reliable and suitable. Gworoŋa provide a known example of incomers who made a deal with autochthons to trade stock for forests. The two groups concerned, the Tija and Wörigöri, provide the remaining link with the early population for whom the woodland would have been vitally important. It would have been less important to a cattle-owning population like the Bora who, I have assumed, migrated into Mandari at an early date. Historical factors—largely forgotten or deliberately unstressed—no doubt have a bearing on contemporary Mandari rituals. Woodland rites may represent strands of continuing ideas and actions belonging to an earlier culture, now become a part of a belief structure produced by a mingling of old and new.

It must be admitted, however, that the Bora themselves claim always to have performed woodland rites and certain statements in their myths seem to bear this out. For instance, Borenye's claim that they owned 'a rain-spear used for the rain and woodland, which guarded the land and fell from heaven'; also significant is the comment of the dominant Gworoŋa, that Wörigöri and Tija were *not* performing forest rites when Gworoŋa took over. The Bora rain prerogative is clearly stated and accepted (although this does not deny the claims of others also to have performed rain rites). The more recent giving of woodlands to retainers—many of whom are known to be non-indigenes—is also, of course, a way of bringing dependants into a direct relationship with their new territory.

PART V

VISUAL AND SENSORY PERCEPTION: SYMBOLIC STATEMENT

21

VISUAL AND SENSORY PERCEPTION: SYMBOLIC STATEMENT

THE Mandari make use of two kinds of symbolic statement, both of which derive from sensory experience and perception. The one makes use of the qualities of certain colours, the other is based on the opposition of hot and cold. In order to assess the qualities and characteristics the Mandari seek to represent through their symbols, it is necessary to bring together ethnographic material already described, attempting then to show why certain colours are used and not others, and the reason why the colours are used in the particular contexts. I shall also show how the symbols of colour and temperature may reinforce each other or make parallel statements. I then consider whether the Mandari colour experience—and therefore the use of colours for the making of statements of various kinds—differs from our own, and in conclusion draw for comparison on experimental work carried out on colour perception in Western societies.

The ways in which colours are allocated and used in any society will, of course, reveal unique features of that society, but we may also consider general, perhaps even universal, principles which would seem to underlie human perception of colour in the external world. These principles will provide a part at least of the explanatory background in any particular instance.

Using colour in order to make abstract statements would seem to be one of the most important ways of concretizing by reference to sensory perception. This is not perhaps surprising if we accept that 90 per cent of all our experiences comes through the eyes.[1]

I

In their symbolic statements, the Mandari make use of the three colours, red, white, and black. These colours have been shown to have a wide symbolic use in Africa, and indeed throughout the world both in modern times and in antiquity. In Mandari, black and white are perhaps the most significant of the three, because they express a strong contrast-relationship. And here we must bear in mind the kind of statement the Mandari wish to make through the colour—that is, what the colour is made to say. The Mandari use colour abstractions to express fundamental moral and affective states and oppositions; they also use them to *change* physical conditions, to reverse a given order. The colours black and white particularly lend themselves to this reversal process. They represent the most direct and obvious of the colour contrasts, and they also stand at the opposite ends of the graduated achromatic scale. In the same way as the colour black—through gradations of grey—can be directly reversed to the colour white and vice versa, in the symbolic context, black changed into white or white into black is seen to affect the actual reversal of the linked situation, thing, or role.

It is essential to stress that the Mandari antithesis symbolism has as much to do with the contrasts light and dark, as with the colours white and black. It is not always clear from the verbal statement whether it is a linked colour pair or a bright/dark image which is intended, and in fact this can sometimes only be inferred from the situation. Much of the time, the Mandari use the same word for white and light, and for black and dark, that is to say, hue and brilliance are often described by the same word. Black is, of course, the typical dark colour and white is the typical light one, so that the oppositions light/dark and black/white, although not identical, are very close. Recent colour studies have emphasized that white and black are colours of a very specific kind, whereas any colour can be light or dark, in the sense that it can have different degrees of brilliance.

Although a verbal distinction between hue (black/white) and

[1] F. A. Taylor, *Colour Technology* (Oxford, 1962)

brilliance (light/dark) may not necessarily be made, the Mandari have words for light and dark in the diurnal and nocturnal context. Thus, while both light and white are rendered by the hue/brightness word *lokwe*, and dark and black by the similar word *luru*, the word *töparan*, 'dayness', is used to describe the lightness of day, *tömudi*, 'nightness', the darkness of night. These terms can also be used to contrast light/dark *locations* during the day or night—the intense darkness of a hut entered at midday, for instance, is *mudi*; re-emergence into daylight, *paran*. When a threatening storm darkens the landscape, day becomes 'like' night, *mudi*, although the actual dark of the sky itself is *luru* (black/dark). The day/night analogy used for light/dark locations is never applied to objects, persons, or animals. One feature of the Mandari colour/brilliance category is thus the general division:

> clear, white or light = *lokwe*;
> opaque, black or dark = *luru*.

These categories combine our ways of distinguishing the qualities of hue and brilliance in colour. The hues that the Mandari place in these brilliance contrasts are, however, limited, partly because though the two classifications are of everyday application, they are also conceptual colour categories, which only cover a restricted area of related hues, thus:

'Dark' colour (*luru*) = black, dark brown, dark grey, dark blue; things giving the feeling of darkness or with a preponderance of dark markings; sometimes very dark blue;

'Light' colour (*lokwe*) = white, whitish grey; things with a predominance of light patterns.

Lokwe (brilliance) is not used to describe light green, light blue, or light pink, neither is *luru* used for the darker shades of these and other colours.

Red is the third symbolic colour. It stands alone epitomizing the experience of pure colour (chroma) and denoting the other main communication the Mandari wish to make, the aggressive, dynamic one. Red appears in a non-contrast unpaired situation, as its 'opposites'—the quiet, neutral, retreating colours, pre-eminently represented by green (perceptually and emotionally a neutralizing contrast to red) are not valued by the Mandari and are therefore not used symbolically. Red as a category colour covers:

Red (*lotor*) = true red, reddish browns, chestnuts, roans, pinks.

In daily life the three category colours must often be more exactly specified, since they are important cattle colours and reference to cattle must be precise. Red, for instance, has a scale of intensity as follows:

lotor = (*a*) Red, the unqualified category term; (*b*) Rich chestnut brown when no ambiguity or disagreement about the colour is likely.

lotor a wot 'very red' = true red; a brilliant saturated scarlet.

lotor madaŋ 'a little red' = reddish, a modified or cooled red, pinkish, or pale reddish-brown, or red where the red content is reduced, but sufficient to place the colour in the red category.

The scale based on intensification or modification to distinguish what we would call intermediate colours, can also be used for all the chromatic colours, and for black and white. The truest colour is the most favoured, blends the least popular.

A colour can also be defined by association with something in nature; the colour *lojöri*, for example, is derived from the words 'lo', meaning 'of' or 'like', and *jöri*, a red millet. It denotes a chestnut brown. There are also names for the main colours: green (*loŋem*), yellow (*lopore*), blue (*lobuli*); and for some intermediates, for instance, *lowaŋe*, a form of pink.[1]

When colour is associated with a hitherto unknown experience, individual perception varies and differences of opinion may be expressed. Thus, when describing a European, it is most usual for the Mandari to speak of 'white' (*lokwe*), stressing the light element, but I have heard Europeans described as 'red' (*lotor*), stress being placed on hue and the skin being seen as a very pale variant of red. A Mandari may also describe the skin of a fellow countryman who, to our eyes, might simply appear black as 'red', because of a reddish tinge in the skin.

Another comparison scale is used to describe patterning. This series is primarily derived from cattle and wild animal markings. The designations are now often in the Dinka language, though traditional, but less rich, Mandari names also exist.[2] Colour pattern

---

[1] Colour terms take masculine or feminine gender, depending on the nouns they qualify. The prefix *lo* (masculine), *na* (feminine) makes 'red' either *lotor* or *nator*.

[2] See Lienhardt, *Divinity and Experience*, pp. 13–14. Certain of these Dinka names appear as Mandari cattle names, sometimes slightly changed.

analogues are common in some Mandari songs in which an elaborate poetic and aesthetic element predominates; they have no symbolic use.

II

The general principles adopted in Mandari colour symbolism are as follows. White is the beneficial colour, used to express preferred moral and intellectual qualities, to represent high status and attributes seen to be embodied in it. White, however, also has an important negative side. Black, often linked to white as a complementary, has an obscuring, malign, low status association; but has a beneficial, veiling side as well. Red, standing alone, is positive and dynamic, the colour of violence, tension, and excitement; it, too, has a hidden element, an association with life.

Black and white lend themselves to statements of contrast, are important in rites which change the status of life-giving social categories like landowning chiefs and their assistants, and feature in the experiences claimed by doctors. These two colours are also used where a death-orientated situation must be changed into a life-orientated one; for instance, in the rain rite where black and white animals feature in conjunction, the explicit explanation being that sky, conceptualized as light, must be blackened: 'If the sky remains light [lacking black thunder clouds] rain does not fall.'

In the rain rite, the black animal actually reverses the existing physical situation—it is seen to darken the sky by both symbolic and real criteria; it is also analogous, in that the black animal and the black rain cloud merge as signs of rain. Here light is bad and destructive. It represents the bleaching effect of excessive sun, the scorching, deadly qualities of over-whiteness which eliminate life and vitality. While this brilliance continues, vital rain retreats and ultimately men, animals, and crops die. Black in the rain context is life-bringing; though, at the same time, it retains its primary 'death' association—here a reversed and secondary characteristic— so that the deliberately induced and desirable darkening still embodies inherent menace. The danger of black is real here as well as conceptual since storms bring lightning, the killer and destroyer.

The Mandari attempt to modify the inherent menace of black by the white ewe, the neutralizer. The ewe—often one already dedicated, and being a female, never slaughtered—is brought to the rite, addressed, and soaked with beer libations, 'to make the rain fall gently and tamely'—in a 'white' mood. The white animal and the black animal together represent the ideal sacrifice, but if only one animal can be found, the black is the essential one, 'because without it there will be no rain'. Failing a white animal people take a chance; those whose guilt makes them feel vulnerable carrying out individual protective cleansings. The principles underlying the rain rite are the changing of destructive light to dark by the use of black, then the modification of the danger of black by the use of white.

When the aim of a rite is to obscure or veil, dark or black animals are absolutely essential. At the rite described on p. 103, where an interim offering was to be made, 'a little black chicken, for the eyes of the Jok, to make them dark', was prescribed to give protection by hiding and masking.

Light/dark symbols are also used passively (analogously), to express inherent mood or condition, shown for example by the colour qualities given to the oppositions celestial/terrestrial. Sky is seen to be actually light, and earth in relation to sky dark. Outside these relational contexts, earth is not considered to have any particular colour qualities. Similarly, Spirit-of-the-Above is light and cool, Spirit-of-the-Below black and hot. This analogy is logically followed out in ritual situations. Rites for ancestors, for dead kin, for Powers for sin-cleansings, which have an earth or world or Spirit-of-the-Below connotation, ideally have sacrificial animals which are dark or red coloured.

In sin-cleansing colour is also analogical. For this reason the hue of the animal actually sacrificed varies. Some elders even told me that colour did not matter, and their statement was correct in the sense that colour here is simply expressive of mood and moral state and has no function of effecting physical change. Wrong colour does not nullify the rite or positively endanger, as it would in a rain rite where the colour role is active. A doctor, on the other hand, told me that a black animal was essential—he was speaking as a ritual expert, concerned with correct symbolic statement and not simply with desired results. Black in a sin rite indeed represents most closely the mood of sin, but the sin itself is not removed by the blackness but by the sacrifice, the anointing, and the confession. In this situation, any animal within reason can be called 'black'.

Black and white also appear in comment on social status. The Mandari describe black as 'an ugly colour, like clientship'— a generalization about the negative qualities and disabilities of subordinate social groups. Here black, in this sense, represents social obscurity, poverty, servility and, by extension, association with witchcraft and the evil eye. 'White is a "good" (*nab'us*) colour like Chief, black is an "ugly" (*loron*) colour like client.' Servile blackness is the direct antithesis of chiefly whiteness conferred at installation, with its positive qualities and its link with life and fertility. While the contrast between the two extremes— chief and client—can be represented in this idiom, I should stress that there is no overall division of people conceptually into 'black' and 'white', and further that this way of representing extremes is only used when preferred and non-preferred roles are directly contrasted, or when qualities abstracted from them are being used metaphorically.[1]

The somewhat similar generalization regarding night and day is not entirely of the same order. Night as absence of light is indeed experienced as the reverse of day, but it is much more than this alone. Night is 'an active counter-principle, day and night represent the dualism of antagonistic powers: they become visual images'.[2] For the Mandari night and darkness have strong emotional overtones based on complex images and perceptions, some involving persons and animals with 'night' qualities, often of a malign kind, particularly creatures having glowing and gleaming eyes. 'Night' eyes are seen as red—the danger colour, advancing, attacking—and it would appear that red showing through darkness can have intrinsic shock qualities. Kouwer has made some interesting comments on the fright–anxiety impact of night and darkness, suggesting that darkness is not disturbing simply because something may be lurking in the dark, but because the darkness itself is felt to be lurking—it 'looks' at us. 'Nothing is so terrifying as eyes gleaming in the dark, since they are experienced as the eyes of darkness itself.'[3] We must be careful when reading

---

[1] I would stress that because the properties of certain colours make them suitable for abstract statement, this does not mean that the special associations are seen to hold *at all levels*. For example, black outside special contexts is not seen to be 'bad', nor white 'good'. Red, the danger colour, is favoured in decoration—in small quantities.

[2] R. Arnheim, *Art and Visual Perception* (London, 1957), p. 313.

[3] B. J. Kouwer, *Colours and their Character* (The Hague, 1949).

psychological overtones which may be true for urban man into the Mandari situation. The Mandari, who lack lamps, are very experienced in night mobility.[1] However, their developed and malign night associations—more numerous and positive than those relating to day—may well derive some of their power from the emotional sensation of the dark as menacing in itself. It may be a human characteristic to be handicapped and disorientated in darkness, partly because complete darkness seems to exert actual solid pressures—'a wall of darkness'.[2]

The conceptual alignment of early world, human condition, and those spiritual agents most closely akin to human beings— ancestors and Powers—with the darker side of things, does not indicate a view of the world as evil, but as having lower, more material qualities, in contrast with the upper, more remote sky which is associated with Creator, the less intimate, and spirituality in general. This dichotomy is, however, far from absolute; earth– terrestrial being neither unrelievedly black, nor sky–celestial un- failingly light; at all spiritual and spatial levels, white and black, light and dark, mingle. The earth is marked with light, the sky with black. Conceptual whiteness in the earth is exemplified by white roles and experiences; and celestial black and white are mingled in the two ritually significant 'birds of the sky' (pp. 246 and 248, above). Human beings, although earth-bound, have characteristics of the celestial in their physical 'moisture' which is rain- and sky-associated, and through the non-material quality of their life.

Certain roles set apart their holders, and are achieved by sym- bolic 'whitening', or the preliminaries to assuming the role may feature experiences centring round light. The supreme example is chiefly initiation, where simply being a candidate for office is not enough; the candidate must receive the white qualities through the symbolic pouring of milk after washing and anointing with clear oil. Permanently whitened, the chief can hold the land and its people, and 'chiefship' can be seen to be 'good', regardless of individual character, because those of a permanently white category cannot be darkened.

---

[1] The actual darkness of any particular night also varies according to moon phases and weather, although the Mandari characterize certain hours of night in general as having greater depth of intensity than others—*warawara*, for instance, denotes the late hour of darkness when the night-witch walks.

[2] Kouwer, op. cit., p. 91.

The deliberate veiling of the dark side of human nature in chiefly office, and the need felt to eliminate the error and failure of the natural man from these roles, could be aptly expressed in Jung's words: 'the shadow must not be seen, it must be denied, repressed . . . There is no room for prestige-diminishing weakness.'[1] The Mandari state categorically that 'the chiefs were good' and only admit on specific questioning that some were less good than others. The special client who acted as the chief's shadow personality was also transferred by 'whitening' from the dark social category to the light one.

The Mandari point out that milk was used in this rite, first, because it is white (white represents the ideal, the transcendental), and secondly, because 'it is a living thing'. White on its own, because of its neutrality as a colour, has a certain negation, even sterility; milk, as the supreme female 'life' symbol, adds the missing element. By combining the two symbols the perfect statement is achieved. Milk is also the appropriate symbol for chiefship, an office vitally concerned with promoting natural and human abundance, since it enhances the lesser creativity of maleness.

Another important life-supporting role, seen to be marked by enlightenment, is that of the doctor. While not specifically a 'white' category entering his profession through translation ritual, the doctor's spiritual selection may involve the equivalent of a dark liminal period (mental and physical suffering), followed by a re-emergence into the light of new creative powers, certainty and knowledge. The claimed encounters with shining light or light beings who reveal the way in dreams, or during the night in dark places, is a feature of Call experiences.

White and black, then, are used in conflict situations, or where an opposition is to be stated. The life-giving/death-dealing qualities of rain are recognized in black/white terms and solved by the different-coloured sheep. Here both black and white are needed to achieve the object. In the chiefly installation, the white/black opposition is recognized; but the black, which is not required here, is eliminated by the predominance of white and cool. Black and white, light and dark are traditionally used in the artistic statements of all cultures to express the unresolved contradictions of existence.[2]

---

[1] *Collected Works*, vol. 14, p. 247.
[2] Such masters as Braque, who illustrate the kind of statement I mean, have

No human state or condition is represented by the Mandari as 'red'. However, in two important violence-associated situations red figures, and from these we can legitimately abstract its meaning. Red symbolism is aimed at bloodshed and is therefore danger-orientated. A positive objective is always present. Before embarking on a cattle raid or a vengeance foray, a red sheep or goat, or two red chickens, were killed at the meeting-tree, and the blood was sprayed over the heaped weapons, 'in order that the spears and arrows may fly straight'—that is, draw blood. The Mandari say that if other coloured animals were used, 'the arrows and spears would fall to the ground'; they would miss their target and there would be no slain enemy. Vengeance killing and raiding are now rare, but hunting ritual performed before each hunting season by professionals features the same red associations. A red chicken is killed over the hunter's heaped weapons to ensure successful kills. As a hunter, whose rite I observed, remarked: the blood of a 'chicken red, like meat'.

When killing is the aim a 'red' mood is created; but a 'red' condition in the psyche would be disorientating and undesirable. The condition of symbolic 'heat' typical of the 'black' sin-pollution tends to embody some of the tension characteristics of red. Both red and black have their value but, in general, menace and destruction are present in the messages carried by both, but particularly by red. The correctly orientated state is cool and white.

III

Certain rituals are characterized by a conjunction of symbols which add weight to their message. In the 'red' (war, hunting) context the experience of blood is the central objective and here blood as a symbol states qualities suggested by the mood of red, namely violence, dynamism, and heat. Similarly, in the white-orientated installation ritual, milk (the supreme fertility symbol) stresses the essentially creative role of the chief and through its whiteness, the non-aggressive, ideal, qualities. In the one situation red and blood in conjunction make the strongest possible statement about lethal aggressive qualities with over-all emphasis on

much to teach about the message for the psyche carried by colour and tone oppositions, but this is outside the scope of this book.

positive achievement; in the other, milk and white make a similar communication regarding life, peace, and moderation.

The associational factor which strengthens the symbolic statement and its emotional power through the linking of two independent symbols, can lead an observer into the error of regarding the separate, but associated, symbol as causally related in some way, rather than as having a relationship of a dialectical or structural kind. (I use dialectical relationship in the sense of a logical and not an actual relationship.)

An explanation in terms of causal relationship is based on the assumption that the value of colours derives from a biological determinant of the kind, 'Blood has a powerful emotional content, therefore red is significant because it is the colour of blood.' This assumption is based on a mistaken notion of the type of association involved. In fact, both red and white, as colours, have a special emotional and perceptual significance which makes them eminently suitable for use in comparable situations to those in which blood and milk can carry a parallel message.

In Mandari, blood and milk have profound significance and the parallel significance of red and white is often clear. As I have already shown, Mandari culture is preoccupied with the problem of fertility, with attempts to promote this and with the preservation of what are believed to be life-elements. Woman as child-bearer and rearer typifies the essentially creative and her creative functions are epitomized by the breasts and breast-milk and by menstrual blood. Although milk and menstrual blood both have fertility associations, the latter is destructive to milk in much the same way as red is incompatible with white, and a red situation endangers a white one. This incompatibility lies in the fact that the statement made by white and milk is largely unequivocal, whereas that made by blood and red always implies a reverse side.

The inherent ambivalence of blood, the fact that its flow can be more or less creative or lethal, lies at the basis of a scale of neutralizations. Where the dangerous side is seen to be the stronger, blood has the power to eliminate those beneficial aspects of fertility it shares with milk—and in general milk lacks its resilience as well as its ambivalent qualities. Red, as a colour, also contains a much stronger inherent contradiction than white, and large areas of red are absolutely hostile to those few qualities it shares with white.

Because the messages carried by red and white are so outstandingly represented in the experiences of blood and milk an extra emotional dimension is added to the experience of these colours in situations where blood and milk also figure as symbols; but this is not the same as a relationship in which the value of the colour is the product of such association.[1]

The evidence from a number of African peoples simply tends to confirm the largely abstract qualities of the three colours. That a biological component is often strongly marked out by the use of colour symbols does not prove a derived association; it is not surprising, after all, that when colour is used to make ideological statements it should make them about significant physiological phenomena and processes.

The fact that the colour red is important in *itself* apart from its blood association is clearly demonstrated in the Mandari context. For while animal blood is continually shed in sacrifice, sacrificial blood specifically does *not* have the aggressive, dynamic, outgoing qualities of red. In the sacrificial situation the symbolic mood of red is not evoked at all, but rather blood is shed in a 'white' mood—a calm and 'cool' one. Only by the aggressive act of spearing is sacrificial blood made dynamic—'hot'.[2] In many

[1] The hypothesis put forward by Turner, therefore, that the value of red, white, and black *derives* from biological associations, from the fact that they are the colours of issues of the human body—like blood, milk, and faeces—whose emission is accompanied by a heightening emotion, appears to me to be inadmissible. Turner demonstrates that the milk/blood symbolism most aptly states essentials of certain relationships, particularly within the framework of Ndembu initiation ritual. The parallelism embodied in the white/red series and the milk/blood series gives an impression of complete fusion between the two sets of symbols, both tending to move together and elements of ambivalence centering in the one set aligning with and repeating the ambivalence of the other. Deliberate 'reinforcing' by the use of a range of things with analogous qualities also occurs. V. Turner, 'Three Symbols of Passage in Ndembu Circumcision Ritual: An Interpretation' in *Essays on the Ritual of Social Relations*, ed. Max Gluckman (Manchester, 1962); and *idem*, 'Colour Classification in Ndembu Ritual', in *Anthropological Approaches in the Study of Religion*, A.S.A. Monograph No. 3 (London, 1966).

[2] That the Ndembu also abstract colour qualities and use them in contradiction of the natural colour of the phenomena which stresses their hue and also in contradiction of the general quality the colour represents in perception, is clear from Turner's statement that 'blood can be either white or black'. The conceptual colour of blood changes with the context ('Colour Classification in Ndembu Ritual', pp. 147–8). The Mandari do not represent the different associations of blood in this way but contrast it as beneficial or destructive— beneficial blood is from a sacrificial animal, destructive blood from the anus of the night-witch.

sacrifices the Mandari are not speaking in symbolic colour statements at all. The fact that the animal's blood or the colour of
the animal is red is then not necessarily significant, but it becomes
so where a red *objective* is embodied in a rite. Then the animal
itself must be red, since the redness of the blood alone is insufficient. Perhaps it is because blood is red, and blood features
in all sacrifice, that the effectiveness of its redness is here de-
valued and lost.

Special complicating factors surround the understanding of
red and white symbolism because these are the colours of other
things which, in turn, spread their own complex 'fan' of reference.[1]
Black, certainly in this respect, makes a clearer and less ambiguous
statement. The only natural phenomenon of significance represented as black is the rain cloud. Black is chiefly used to denote
conceptual conditions and states, or the qualities of roles and things.
Perhaps for this reason, black may give the impression of playing
a less important part than red and white: a fact noted by Turner
for the Ndembu.[2]

Essentially the distinctness and the unique emotional character
of the three colour statements is quite clear. The dynamic, intense,
positive side of things, cannot be represented by either black or
white. Both lack the required tensions, and it is impossible to read
into a colour a quality which is entirely opposed to its intrinsic
properties. Hence the fact that blood must sometimes be referred
to as 'white'.

All colours, however, have a variety of potentials, their qualities
are not absolutely fixed. A secondary, often ambivalent, side exists,
even for white. All colours also have both neutral and positive
elements. Those overlap areas of emotional emphasis which the
Mandari stress between the three colours red, white, and black,
are just those areas shown to be overlapping by Kouwer in his
psychological colour tests.[3] Kouwer uses the word 'polyvalence'
to describe these many potentials. He shows how systems of

---

[1] Ibid.

[2] Ibid. Turner seeks a biological explanation for the importance of black on
the basis of the fact that faeces carry a 'black' association for Ndembu, although
it seems clear that here also black has largely *abstract* qualities. The reference
to faeces as 'black' is quite logical where they are seen to have malign
associations.

[3] See Appendix V. The reader may be interested to make his own
comparisons.

colour symbolism in many cultures have taken note of this characteristic, which is also brought out clearly in his own tests, together
with the way in which colours 'take' or 'borrow' from each other.

IV

The other symbolic statement used by the Mandari, which
parallels the colour statement, is the hot/cold opposition. Conceptual 'heat' denotes pollution, sin, sickness, or peril, a condition
the Mandari describe as being 'hot in the self' (*mugan tomaka*).
The healthy, well-orientated psyche is the 'cool' one (*mugan tato*).[1]
Personality and disposition are also described in these terms;
tö'ly tomaka portrays the enraged, vindictive, revengeful, aggressive mood: *tö'ly tato* the benevolent, well-disposed, and even-
tempered one. The association of undesirability with heat in the
psyche and the desirable with the cool, is very widespread.[2]

Heat surrounds burial, corpses and mortuary rites, killing,
wounding, and bloodshed. Because dangerous heat is generated
by human disposition, ceremonial occasions when large crowds
gather are potentially hot, hence the cooling measures like sprinkling water. Daylight hours also follow the hot/cool antithesis,
dividing into the physically and conceptually cool morning and
evening, and the similarly hot midday. Full sunlight is always
incompatible with ritual performance.

The important creative categories—fertile women and landowning chiefs—are vulnerable to conceptual heat released by sin
or disposition. Because heat is stronger than coolness and endangers it, these categories must be protected. Illness is a hot

[1] The Mandari have a number of words for 'cold'. *Tato*, often used in relation to cold food, has the sense of 'calm, quiet', when used in reference
to disposition. This is the word used in the ritual context. *Kararut* describes
cold and chilly weather, or the sensation of being cold, and also a 'cold-in-the
head'. *Lilik* has the sense of 'cool, moist, fresh', and is used to describe dawn
and evening—'*kak lilik*'—'the earth is cool'.

[2] One has only to consider our own 'hot-tempered', 'his blood boiled',
and the opposite, 'cool-headed', a 'cool hand', etc. In our case, the hot is
also favourably represented, however, 'a warm heart' is preferred to 'a cold
fish', two cold images in the latter suggesting an excessive coldness. Mandari
do not use warmth to stress favourable aspects of personality as we do, a point
to which I return later.

state, although some illnesses have cold symptoms within this over-all classification, because some religious agents are 'hot', others 'cold'. A dangerous confusion can therefore be involved unless animals used in sacrifice follow the correct temperature alignment of the demanding religious agent. Terrestrial spirits and associated agents are 'hot' and require 'hot' animals—goats; 'cool' Celestial Spirits require 'cool' sheep. Creator, representing universals, does not receive animal sacrifice nor is Creator bound by the specifics of temperature and colour.

The alignment of animals in relation to temperature reflects careful observation of actual animal nature and behaviour. Sheep are, as a rule, mild, docile, and controllable: goats are temperamentally rough, aggressive, randy, and prone to butt. Inadvertently to confuse these two classes of sacrificial animal leads to sickness; as the Mandari put it, 'If a hot animal is sacrificed to cool Spirit-of-the-Above, it suggests that on the contrary a hot spirit, like a ghost, is being addressed.' Nullification or positive harm follows such a mistake. In default of the correct animal a stop-gap neutral offering such as chicken or beer is made. Cattle have an over-all suitability since they are also neutrals—'neither hot nor cold'.

In ritual for sin-cleansing the position is not perfectly clear. A 'cool' sheep is generally said to be required, although sin is a 'hot' state. A doctor explained that a goat 'would only make the sinner hotter'. I have, however, heard the Mandari speak of 'a goat of purification', and while this may be a statement of the general classification of all small stock as 'goat' (*kini*), there seems to be a genuine difference of opinion here. Whatever the correct procedure, goats may sometimes be killed in the sin-cleansing of ordinary people, but as sin-cleansing is often effected with 'cooling' oils, sacrifice is rare here. A sheep is essential for the cleansing of a landowning chief.

The ritual oils likewise divide under light and dark, 'cool' and 'hot'. Sesame and liquid butter (clear and light) are 'cool', shea-butter (dark and sticky) is 'hot'. 'Cool' oils are used for ritual anointings and as general cosmetics, 'hot' shea is basically a food oil, a basis for sauces. It is not a cosmetic nor is it used in ritual (with the exception of its use on the corpse). Water is a minor 'cool', light cleanser, but as it lacks the life-giving quality of oil and is described as a 'dead thing', its ritual use is limited.

V

There is clearly an overlap between the red/white/black and the hot/cold schema, which shows the implied identification of white with 'cool', and 'hot' with both black and red. The white and the 'cool' have the association of life-giving things, like dawn (and the east), water, and sight. The 'hot', together with black and red, carry the generally destructive associations of dark (sunset), blindness, and fire.

'Hot' can apply to both red and black because it embodies both the lower/earth/evil/death aspects of black and the violent/dynamic/danger elements of red.[1] Colour has a greater specificity and a more extensive range of communication than temperature; thus while killing is 'hot' and red it is not black, and the thunder cloud is 'hot' (menacing and black) but not red. It would be a mistake to attempt to reduce Mandari colour symbolism to simple opposition, though this is valid in the case of temperature.

The Mandari use temperature and colour to make parallel statements, but it cannot be assumed that there is an absolute relationship between the two scales of the kind, 'hot' animal—'hot' colour: 'cool' animal—'cool' colour. Both colour and temperature are used in a much more subtle way in order to comment on conflicting or complementary elements seen to be present within the situation and in the symbol itself.

One category of animal (goat) is certainly 'hot' in direct contrast to the other (sheep), and in ritual statements where temperature symbols are primary, this alignment is absolute and cannot be modified. In situations where the colour statement is the one of paramount importance, temperature may be less stressed. The quality seen to be essential to the objective is always the one emphasized. Thus in the purification rite for a chief the animal must be 'cool' (sheep) and, while ideally it should be black, it may in fact be of another colour—although this animal will be described as 'black'. In a war or hunting rite where stress is on the red colour and not on the animal's temperature designation, either a sheep or goat may be used provided the animal is red. In a rain rite, on the other hand, the animal's temperature designation and colour must be of the same order.

It would appear from what has been said that a white ewe is

---

[1] The redness of fire as well as its heat may help to stress this.

the 'coolest' animal and a red or black goat the 'hottest'; however an animal's 'hot/cold' condition, as opposed to its colour, can be altered in particular ritual situations by the manner of its killing. I have described the transformation of an animal at burial, where the blood of the neutral ox is 'heated' by spearing. Spearing, 'like war', is 'hot', cutting the throat is 'cool'. The latter is therefore the standard method of sacrificial killing since sacrifice aims to cool. The speared burial ox's blood is directed at persons or forces potentially responsible for the death. Here 'heat' is appropriate; it is inappropriate and destructive in the 'cooling' sacrifice for illness. Paradoxically, perhaps, even a 'hot' animal killed correctly in sacrifice has a 'cooling' effect. The 'hot' goat killed for the ancestors aligns with the 'hot' causal agent to produce a 'cooling' and ameliorating effect. A 'hot' goat offered to a 'cool' spirit, however, makes the situation 'hotter', the 'heat' of the animal destroying the aim of 'coolness' by producing a confusion of sensory images.

How far do the Mandari consider it essential to adhere to correct temperature and colour designations in sacrifice and how far are these seen to underlie success in ritual? In practice a greater range of allowable substitutes exists in some contexts than in others. In relation to colour in a rain rite, for instance, it is not enough to state that the sacrificial animal is 'black' (*luru*). It must be *seen* to be dark, as one falling in the light or red category 'only makes the sun hotter or the sky lighter', and further it must not be 'hot', so the choice is confined to sheep, ox, or chicken. Some latitude may be allowed as to the degree of darkness—the animal may be a dark brown or have extensive dark markings. All rain sheep I have seen killed, however, have been 'black'.

Here we return again to a basic premiss of Mandari colour symbolism, namely that where the colour must effect *physical change* precision is essential, but where the colour is used to represent moral states or conditions modification of the ideal is admissible. Modification can never be allowed, however, in relation to the sensory guides of 'hot' and 'cold', perhaps because the Mandari do not represent gradations of the ideal temperature in animals—the animal is either 'hot' or 'cold', it cannot be something in between (a possibility with regard to its colour, particularly when two colours combine in markings).

A problem still remains, however, concerning the real and the ideal in relation to colour, since too great a deviation from the ideal may be inadmissible. How, therefore, do the Mandari determine the colour of an animal where there is a possibility of a difference of opinion? Do they see a dark brown cow as red or black? Is a black-and-white piebald black or white? To some extent an indeterminately coloured animal can work in either role. It must also be remembered that in the context of sacrifice the Mandari are dealing with three broad category colours and not with intermediates which may be relevant in the situations of daily life. Category colours can be treated as light, dark, and red-brown. Animals fall quite easily into light, dark, and red as main groupings containing a number of related hues. Cattle are often roan or chestnut; sandy-coloured ones if placed beside a roan can also be seen to belong there—the sandy colour has a reddish tinge. 'Red' is therefore the designation of most bovine animals which are not black, darkly patterned, or light-coloured. It is not therefore as difficult as might be supposed to find a correctly coloured creature from the range cow, goat, sheep, or chicken. However, sacrifices can be seen to fail, and then a number of explanations will be given, one of which may be that the colour attribute was wrong. Mandari must select sacrificial animals as best they can, convinced that 'a spirit understands that a man can only offer what he is able'. What is reasonable by general consensus is usually assumed to be allowable.

Substitution, however, may mean only partial success and necessitate a further offering. There is a limit to the allowable latitude. The diviner who specifies the allowable modifications and substitutes (taking into account the economic situation) is always called where sacrifice is involved, and he may insist on exactness and refuse to sanction substitutes. Extreme deviations from the ideal are always avoided.

In sickness rituals the criterion of 'hot/cold' in the animal overrides all other considerations because illness is seen to derive from spiritual agents with sensory designations based on this opposition. Colour, on the other hand, assumes importance in rites which deal with changing a physical condition where the animal's colour matches some feature of the desired result, generally those performed on behalf of the community such as rain or war rituals. Here temperature designations may, or may not, play a part.

The chains of substitutions allowed in sacrifices based on temperature qualities alone, are set out in Fig. 14. In the rain rite an
ox and sheep are equivalent: economically the ox is the most
valuable domestic animal, but the sheep, although less so, is
especially favoured for rain ritual because of its strong association
with 'coolness'. This gives it equality with the economically more
valuable, but neutral ox.

The same applies to 'hot' animals, particularly goats in ghost

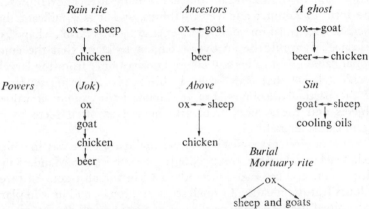

NOTE: ←—— indicates substitution. ←—→ indicates equivalents.

FIG. 14. *Temperature designations—chain of substitution*

offerings where a large neutered goat (*qweto*) is equivalent to
a neutered ox (*budösho*). Beer, a substitute offering for terrestrial
agents, cannot be offered on its own to celestial ones, although
beer drinking is a *background* to all ritual. Burial and mortuary rites
require the killing of an ox (killings of goats and sheep are subsidiary) since at death cattle are the only equivalent of human life.

VI

Psychological studies of human responses to colour shed light
on several of the questions with which this chapter is concerned.
The choice of symbolic colours and theoretical rejection of others,
the significance of each symbolic colour and the message it bears
in Mandari, can be seen to be related to human colour response
over a wider field.

Kouwer has pointed out that the perception of colour is the

experience of both its concreteness and its abstractness, and it is clear that, for the Mandari, colour has importance both as object colour and as abstract colour. I now want to consider for a moment the question of object colour since the colours of objects in the visual field have an important bearing on symbolic selection. In a simple rural community lacking artificial dyes and paints, red, white, and black tend to be the colours of objects of the immediate foreground and near distance. They feature in men, animals, and crops, and in the important objects of daily life. They represent the form of familiar and valued things, and it is significant that the Mandari word for colour, *gweya*, also means 'form', 'shape', or 'essence'. It would be an overstatement to claim that the emotional value given to certain colours derives only from the largely accidental fact that many valued objects give a strong sensation of the particular colours, but in Mandari the colour of valued objects and the symbolic colours themselves often seem to be significantly linked.[1]

Some random examples will suffice to illustrate the way in which red, black, and white are strikingly present in the Mandari environment, and are also constantly used in the abstract. All three colours feature in cattle, in small stock and fowls, and in wild plant and animal life. We have seen how domestic stock can be placed in one or other of these categories, particularly if we eschew the assumption that 'red' means saturated, brilliant scarlets. These three colours abound in seeds, fruits, and grains, and particularly in the three main classes of millet which have russet, black, or white grain heads.[2] If one looks into a gourd of millet seed mixed for sowing, red/white/black speckling is clearly visible.

Mandari lack artificial dyes, but have standard whitening, reddening, and blackening materials. The red paste *meje*, prepared by a process of grinding, boiling, and mixing red ochre with sesame oil, is a cosmetic, a medical sealing preparation for wounds, and a ritual medium. Women use red ochre powder to reduce their goat-skin loin-coverings to a rust colour, a use now extended to reddening trade cloth. The coarse, unprinted, undyed calico is treated in this way; untreated it is said to be 'unattractive', and

[1] Kouwer observes the same thing when he points out that an object has a meaning, a colour has a meaning, and the colour character and the value of the coloured object are often integrated in a special mutual relationship.

[2] These three species are *jöri lotor* (red), *jöri luru* (black), and *jöri lokwe* (white).

the rust colour is described as 'better' or 'more pleasing'.[1] The more costly cloth with woven patterns criss-crossing in stripes of reddish browns, ochres, and black (a form of 'tartan') is worn untreated, since it combines favoured colours.

Black and white as the contrast colours are widely used in design and decoration. Incised patterns on gourds and clay pots are blackened with a heated knife or spear-point, white contrasts are made by rubbing white clay or white ash into incised black or red surfaces. Young people decorate their faces with white ash to imitate the facial markings of oxen and cows. The circular band of white clay round the doorway of girls' courting-huts serves to locate them (and may also carry the conventional, though perhaps unjustified, association of virginity).

In the traditional bead ornaments, the dramatic effect of white on a dark skin, and the combination of white and black, is clearly portrayed. White beads were made from ostrich-egg shells, black ones from wood, probably ebony. A favourite traditional necklace alternated a white and black bead. Another of white beads called *toto ko meda*, 'asleep and watching', refers in its name to watchful nights in cattle-camps and also, perhaps, since three strings may be worn around the forehead by youths visiting girls' huts, the object of the visit—to look out for, and sleep with, girls. Heavy ivory arm-bands are prestigious ornaments for older men (see Plate 6).

Of the three colours in artistic design, red is traditionally used on its own and black and white in planned contrast. On my return to Mandari in 1958, however, I found a dark navy-blue trade-bead used in combination with an orange bead in the waist-bands worn by girls. The combination gave broad alternating bands of vertical colour—perhaps a variation on a black–red theme?

Many old beads exist (some cylindrical and made of opaque glass) and are now valuable heirlooms. Most are in dark muted shades: one kind which I never saw, but heard described as 'large' and 'very dark blue', formed part of the chiefly regalia. The origin of the old beads is obscure; some may have been early Portuguese trade-beads which circulated outwards from the East African trading posts.

[1] In the use of red the *bright* reds are confined to splashes of colour as in beads and the patterns on small head-cloths, and are not used as solid, all-over colour. (One might contemplate in our own context the sensation created by large areas of red, for instance in a room with all-red walls.)

While the colours used in design are partly used because these are the only colours which are available, the Mandari experience of colour has considerably widened during the last decade since the introduction of trade-beads. But the demand for these is still largely controlled by conventional aesthetics. Among trade-beads red is very popular, and black and white are still highly rated. Necklaces of all-white or all-red beads are thought to look well on a dark skin; alternating red and black is another favourite combination. Other colours including a purplish pink have enjoyed a run of popularity. This bead, named *remeyor*, was at the height of its popularity as a 'set'-bead in 1950–2 but was losing its appeal among the young men, who were passing it on to their sisters, when I returned to Mandari in 1958. Yellow beads have a limited success as a set-bead, blue and green ones less appeal. When I speak of a particular bead having a successful run as a set-bead, I am referring to those beads selected by a group of youths who are age-mates, to be worn as a threaded bead corslet. The latter differ from single necklaces, made by individuals, where the arrangements show personal experimentation, and have a much wider variety of colour and colour combination. Set-beads show group preferences determined by consensus; personal necklaces reflect individual likes and dislikes and idiosyncrasies of individual taste, not uncommonly contradicting the cultural preferences and representing innovation.

Since there is a real predominance of red, white, and black in the colours of the foreground objects of the Mandari experience, it is reasonable to suggest that colours which are prominent and constantly handled in objects of day-to-day value may be given more significance than those seldom seen or noticed and those of objects of little interest to the observer.

Other colours are, however, represented in the Mandari field of experience, some abundantly, yet they are ignored by them as designations in symbolic communications. Of these I will consider green and blue in more detail.[1] The lack of value accorded to green cannot be explained by a lack of a word for 'green' as we would recognize it. There is no gap between the perception of the

---

[1] Blue and green, together with yellow and purple, have been shown to be important in classical literature, particularly in the symbolism of the archaic Eastern world, in ancient Christianity and Judaism. See Jung, *Collected Works*, vol. 14.

experience of 'greenness' and the ability to describe it.[1] The word *loɲem* covers roughly what we would see to be a clear fresh green (as in new vegetation and leaves, and also the green of a trade-bead). But our and the Mandari categories may not exactly correspond on the boundaries of the green experience—thus dark green may be referred to as 'black'.

Green is predominantly a non-social colour for the Mandari, limited to the colour of the natural background and unrepresented in homestead objects and animals. It provides the neutral scenery, on a vast scale, against which the strong-action colours like red stand out in sharp contrast. In providing this background, green gives an unobtrusive reposeful impression, and the Mandari do not wish to say anything about qualities of this kind in their symbolic statements.[2] Mandari statements are positive and often the dialectic of opposition is crucial.

Blue is an even more indeterminate colour. Although the Mandari have a name for it, blue is so rarely encountered or referred to that I could not at first remember the word when preparing this chapter.[3] On one occasion something blue was described to me using the word for green, and it seems certain that the definition of blue varies considerably. Strong, very dark blue, the colour of antique beads, is a valued colour, but is seen more usually as a variant of black.

The Mandari do not have a stereotype of sky as blue and in their climate it is only blue at certain times of day and at certain seasons. The sky over Mandari-land can be anything from a brilliant, colourless glare (and the effect of great brightness on colour is a factor to bear in mind)[4] through intense blue to grey or menacing black. What the Mandari see in sky is light rather than colour; movement, as in cloud forms; and mood, as in the sensation of

[1] Dr. Lienhardt tells me, on the other hand, that there is no specific word for 'green' in Dinka as opposed to words for qualities of 'freshness' in vegetation, and so on. See also the variants of a word describing green among the Hanimoo. H. C. Conkin, 'Hanimoo Colour Categories', *S.J.A.*, vol. 2 (1955).

[2] Kouwer notes the negative nature of green; op. cit., p. 122.

[3] It is possible that the word for blue has been introduced from the Bari, a people in contact with Arab and other influences. As, however, all Mandari names for primary colours are in the Bari language (the Mandari and the Bari are closely related and share many common words) terminology alone is not a significant guide. None the less, new and convenient words soon spread across areas where there may be occasional contact, and the Mandari may visit Juba, a Bari township.

[4] See also Arnheim, *Art and Visual Perception*, p. 315.

violence in the storm, and signs of hope in the rain. They usually describe sky as *perere*, transparent or translucent; the word may derive its use here from the sensation created by distance or depth or by movement, as when clouds float across each other or the sun. It also means something similar to shimmering or luminous; in this sense it is used to describe the incandescent ring around the full moon, which is often striking in the night sky over Mandari.[1]

Sky is most often described by reference to a percept other than that of colour, but one we should also recognize in descriptions of things which give the appearance of inner activity, and which is represented for us by words such as 'glittering', 'shimmering', 'luminous'. If, therefore, a Mandari described his impression of the sky he would probably only give a hue after first enumerating these other properties. Hue would not be the first characteristic that he would isolate, as we might. The Mandari perception of the colour of liquid may also be secondary to the perception of its other characteristics since water is described by its clearness, depth, and so forth, rather than by its colour.[2]

Because of the background, retreating characteristics of green and the contingent nature of the Mandari experience of blue, both colours are inadequate for making positive statements, the value of colour to the Mandari for use in statement being to a large extent fixed in proportion to its sharpness of contrast and clarity.[3]

VII

Certain tests which have been carried out to show the influence of colour on the organism may also be mentioned, particularly as they bear significantly on problems of colour symbolism. Studies of response to colour suggest that an underlying pattern of perception, and more particularly a basic structure of colour

---

[1] Thus *perere ko yapa*—'moon rays'—a phrase in the Mandari hymn recorded on p. 339.

[2] It may be, though this is difficult to substantiate, that the Mandari make an implicit distinction between what is termed 'film colour', and 'surface colour', and imply that phenomena with film colour, such as sky, have a quality of their own that is not precisely hue. (For a description of film, surface, and volume colour, see David Katz, *The World of Colour* (London, 1935), pp. 9 and 17. For a description of sky as typical of film colour, see his pp. 71–4.)

[3] Conkin mentions the lack of value given to green by the Hanimoo, because green is the colour of the surroundings; op. cit.

perception, does exist, regardless of marked cultural or personal variations.[1]

The studies also reveal the real properties present in colour and emphasize the direct effect the perception of colour has on the psyche. Kouwer points out that 'the perception of colour is more than a visual event': that 'we must ask how the observer, as a total individual, is affected by a colour experience and not simply how the retina is stimulated'. He stresses that observed phenomena must be seen as an integral part of an actively experienced situation, rather than as tests laid out in the laboratory; and that the observer and what is observed must not be separated because, when taken together, the 'meeting' they present can give a special and true kind of insight.

Kouwer's phenomenological study of colour character (which I read later) has helped me confirm my views as to the reasons why the Mandari choose certain colours to represent particular moral and existential situations. Kouwer based his findings partly on his assessment of the work of other writers, including anthropologists, but mainly on his own experiments with 'colour words' in which he aimed to arrive at the direct emotional experience in which colours and words with a strong affective association formed part of a single experience.

I have discussed the standardized colours used by the Mandari, and it could be argued that colour values in this sense have little to do with the individual's psychological responses; but it may also be allowed that cultural selections are ultimately based on ways of perceiving which must originally have arisen in the individual consciousness or, at least, that must evoke some meaningful response in the individuals who use them. Leaving aside recognized social and cultural determinants, such as conventional associations acquired through learning, experience, fashion, religious symbols, and so forth, Kouwer's results suggest that certain 'affective dimensions were already present in the colours'.

In his tests Kouwer used ten colours: Mandari symbolism is only concerned with three, and the number of colours involved can be very significant because colours tend to 'take from each

[1] While no account is taken here of work published after 1967 on this subject, it seems that a working hypothesis has not yet been formulated to account for the psychological processes involved in the colour influences. See also M. D. Vernon, *The Psychology of Perception* (Harmondsworth, reprinted 1966).

other'. Kouwer found, for example, that other dark colours—
purple, dark brown, dark grey—assumed some of the unpleasant,
depressing 'dark' qualities of black when included with black, and
took over all the 'black' qualities in a test where black was excluded.[1]

In the Mandari system, not only is less said, but the system is
cruder in the sense that each colour must make a more generalized
kind of statement.

As far as red, white, and black are concerned, Kouwer showed
that red attracted a high ratio of words for passion, emotion, action,
and temperament. White attracted words indicating integrity,
purity, sublimity, and quietness. White was always opposed to the
inferiority accorded to black, and the restlessness of red. The outstanding significance of these three colours appeared in all the
tests, and Kouwer found there was a greater measure of agreement about them than there was about any other colours.[2]

The Mandari stress many of the characteristics noted by Kouwer,
for red, white, and black; moreover some moral qualities and
affective states are verbally associated by them with the colours
as, for instance, 'black is like client' and 'white is like chief'. From
the stereotypes black/client, white/chief, secondary meanings can
be deduced. The qualities of black are more fully understood when
the bundle of associations represented by the word 'client' is
unravelled. Client/thief/witch represent generalized low status
images; taken further, each of these elements breaks down into
a number of subsidiaries. Thus, 'black' is also:

(a) witch/evil eye = jealousy, malignance, evil, night, hidden,
and death;

(b) thief = stealthy, unseen, hidden, night.

While the negative sides of black are the most fully represented,
as I pointed out, black also has its positive and helpful 'veiling' side.

White also has a number of secondary associations since 'white
is like chief', and 'chief' represents:

(a) high status;

(b) intelligence, leadership, true judgements;

---

[1] The results of two of Kouwer's tests may be compared (see Appendix V)
with the Mandari colour statement where all that needs to be said is placed
under three 'colours'.

[2] This brief summary can be amplified by a glance at the colour ratings in his
tables.

(c) calm, peace, unity (the qualities of 'cool');

(d) detachment: not being too close to subjects or divisive situations; avoidance of involvement like the involvement in 'red' states, typified by aggression and hate.

Because of its detachment, white embodies the adverse combination of sterility and negation, hence it can also have a death association. The Mandari express the negative side of white—the over-whiteness and brightness of the light sky when it should be rain-darkened.[1] Red is not used by the Mandari to express moral states and qualities, nor to express opposition (although a recognized opposition is seen to exist between some red and white things, e.g. blood/milk). Red is used only in the direct statement of achievement sought in socially sanctioned bloodshed like war, raiding, and hunting. All these activities, however, carry secondary associations:

(a) aggression, danger, killing;

(b) vitality and maleness, action and strength (red destroys white);

(c) implicit association with sexuality: (i) unregulated sex is 'hot', red is 'hot'; (ii) suitors in courting-huts become smeared with the red ochre (meje) worn by girls, and to display this on the shoulder and chest the day after courting is a sign of successful philandering.

The positive, successful, hopeful qualities of red are stressed by the Mandari as well as its violence. But red always has an undertone of tension, and a continuous red state would be difficult to support, because of its ambivalence. The red mood only appears in short episodes, as does the colour red in the environment. The white and 'cool' has permanence. Red is also, in an absolute sense, the supremely 'warm' colour (comparatively, of course, any colour can be 'hot' or 'cold'; a 'cooled' red may be 'colder' than a 'warm' green). The association of red with warmth was strikingly revealed in Kouwer's colour tests. But it is not surprising that, in a climate where heat and drought are the overriding problems and cool and moist the ideal and sought-after conditions, the warm side

---

[1] In China white is the colour of mourning. White may be used as a marker on the corpse or the mourners, the mark of negation. This adverse side of white needs further investigation.

of red is not positively valued and that in the 'hot/cold' Mandari schema the 'hot' is always the undesirable.

The role a colour has been chosen to play will always partly be determined by the character of the colour itself, and as Kouwer points out, we must begin by asking 'what a particular colour experience represents'. One important determining factor in selection would seem to be the degree of prominence. The distinctness of the primaries—white, black, yellow, blue, and red—tends to make them easier for conceptual abstraction than the intermediate colours or blends. The sensations these colours give are fundamental in the sense of being irreducible perceptually.[1] (There is difference of opinion as to whether green should be considered a primary colour in this sense.) Brightness and light saturation are other factors. Hues corresponding to vibrations of long wavelength are known to produce excitement, although we do not know much about why this should be so. The warmth or coldness of a colour may be relevant.[2] Katz in his colour testing shows the 'open', advancing and retreating character of colours, and their difference in insistence; he finds that 'reds seem to stand nearer than blues.' His experiments with red and blue nails showed that red nails stood half a centimetre nearer than blue ones when viewed binocularly from about 80 centimetres (although by altering the light he was able to reduce this sensation).[3] Goethe drew a contrast between red (active) and blue (passive). Kouwer points out 'the concentration of colour (chroma) in red, its dominant emotional intensity, and the fact that it is never neutral. It is the colour of maximum warmth; a symbol of life and vitality—in both the physical and the emotional aspect—of emotional ties and contact.' But he considers it wrong to reduce the life-symbolism of red simply to the experience of blood. The dynamic elements are present in red itself, and blood, through its essential life properties simply emphasizes the function of red.

Kouwer confirms that the importance of white lies partly in its contrast value with black or, sometimes, with red. He characterized

---

[1] Arnheim, *Art and Visual Perception*, p. 341. See also Leo M. Hurvich and Dorothea Jameson, 'An Opponent-Process Theory', in *Colour Vision*, ed. Richard C. Teevan and Robert C. Birney (New York, 1961).

[2] Arnheim, *Art and Visual Perception* pp. 327–33. Arnheim considers the theories of Kandensky, Allesch, Goethe, and others, then puts forward his own theory regarding 'hot' and 'cold' qualities in colour.

[3] Katz, *The World of Colour*, p. 69.

white by neutrality, by a lack of colour fullness, and by the fact that it has a light stimulus but no specific kind of light. Its qualities are abstract and transcendental, while its tensionlessness raises it above conflicts which accompany differentiation. But white can easily be soiled—changed or deprived of its abstractness —by other colours. This is clearly stated in the Mandari idea of danger to white—the chiefly role—from all kinds of black (sin and pollutions), or red (aggression, blood, killing).

White and black are important not only because of intrinsic mood, but because of their significance as a linked pair. No other colour pair represents such a clear contrast, other opposing pairs— red/green, yellow/blue—do not have the same emotional appeal, neither is the contrast they provide so directly apparent. Laymen may not even see yellow/blue as a contrasting pair. In the white/ black example the opposition is already there in experience, above all in the night/day dichotomy. Tests for illumination led Katz to conclude that there is a non-derived, non-inferred, primary impression of illumination of the visual world which is a prior experience to the experience of the individual colours of objects in the visual field.[1]

Psychological testing, and evidence from the pictorial art of the mentally ill, gives some support to the hypothesis that colour may exact certain kinds of physical response or signify a disturbed emotional condition. An artist or a layman's use of colour can be modified during mental illness, and the ordinary observer can follow these changes if he looks carefully at the work of certain artists. The use of dark colours appears during some kinds of psychosis—heavy black outlining, blotting-out, and accenting, for instance. Kouwer remarks, 'depression is closely related to anxiety and experience of death, and both experiences are characterized by black.'[2] Tests with red have shown bodily responses. Goldstein and Rosenthal's tests suggest that deviations in cerebrally diseased patients became more intense under red. Wallen, using Rorschach colour-blot tests, reported that 'colour shock' occurred when multicoloured plates were followed by the first of a series of red spots and black spots in combination. A marked response to red

[1] Ibid., p. 41.
[2] Reitman, who is not specifically concerned with the use of colour by the mentally ill, makes some mention of it. Francis Reitman, *Psychotic Art* (London, 1950) (see Index).

has been noted in infants, and painting tests with psychotics showed that patients applying red with heavy pressures thus externalize sadistic aggressiveness in a non-dangerous way. The importance of green appears in many tests and is especially evident in the results which follow when red is replaced by green. Kouwer gives an example of factory workers becoming noisy, excited, and tired until red windows were replaced by green.[1] Colour testing of infants and very young children has shown strong response to, and preference for, red.

VIII

Evidence from the writers quoted in the last section suggests that certain qualities are present in colours themselves and, in the sense that colours have certain effects on the human organism, these play an active role in perception. In addition, however, to the innate response secondary, derived reactions to colours are of great importance. These include emotional responses acquired through learning, knowledge, and associations, and psychological responses arising from conditioning at a very early age—the blood-red association is of this kind. It may be difficult to determine where a reaction is a pure sensation reaction and where it is a reaction through the association of ideas; there is no doubt, however, that in all cultures reaction to colour is a combination of both, and that both must be recognized in an attempt to understand symbolic colour communications.

Variations will be found between cultures in the way in which each will use what is given, and further variations will occur because of the emotional alternatives presented in any one colour message. Symbolic statements will vary according to the message the colour bears for a particular society. Nevertheless, it would seem that a basic cross-cultural similarity of response can be discerned and that tests on Europeans bear out evidence collected in the African field and vice versa.

[1] Katz, op. cit., pp. 69–70.

CONCLUDING NOTE

I

ON the basis of their observations, the Mandari assume that they can discern an underlying order and predictable response in elemental forces, in the physical world, and in human and animal physiology (humans in their physical nature being assumed to be matter). As I have demonstrated, one constituent of theoretical ordering which allows control, prediction, and classification, is the principle of moderation with its rule based on the qualities of cold and hot and their assumed determinants such as neutralization–amelioration and positive–negative response. Another constituent is the theory of three-dimensional orientation such as falling down/raising up, facing up/facing down, separating out/bringing together, and so on.

This 'law of connection' is supported by a body of proof drawn from the careful observation of the real or the supposed properties of matter at the level of practical experience,[1] although at the higher level of theory the hypotheses formulated have little to do with empirical observations or procedures. Connections assumed in the general law cannot in fact be proved or disproved at the level of direct experience. At its highest level, the law also governs the Spiritual Beings posited as its controlling agents. Spiritual Beings are therefore bound by the law as well as explaining its operation. Creator, the final cause, is seen to be outside the universe and beyond the control of the law which regulates it.

Since the law of connection operates at all levels, the religious, the magical, and the concrete are in this respect governed by one set of principles. The law has a generalized application, operating throughout the universe to all orders of reality; but it is also specific, in the sense of being restricted to certain conditions and situations at each level—the qualities of hot and cold, for instance,

---

[1] Observations at this level correspond roughly to what Lévi-Strauss has called 'the science of the concrete'. *The Savage Mind, passim,* especially chap. i.

are applied in controlled (restricted) situations only, and cannot be used randomly outside these.

The fact that certain processes are assumed to be involved where they cannot be directly demonstrated, is well shown by the Mandari assumption that touching the rainbow where it joins the earth precipitates mental illness. This theory uses observations about the shock symptoms of mental illness, the nature of weather phenomena, and the effect of lightning strike on matter. The supposition here is that causal links of a physical kind are present and reinforced by links of associational analogy. Not only is an ideal association made of the kind, 'attributes of mental illness have something in common with attributes of lightning shock', but a physical force is actually assumed to be harmfully directed.

Since language is the essential tool of differentiation and categorization, and since Mandari theory regarding physical matter and neutral force is presented in religious terminology, the kind of distinction which can be stated explicitly through a specialist vocabulary is not made. Their non-specialized terminologies effectively accommodate the intellectual inquiry and the statement of mystical and psychic experience. While the need to make an explicit distinction between these different orders of reality is not generally felt, therefore, the way in which the Mandari proceed in some situations seems ultimately to depend upon implicit distinctions.

Moreover, the Mandari theoretician waits for new evidence to be revealed and does not directly seek for it to support a particular proposition. But when the nature of any new evidence must be established, those responsible for giving interpretations will ask 'why' and 'according to which principles'. A preoccupation with promoting new synthesis and building new models is, however, generally absent, and adaptations confirm the law rather than contradicting it because the Mandari believe that they can answer unsolved problems by re-examining the relations between parts of the concrete, or between the concrete and the controlling principles, as these are already apprehended. Thus they reassemble or modify what is already given, proceeding by trial and error within recognized boundaries.[1]

The fact that accepted boundaries are seldom fundamentally challenged relates essentially to their lack of the necessary knowledge for carrying out testing. But the reassessments that they make

[1] As in their reassessment of burial procedures (pp. 360-1).

are often radical within their context. Without a different *kind* of yardstick for comparison, there is no reason why the Mandari should be dissatisfied with the results of their explorations, and indeed, their adaptations appear to them to show reasonable theoretical advance. Different kinds of comparison of success or failure may be made by the Mandari who have travelled.[1] Modifications always arise from the scrutiny of the personal or group experience, and as I have shown, the direct experience, particularly in relation to medical practice, provides the impetus to theoretical advance.

A characteristic of the way in which the boundaries of indigenous Mandari knowledge are extended is the acceptance, in certain conditions, of proof from the single instance when one event alone, if accepted as sufficiently conclusive, may constitute a contribution to knowledge, particularly if it embodies an accepted pattern making a great weight of new supporting evidence unnecessary.[2] Through the evidence provided by an event and its final interpretation, a new component is added to the theory of matter and to religious doctrine at one and the same time. The Mandari advance their religious understanding and their theoretical knowledge together without conflict between the two.

Another factor which would seem to inhibit a radical revision of traditional assumptions is the fact that Mandari theory is framed in so generalized a form that it fails to compel the close observation of phenomena, ultimately essential to proving or refuting a hypothesis. Or rather, more exactly, since scientific laws are also often simple or generalized, the Mandari lack the experimental method and therefore their theories cannot ever be validly tested, in spite of what I have said regarding their preoccupation with matter. Proof established through the observation of results after a law of contingent connections has been assumed, is not very helpful in establishing probabilities. Ultimately theory cannot be proved to be wrong or right.[3] To the extent also that inquiry

---

[1] Those Mandari who have visited urban centres, for instance. But the comments of those who have visited neighbouring peoples are also relevant. See comments of Wale on medical practice among the Nile Köbora (p. 286).

[2] An isolated event advancing theory and also proved by it was given on pp. 345–6 where sickness followed from seeing a *raga* 'walking'. This new event and its interpretation fall within the conditions of the law of weather control and objects relating to it—the effect of sky phenomena on the human body, and so on.

[3] Some comparison might be made here with the theory and practice of blood-letting so widely used as a cure-all in the nineteenth century. Physicians

proceeds intuitively on the basis of psychic experience, and that a proposition rests on a very small sample of cases (even on one alone), it is impossible for the Mandari to judge whether a cure is spontaneous or results from the 'treatment' given. In the final analysis it cannot even be shown *why* the treatment works.

II

While I have been concerned in this book with the cognitive processes and their manifestation in traditional religious thought, action, and healing, I have also been concerned to provide examples of religious beliefs, of ritual action, and of sacred symbols operating at the more generally accepted level of the spiritual, that is the level of psychic experience. I have shown how symbols stand out clearly in support of the moral truth, the value of special states, the fundamental precept obscurely apprehended. The greater part of Mandari rite and symbol is, in fact, concerned with this, particularly the rites of role-change, life-crises, purification, elimination, and so forth.

A whole range of representational symbolism also lies at the basis of protective magical acts and charms and is also clearly present in the homoeopathic associations in many healing techniques. Here the connections are so specific and varied, so short and broken—although with a general underlying pattern—that they should not be assumed to be attempts at control by the theoretical law of matter just discussed. Indeed, the Mandari themselves accept these linkings as contingent models mainly efficacious at the level of psychological reassurance. A charm is recognized, to some extent, as of limited value *because* its special operation involves the emotional attitude of the wearer (the strength of his 'belief' or 'faith') as much as the control of the external factors; and many Mandari do not use charms, or believe them to have a limited value.[1]

were also working with a wrong set of assumptions regarding physiology which could not be corrected because of the lack of a valid experimental procedure.

[1] It was partly from his observations of these short chain magic connections that Frazer conceived his theory of Homoeopathic (or Sympathetic) Law. Since he assumed that 'primitive' thought was not guided by any theoretical hypotheses, he found it hard to understand how the associations could have been formed except at the level of a mistaken attempt to explain concrete associations. He also failed to understand the dual role played by symbols, and therefore confused representational symbols with symbols of concrete

Since in the Mandari context, one symbol can carry diverse meanings, be used to make statements at different levels of reality, or to produce effects of different kinds in a single ritual situation, the anthropologist is faced with the problem of separating out the different messages and objectives of the one statement with little more than personal intuition as a guide.

III

On the evidence, the Mandari seem to show a marked concern with understanding the nature of universal principles, and, to some degree at least, a preoccupation with speculative inquiry. It is therefore of interest to ask why this should be so, in view of the rather different direction of interest often reported by observers for other non-scientific cultures. A different emphasis of interest even seems to be present among such close neighbours as the Nuer and Dinka. The evidence from these latter peoples suggests that they have a more dominant concern with effecting control at the level of the moral statement and with using symbols as mediaries at the meeting-point between man and Spirit. Consequently Nuer and Dinka show a more passive attitude to empirical fact and even a lack of concern with it since a correct understanding of the religious law is the desired objective, and not a science of matter.[1]

As Professor Evans-Pritchard has pointed out, 'at the core of mystical thought we find recognition of natural causation and other scientific observations which lie, as it were, dormant, known yet socially inhibited because they are irrelevant to the particular situation which evokes the pattern of thought or because they contradict it. If this were not the case it would be difficult to understand how scientific thought could ever have emerged.'[2] In

instrumentality, regarding all symbolic statement as of the same order. Sir James Frazer, *The Golden Bough*, abridged ed. (Macmillan & Co: London, 1929), *passim*.

[1] Whether this is the case with all pre-scientific cultures is debatable, in view of the evidence presented by Robin Horton, who argues in support of the primacy of the cognitive in primitive religious thought. From a series of his articles, see 'African Traditional Thought and Western Science', *Africa*, vol. 37, no. 1 (1967), and 'Neo-Tylorianism: Sound Sense or Sinister Prejudice', *Man*, N.S., vol. 3, no. 4 (1968).

[2] From a paper by Evans-Pritchard on Lévy-Bruhl's Theory of Primitive Mentality, *The Bulletin of the Faculty of Arts* (Cairo), vol. 2, part i (1933).

the Mandari case, the 'closed circuit' of thought which often seems to inhibit the direct awareness of contradictions within a belief system has never existed. Significantly, it is at the point where contradictions arise and are faced that intellectual curiosity begins. The particular Mandari situation and the historical influences to which they have been subjected have constantly been a challenge to traditional theories and compelled reassessment in the light of new ideas. Concern with this kind of inquiry has not however in any way impoverished the moral and psychic experience; on the contrary, the vitality and richness of cultural and emotional life may be in part the result of intellectual preoccupations.

APPENDICES

APPENDIX I

RITUAL MEAT

THE division of sacrificial meat varies according to the particular sacrifice, including the agency to which it is offered, and the number of persons who attend and their relationship to each other.

Certain principles, however, must be observed. The crucial distinction involved is that between the 'ritual' or classified parts and the meat which is unclassified. Classified meat 'belongs to the owners of the sacrifice'—the persons for whom it is offered and their close lineage elders. Unclassified meat belongs to less closely related persons, clan members, affines, or neighbours. When attendance is limited, all meat—of both classes—may be consumed within the family. The animal will then be small (sheep or goat) since cattle are not killed in minor ritual.

Some parts of the classified ritual meat must be eaten at the ritual meal which follows the sacrifice itself. These include the head (which 'belongs' to the owner), and the vital organs—the liver, kidneys, and heart. Chest meat (*kido*) is also ritual meat, and divides into the front ribs (*lama*, sing. *lamasho*) and the back ribs (*polyat*, sing. *poliso*). But while all the internal organs must be eaten at the ritual meal, chest meat may be eaten later or may be dried and stored for entertaining. It is not essential for the whole of the chest meat to be eaten within the family. The intestines and stomach lining belong to the homestead women and women elders. These are not eaten by distantly related female elders who attend mortuary rites; the latter simply drink beer. Any ritual meat not eaten at the sacrifice is stored, some in the 'pot-of-the-back-of-the-hut'. The blood is carefully retained and used, mixed with water, for the boiling of the sacrificial meat at the ritual meal. A sacrificial chicken is boiled whole.

Non-ritual parts may be roasted. These include the legs—particularly given to visitors. The meat at the base of the spine (*gole*) and the *lower* back ribs (*tiar*) may also be consumed *outside* the homestead. Non-ritual portions are the animal's extremities, its less essential parts furthest from the vital centre.

Young unmarried persons do not attend rites (unless directly involved). They receive allocations from the meat given to older relatives who take their meat home and divide it between wives who make further allocations for sons and daughters. Parts said 'to make people promiscuous' are not given to young people.

When several spiritual agents are involved, each receives its own meat; the same goes for sacrifice offered to one agent where there are several agents in the homestead with shrines. Mixing up meat is endangering and meat must be cooked in the correct pots. One spiritual agent takes the meat of one side of the animal, the other agent the meat of the other side. In principle, the meat of Spirit-of-the-Above is on the animal's right side, 'which shows uppermost towards the sky, when the beast falls on its left side'. The meat of ancestors and Powers is then that 'facing the ground'.

The meat of a patient's first sickness sacrifice, or the meat from a sacrifice which is consumed in his homestead, is proscribed to him. This meat contains the *nyök* of sickness in general. After refraining from this, a patient eats meat of further sacrifices offered for him or for relatives. Small pieces of tender meat are selected for very sick persons; chicken meat is seen to be particularly good for them since it is 'tasty' (*pedede*).

APPENDIX II

SHRINES FOR POWERS (KÖDI LO JOK)

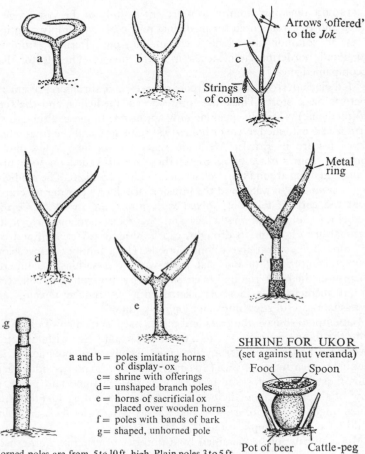

Arrows 'offered'
to the *Jok*

Strings
of coins

Metal
ring

a and b = poles imitating horns
       of display- ox
c = shrine with offerings
d = unshaped branch poles
e = horns of sacrificial ox
     placed over wooden horns
f = poles with bands of bark
g = shaped, unhorned pole

SHRINE FOR UKOR
(set against hut veranda)

Food   Spoon

Pot of beer   Cattle-peg

Horned poles are from 5 to 10 ft. high. Plain poles 3 to 5 ft.
Siting is very important. Poles for Muŋork, Myom, and Mutiaŋagok sited
in *Bop* (veranda). Those for Adwegdwor, Agok, and Malual in open yard.
Poles similar in shape are also raised for Spirit-of-the-Above.

HERBS AND ROOTS USED IN TREATMENT OF ILLNESS

THIS note does not attempt to represent a study of the vast range of herbs and tree-roots used for medicinal purposes, but simply mentions a few in common use which I collected in one afternoon from the woodland bordering homesteads in Dari village. The doctor Kok accompanied me.

Medicines derived from the roots of trees and shrubs represent the doctor's basic store. These are 'professional' medicines and the term *ini* (medicine) is strictly speaking only applicable to these, although the term is also extended to cover homestead remedies, and the trees whose leaves feature in rituals. Medicine roots are sections a few inches long cut from surface-lying roots; these are threaded on to a fibre string and hung around the neck when attending a patient. The medicine root is pounded in water and the infusion drunk or a powder is scraped from the core of the root, mixed with water and drunk. Tree-root medicines, unlike leaf medicines and the roots of plants which are seasonal or vulnerable to drought, can be dug at any season, and can be stored for comparatively long periods. On a number of occasions doctors complained to me that their work was seriously hampered because medicinal herbs had been affected by drought. The collection of rare medicines, or those associated with a particular terrain, may necessitate careful searchings and long expeditions.

I attempted to have the trees and plants used as medicines identified from the drawings made at the time of collection.[1] But without actual specimens and working from drawings which were botanically inadequate, identification was extremely difficult. Tentative identifications must not therefore be taken as definite—an important point, in view of the fact that medicines are *eaten*, and a wrong identification which might at some future time find its way into the local classification could have serious implications.

Medicines might be classified by a number of criteria. Those used on the basis of 'sympathetic' analogy to accompany certain ritual gestures—such as leafy twigs of ritual trees waved or brushed over patients

---

[1] In this connection I would like gratefully to acknowledge the assistance of the Natural History Museum and the Royal Botanical Gardens, Kew. Mr. Wickens of Kew gave an afternoon to go through my drawings and the tentative identifications given here were made by him.

—and therefore of no scientific value, could be distinguished from those used 'medically' (albeit in their 'raw' state) in a more acceptable way—administered orally, rubbed into the skin, or bound on wounds. Some of the latter medicines might on analysis be found to have no value whatsoever, others might have properties other than those imputed to them, others perhaps have real value. I do not attempt any kind of classification here, but simply list the species giving the agents and symptoms Mandari associate with their curing powers.

The following are the ten medicines collected during my hour's walk:

1. *Tirioti* (possible identification: *Grewia bicolor*)

Branches of this little tree which has numerous small fluttering leaves and looks rather like acacia, are regularly used for brushing over patients to drive away evil influences (Powers, Celestial Spirits, etc.). A twig may also be split down and placed on the neck or back of a patient during a rite.

2. *Rurupi* (No botanical classification possible. Father Spagnolo, however, lists '*Rurupi*' under the heading '*Rhamnaceae* and *Rutaceae*', subheading *Anacardiaceae: Sclerocarya* near *Sc. Caffra*. See *Bari Grammar*, p. 421.)

A small tree, the branches and leaves used as in 1 above.

3. *Kirili* (Illustration I: *Harrisonia abyssinica*?)

The leaves of this tree are used similarly, particularly for chest disorders from Celestial Spirit. The leaves may also be shredded and put in the beer which is drunk at sacrifice.

4. *Kirot* (*Combretum fragrans*?)

One of the trees used together with others for cleansing the possession of a dead person. A tall, waving tree, resembling the silver birch, the bark of the main trunk being strikingly patterned white and black. A red substance 'like blood' exudes when the bark is scored.

5. *Porsho* (a species of *Ziziphus*?)

A small tree. The thick reddish-coloured tuberous roots are eaten. Porsho is used to treat diarrhoea, and sometimes as follow-up treatment after Joicputch (see below) to 'harden the bowels'.

6. *Lugusho* (*Nauclea latifolia*?)

A large shrub with dark shiny green leaves borne on red stems. The tuberous root is eaten for pain in the abdomen, hernia, or a swollen belly.

7. *Medicine for the Powers Mulual and Mutiaŋagok* (vernacular name not recorded. Is generally referred to as 'medicine of Powers'; *Cistus populnea?*)

A large spreading shrub-like creeper with tentacles. Tuberous roots (black-skinned with white insides) are chewed, or pounded in water and drunk if the patient is very ill. Before plucking a piece of this plant Kok made protective passes over me and spat on my head. The medicines of Powers are particularly 'potent' (pötö), and if picked at random are endangering.

8. *Medicine for Celestial Spirit (Ki) particularly for Kuluŋ* (Illustration II: *Gloriosa simplex?*)

This medicine is for symptoms associated with the chest. The compound root is chewed or pounded and drunk in water.

9. *Medicine for Mutiaŋagok* (unidentified)

The tuberous roots of this small tree with a habit similar to Acacia, are chewed or pounded in water.

10. *Joicputch* (Illustration III: *Jatsyha?*)

Small weedy bushy plants 3 or 4 feet high. Root pounded in water and used as a common household purgative.

After drinking medicine the patient is circumspect in his eating, firstly because he is ill, and secondly in order not to mix the medicine indiscriminately with mundane food.

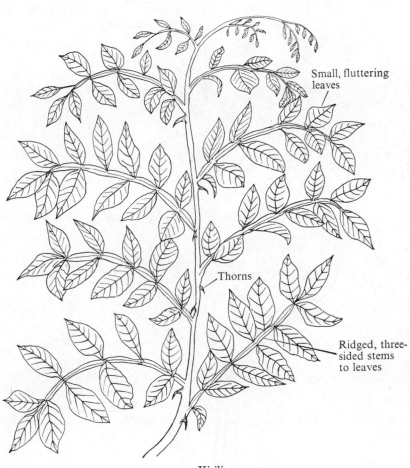

Small, fluttering leaves

Thorns

Ridged, three-sided stems to leaves

1. Kirili

Root

11. *Medicine for Celestial illness* (*Kuluŋ*)

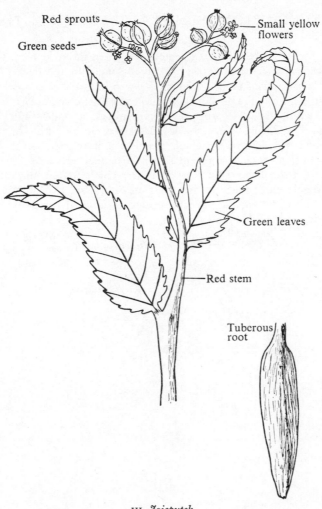

Red sprouts

Green seeds

Small yellow flowers

Green leaves

Red stem

Tuberous root

III. *Joicputch*

APPENDIX IV

DELEGATION OF SHEA-TREES IN MIJIKI

SHEA rituals in Mijiki are delegated to a client group named Togole. Mar Rengo, their founder (said to have 'come from the bush') settled with Mar Mujör of Nolija. The chief rewarded his skill as an elephant and buffalo hunter with the skin of a leopard (the symbol of the predatory wild), also delegating the game animals and shea-butter trees to him. The Mijiki lagoon is also described as 'his', but 'rain' until its loss was retained by the chief. Togole also have clients of their own who help them to collect shea fruit for the annual ceremony. There are, therefore, three levels of delegation in this chiefdom (see diagram).

A Togole elder told me that their ancestor, said by Mijiki to have 'come from the bush', was the leader of an early migration from Somöring clan of Mandari Bora.[1]

[1] See *Chiefs and Strangers*, p. 59.

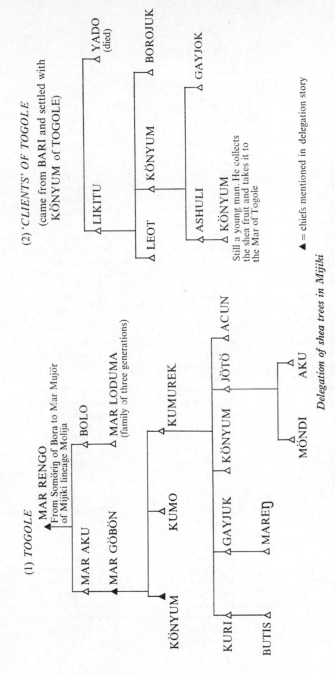

(1) *TOGOLE*

MAR RENGO
From Somörig of Bora to Mar Mujör
of Mijiki lineage Molija

(2) *'CLIENTS' OF TOGOLE*

(came from BARI and settled with
KÖNYUM of TOGOLE)

ASHULI ... KÖNYUM
Still a young man. He collects
the shea fruit and takes it to
the Mar of Togole

▲ = chiefs mentioned in delegation story

Delegation of shea trees in Mijiki

NOTE. For details of Mijiki landowning clan, see *Chiefs and Strangers*, Fig. 5. p. 47.

APPENDIX V

KOUWER'S APPENDICES ON COLOUR TESTING

TABLE C

BLACK	WHITE	RED
64 death	63 peace	75 passion
58 night	59 nude	71 emotion
44 murder	51 baby	69 temperament
36 anxiety	51 soul	65 action
30 misery	48 simplicity	52 mutinousness
30 defeat	48 child	50 force
30 disgust	40 mind	48 sexuality
28 deceit	30 reverence	46 tension
25 lie	30 molten	43 lone
21 theft	27 religion	40 spontaneity
21 disadvantage	27 solitude	38 victory
21 poison	27 freedom	36 shame

YELLOW	ORANGE	BLUE
28 jealousy	38 fun	49 confidence
25 hatred	27 laughter	38 co-operation
25 pleasure	25 fertility	36 harmony
22 lust for power	25 pleasure	36 devotion
22 laughter	25 morning	36 man friend
21 fun	23 victory	31 responsibility
21 pain	23 joy	30 personal
21 joy	21 originality	30 woman
20 ambition	19 success	30 son
21 festivity	15 harmony	29 willingness to help
26 spontaneity	15 advantage	29 mother
		29 satisfaction

GREEN	PURPLE	BROWN
62 nature	34 deceit	26 man (male)
30 naturalness	26 prison	23 masculine
25 prison	25 misery	23 disgust
18 youth (childhood)	24 theft	21 father
16 wish	22 tears	21 business
16 goodness	21 sorrow	20 dependence
15 advantage	21 illness	19 profession
15 charity	20 anxiety	19 brother
15 willingness to help	20 evening	19 theft
	20 constraint	19 disadvantage
	19 jealousy	19 hindrances
	19 adversity	

GREY

51 boredom	40 worry
47 discouragement	38 business (things)
47 past	36 adversity
42 old age	32 sorrow
42 theory	30 solitude

Theme. Words most frequently combined with each colour.

The numbers represent the percentages of subjects arranging the corresponding word with the colour under consideration.

TABLE D

Spontaneous judgements	Black	White	Red	Yellow	Orange	Blue	Green	Purple	Brown	Grey
STRONG, forceful, masculine, solid	8	2	27	6	7	19	6	9	26	—
INTENSE, fiery, fierce, exciting, striking	—	2	55	19	20	3	9	5	2	2
WARM	—	—	27	7	12	13	5	8	5	—
ACTIVE, spontaneous, tension, lively, emotional, erotic	1	2	78	14	25	10	13	6	4	—
MERRY, glad, joy, cheerful, sunny, festive, gay	—	10	22	34	43	15	8	4	—	—
AGREEABLE, beautiful, good, nice, pleasant	3	22	17	24	17	33	29	11	7	2
SOCIAL, cosy, friendly, love, faithful, personal	1	17	24	10	17	41	24	13	18	6
QUIET, harmonious, peaceful, sedate, soft, free	3	21	4	6	5	31	29	15	11	28
SPIRITUAL, abstract, divine, awe, sacred, duty, ideal	—	41	2	12	2	31	8	16	—	—
PURE, clear, fair, innocent, feminine; subtle	—	69	1	15	3	19	8	2	—	—
YOUTHFUL, fresh, natural, hopeful, future	—	29	7	16	7	16	49	2	2	9
VAGUE, indeterminate, uncertain, dark, deep	40	13	—	5	2	14	5	12	22	47
NEUTRAL, noncommittal, dull, boring, colourless, lifeless, dead, old	37	28	—	12	18	15	25	33	26	62
DISAGREEABLE, unpleasant, awful, repulsive, ugly, bad	43	3	10	27	5	10	24	41	38	9
AGGRESSIVE, mean, selfish, unreliable, sharp, hatred, poisonous, terrifying	10	1	16	33	2	1	25	21	2	2
HARD, pressure, oppressive, inescapable	26	1	2	8	2	8	7	20	6	15
SAD, sombre, grief, serious, worry, misery	62	1	1	2	2	9	3	38	19	42
COLD	—	5	—	11	—	11	3	2	—	4
IMPERSONAL, unemotional, business, objective, cerebral	7	20	3	11	5	32	16	7	21	15
Number of subjects	92	143	143	143	60	143	143	102	85	53

Spontaneous judgements on his columns under instruction II and IV. The judgements have been subdivided subjectively into 19 categories. For each colour the percentage is indicated of the subjects in whose protocols the corresponding judgements occur. Eight per cent of the subjects, e.g., judged black for its forcefulness, nought per cent for its intensity and warmth This table also includes the results of the experiments with colour samples (27 subjects).

BIBLIOGRAPHY

ARNHEIM, RUDOLF, *Art and Visual Perception* (English edition). London: Faber & Faber, 1957.

BEATTIE, JOHN, *Bunyoro: An African Kingdom.* New York: Holt, Rinehart, & Winston, 1960.

—— 'Group Aspects of the Nyoro Spirit Mediumship Cult', *Rhodes-Livingstone Journal*, vol. 30 (1963).

—— 'The Ghost Cult in Bunyoro', *Ethnology*, vol. 3 (1964).

—— 'Ritual and Social Change', *Man*, N.S., vol. 1, no. 1 (1966).

—— and MIDDLETON, JOHN (eds.), *Spirit Mediumship and Society in Africa*. London: Routledge & Kegan Paul, 1969.[1]

BEIDELMAN, T. O., 'The Ox and Nuer Sacrifice: some Freudian Hypotheses', *Man*, N.S., vol. 1, no. 4 (1966).

BURRIDGE, KENELM. *New Heaven New Earth*. Oxford: Basil Blackwell, 1969.

BUTT, AUDREY, 'Trial by Trance', in *Trances*, by Wavell *et al.* London: George Allen & Unwin, 1966.

BUXTON, J. C., *Chiefs and Strangers*. Oxford: Clarendon Press, 1963.

—— 'Mandari Witchcraft', in *Witchcraft and Sorcery in East Africa*, ed. John Middleton and E. H. Winter. London: Routledge & Kegan Paul, 1963.

—— 'Girls' Courting Huts in Western Mandari', *Man*, no. 56 (1963).

—— 'Animal Identity and Human Peril: some Mandari Images', *Man*, N.S., vol. 3, no. 1 (1968).

CONKIN, H. C., 'Hanimoo Colour Categories', *S.J.A.*, vol. 2 (1955).

DEREN, MAYA, *Divine Horseman*. London: Thames & Hudson, 1953.

DOUGLAS, MARY, *Purity and Danger*. London: Routledge & Kegan Paul, 1966.

EVANS-PRITCHARD, E. E., 'Lévy-Bruhl's Theory of Primitive Mentality', *Bulletin of the Faculty of Arts* (Cairo), vol. 2, pt. i (1933).

—— 'Customs and Beliefs Relating to Twins among the Nilotic Nuer', *Uganda Journal*, vol. 3 (1936).

—— *Witchcraft, Oracles, and Magic among the Azande*. Oxford: Clarendon Press, 1937.

—— *The Nuer*. Oxford: Clarendon Press, 1940.

---

[1] This book deals with many of the themes I am concerned with, but specific reference has not been made to it as it appeared after I had completed the present study.

—— *Kinship and Marriage among the Nuer.* Oxford: Clarendon Press, 1951.

—— *Nuer Religion.* Oxford: Clarendon Press, 1956.

—— Introduction to Hertz's *Death and the Right Hand* (1960).

FIELD, J. M., *Search for Security.* London: Faber, 1960.

FORTES, M., *The Web of Kinship among the Tallensi.* London: Oxford University Press, 1949.

FRAZER, SIR JAMES, *The Golden Bough* (abridged edition). London: Macmillan & Co., 1929.

GENNER, ARNOLD VAN, *The Rites of Passage,* trans. Monika B. Vizedom and Gabrielle L. Caffree. London: Routledge & Kegan Paul, 1960.

GIRLING, F. K., *The Acholi of Uganda.* London: H.M.S.O., 1960.

GLUCKMAN, MAX, *Judicial Processes among the Barotse of Northern Rhodesia.* Manchester: Manchester University Press, 1955.

—— *Politics, Law and Ritual in Tribal Society.* Oxford: Blackwell, 1965.

GOODY, J., *Death, Property and the Ancestors.* London: Tavistock Publications, 1962.

HAYLEY, AUDREY, 'Symbolic Equations: the Ox and the Cucumber', *Man,* N.S., vol. 3, no. 2 (1968).

HORTON, ROBIN, 'African Traditional Thought and Western Science', *Africa,* vol. 37, no. 1 (1967).

—— 'Neo-Tylorianism: Sound Sense or Sinister Prejudice', *Man,* N.S., vol. 3, no. 4 (1968).

HOWELL, P. P., 'Some Observations on "Earthly Spirits" among the Nuer', *Man,* no. 53 (1953).

HURVICH, LEO M., and JAMESON, DOROTHEA, 'An Opponent-Process Theory', in *Colour Vision,* ed. Richard C. Teevan and Robert C. Birney. New York: D. Van Nostrand Co. Inc., 1961.

JUNG, C. J., *Collected Works,* vol. 11, 1958; vol. 12, 1953; vol. 14, 1963. London: Routledge & Kegan Paul.

KATZ, DAVID, *The World of Colour.* London: Kegan Paul, Trench, Trubner & Co., 1935.

KOUWER, B. J., *Colours and their Character.* The Hague: Martinus Nijhoff, 1949.

LEIGHTON, A. H. *et al., Psychiatric Disorder among the Yoruba.* New York: Cornell University Press, 1963.

LÉVI-STRAUSS, C., *Totemism,* trans. R. Needham. Boston, Mass.: Beacon Press, 1963.

—— *Structural Anthropology,* trans. Jacobson and Grundfest Schoepf. New York: Basic Books Inc., 1965.

—— *The Savage Mind* (trans.). London: George Weidenfeld & Nicolson, 1966.

LEWIS, I. M., 'Spirit Possession and Deprivation Cults', *Man,* N.S., vol. 1, no. 3 (1966).

Ff

LIENHARDT, Godfrey, 'Modes of Thought', in *The Institutions of Primitive Society*, by E. E. Evans-Pritchard *et al*. Oxford: Clarendon Press, 1954.

—— 'The Shilluk of the Upper Nile', in *African Worlds*, ed. Daryll Forde. London: Oxford University Press, 1954.

—— *Divinity and Experience*. Oxford: Clarendon Press, 1962.

MAUSS, MARCEL. *The Gift*, trans. Ian Cunnison. London: Cohen & West, 1954.

MIDDLETON, JOHN, *Lugbara Religion*. London: Oxford University Press, 1960.

MIDDLETON, JOHN, and WINTER, E. H., *Witchcraft and Sorcery in East Africa*. London: Routledge & Kegan Paul, 1963.

MILLAIS, J. G., *Far Away up the Nile*. London: Longmans, Green & Co., 1924.

NALDER, L. F., *A Tribal Survey of Mongalla Province*. Oxford: Clarendon Press, 1937.

NEEDHAM, R., 'Percussion and Transition', *Man*, N.S., vol. 2, no. 4 (1967).

NEHLER, A., 'A Physiological Explanation of Unusual Behaviour in Ceremonies Involving Drums', *Human Biology*, vol. 34 (1962).

P'BITEK, OKOT, *Song of Lawino*. Nairobi: Modern African Library, East African Publishing House, 1966.

RADCLIFFE-BROWN, A. R., *Structure and Function in Primitive Society*. London: Cohen & West, 1952.

REITMAN, F., *Psychotic Art*. London: Routledge, 1950.

SELIGMAN, C. G., *Pagan Tribes of the Nilotic Sudan*. London: George Routledge & Sons, 1932.

SPAGNOLO, Fr. L. M., *Bari Grammar*. Verona: Missioni Africane, 1933.

STIGAND, C. H., *Equatoria, the Lado Enclave* (new impression). London: Cass, 1968.

STURTEVANT, W. C., 'Categories, Percussion and Physiology', *Man*, N.S., vol. 3, no. 1 (1968).

TAYLOR, F. A., *Colour Technology*. Oxford: Clarendon Press, 1962.

TURNER, V., 'Three Symbols of Passage in Ndembu Circumcision Ritual: an Interpretation', in *Essays on the Ritual of Social Relations*, ed. Max Gluckman. Manchester: Manchester University Press, 1962.

—— 'Colour Classification in Ndembu Ritual', in *Anthropological Approaches in the Study of Religion*, A.S.A. Monograph no. 3. London: Tavistock Publications, 1966.

WORSLEY, PETER, 'Groote Eylandt Totemism and Le Totemisme Aujourd'hui', in *The Structural Study of Myth and Totemism*, A.S.A. Monograph no. 5. London: Tavistock Publications, 1967.

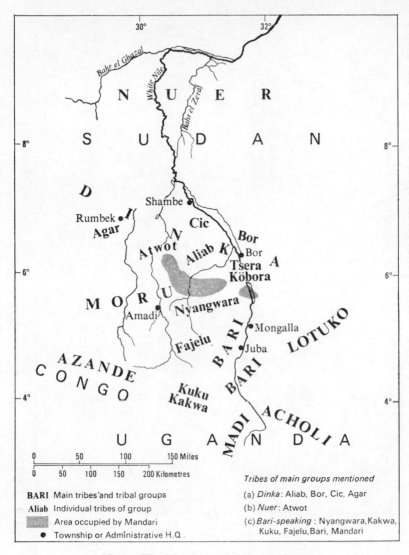

Map 1. The Mandari and their neighbours

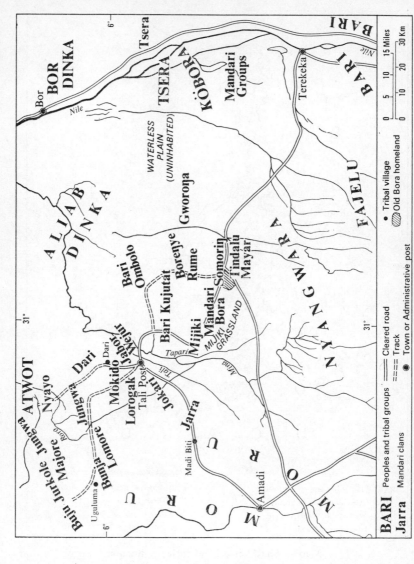

Map 2. The Mandari clan locations

INDEX

Abyel, a Power, 75.
Acholi, people, 344.
Administration (Sudan Government), 9, 12, 64–5, 112, 132, 134, 150, 315, 332 n., 332–3.
Adwegdwor, a Power, 75, 108.
Agar Dinka, 284.
Agaraŋ, a Dinka practitioner, 284.
Agok, a Power, 75, 108.
Agor, a female doctor, 290.
agoratit, 355 f.
Agoya, archetypal female, 24, 203, 206, 248.
Ajak Patis, 86–92, 140–1.
Ajara lineage, 374–5.
Ajayich (*see* Kok), 283.
Akawio, people, 307.
Ako Akurukway, a doctor, 56–61, 71, 73, 78–84, 87 f., 97, 102–4, 143, 285, 287, 294–6, 301, 309 n., 310, 313, 319, 326, 366 n.
his Call, 280–3.
Aliab Dinka, people, 64–7, 69, 71, 107, 338.
language, 81, 94.
Aliŋakway, 86–92.
ancestors (*mulökö*), 29, 72, 129, 133, 135, 155–9, 164, 166–8, 171, 172, 177 f., 187, 203, 206, 238, 286, 315, 321, 336, 339, 343, 347 f., 366 f., 370, 372, 386, 388, 399, 418.
ancestor commemoration rite, 161.
female ancestors, 165–6, 177, 217.
animal characteristics, 259–61, 266.
classification, 251–3.
markings, 258–9, 269–70, 384, 397–8.
metamorphosis, 105, 249 n., 255 f., 261–5.
personality, 254–8.
stereotypes, 266–72.
symbolism, in Call experiences, 286, 289, 294.
Anok Pilari, Chief of Dari, 181 n.
Anuak, people, 266.
Apu, a female doctor, 294, 296.
her Call, 289–90.
Are, an elder of Dari clan, 230.

Are lineage, 372.
Arnheim, R., 259 n., 387 n., 403 n., 408 n.
Asek, a doctor, 78–84, 85, 296.
his Call, 285.
assimilation of foreign peoples and ideas, 1, 3, 18, 26–7, 64–70, 106–13, 264–5, 268, 280, 286–7, 371.
Atwot, people, 5, 56, 58, 64–7, 70, 105, 108, 268, 282, 283–4, 305, 325, 338, 378.
country, 102.
language, 56.
avoidance relationships, 125, 217–19.
Awor, a man, 57, 116–18.
Awuk, wife of Korondo, 377.
Azande, people, 68, 166, 167–8, 269, 360 n.
dreams, 294 n.
Azande scheme, 14.
Aznaba Lakuli, Chief of Mandari Bora-Somöriŋ clan, 346, 347, 375.

Bari, 22, 342 n., 346, 355, 357 n., 371.
language 15, 273 n., 286, 403 n.
Bari Kujutat clan, 142, 267, 267 n., 343, 375.
Bari Tapir lineage, 375.
Barisho, Chief, 347, 348, 375.
Bariyei lineage, 280, 366.
Beattie, J., 107 n., 109 n., 359 n.
Beidelman, T., 8 n.
Bekat clan, 347.
birth variants, 244–50.
abnormal births, 247, 250.
animal resemblances due to contact during pregnancy, 268–70.
breech-birth, 247, 249.
deformities at birth, 36 n.
story of assistance by a mouse at birth, 266–7.
black (*luru*) (*see also* colour symbolism, red, white), 76, 82, 90, 92, 103, 115, 196, 246, 248, 256, 259, 338, 382–3, 392 n., 393, 393 n., 396 f., 400, 406 f., 428–9.
contrast with white, 385–9.
blood antipathy, 211–12.